Joint Management and Employee Participation

Joint Management and Employee Participation

Labor and Management
at the Crossroads

Neal Herrick

 Jossey-Bass Publishers

San Francisco • Oxford • 1990

JOINT MANAGEMENT AND EMPLOYEE PARTICIPATION
Labor and Management at the Crossroads
by Neal Herrick

Copyright © 1990 by: Jossey-Bass Inc., Publishers
350 Sansome Street
San Francisco, California 94104
&
Jossey-Bass Limited
Headington Hill Hall
Oxford OX3 0BW

Library of Congress Cataloging-in-Publication Data

Herrick, Neal Q.
    Joint management and employee participation : labor and management
at the crossroads / Neal Herrick. — 1st ed.
        p.   cm.—(The Jossey-Bass management series)
    Includes bibliographical references (p.
    ISBN 1-55542-238-1 (alk. paper)
    1. Management—United States—Employee participation.   2. Work
groups—United States.   3. Collective bargaining—United States.
I. Title. II. Series.
HD5660.U5H46   1990
658.3'152—dc20   89-26949
                                                              CIP

Manufactured in the United States of America

JACKET DESIGN BY WILLI BAUM

FIRST EDITION

Code 9040

The Jossey-Bass
Management Series

Contents

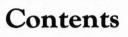

Preface

Management can benefit from worker participation through improved product quality and increased productivity, but can be hurt if workers become disillusioned and alienated. Labor can benefit from worker participation through the retention of jobs and creation of more satisfying work, but can be hurt if workers turn against workers, plants turn against plants, and workers turn against their unions. Participation is indeed a paradox: a situation full of contradictions. These contradictions, however, are not an inevitable result of participation. Instead, they result from the specific characteristics of the participative systems being used by labor and management. *Joint Management and Employee Participation* proposes an approach to participation aimed at resolving these contradictions. This approach, which involves incorporating worker participation systems into the existing collective bargaining process, is called *extended bargaining.*

Participative systems are becoming more and more common in North American workplaces. They are being designed jointly by managers, union leaders, and, in more progressive instances, rank-and-file workers. These managers, union leaders, and workers should be aware of the lessons learned through efforts such as those undertaken at the Detroit-Hamtramck Cadillac plant, by the Pima

County (Arizona) government, at the Shell-Sarnia chemical plant, and at the Saturn assembly plant (see Chapter Five). In this book, I discuss the pitfalls of participation and propose a strategy (extended bargaining) aimed at avoiding these pitfalls.

Many of the activities that now fall under the rubrics "worker participation," "employee involvement," "quality of working life," and so on are, in fact, weak and watered-down forms of collective bargaining. In the past, unions and managements mixed integrative bargaining (that is, problem solving) with distributive bargaining (that is, determining who gets more and less of a limited resource) in their regular bargaining sessions. In recent years, the amount of integrative bargaining has increased greatly, has been separated from distributive bargaining, and—disguised as worker participation—has become largely controlled by management. For the most part, management conducts this integrative bargaining directly with workers. These workers, however, do not bargain as union representatives. This situation has caused confusion among the leaders and members of many North American unions. It has also impaired the ability of labor to organize nonunion plants and has, in some cases, contributed to the alienation of workers from their unions in unionized plants. This present state of affairs is also disadvantageous to management. Middle- and lower-level managers often find subtle but effective ways to resist giving workers a genuine influence in the decision-making process. Thus, many participative systems offer only pseudo-participation and, for this reason, fall far short of their potential benefits: increased productivity and worker satisfaction.

An extended bargaining strategy can help both labor and management. By identifying integrative bargaining as a union function, workers can be made aware that they have their unions to thank for the benefits of participation. By making participative behavior on the part of managers and supervisors enforceable, participative systems can operate more effectively, thus increasing both productivity and worker satisfaction.

An extended bargaining strategy leaves intact the existing collective bargaining process. However, it extends this process in terms of scope, time, and space. The scope of collective bargaining is extended to cover matters now being addressed in participative problem-solving teams. Collective bargaining is extended in terms of time in that it is conducted on a monthly, weekly, or even daily basis, depending on the level of the organization involved. Collective bargaining is extended in terms of space in that it is carried on in every unit and subunit of the organization. There is no question that this kind of bargaining is possible; it is already being done, albeit in a weak and disorganized way. The pressing question is whether labor and management can take the steps necessary to bring extended bargaining under control and make it a positive force for unions and their members, management, and society as a whole.

Background

In 1972, the United Auto Workers and the then Jervis Corporation launched an employee participation experiment in an auto mirror plant in Bolivar, Tennessee. This experiment borrowed from the Scanlon Plan in setting up a three-tier parallel organization. Labor and management used this parallel organization (consisting of an advisory committee, a plant-level working committee, and thirty-three "core groups") to jointly design and operate the participative program (Macy, 1982). Since that time, many other unions and managements have followed suit. In most instances, these "joint management" programs (for example, quality circles and the team concept) have been management dominated and have been tied to the management—but not to the union—administrative structure. In virtually all instances, these programs have used at least a one-tier parallel organization (that is, a plant-level labor-management steering committee). In some instances, these programs have achieved participation through involving workers at lower levels of the organization in what amounts to a new and unique form of collective bargaining. In most cases, however, the parallel organizations involved have been weak, flawed, incomplete, and unconnected to the mainstream collective bargaining process. Nevertheless, even in their imperfect state they have been remarkably effective. This book builds on seventeen years of work with parallel organizations to develop a set of principles aimed at improving their flawed and incomplete state and to devise an approach for integrating them with mainstream bargaining.

Current Opinion

Employee participation, as it is now practiced in North America, is the subject of an important debate within organized labor. United Steel Workers of America President Lynn Williams states that his union champions worker involvement and negotiates for it in collective bargaining contracts, and he cites a number of cases where it has made steel companies more competitive (Williams, 1988). Communications Workers of America President Morton Bahr writes that America will not successfully renew its competitive position without employee participation (Bahr, 1988). Both Williams and Bahr agree that employee participation is unsuccessful where it is "managed" by management without the active involvement of the union.

Other unionists and observers take a less favorable view. Mike Parker and Jane Slaughter (1988) attack the team concept (at this time perhaps the most widespread form of employee participation) as a management tool for speeding up production and busting unions. Victor Reuther told me in a May 1989 telephone conversation that "labor must find ways and means to protect itself from the dangers of the team concept in order to reap its potential benefits." Labor-management cooperation and the team concept are prime targets of what appears to be a growing "New Directions" movement within organized labor. A New Directions conference, held in Detroit on January 8, 1989, attracted nearly 900 southeast Michigan UAW members. A May 19–21, 1989, New Directions conference (also held in Detroit) attracted over 1,000 rank-and-filers and local leaders from a wide variety of private- and public-sector unions. The announcement for the May conference listed recent gains in the fight for a new direction, including the statement "Auto Workers are rejecting 'jointness' and the team concept, and are sending their top union leaders a message that it's time for a change" ("New Directions," 1989). *Jointness* is a term used to describe any activity that labor and management engage in together. Joint activities often involve only managers and top union leaders. However, when managers and union leaders jointly meet and agree to an approach like the team concept, this leads to jointness at the work unit level.

There also seems to be a feeling among American unionists

that Japanese-style participation will not wear well in North America. CAMI Automotive Inc. has negotiated an agreement with the Canadian Auto Workers (CAW) that includes a teamwork provision. However, Ron Pellerin of the CAW wrote to me on June 22, 1989, that, while CAMI has treated its 700 new employees with kid gloves, "there is frustration surfacing in dealing with the Japanese. Empowerment is now being curtailed, and workers are beginning to realize that empowerment means the ability to affirm management's decisions, not freedom to make their own decisions." When I called Dick Greenwood of the International Association of Machinists (IAM) in mid 1989 to discuss this book, he asked, "You aren't trying to run off any of that Japanese crap on us, are you?"

At the plant level, the debate has become divisive and extremely painful for the hourly workers involved. For example, an hourly employee involvement coordinator in a Midwestern manufacturing plant says:

> I'm in an untenable position. We had a layoff in the summer of 1988, and I have a lot of personal friends who are out on the street. They haven't got enough food, some of them. We have to do a better job in order to get a bigger share of the market and get them back to work. We have to work together with management to solve problems and work out better ways of doing things. But I can't even carry on a decent conversation with management without them [workers who are against labor-management cooperation] telling me I've sold out. It hurts. They don't understand that a person can talk to the other side and not have the other side's values and beliefs. I'm a good union person and I come from a good union family. But I know that times have changed. The fight between labor and management has got to be carried on in a more sophisticated way. We can't just screw each other back and forth the way we used to do—or we'll all end up screwed.

The debate that is raging, especially within the bellwether United Auto Workers, is broader than employee involvement versus no employee involvement. It is about the overall strategy of cooperating with management versus confronting management. However, this overall strategy issue is inextricably tied to the employee involvement issue. Because the team concept and employee participation generally have been based on labor-management cooperation, they have been placed at the center of the debate. As a recent *New York Times* article (Levin, 1989) comments, "the rest of industrial America, which has taken some steps towards jointness, is watching the UAW closely to see how its leaders and members resolve their differing approaches to workplace restructuring."

I believe that both the New Directions and establishment positions on employee involvement are valid. I also believe they can be reconciled by making employee participation a labor issue, thus removing it from the arena of top-level labor-management cooperation. I recognize that the nature of employee participation requires cooperation at lower levels of the organization. However, cooperation below the bargaining unit level does not raise the problems between union members and their union that are raised by cooperation at higher levels.

Employee participation systems can be highly beneficial to both labor and management. They can also be detrimental to both parties. It all depends on the specific features of the participation system being used; the most important feature is the extent to which employee participation is folded into the collective bargaining process. These features determine the extent to which the workers and their union are able to exert control over the system. They also determine who the workers thank for the system's benefits: labor or management.

The movement toward participative management is not, of course, limited to unionized firms. Neither is it limited to North America. It is a "global" phenomenon (Cohen-Rosenthal and Burton, 1987, p. 58) that "is moving to a new stage in the U.S. and many other places throughout the world" (Sachs, 1988). This book, however, limits itself to suggesting approaches, principles, and practices aimed at producing employee participation systems beneficial to both labor and management in North America. The central argument of this book is that, in order to successfully serve the interests of both labor and management, these systems must be reshaped into extensions of the collective bargaining process. It is not enough for them to be based on "collective bargaining" (Bahr, 1988).

The Concept in Brief

In 1965, Richard Walton and Robert McKersie published a landmark study of collective bargaining. They noted that two different activities took place at the bargaining table and termed these activities *distributive bargaining* and *integrative bargaining.* Distributive bargaining deals with issues (matters on which there is a conflict of interest) and is win/lose in nature. Integrative bargaining deals with problems (matters on which solutions can benefit both parties) and can be win/win in nature. The general theory of integrative bargaining is summarized in Chapter One. The special features it takes on, when practiced in the context of joint management, are discussed in Chapter Four.

This book proposes that integrative bargaining be separated from distributive bargaining, that it be extended to every level and every unit of the organization, and that its processes and its products be enforced. In 1965, this would have seemed an outlandish and unmanageable proposal. After all, uniformity has been basic to collective bargaining. And how can there be uniformity if bargaining is going on in every nook and cranny of the organization? Wouldn't the labor-management relationships get out of control?

However, beginning in 1972 with the Bolivar experiment, participative systems have been successfully developed by unions and managements to include many of the elements of integrative bargaining. We have discovered that uniformity is not as necessary to integrative as to distributive bargaining. We have also discovered that integrative bargaining at lower levels is not so difficult to control.

Recently, union leaders have begun to recognize the need for some link between employee participation and collective bargaining, saying that participation should be "accomplished under the framework of, and in no way be a substitute for, a collective bargaining agreement" (Williams, 1988, p. 11). This book goes a giant step further: it argues that the most effective and meaningful way for employees to participate is for them to conduct integrative bargaining themselves at every level of the organization, including the work unit level. At present, only a few union officers and staff members participate in collective bargaining. Under the approach proposed in this book, as many as one-half of the employees in a bargaining unit could represent their co-workers on integrative bargaining teams over the course of a single year. Further, all employees could be involved in hour-to-hour and day-to-day integrative bargaining in their autonomous work teams.

In order to follow the argument of this book, it is necessry to understand the way the following three terms are used: *joint management, parallel organization,* and *integrative bargaining.* In brief, *joint management* occurs in any workplace where labor and management jointly sponsor an employee participation system. The *parallel organization* is the labor-management committee, or system of committees, that is almost always set up to carry out the joint management process. These committees are "parallel to" the units of the primary organization. The labor-management committee that is normally set up at the bargaining unit level is also "parallel to" the traditional collective bargaining structure. *Integrative bargaining* is the joint management process itself. Thus, the parallel organization is the structure, integrative bargaining is the process, and joint management is the result.

Potential Benefits of Employee Participation. Employee participation programs can benefit both labor and management. They can benefit labor by meeting workers' needs for "a say" in decision making. They can benefit management (and labor) by increasing productivity. In a time of fierce international competition, management needs increased productivity to maintain profits and labor needs it to maintain jobs.

Potential Pitfalls. Worker participation systems do not always provide these benefits. An ill-designed participation system can have quite different results. It can be a problem to labor when it is used as a subtle management tool to speed up production at the expense of the worker. It can also be a problem to labor when it is used as a device to weaken or bust unions (Parker and Slaughter, 1988). For example, when the team concept is used as a coercive speed-up tool it is very difficult for the worker to resist, because it brings to bear a strong element of peer pressure. A worker participation system is effective in weakening or busting unions to the extent that management can claim credit for its benefits to employees. Employee participation can be a problem to management because, used as a speed-up tool or as a way to weaken the union, it serves management's needs for only a limited period of time. A participation program that includes the union only as a passive partner is a "quick fix." After a period of time, workers often resist, sometimes becoming angry not only with management but with their union for going along with management. These abuses of employee participation create serious problems for both management and labor. They prevent the parties from realizing its tremendous potential benefits. Management abuses kill the goose that lays the golden eggs. In the process, labor loses an opportunity to both save jobs and gain better working conditions for its members.

The Problem

Except in the case of pure production problems, the problem-solving activity that goes on under the guise of employee participation is really a form of collective bargaining—one that has not been recognized as collective bargaining by organized labor. Because it has not been enforceable and has not been carried on by workers acting in the capacity of union officers, labor has looked on employee participation as basically a management concern. In addition, it requires time, energy, and money to become visibly and substantially involved in an employee participation system.

The problem is that labor has simply not considered employee participation a high enough priority to justify the expenditure of this time, energy, and money. But now grass-roots union resistance to employee participation (for example, the New Directions movement) has created a crisis of its own. Ironically, this crisis has occurred, in part, because local unions have been giving less and less, instead of more and more, attention to developing and maintaining their parallel organizations. In the 1970s, when joint management was in the early experimental stage, international unions and foundations contributed time, energy, and money to the experiments, and it was possible for local unions to give closer attention to the way parallel organizations were designed and operated. Now that local unions are on their own, it is more difficult for them to deal with the situation. Well-designed parallel organizations, vital though they are to the interests of organized labor, have three strikes against them. First, they are a drain on the limited resources of labor. Crises and higher-priority activities prevent staff unionists from devoting substantial time to negotiating parallel agreements and maintaining parallel organizations. Second, they are attacked by management (and by some unionists) as "just another layer of bureaucracy." Management doesn't want to be constrained, and unionists, unaware of their need for protection, don't want to be bothered. Finally, some managements and unions have accepted the idea that worker participation programs should be based on an unquestioning trust between management and labor and that parallel organizations and agreements are evidence of mistrust.

During the past several years, participative programs have more and more become "the direct responsibility of regular management" (Sachs, 1988). The focus is now on autonomous work teams that can be fully integrated into the management structure and removed from the influence of organized labor. Employee participation becomes "just the way we do things around here" (Sachs, 1988). There is, of course, a joint labor-management steering committee at the top level of the organization, but—because the actual participative process is integrated into the management structure— the steering committee's function is more to bless worker participation than to control it.

As participative management has moved away from the influence of labor, it has encountered increasing resistance from local unions and workers (Feldman and Betzold, 1988; Parker, 1985; Parker and Slaughter, 1988). The 1985 AFL-CIO committee recommendation to accelerate the development of joint programs (AFL-CIO, 1985) does not seem specific enough to meet the situation as it has developed. What kinds of programs merit acceleration? How are they to be accelerated? What should be labor's specific role in their acceleration? In this book I take the position that unions should take the initiative and redesign the parallel organization so that it can be used as a mechanism for extended integrative bargaining.

Employee Participation and Collective Bargaining

In the 1970s it was an article of faith among unions and managements that employee participation should be kept separate from collective bargaining. By the mid 1980s, this article of faith had been largely abandoned. Academics and international union leaders were saying that employee participation should be based on or linked to collective bargaining. They appeared to mean by this that employee participation programs should be legitimized by being mentioned in the basic labor contract. But, at the local level, jointly managed workplaces had already been linking participation to bargaining in a far more important way. They were using the parallel organization to engage in an activity that has many of the elements of collective bargaining itself. The problem is that this innovation has been management dominated. In effect, it has created "company unions" within unionized workplaces.

Despite its weaknesses, most of which can be traced to the fact that it has not been tied to the regular collective bargaining process, the parallel organization points toward a whole new approach to employee participation: the extension of collective bargaining. This extended integrative bargaining would deal with employee problems not already dealt with in the contract and, to the extent labor can negotiate the right to bargain them, with production problems.

In the early 1990s, at the same time that some unionists are calling for a closer relationship between participation and collective bargaining, the two activities are, in actual practice, being further separated. While lip service is given the "closer relationship" by mentioning participation in the labor contract, participation itself is more and more being limited to the top and the bottom levels of the organization. At the top level, there is a joint labor-management committee. At the bottom level, there are autonomous work teams. The rules and procedures governing the team concept are being integrated into the management structure (Sachs, 1988). The parallel organization is less and less "whole." Employee participation, which promised to lead us toward a radical innovation in collective bargaining (that is, direct employee participation in the bargaining process) is, with the acquiescence of organized labor, becoming a management device for increasing productivity on the shop floor.

This is not to say that the autonomous work team (that is, the team concept) is a bad thing. It can be a very good thing indeed—for both labor and management. But it can be good for labor and management only if it is jointly designed and implemented and then monitored by labor. The existing bargaining structure, however, is not equipped to effectively design and monitor autonomous work teams. The existing structure can control them only by opposing them. The action and planning teams of the parallel organization, on the other hand, are well situated to design, implement, and monitor the team concept through the integrative bargaining process.

Participation in making decisions on the job is not enough. Job enrichment, quality circles, and the team concept, when they are attempted without representative participation at each level of the organization, are easily manipulated by middle- and lower-level managers. A well-designed parallel organization (and the integrative bargaining process it could support) would allow employees and their unions to participate not only in solving problems and in developing organizational plans but in designing, implementing, and monitoring the team concept and all the other components of the participative system itself.

Theme of This Book

The assumption on which these chapters are based is that employee participation systems can be designed to be highly beneficial to both labor and management. I will argue, however, that they cannot benefit either labor or management in the long run unless they are jointly controlled. I will also propose that parallel agreements and parallel organizations (designed in accordance with the principles set forth in Part One) are necessary for this joint control and that these parallel agreements and parallel organizations should be recognized by both labor and management as legitimate extensions of the collective bargaining process.

It is natural and understandable that management should want unions to support participative systems but should not want unions to get too involved in the operation of these systems. Further, it is true that management-dominated systems can in a limited way meet management's needs over the short run. Over the long run, however, even management's goal (productivity) is difficult to sustain without joint union control. As one manager put it: "Management would drop the uncomfortable parts of the system (such as having regular meetings, making up committees by election rather than appointment, genuinely sharing information, discussing problems on an equal footing with employees) and retain the comfortable ones (having employees develop suggestions and solutions for management problems)" (Showalter and Yetman, 1983, p. 124).

A system that cannot improve productivity over the long run cannot meet labor's need to maintain jobs. A system that is controlled by management and passively blessed by the union is not likely to make workers more loyal to their unions. However, a system that includes labor and management as equals (that is, an extended collective bargaining system) can serve the interests of both parties.

Organized labor not only needs to maintain jobs and improve working conditions, it needs to survive. With union membership at about 17 percent of the work force, unions need to adapt (and to become more adaptable) in order to attract new members. Extended integrative bargaining is a way of adapting to a changing competitive climate, changing management methods, and changing employee needs. It also sets up a structure (the parallel organization) that is capable of responding quickly to further changes as they occur.

Overview of the Contents

Until now, no book has been written that focuses on worker participation in *unionized* workplaces. Yet the implications of worker participation systems are quite different in unionized and nonunion organizations. In the unionized workplace, a participative system can potentially provide employees with the right to influence their day-to-day working conditions and work methods. In the nonunion workplace, employees cannot have the right to share in designing the decision-making process. This difference is pivotal. In the nonunion workplace, management unilaterally decides the nature, the extent, and the structure of participation. Employees exert influence only within the constraints established by management. Because nonunion workers have no right to participate, they are especially vulnerable to pseudo-participation and manipulation. Further, the company union provision of the National

Labor Relations Act generally limits the scope of participation in nonunion plants to matters other than working conditions. This book is intended to assist labor and management in dealing with the problems presented by worker participation systems, and in converting these problems to mutual opportunities, by proposing a specific approach and providing detailed guidelines for designing, implementing, and maintaining this approach.

The Introduction provides the information and conceptual tools the reader needs in order to understand the concept of extended, integrated bargaining. It gives a brief history of management philosophies and ends with a discussion of the practices and assumptions of joint management.

In Part One, I propose a theory of joint management based on extending the collective bargaining process by adding integrative bargaining structures at the bargaining unit and lower levels of the organization. I then relate this theory to the experience of four jointly managed workplaces. Chapter One summarizes the various theories of participation and industrial relations that contribute to this proposal. Chapters Two, Three, and Four set forth the design principles, operating principles, and structure of joint management (that is, the parallel organization), and identify the differences between traditional integrative bargaining and integrative bargaining within the context of the parallel organization. In Chapter Five, I present the histories and descriptions of four jointly managed workplaces: the Detroit-Hamtramck Cadillac assembly plant, the Shell-Sarnia chemical plant, the Pima County (Arizona) government, and the Saturn assembly plant in Spring Hill, Tennessee. Each of these workplaces is analyzed in terms of the extent to which its participative system follows the design principles proposed in Chapter Two.

Parts Two and Three discuss the new aspects taken on by the various management functions under joint management. For example, the role of the manager changes from directing, controlling, coordinating, and disciplining subordinates to educating them and providing them with the tools, materials, supplies, skills, and services they need to get the job done. Planning is engaged in by all organization members. Internal controls are substituted for external controls. The use of conflict and competition to stimulate activity decreases.

Because jointly managed organizations rely heavily on group activity, Part Four provides a general discussion of group dynamics and sets forth the roles, functions, compositions, and operating methods used by the three kinds of groups (action team, planning team, and autonomous work team) used in joint management.

In Part Five, I discuss three skills that are required of both managers and workers under joint management: communication, problem-solving, and proposal-writing skills. Part Six addresses one of the major problems/opportunities presented by joint management: its implications for compensation systems. Chapter Nineteen points out the necessity for revising jobs and performance evaluation systems in jointly managed organizations. In Chapter Twenty, I discuss gain sharing as a means of distributing increases that result from greater productivity due to worker participation. In Chapter Twenty-One, I recommend that attention be given to worker ownership as a societal approach to providing more equitable compensation.

Part Seven discusses the specific steps involved in designing, installing, and operating an effective joint management system. Chapter Twenty-Two suggests a series of steps to be taken in order to extend the collective bargaining process. Chapters Twenty-Three and Twenty-Four describe the kinds of changes management and labor must make in their administrative policies in order to make these policies consistent with and supportive of the joint management system.

Part Eight places the rest of the book in context. In this part, I address the questions "Can joint management increase productivity and human well-being?" and "What steps might be taken by the institutions of society to promote well-designed joint management systems?" Chapters Twenty-Five and Twenty-Six take a broad view and are addressed mainly to policymakers in labor, management, government, education, and religious organizations.

Audience

This book is intended primarily for the use of three groups: policymakers in labor, management, education, and government; plant-level managers, union officers, and rank-and-file workers;

and the academic and consulting community. It aims at creating a heightened awareness of the "the participation paradox" among policymakers and at stimulating their thinking regarding strategies for reconciling the contradictions of this paradox. It is also designed to assist plant-level managers, union officers, and rank-and-file workers as they design, implement, and operate participative systems. Whether a local union and management decide to adopt the recommended extended bargaining approach or elect to stop short of enforceable integrative bargaining, this book can be used as a text in training managers, union officers, and workers (especially those who are members of action, planning, and autonomous work teams) in the philosophy of joint management and in the communication, problem-solving, and proposal-writing skills it requires. Professors and students of industrial relations, organizational behavior, and organizational theory will also find this book useful as a primary or supplementary text. Finally, consultants who work with unions and managements in developing and installing participative systems will find this book helpful.

Acknowledgments

I wish to thank all the many people who gave me advice and moral support during the period from 1972 to 1989, which I spent as a consultant to various experiments in joint management. Throughout these years Elliot Leibow and Eric Trist, in particular, gave me much-needed collegial and emotional support. Elliot also reviewed portions of the manuscript for this book and made valuable comments. Without the support of Joe Tomasi and Jim Vainer of the United Auto Workers, and Warren Jennings and John Reed of the American Federation of State, County, and Municipal Employees (AFSCME), my years in Ohio during the early 1970s would have been less productive. Jon Showalter and Jim Wright, then of AFSCME, guided me through the minefields of unionism in a right-to-work state (Arizona) during the late 1970s and early 1980s. Emil Franzi, grass-roots philosopher and behind-the-scenes politician, delivered three Pima County Board of Supervisors votes each time the Pima County experiment needed them. Terry Mazany and David Olsen read and commented on an early draft of the manuscript. Sue Schurman read and commented on a later draft. I am especially indebted to Hy Kornbluh for the insightful comments he made during our many discussions of *Joint Management and Employee Participation* while this book was being written. Colin Clipson, director of the Architectural Planning and Research Laboratory (APRL) of the University of Michigan's College of Architecture and Urban Planning, provided me with a visiting professorship and the support that went along with it while I was working on the manuscript. Paula Bousley of APRL did an excellent job of drawing the figures and preparing the text for copyediting.

Ann Arbor, Michigan   Neal Herrick
February 1990

The Author

Neal Q. Herrick received his B.A. degree (1953) from the University of New Hampshire in English literature and his Ph.D. degree (1976) from the Union Institute in industrial relations.

A charter member of UAW Local 422 in Framingham, Massachusetts, Herrick has been an auto worker, construction worker, gandy dancer, municipal worker, salesman, retail clerk, meteorological aide, football coach, and reporter. As chief of policy development for the Federal Wage and Labor Standards Administration, he headed the HEW/Labor Task Force that drafted the Occupational Safety and Health Act first submitted to Congress in 1968 and chaired the Department of Labor's seminal labor-management conferences on the quality of working life in 1971–1972.

Herrick coauthored *Where Have All the Robots Gone?* (1972, with H. L. Sheppard), served on the task force that produced *Work in America* (1973), and edited *Improving Government: Experiments with QWL Systems* (1983).

Joint Management
and Employee Participation

Introduction

Participation, Joint Management, and Integrative Bargaining

This book seeks to give the reader an idea of the meaning, history, and practice of joint management. It then proposes a specific approach to joint management, discusses management functions and skills in the context of joint management, outlines some compensation issues, recommends some strategies for organizational change, and suggests some societal implications of joint management.

This introduction gives the background information necessary to understand the nature and historical significance of joint management. Part One discusses the theoretical bases for joint management, describes the principles, structure, and process of the parallel organization, and presents four examples of joint management in North America. Part Two deals with the special forms taken by planning, power, and conflict in jointly managed organizations. Part Three examines the impact of joint management on needs, attitudes, behavior, motivation, and leadership. Part Four discusses the relationship of group dynamics to joint management and describes two components of the parallel organization in detail (the action team and the planning team). It also describes the autonomous work team and its relationship to the parallel organization. Part Five discusses the skills that are so important in jointly managed organizations (communication, problem solving, and pro-

1

posal writing). Part Six discusses some of the economic rewards that are appropriate in jointly managed organizations. Part Seven defines the roles and responsibilities of the two institutional parties to joint management and presents the process of converting from traditional management to extended integrative bargaining (and of adapting to the new system). Finally, in Part Eight, there is a brief discussion of the implications of joint management for workers, for institutions, and for society.

This is a new kind of book on management. It is written not just for supervisory personnel but for union officers and rank-and-file workers. It is designed to meet the need for a book on how to manage in a new kind of unionized workplace: a workplace where all employees have roles to play in the management process.

More specifically, it is written to meet the needs of organizations where organized labor and management have joined together to sponsor employee participation programs. Unions and managements that join together in this way are said to engage in "joint management." The structure used in jointly managed organizations is termed the "parallel organization." Some parallel organizations are highly centralized and consist only of top-level labor-management committees. Others are more complete or "whole." Based on our North American experience with parallel organizations, this book creates and proposes a model aimed at making employee participation an integral part of the collective bargaining structure. It also treats the autonomous work team and other subjects (like power, leadership, group dynamics) in the context of joint management.

Even more specifically, this book sets forth principles and practices that can be used by labor and management to ensure that employee participation efforts do not degenerate into "quick fixes," with long-term consequences harmful to both parties. However, these chapters do not pretend to describe a "tried, true, and tested" best way of structuring employee participation. I know of no organization where labor and management follow all the principles and use all the practices set forth in this book. This book proposes a "vision." It does not describe an accepted and widely used approach.

Neither does it propose a panacea. It does not claim to have the one solution to the problems presented by joint management. Each industry, corporation, international union, local union, and workplace must find its own solutions to these problems. It is my intention to stimulate the discussion of these problems and to provide a point of departure for this discussion. Because I believe that specific proposals stimulate discussion more effectively than do abstractions, I have tried to make my proposals as specific as possible.

The notion that employee participation might best be accomplished by extending the existing collective bargaining process has not yet been tried out. The concept of extended integrative bargaining as a desirable form of worker participation and as an integral part of the collective bargaining process was first proposed only recently (Herrick, 1986). However, Chapter Five presents an example of an effort that comes close to this vision (Shell-Sarnia). It also describes some efforts that use weak or highly centralized forms of the parallel organization.

The Traditional Split Between Thinking and Doing

Many books on management, while they may include sections on participation, make the basic assumption that workplaces are made up of two classes of people: people who figure out how to get the job done and people who do it. They are written for the former group and focus on two skills: (1) figuring out what should be done and (2) figuring out how to get somebody else to do it. Such books are, in a sense, consistent with the way things are arranged in many workplaces. Many organizations continue to follow Taylor's (1911) fourth principle of scientific management: there should be a division of labor between the thinkers and the doers. Put very simply, this explains why there have been, until very recently, no books written for labor on "how to manage."

But now there are many organizations that do not appear to follow Taylor's fourth principle. Some of these organizations are nonunion or are organized by unions that do not want to be involved in employee participation. They use techniques such as quality circles, job enrichment, and autonomous work teams (without parallel organizations) to give workers some scope for thinking. Others are organized by unions that wish to be in joint control of whatever participatory technique is used. They tend to use autonomous work teams linked to parallel organizations as their means of providing people with opportunities for participation and autonomy.

The next few sections of this introduction answer some basic questions about joint management, parallel organizations, integrative bargaining, and autonomous work teams. They set the stage for the more detailed treatments of these subjects in later chapters.

General Management Principles

The general management principles implicit in joint management can best be understood by contrasting them with Taylor's four principles of scientific management (1911).

Table 1. The Principles of Scientific and Joint Management.

Scientific Management	*Joint Management*
1. Specify the way each task should be performed	1. Let the worker decide how best to do the job
2. Reward each worker according to the amount he or she produces	2. Promote cooperation through group rewards
3. Hire people who will accept detailed instructions and train them to do so	3. Hire people who can take responsibility and train them to do so
4. Let management do all the thinking and require workers to do exactly as they are told	4. Let workers combine thinking and doing; let workers and managers think together

Most present-day organizations follow principles that lie somewhere between these two extremes. Some people think that we have moved a long way from the scientific management principles of the early twentieth century. Others, like Braverman (1976), believe that scientific management is still the dominant way of organizing work. Parker and Slaughter (1988) believe that the "team concept," which is perhaps the most common form of employee participation in current use, is an "intensification of Taylorism."

Joint Management Means Many Things

Joint management has many names. For example, the United Auto Workers (UAW) and General Motors use the term "quality of working life" (QWL). The UAW and Ford use the term "employee involvement" (EI). Groups of workers and managers who meet to identify and solve problems may be called quality circles in one organization, production committees in another, and planning teams in a third. Some participative systems bearing the labels QWL and EI follow many of the principles and practices suggested in these chapters and others do not. In this book, the term "joint management" is used to describe any situation where labor and management have entered into an agreement to sponsor an employee participation program.

Not only does joint management have many names, it also has many forms. No two workplaces have implemented it in the same way and no two consultants recommend the same design features. One reason for this is that joint management has evolved independently in many widely separated workplaces. While networking conferences were held as far back as early 1974 and organizations did learn from each other at these conferences, there was no one model that organizations could use in designing their joint management systems. Another reason for the many forms of joint management is that each workplace has tailored its system to fit its own unique circumstances. The evolutionary process through which joint management has developed in North America is in sharp contrast to its legislative base in some other countries. For example, Swedish law is very specific about the forms that worker participation can and cannot take.

Despite all this, it is nevertheless true that a measure of general agreement has evolved over the past decade or so regarding many of the principles and procedures that should be followed in jointly managed organizations. Some of the positions taken in this book reflect this general agreement. However, many of the other positions taken either depart from this general agreement or deal with issues on which no general agreement exists. In the final analysis the reader must judge.

The Benefits of Joint Management

Why should managers give up the ease with which they can make arbitrary decisions? Why should workers take on the headaches that come with getting involved in management? Why should unions become involved? The answer to the first question is fairly straightforward. The country is in a productivity crunch. Involving workers in decision making is a viable approach to increasing labor productivity (Kanter, 1983; Pasmore, Francis, Haldeman, and Shani, 1982; Nicholas, 1982). Therefore, many top managers are requiring middle- and lower-level managers to manage participatively.

There are several answers to the questions about why workers should participate. First, workers also have a stake in the health of the enterprise and in the state of the economy. Second, people like to be in control of their lives. It is true that some people fall into the rut of "just letting things happen" and then blaming others for their problems. Given a reasonable chance of success, however, most people will take the opportunity to be in control themselves. Third, by influencing the rules, policies, procedures, and work methods of their workplace, people can make their work a more satisfying experience. Finally, the experience of working on common problems in groups is personally enriching. People get fulfillment and satisfaction out of doing meaningful work—and influencing the way an organization operates is meaningful work to most people.

Unions should become involved because their continued existence depends on it. The work force is changing. White-collar workers now make up over 50 percent of the work force, compared with 36 percent in 1950. Management is changing. In both the union and nonunion sectors, management is becoming more participative. The economy is changing. International competition is forcing internal change. Unions, which now organize only about 17 percent of the work force as compared with 35 percent in the late 1940s, must adapt themselves to their new circumstances. For example, they need to appeal to additional groups of workers (for example, semiprofessionals). They need to involve more rank-and-file members in union activities. They need to become identified with the movement toward increased participation.

Recent History of Joint Management

The joint union-management sponsorship of employee participation efforts is a creature of economic necessity. Until 1972, joint management in North America occurred mainly in a few private-sector workplaces that used the Scanlon Plan. These firms often set up parallel organizations. Their committees, however, did not deal with conditions of employment but limited themselves to solving production problems. Frequently, companies adopting Scanlon and other gain-sharing plans were motivated by economic difficulties. With these firms it was often a case of "do something or shut down."

In 1972, the United States had its first twentieth-century balance of payments deficit. It then seemed to some union leaders and managers that, for the nation, it was a case of "do something or shut down." The executive and legislative arms of the federal government were also concerned. The secretary of Health, Education, and Welfare convened a task force that produced a widely read book titled *Work in America* (U.S. Department of Health, Education, and Welfare, 1973). Senator Edward Kennedy's Subcommittee on Employment, Manpower, and Poverty held hearings on worker alienation (U.S. Congress, 1972). Irving Bluestone, a vice-president of the United Auto Workers, met Sidney Harman, president of the then Jervis Corporation, at the Kennedy hearings and the two men subsequently entered into a historic agreement. Their agreement was to initiate a joint labor-management effort to improve the quality of working life and to increase productivity at Jervis's auto mirror plant in Bolivar, Tennessee. This was the first non–Scanlon Plan U.S. experiment in joint management during post–World War II years. In 1973, the UAW/General Motors contract included provisions for joint quality of working life experiments (Vogl, 1984). In 1980, the Communications Workers of America and AT&T negotiated similar provisions in their labor contract.

Participation in Nonunion Firms

While this book is concerned only with unionized organizations, it is necessary—for the sake of clarity—to give a brief account of the status of participative management in the nonunion sector. Until 1972, participative management followed much the same course in nonunion as in organized workplaces. With the coming of the "human relations" approach to management in the 1930s and 1940s, it occurred to some managers in both sectors that, in addition to treating employees more considerately, it might be well to seek their help in finding solutions to problems. These managers quite naturally wished to gain the advantages of worker involvement without giving up any of their control over decision making. Therefore, they relied on interpersonal approaches to encourage worker involvement (for example, training supervisors to be more open to employee ideas). During this period, interpersonal approaches were also used in unionized firms, since most unions maintained "hands off" policies when it came to employee participation efforts. Beginning in 1972, when unions did become involved in these efforts, they caused provisions for employee participation to be defined by rules, policies, and procedures. Participation systems became more structured and therefore more subject to being monitored by organized labor.

In recent years, employee participation systems in nonunion enterprises have become somewhat more structured. For example, by far the most common participatory technique used in these organizations is the "quality circle." These circles "seek to increase an organization's productivity and the quality of its products through direct employee participation" (Blair, Cohen, and Hurvitz, 1982, p. 9). The scope of these nonunion circles is limited, however, in firms covered by the National Labor Relations Act. These firms risk violating Section 8(a)(2) of the act if their circles address worker concerns as well as production problems (Bohlander, Jorgensen, and Werther, 1983). This section of the act, which is now threatened by a 1982 decision of the Sixth Circuit Court of Appeals (*NLRB* v. *Streamway Division*), is aimed at protecting workers from the formation of company-controlled unions. The 1982 Sixth Circuit decision, in essence, gave employers "a free hand in establishing their own systems of worker representation" (Heckscher, 1988, p. 135). If I am correct in thinking that the labor movement could strengthen itself by establishing well-designed systems of worker representation *within* workplaces, it cannot afford to lose the monopoly on this activity given it by Section 8(a)(2).

Joint Management, the Parallel Organization, and the Autonomous Work Team

Joint management occurs when a union and a management enter into an agreement to provide employees with greater opportunities for participation in the decision-making process. In most cases, these agreements specify the parallel organization as a means of providing these opportunities. Sometimes, units of the parallel organization are set up at every organizational level and are used to design and support autonomous work teams. In other cases, the parallel organization consists of only one top-level labor-management committee. In these cases, participative practices such as the autonomous work team are integrated into the management structure. This book proposes a form of joint management that is based on written agreements and administers these agreements through a visible structure of joint labor-management teams at all levels of the organization.

The Need for Visible Structure in Employee Participation Programs

All employee participation arrangements are structured. Structure is simply the set of rules and procedures that governs an activity. The issue for employee participation efforts is not so much whether they should be structured as how they should be structured. I believe the structure should create trust among the participants, provide for continuing joint control by labor and management, be clearly understood by the participants, be enforceable by the parties, and provide for the participation of large numbers of employees in making significant numbers and types of decisions. I will argue in the following paragraphs that an employee participation system should meet all these criteria in order to be effective for both parties. A system that does meet all these criteria is, in effect, an extension of the collective bargaining system.

Trust Among the Participants. Trust is desirable in distributive bargaining. In integrative bargaining it is essential. The parties must trust each other to abide by agreements. They must also trust each other to be open, honest, and respectful during the bargaining process. Trust can be sustained only by performance. Each party must come reasonably close to living up to the expectations of the other. If this does not happen, the aggrieved party will lose its trust and the system will lose a good measure of its effectiveness. It is clearly unrealistic to expect either labor or management to perform according to the expectations of the other party when these expectations are not known to them. Without a written agreement setting forth the policies and procedures of the participative system, it is impossible for either party to know whether or not the other party's actions are trustworthy—or even to be clear on what is expected of them. A parallel agreement needs to be negotiated for every unit of the organization. And without a network of joint labor-management teams to operate the participative effort, the participants cannot know with any certainty whether or not the other party has performed according to these agreements. A participative system without a visible set of rules and procedures or without a means for the parties to monitor its operation has no tools with which to build trust.

Continuing Control. It is not enough for labor to participate in the design and installation of a participative system. The system may start out with good intentions and sound rules and procedures. But there is a natural tendency for management, if it is left to its own devices, to (in the words of Yetman, 1983, p. 124) "drop the uncomfortable parts" (of worker participation) "and retain the comfortable ones." The workers (through their union) must be in a position to continually monitor the system and ensure that meetings are being held, that workers' concerns are being addressed, and that management is fully aware of the implications of its decisions for employees. The most feasible way for the parties to monitor the system is through a network of labor-management teams formed for this purpose (as well as for the purposes of reviewing proposals from lower-level teams and reaching consensus on solutions to organizational problems). In short, the basis of participative management, even at the worksite level, is integrative bargaining (that is, problem solving). And how can bargaining be effectively accomplished without duly authorized bargaining teams?

Clear Understanding. It is necessary that all members of the organization understand the goals, rules, and procedures of the integrative bargaining system. In addition, they need to understand the decision-making process that creates these goals, rules, and procedures and the process by which they can be changed. If organization members do not understand the system, they will be inclined to resist it and will certainly not be in a position to support it effectively.

Written parallel agreements, one of which should be negotiated by each unit and subunit of the organization, are necessary tools to create understanding. These agreements should be printed in pocket-size handbooks and distributed to all organization members. This, however, is not enough. In addition to the availability of the written agreements and the provision of periodic training in the goals, rules, and procedures of the participative system, a network of interlocking labor-management teams is necessary to provide a continuing means of explaining the parallel agreement to all organization members. Every organization member should have a representative on the parallel organization team serving his or her unit. These representatives are responsible for maintaining two-way communication with their constituents on the current activities of the parallel organization and for answering questions about participative goals, rules, and procedures as they arise.

Enforceability. A participative system will not work well if its rules and procedures are disregarded by any of the participants. If the procedures are not closely followed, people will become disillusioned and resistant or indifferent to the participative process. This has been perhaps the most serious problem faced by joint management in the past seventeen years. It is usually labeled "lack of top-level commitment." By the same token, one of the great advantages of making participation an integral part of the collective bargaining process is that its rules and procedures become enforceable and must be taken seriously by the parties. This point is illustrated by the Shell-Sarnia case described in Chapter Five. When the *Good Work Practices Handbook* became grievable in 1988, management began to treat it with respect. When this happened, the workers—who had become cynical about the participation system—regained their enthusiasm.

Obviously, rules and procedures that are not in writing cannot be enforced. Written parallel agreements are a necessity. Of course, informal means of enforcing the parallel agreement are most desirable—just as they are most desirable in enforcing the basic labor contract. Deterrence is the best informal means and informal discussion is next best. These informal means, backed up by the existing grievance procedure, are probably the best means of enforcing parallel agreements and the rules, policies, and procedures they produce. Where the offending party is a labor representative, there are two possible means of redress. First, his or her constituents should have the right of recall. Second, employees or management could appeal to his or her superior officer in the union hierarchy. These two means of redress should be detailed in the parallel agreement.

Scope. There are two kinds of participation available for use in joint management programs: direct participation and representative participation. Direct participation involves employees in the decision-making process without any intermediaries (for example, the members of an autonomous work team all participate directly in planning and coordinating the work of the team). Representative participation is used where the number of people affected by a decision is too large for all of them to sit down and solve problems together. It is extremely difficult to solve problems effectively with more than seven to nine people. Therefore, if employees are to be involved in decision making above the autonomous work team level (or where the autonomous work team has more than seven to nine members), representative participation is necessary. The parallel organization provides for representative participation at each decision-making point in the organization.

Direct participation alone is not enough. This is so for two major reasons. First, many decisions that substantially affect productivity and conditions of employment are made above the work unit level. These decisions benefit from employee input and employees benefit from giving their input. Second, without labor-management teams at all levels of the organization to monitor the direct participation (autonomous work team) system, it is vulnerable to use by management as a speed-up or union-busting tool.

The Parallel Organization: A Visible Structure

The principles and procedures of the parallel organization and the integrative bargaining process it supports are discussed in detail in Part One of this book. However, it might be well at this point to give a brief description of its structure. Our ideal parallel organization consists of integrative bargaining teams (called "action teams") at each level of the organization. Each organizational unit at each level has its own action team. At higher levels, an action team might have as many as six or seven "planning teams" to do its actual problem solving and proposal writing for it. Both action and planning teams consist of elected representatives from the various labor and management workplace interest groups that are affected by their bargaining. First-line and middle managers, as well as workers, elect their own representatives. These representatives do not represent the views of top management. They represent the views of their constituents. Worker representatives are titled "participation stewards" and are authorized in the union's bylaws. At the bargining unit level, the action team handles integrative bargaining and the bargaining committee handles distributive bargaining. Action and planning teams meet frequently (weekly, biweekly, or monthly). This contrasts with the bargaining committee, which normally meets only at contract time. See Figure 2 in Chapter Three for a model parallel organization.

The Dynamics of Parallel Organizations

In extended integrative bargaining—as in traditional collective bargaining—the authority to make final decisions still rests with management. In extended bargaining, however, labor agrees not to strike over any disagreement that might arise. An integrative bargaining problem can become a factor in a strike decision only if the union reformulates the "problem" as an "issue," takes it to the next round of contract talks, and fails to resolve it at these talks. Does this mean that, in the final analysis, there is really little difference between even the strongest form of joint management and the traditional way of doing business? There are two major reasons why the answer to this question is no. First, the well-designed parallel organization provides a forum for the effective use of persuasion and influence. For all practical purposes, decisions often are made before the decision maker formally gives consent. Where workers and subordinate managers have jointly developed a given rule, policy, or procedure and are committed to making it succeed, a wise top manager will hesitate to veto it. As John Lance, a senior heavy equipment operator involved in a participative system, expressed it: "But anyone who's come up with an idea in a QWL meeting and then written it into a proposal that's broken a log jam knows that there's more to it than who has the final say. Sometimes the decision gets made before the final say gets said" (Herrick, 1983, p. 63).

The second reason has to do with the worker's ability to make final decisions on his or her own job. It is normally within the power of the immediate supervisor to further delegate authority given by higher authority. Therefore, workers and supervisors can jointly develop plans for increased delegations of authority within the work unit (or autonomous work team) while meeting in their worksite-level action teams. Once a final decision has been made with regard to a delegation of authority, subsequent final operating decisions are made by the worker to whom the authority has been delegated. A comprehensive approach to delegating authority and fostering teamwork within the work unit is discussed in Chapter Fifteen.

The Parallel Organization as Reconciler

The ability of the parallel organization to produce decisions that reconcile the views and feelings of all the organization members affected by them—workers and managers alike—is termed "social integration" (Herrick, 1985). Social integration leads to important psychological and economic differences in enterprises using parallel organizations. These differences flow from an increased commonality of purpose created by the parallel organization. Conflict is limited to those matters where it is appropriate and necessary (that is, matters dealt with through distributive bargaining) and minimized in those areas where everyone in the organization has the same self-interest (that is, operating a productive organization that provides its members with secure and fulfilling work).

Where conflict exists in an organization, it is often due to the existence of a variety of ideas and feelings about how things should be done (about the rules, policies, and procedures by which the organization is governed). The conflict stems from the primary organization's inability to reconcile these different ideas and feelings. The parallel organization is designed for multilateral bargaining (bargaining among a number of workplace interest groups). Accordingly, it has the ability to reconcile these conflicting interests and points of view. This operates to the advantage of both labor and management.

The Workplace Interest Group

The structure of the parallel organization assumes that different members of an organization look at things from different points of view and often have different interests that they wish to pursue. It further assumes that members with similar points of view and interests form groups and that these groups seek to influence the policies and operations of the organization. In this book, these groups are called "workplace interest groups."

The workplace interest groups of many organizations are in a continual state of conflict. With regard to some matters, the conflict is open and therefore has a chance of being resolved. With regard to others, it is repressed and manifests itself in indirect ways that interfere with both productivity and personal relationships among organization members.

The parallel organization provides a process (integrative bargaining) through which the differences among the groups can be acknowledged, discussed, and reconciled. Often, it develops proposals to solve problems in ways benefiting all the groups. In those few areas where the goals of the groups are fundamentally in conflict, of course, they must use another process (distributive bargaining) and another forum to resolve their differences.

The parallel organization does not seek to blur the interests and identities of the workplace interest groups. It is based on the belief that their different interests and identities must be acknowledged and clarified as a first step toward reconciling their differences. Some workplace interest groups are based on occupation or level in the hierarchy. Others are based on membership in an organizational unit. Most people belong to at least two such groups. For example, a nurse assistant on the graveyard shift in Ward A would probably belong to three workplace interest groups: rank-and-file worker, member of the graveyard shift, and member of Ward A. The following workplace interest groups are common to most organizations.

Rank-and-file union workers
Nonaffiliated (office) workers
First-line supervisors
Middle managers
Top managers
Union stewards
Localwide union officers
International union officers
Members of an organizational unit

The parallel organization legitimizes the differences in the points of view of these groups and provides forums in which organizational rules, policies, procedures, and programs can be developed to reconcile these differences.

Where the Autonomous Work Team Fits In

The autonomous work team is the point at which the parallel organization dovetails with the production process. It is the point at which the parallel and the primary organizations merge. The lowest-level action team of the parallel organization is made up of the leader and several elected members of the autonomous work team. Where the work team has fewer than ten members, the lowest-level action team is often made up of the entire work team. They are one and the same. Often, the lowest-level action team is formed before the traditional work unit converts itself into an autonomous work team. In these instances, the action team designs the primary task, goals, and working arrangements of the autonomous work team. It then takes the lead in bringing about the shift from traditional to team management. After this shift has been completed, the action team continues to perform the full range of integrative bargaining functions for its autonomous work team. Due to the close relationships between representatives and constituents, integrative bargaining is often most effective at the work unit level—whether the work unit is traditional or has organized itself into an autonomous work team. It should also be noted that the hour-to-hour problem solving that goes on among the members of an autonomous work team as they do their work is a form of integrative bargaining. It is unique, however, in that it normally occurs among employees and does not involve the first-line supervisor (team leader). While this book uses the term "autonomous work team" for the sake of simplicity, work teams are almost never fully autonomous.

The Need for This Book

Joint management brings with it many difficulties and questions. How is management to be prevented from using employee participation as a tool to erode worker solidarity and speed up production? How is labor to be convinced that it must invest substantial resources in joint management programs? How are employees who perform management tasks to be compensated? In short, how can things be arranged so that both labor and management can realize the potential benefits of employee participation?

Many unionists are resisting joint management because they do not believe that these questions can be satisfactorily answered. Many managements are experiencing difficulties with worker participation because they do not have the support of their unions. This book proposes a set of approaches, principles, and practices aimed at helping unions and managements create mutually beneficial worker participation systems. The idea that parallel organizations and autonomous work teams can serve as structures for collectively bargaining solutions to problems of mutual concern to labor and management (Herrick, 1986) is central to this book. Through the use of the parallel organization, this integrative bargaining can be extended to lower levels, yet continue to be controlled by top management and the local union.

This book argues that worker participation systems based on top-level labor-management cooperation (that is, systems that cannot be entered into without the mutual desire of both parties and that can be abandoned by either party for no reason) are serviceable to neither labor nor management. They were necessary during the experimental years (1972-1982), but are now counterproductive. Now that we have learned, through experimentation, the principles and practices that work best, it is time to bargain and enforce them. We have only to contrast the Shell-Sarnia and General Motors Detroit-Hamtramck cases described in Chapter Five to see that grievable participation systems bargained by the union best meet the needs of both labor and management. Shell-Sarnia's system was in disrepair until 1988, when Energy and Chemical Workers Union (ECWU) Local 800 won the right to enforce it. Now it is operating smoothly. GM Detroit-Hamtramck uses a highly centralized, management-dominated system, and a slate that was perceived by workers to be "anti-team concept" won UAW Local 22's March 1989 election. This is not to say that cooperation is unnecessary when engaging in the integrative bargaining process. Integrative bargaining can work only if the parties do adopt open and cooperative behaviors. It is to say that they are more likely to adopt these behaviors if the "rules of the road" are clearly understood and enforceable. Therefore, the basic labor contract should make the participative process (and the rules, policies, and procedures it produces) grievable.

In order to gain and protect their members' opportunities for participation and autonomy, unionists need to learn the skills and approaches necessary for them to (1) bargain the right to extended integrative bargaining, (2) integratively bargain parallel agreements, and (3) monitor the administration of these agreements by management. In order to realize long-term productivity gains, management needs to learn its special role in joint management and to master the same skills and approaches. This book is intended to familiarize unionists and managers with the concept of the parallel organization as a mechanism for extended bargaining and with the principles and practices that should be followed in designing, implementing, and operating an effective parallel organization.

A manager or unionist who has mastered the material presented in these chapters (through reading, discussion, and experiential training) and who has done some outside reading selected for its relevance to his or her particular organization should have gained the foundation skills and knowledge necessary to begin functioning in an action team, planning team, or autonomous work team. It should be noted, however, that the help of internal or external consultants may be needed to facilitate the design and installation of these structures.

Part I

A Proposal for Jointly Managed Organizations

This part first discusses the theoretical roots of joint management. Then it draws on this theory and on our past eighteen years of experience with joint management to propose a set of principles, a structure, and a process that I believe could make joint management work to the advantage of workers, their unions, and management. In some of the instances of joint management that have occurred during the past eighteen years, the unions have actually exerted some day-to-day influence over the participative systems. In others, the systems have been totally management driven and the unions have been passive "cosponsors." These latter instances are the ones that have incurred the wrath of the New Directions movement. This movement, endorsed by Victor Reuther, is concerned about the potential dangers posed by the team concept and other practices based on labor-management cooperation. The principles, structure, and process proposed in this book are simply an idea: a form of joint management that does not exist out there in the world. Only a few workplaces (for example, Shell-Sarnia) come even close. This proposed form is union driven. In this form, employee participation is achieved by extending the bargaining process from the bargaining unit level down to the worksite level and involving virtually all employees in direct collective bargaining. The mechanism proposed for carrying on this extended bargaining (the parallel organization) is not new. Its prototype was conceived by United Steelworkers of America official Joe Scanlon in the 1930s, and weak versions of it have been used in some joint management situations since the early 1970s. The parallel organization has shown great potential. In its present form, however, it has both alienated some workers and failed to live up to its full potential for improving working conditions and increasing productivity. This part proposes principles, a structure, and a process that would enable the parallel organization to fulfill its potential. It describes the way a parallel organization would look under ideal conditions, as a mechanism for extended integrative bargaining. Chapter One summarizes the theories that are especially relevant to joint management. Chapter Two proposes sets of design and process principles. Chapter Three describes the structure of the parallel organization and Chapter Four comments on the integrative bargaining process.

Chapter Five describes four instances of joint management: three in the private and one in the public sector. In each of these cases, labor and management have joined together to jointly sponsor an employee participation system. I discuss each of these cases in light of how it meets (or fails to meet) the four design principles set forth in Chapter Two. These design principles make up the heart of this book. Viewed in this light, the cases differ greatly. For example, the Pima County government participative system is the most whole, representative, and self-designed of the four. Pima County unions and management, however, have done almost nothing to adapt their policies and procedures to joint management. This case is important because it reflects the special problems presented by the public sector and by weak unions. Shell-Sarnia appears to come closest to meeting our four principles. Yet its system is incomplete and centralized and—while ECWU Local 800 has taken the decisive step of bargaining for enforceability—does not identify worker representatives as union officers. Shell-Sarnia is important because it demonstrates both the feasibility and the desirability of folding worker participation into the collective bargaining process. The participation system at the Cadillac Detroit-Hamtramck plant and the planned system for Saturn are important because they give us an idea of the general direction being taken by a bellwether industry.

They are highly centralized and the union involved has not folded them into the collective bargaining process. The managements involved, however, have done an excellent job of adapting their policies to the principles of joint management. I believe that organized labor could convert worker participation from a problem to an opportunity if it were to bring the prevailing approach closer to the Shell-Sarnia model and to the four design principles.

Chapter 1

The Roots of
Joint Management

American unions have not been involved in the operation of participative systems long enough for a theory of joint management to
have evolved. While there has been a good deal of experimentation,
each experiment has been shaped by somewhat different organizational, social, and economic circumstances. Accordingly, each
experiment has used a somewhat different set of preexisting theories
and has developed a somewhat different set of participative practices. This is not to say that the preexisting theories were the determining factor in shaping the practices. In most cases, the circumstances determined the practices both directly and through
influencing the participants to select one theory over another.

Theory, of course, is most often based on practice. It is a set of
assumptions and principles devised to explain a set of existing practices and their consequences. Since the practice of joint management was almost nonexistent until the early 1970s, no preexisting
theories were quite on target. A number of related theories were
present, however, in the minds of the managers, unionists, and
third-party advisers who were involved in the experiments. These
theories were of some use in guiding or justifying the development
of new practices. The fact that they were often present in a highly
simplified form (for example, "Workers want more say over their

jobs and will work better if they get it") strengthened rather than diminished their influence. By the early 1970s, this kind of theory/ assumption had become an element of popular culture. Among the theories that have been used to shape joint management practice are participative management theory, political participation theory, labor-management relations theory, systems theory, sociotechnical systems theory, Scanlon theory, group theory, and design theory.

Participative Management Theory

Participative management theory proceeds from the idea that the "ultimate aims of the organization are efficiency and effectiveness" (Webber, Morgan, and Browne, 1985, p. 209). Given this starting point, participative management theory naturally focuses on productivity and tends to give little importance to the well-being of the worker. It focuses on situations where there seems to be a direct link between participation and productivity and develops practices that strengthen this link. Since the aims of political participation theory, labor-management relations theory, and so on are more "people oriented," the practices proposed by these theories are quite different.

Management textbooks often treat participation as a sub-topic under leadership. This reflects the idea that the extent to which an organization allows participation should be a unilateral management decision. One theory of leadership that has influenced many joint experiments is the "normative" theory (see Chapter Eleven for a more detailed description). In "normative" theory, Vroom and Yetton (1973) describe five levels of participation, ranging from decision making in isolation by the leader to consensus by the group. They propose that the leader select one of these five levels, depending on whether he or she has the information to make the decision alone, whether the decision is important, and whether other people in the organization need to accept the decision in order for it to work well.

By focusing on the efficiency and effectiveness criteria, this theory overlooks the long-term impact of participation both on the well-being of the worker and on the worker's general identification with the organization's goals. The normative leader selects certain decisions that make no difference, require information the manager doesn't possess, or need the worker's support. These decisions are made participatively.

This theory, of course, has influenced the development of even the most carefully designed joint management systems. For example, workers are rarely consulted on investment or marketing decisions. The clearest manifestation of normative theory, however, is the quality circle. "Quality circles seek to increase an organization's productivity and the quality of its products through direct participation" (Blair, Cohen, and Hurvitz, 1982, p. 9). They do this by utilizing groups of workers to solve problems around decisions where management will accept any conceivable solution, requires information, or needs the workers' support to function well. Most decisions that meet these criteria involve production problems. Unions have come to resist quality circles, however, and to insist that participative management systems be tied to worker concerns (Parker, 1985, Chapter Ten).

Political Participation Theory

Political participation theory also accepts efficiency and effectiveness as legitimate goals of participation. However, many political theorists place even greater emphasis on a third goal: the impact of participation on people's social character. Pateman tells us that Rousseau's ideal democratic system "is designed to develop responsible, individual social and political action through the effect of the participatory process" (Pateman, 1970, p. 24). J. S. Mill saw the two measures of a good government as the extent to which it utilized the existing moral and intellectual energies of its citizens and the extent to which it further developed these energies (Mill, 1961). Arnold Kaufman writes, "A democracy of participation may have many beneficial consequences, but its main justifying function is and always has been . . . the contribution it can make to the development of human powers of thought, feeling, and action" (Kaufman, 1969, p. 13).

Nagle, a contemporary political science theorist, describes three kinds of benefits from participation: instrumental, developmental, and intrinsic. Instrumental benefits are the concrete gains that specific people or groups of people can obtain for themselves through participating in the political process. Developmental benefits are those that accrue to society as a whole, including the development of a more politically efficacious, tolerant, and committed citizenry. Developmental benefits correspond most closely to the "efficiency and effectiveness" criteria espoused by management participation theory. Intrinsic benefits are those that accrue to individuals through their involvement in the process of political participation. Chief among these is the participator's enhanced sense of his or her own worth (Nagle, 1987, Chapter Two).

Macpherson (1977) characterizes the kind of democracy that now prevails in the Western world as the "equilibrium" model. This model is pluralist (it fits a society made up of individuals and groups with competing interests) and elitist (it assigns the main role in the political process to an elite group of leaders). It maintains equilibrium between the demand and supply of political goods. Macpherson maintains that a more equitable and humane society requires a different model of democracy. He proposes a "participatory" model. This model would consist of a pyramidal system with direct democracy at the base (the neighborhood or the factory) and delegate democracy at every level above that. Macpherson sees the movement for democratic participation in the workplace as the most important sign that a participatory model of democracy is possible in society as a whole.

Of course, not all political theorists are in favor of participation. Schumpeter's "classical doctrine" of democracy limits the individual's participation to voting for representatives. These representatives then make the necessary decisions (Schumpeter, 1950). This "classical doctrine" is based on the same assumption that underlies management participation theory: that the sole aims of participation are to achieve efficiency and effectiveness. Along with later theorists (like Eckstein, 1966), Schumpeter warns against too much participation on the grounds that it may have a destabilizing effect.

Pateman (1970) points out that the case for participatory democracy depends on the validity of the idea that participation provides developmental and intrinsic benefits. Macpherson (1973) concurs when he suggests that the Western idea of democracy justifies itself on two grounds: that it maximizes individual utilities (provides people with the maximum satisfaction of their consumer needs) and that it maximizes individual powers (provides people with the maximum opportunity for developing their unique individual capabilities). It is interesting to note that the idea of joint participative management must justify itself on two somewhat similar grounds in order to satisfy both labor and management: (1) that it increases productivity and (2) that it improves worker well-being.

Political participation theory played an important role in shaping the early American experiments in joint participative management. This was due, in large part, to the views of Irving Bluestone, then a vice-president of the United Auto Workers and the principal union advocate of worker participation during the 1970s. Bluestone's views were essentially political. For example, he argued for the adoption, in the workplace, of the political rights and mechanisms available to citizens in their nonwork lives.

Labor-Management Relations Theory

Walton and McKersie's classic analysis, *A Behavioral Theory of Labor Negotiations* (1965), pointed out many of the elements that underlie the currently evolving set of labor-management practices. Walton and McKersie analyzed four subsystems of the collective bargaining process: distributive bargaining, integrative bargaining, attitudinal structuring, and intraorganizational bargaining.

Distributive bargaining occurs when the interests of labor and management are in conflict. It deals with matters where each party tries to maximize his or her share in what Walton and McKersie call a "fixed-sum payoff." These matters are termed "issues" and involve situations where the gain of one party is necessarily the loss of the other. The amount of compensation that labor receives for its services, for example, is an issue. Distributive bargaining involves proposals, counterproposals, and compromises. Each side has decided beforehand what it wants and what it is willing to accept. Each side seeks to mislead the other side on these points. Each side postures, conceals information, and misrepresents its intentions.

Integrative bargaining occurs when labor and management have a common concern that can be addressed by the same action.

These matters are termed "problems." A problem in its purest form is a matter where the parties would assign the same priorities to all possible outcomes and about which the two parties are equally concerned. For example, the loss of a major business contract might be a pure problem if the potential losses in profits concerned management to the same extent that the possible losses in jobs concerned labor. In integrative bargaining, the parties (ideally) work together to define the problem, analyze it, gather information, develop alternatives, and agree on a solution.

Attitudinal structuring is the process of shaping the continuing relationship between the parties. Walton and McKersie suggest that negotiations are used by each party to create attitudes of friendship, hostility, competition, cooperation, trust, and so forth on the part of the other party. Interorganizational bargaining is a set of activities engaged in by the negotiators to achieve consensus within their constitutencies (that is, labor or management).

Integrative bargaining is the element of Walton and McKersie's theory that is most relevant to joint participative management. Indeed, the parallel organization can be viewed as a structure specifically designed to facilitate integrative bargaining—not only at the bargaining unit level but at all levels of the organization, including the work team. They recommend the use of integrative bargaining to establish (and maximize) the total benefits to be distributed. Then, say Walton and McKersie, the parties should shift to distributive bargaining in order to decide how the total benefits are to be divided. However, they identify a number of collective bargaining features that make this extremely hard to do (for example, the difficulty of trusting the other party in the collective bargaining situation and the difficulty people experience in shifting from one kind of bargaining to the other).

The parallel organization, by establishing a new relationship separate from the distributive bargaining relationship in terms of space and time, minimizes most of the difficulties pointed out by Walton and McKersie.

Systems Theory

The proposition of systems theory that has had the most influence on the management of organizations is put by Emery

(1969, p. 14) in these words: human organizations "have to be analyzed as 'open systems,' i.e., as open to matter-energy exchanges with an environment." This idea is presented in management texts in terms of models that "receive inputs from their environments (raw materials, energy, new employees, new equipment, information, and so on), transform these inputs, and return outputs" (Wofford, 1982, p. 22). This "open systems" perspective has led to an emphasis on the "interrelationship of the parts of an organization and its environment as they influence effectiveness" (Steers, Ungson, and Mowday, 1985, p. 77). This aspect of systems theory is often expressed by managers and unionists in words such as these: "Don't change one part of the organization without thinking about how the change will affect the other parts."

Prior to 1972, most U.S. work-restructuring experiments were conducted with small units within organizations and, as a rule, had very short lives. The first widespread application of systems theory occurred in the labor-management experiments of the early 1970s, where changes were implemented on an organization-wide basis. However, these later experiments were done with total organizations because most union leaders found it politically unwise to provide benefits (whether economic or psychological) to some members of their bargaining units while withholding them from other members.

Where members of the same bargaining unit were treated differently, the predictions of systems theory (and the political intuitions of union leaders) were generally borne out. For example, Goodman describes an early experiment in which part of a coal mine experimented with autonomous work teams while the remainder of the mine continued its traditional working arrangements. One of the reasons given for the failure of the experiment to last and to be extended to the rest of the mine was that "the original program created inequities within the mine . . . the negative feelings generated led to a general resistance to the mine-wide program" (1982, p. 249).

Sociotechnical Systems Theory

The term "sociotechnical system" was coined by the British theorist Eric Trist (Trist and Bamforth, 1951). Its main assumption is that "any work site contains two interdependent systems, a technical system and a social system" (Trist, Susman, and Brown, 1977, p. 207). The technical system (machines, tools, conveyances, and so forth) and the social system (people's attitudes, beliefs, and feelings) should be designed concurrently so that the total system can find the best match between them. In practice, the term "social system" has come to include the rules, policies, and procedures that arrange relationships among people and between people and the technical system.

Sociotechnical systems theory was especially influential in the early joint participative management experiments because some of the leading formulators and proponents of this theory acted as "third parties" in these experiments. For example, the first such experiment, entered into by Harman International Industries and the United Auto Workers, used the advice of Einar Thorsrud, a Norwegian theorist and practitioner (Macy, 1982). Eric Trist (mentioned above) led the team of consultants that advised the United Mine Workers and the Rushton mine.

More important, the joint nature of these experiments made it politically necessary that they take into account the beliefs, attitudes, and feelings of the workers as well as the features of the technical system. Once it became involved in the restructuring of working arrangements, labor naturally represented the interests of its constituents in this new area of concern.

Scanlon Theory

The Scanlon Plan is a joint labor-management system developed in the 1930s by the brilliant United Steelworkers official Joe Scanlon, for the use of distressed firms. It combines the participation of workers in solving production problems with productivity gain sharing. The genius of the Scanlon Plan is that its participation and equity mechanisms act in concert to promote cooperative and helping, rather than competitive, behavior. This behavior often leads to an increase in productivity that is shared by labor and management.

Moore and Ross (1978) state that the two basic assumptions of Scanlon theory are (1) most of us desire personal growth and development and (2) most of us wish to contribute to organizational goals. The Scanlon Plan creates a set of circumstances that make it both rational and feasible for us to do so. Scanlon plans make it rational by giving us a share in productivity increases. They make it feasible by setting up a committee structure through which we can influence work process decisions.

The parallel organization draws heavily on the Scanlon committee structure. Most parallel organizations differ from Scanlon plans, however, in two important respects. On the positive side, they are not generally restricted to production problems, but address a wide range of worker and management concerns. In addition, they can be used to design and support autonomous work teams and to protect workers from possible abuses of the team concept. On the other hand, the Scanlon Plan includes a vital component lacking in many parallel organizations: a direct economic incentive for cooperative and participative behavior. There is no reason parallel organizations in the private sector should not utilize Scanlon gain-sharing practices. Indeed, these practices and the parallel organization go together like "ham and eggs." Even in the public sector, Scanlon principles can be applied (see Chapter Five). Gain sharing gives people a strong motivation for doing the hard work involved in problem solving and for putting up with the frustrations that often go along with the hard work. Also, the planning teams of the parallel organization are ideal forums for the development of gain-sharing plans (see Chapter Twenty). Nevertheless, most unions prefer to rely on after-the-fact distributive bargaining as a means of getting the workers' share of any productivity gains achieved through worker participation systems. For example, not one of the three private-sector organizations described in Chapter Five uses a productivity gain-sharing plan.

Group Theory

Most forms of participation involve three or more people getting together to solve a problem or to accomplish some other task. In the parallel organization, these groups are called action teams, planning teams, and—at the worksite where the parallel and primary organizations merge—autonomous work teams. Since most day-to-day participative activities occur in groups, group theory is an important part of participative theory.

The use of groups to perform tasks rests on the idea that groups can be more effective than individuals in solving problems where a wide range of skills and knowledge is required and in performing complex work (Wofford, 1982). By bringing more information to bear, they can produce sounder solutions to difficult problems. By bringing more skills to bear and by providing a framework for cooperative behavior, they can be more productive in performing complex work.

A great deal of research has been done on the factors that determine the effectiveness of groups (see Chapter Twelve). For example, Seashore (1954) found that cohesive groups with high productivity goals ranked higher than others in productivity. Wofford defines cohesiveness as the degree to which members are motivated to remain in the group. Some of the conditions that affect group cohesiveness are the group's success, the existence of an outside threat to the group, amount of time members spend together, and the extent to which members agree on group goals.

Design Theory

Design theory is relevant to joint management at two levels. First, the joint management system itself must be designed and the design process is crucial to its success. Second, once the joint management system is in place, it is used to design work processes and the administrative systems of the organization.

We have already discussed one design theory: the sociotechnical approach. Now we will place this approach in the context of current Scandinavian systems design research. Bansler (1987) identifies three design approaches from the 1960s to the present: the infological approach, the sociotechnical approach, and the collective resource approach. The infological approach focuses on the efficient use of information. The sociotechnical approach seeks to discover the optimum "fit" between the social and technical systems of an organization. The collective resource approach recognizes the conflicting interests within an organization and focuses on ways to involve workers and their trade unions in the design process.

A Beginning Theory of Joint Management

The approach to design taken in this book falls clearly within the collective resource approach identified by Bansler. This book regards the workplace as a political organization, made up of a number of workplace interest groups—all with different and sometimes conflicting interests. In order to reconcile these different interests and agree on common courses of action, an integrative bargaining structure is needed at each level, from the bargaining unit down to and including the work unit. Since the workplace is not regarded as only two monolithic groups, the parallel organization must be designed to accommodate multilateral bargaining.

Before unions became involved in participative programs, participation was simply a management tool for controlling the work force and increasing productivity. The emphasis was on understanding the factors that affected control and productivity so that management might more effectively manipulate these factors. The well-being of the worker was important only insofar as it affected control and productivity.

Now that unions are involved, the context of participation theory has changed. The well-being of the worker must be given an importance at least equal to that of productivity, and ways must be found to ensure that the worker shares in any productivity gains. Further, the factors affecting control and productivity can no longer be manipulated solely by management. The workers must now participate in any decisions about these factors. A new body of participation theory is needed. This new body of theory should deal with participation, not as a management tool but as a political structure within the workplace. One of the purposes of this book is to begin the development of a theory in this new area of participation.

As a first step, I am proposing a set of relationships among joint management, the collective resource approach to design, extended bargaining, the parallel organization, and the autonomous work team. Joint management is any situation where a union and management agree to work together to involve workers in the decision-making process. This involvement may occur only at certain levels of the organization (like the autonomous work team) and may be restricted to certain kinds of problems (like production problems), or it may occur at all levels of the organization, include all kinds of problems (like production and working-conditions problems), and be an integral part of the collective bargaining process, as proposed in this book.

The collective research approach to design advocates the influential involvement of workers and their unions in a broad range of systems design problems. Accordingly, it can be described as a political approach to joint management that is not limited by management to the worksite level. Extended integrative bargaining is a specific collective resources approach to design that fits well with the North American collective bargaining process.

The parallel organization is a structure within which extended, integrative, multilateral bargaining can take place. This bargaining produces "social integration"—harmony within the social systems of complex organizations (Herrick, 1985). I hypothesize that the effectiveness of integrative bargaining is determined by the extent to which the parallel organization adheres to the four design principles discussed in Chapter Two. The autonomous work team is a method of organizing the work unit so that its members can participate to a greater extent in making day-to-day and hour-to-hour decisions. This day-to-day and hour-to-hour participation is a part of the integrative bargaining process. Autonomous work teams can exist in nonunion workplaces where there is no parallel organization or in union workplaces where it is incomplete. Where there is a parallel organization and where it includes worksite action teams, each of these teams can be useful in the design and maintenance of corresponding autonomous work teams.

Chapter 2

Principles for
Designing and Operating
the Parallel Organization

The vision set forth in this book is a parallel organization that is whole, representative, self-designed, and installed in a workplace where the policies of labor and management have been made consistent with the principles of joint management. Such a parallel organization could serve as a mechanism for extended integrative bargaining. This bargaining would occur at all levels of the organization around problems that concern both labor and management. The end products of this bargaining would be mutually agreed-upon plans in the form of enforceable rules, policies, procedures, programs, and work methods. The parallel organization would produce these plans through three kinds of teams: the action team, the planning team, and the autonomous work team. Where a work team has fewer than about ten members, all of them would normally sit on its action team. Even small work teams, however, might choose to form two- or three-member planning teams to develop their plans. At the intermediate levels of the organization, action teams would review and approve plans developed at lower levels. At the upper levels, each action team would be served by a number of planning teams. These planning teams would develop proposed plans and submit them to their action teams for approval. Figure 1 in Chapter Three shows, in chart form, a generalized structure for the parallel organization.

Parallel organizations—both in their present form and in the form they would take if they were folded into the collective bargaining process—plan by first identifying problems (either present or anticipated) and then developing rules, policies, procedures, programs, or work methods that solve the problems or prevent them from occurring in the future. Thus, the activities of the parallel organization are problem oriented. Worksite action teams and upper-level planning teams keep themselves focused by using formal problem-solving steps (see Chapter Seventeen).

The introduction to this book talks about the underlying principles of joint management. This chapter first discusses the relationship of joint management's vehicle (the parallel organization) to the union and then sets forth some principles for use in designing and operating it. The design principles have a concrete nature and can be easily monitored. The process (operating) principles deal with the ways people behave as members of action, planning, and work teams. This makes them more difficult to monitor and enforce.

The Parallel Organization and the Union

Parallel organizations have been used by labor and management to involve employees in decision making. This book proposes that these structures be more fully developed and used by labor and management to conduct extended collective bargaining. This would enable organized labor to directly involve large numbers of members in the bargaining process. Parallel organizations could provide employees with opportunities to participate in a solid and meaningful type of decision making: collective bargaining. Further, by merging participation and collective bargaining, unions could exercise control over participative practices and prevent these practices from being used to weaken them. The parallel organization gets the participative process out in the open where it can be monitored, brings participation to bear on organization policies and programs at all levels, and, if it were folded into the collective bargaining process, could make it clear to members that their union is responsible for any benefits achieved through participation.

Getting Participation Out in the Open. Some jointly managed organizations use a very limited form of the parallel organization. They establish their parallel labor-management team or teams only at the top level. Then, instead of including the procedures governing autonomous work teams in the worksite-level parallel agreements, they integrate them into the management structure. This makes it extremely difficult for the union to keep track of these procedures and the way they are put into operation. This difficulty has contributed to a feeling on the part of some unionists that autonomous work teams are being used by management to enforce Tayloristic management practices and to speed up production (Parker and Slaughter, 1988).

Well-designed parallel organizations get the "nuts and bolts" procedures of a participative system out in the open. The parallel agreements that are negotiated by each organizational unit make these procedures a matter of record. The union participates in developing the participative procedures at every level of the organization and agrees to them before they are implemented. It is also in a position to bring about changes in these procedures if they are not working well. It can bring about these changes by establishing an official union presence on action and planning teams at all levels of the organization. Among the responsibilities of the action and planning teams of the parallel organization are monitoring the operation of the participative system and changing its procedures where necessary.

Bringing Participation to Bear at All Levels. Organizations often have four, five, or even more levels of hierarchy. Decisions made at all of these levels can weaken or strengthen a participative system or weight it in management's favor at the expense of the workers. Other decisions are also made at all of these levels that affect employee well-being and productivity. A well-designed parallel organization can ensure that these decisions are made with the knowledge, input, and concurrence of the employees and their union. It includes action teams at each level of the organization. These action teams monitor and continually redesign the participative system. Each action team has official union representation. Of course, only a small portion of a parallel organization's time is spent monitoring and modifying the procedures of the participative system. It spends most of its time working on other matters affecting both employee well-being and productivity.

Making it Clear to Members Where the Benefits Are Coming From. Without a well-designed parallel organization, employees are almost certain to give management the credit for the benefits they gain through participation. They see managers operating the participative system and they are often not aware that, when participation was first adopted, their union was involved in its design. Most parallel organizations now in existence are not well designed. Because of this, management gets the credit and employees sometimes ask themselves, "Why are we paying dues to the union when the parallel organization is free?" If the union wishes to retain the loyalty of its members, it must take a highly visible, influential, and continuing role in operating and monitoring the participative system. The parallel organization, if designed and operated according to the principles set forth in this chapter, can provide this highly visible, influential, and continuing role.

Design Principles

Many of the specific principles that affect the success or failure of a parallel organization can be built into its design. They are translated into system procedures and, in this form, set the stage for the operation of the parallel organization. The extent to which a parallel organization meets these design principles determines, in large part, the extent to which it is capable of engaging in extended collective bargaining. A parallel organization should be whole, representative, and self-designed. It should also exist side by side with labor and management primary organizations that are adapting their policies to be consistent with the philosophy of joint management. If these four design principles (wholeness, representation, self-design, and adaptation) are met, the parallel organization can function effectively as an integral part of the collective bargaining process. The more fully the parallel and primary organizations meet these principles, the more beneficial joint management can be to both parties.

A Parallel Organization Should Be Whole. Workplaces are often assumed to be made up of two groups of people (labor and management), and each group is assumed to have homogeneous sets of interests and points of view. Our collective bargaining system reflects these assumptions. Now, however, I think it is more useful to assume that workplaces are made up of a number of groups of people, each group with its own special—sometimes conflicting—interests and different ways of viewing the world. These workplace interest groups are formed along hierarchical, organizational, and occupational lines. For example, top management, middle management, and first-line supervision are three different groups with different concerns and points of view. The members of an operations division often see things differently from the members of a staff office group. Different occupational groups (for example, registered nurses, licensed practical nurses, and nurse assistants), while they may be concerned with the same field of work, have different career and work concerns.

In order to accomplish its main objectives, which are to reconcile the views of these workplace interest groups and to establish work methods and administrative guidelines that are consistent with these reconciled views, the parallel organization must be equipped to engage in multilateral bargaining. That is, each action and planning team must be internally whole. It must include all the interest groups that have a stake in its activities. If it is not whole, it will simply create new conflicts and polarize the organization along new lines. For example, let us suppose that a school action team did not include students. Such an arrangement might reconcile the views of teachers, support staff, administrators, and parents. However, it would further polarize relationships between these groups and the students.

In applying this principle, the key question becomes "What are the separate workplace interest groups that have stakes in the activities of a given action team or planning team of the parallel organization?" Since it is difficult for an action team with more than seven to nine members to discuss issues in the depth required for true understanding, compromises must sometimes be made in the number of workplace interest groups that are entitled to an exclusive representative. These compromises often mean having interest groups with somewhat dissimilar concerns served by the same representative. This problem is especially severe with action teams at higher levels in the organization. Action teams at lower levels often serve only a few interest groups and, accordingly, have only a few members. Planning teams, since they are usually organized into miniteams, can be much larger.

The wholeness principle adds a new dimension to collective bargaining. Integrative bargaining, as it is carried on in the parallel organization, is multilateral. It does not involve just two parties, labor and management. Instead, it sees labor and management as being made up of subgroups, each with somewhat different interests. Sometimes it even includes workplace interest groups (for example, students and parents) who are neither labor nor management. It also requires the inclusion of employees who are not unionized, like office and administrative staff. This part of the wholeness principle is often violated even in the most advanced participative systems. For example, the Shell-Sarnia system (see Chapter Five) has not yet included its administrative and engineering staff. The special nature of bargaining in the context of the parallel organization is discussed in Chapter Four.

It is not enough for each action and planning team to be internally whole. In order for all workplace interest groups to be substantially involved in the bargaining process, the system itself must be vertically and horizontally whole. To be vertically whole is to have action teams at every level of the organization. To be horizontally whole is to have an action team for every organizational unit at each of these levels. This includes autonomous work teams of more than nine or so members. Where autonomous work teams are very small, it works well for all of their members to attend planning meetings. In these cases, the work team and its action team are one and the same.

Finally, the wholeness criterion requires converting all work units to autonomous work teams. If this is not done, two sets of inconsistencies will be created. First, the employees who are assigned to traditional work units will find inconsistencies between their day-to-day work lives and the experiences they have while serving on action and planning teams. Second, they will be acting according to traditional assumptions about work while their brothers and sisters in autonomous work teams will be living their day-to-day work lives according to joint management assumptions (see Table 1 in the Introduction).

A Parallel Organization Should Be Representative. The overriding virtue of the parallel organization is not that it provides technically sound solutions to problems involving work methods or administrative policies. It does provide these technically sound solutions and this is certainly important. Far more important, however, is the parallel organization's ability to provide solutions that represent the reconciled views of the many interest groups involved. Both the process of developing these solutions and the reconciling nature of the solutions themselves lead to a socially integrated enterprise (Herrick, 1985). In a socially integrated enterprise, the organization members work together in mutually acceptable ways to achieve mutually agreed-upon objectives. Each interest group, however, maintains its own separate identity and recognizes the fact that its interests are sometimes in conflict with those of other groups.

The concept of social integration is central to translating the principle of representation into reality. A union and management that give priority to the technical quality of solutions and the promptness with which they are produced may err in their interpretation of the representative principle. They may think that the principle has been sufficiently observed if there are members from the concerned workplace interest groups sitting on a given action or planning team—regardless of how they got there. Indeed, one writer on the subject talks about the importance of "handpicking people for teams or task forces who have the skills and enthusiasm for carrying out the activities" (Kanter, 1983, p. 247). However, little if anything in the way of technical competence is gained by "handpicking" and virtually everything is lost in the way of social integration. People who do not control the selection and recall of their representatives have less understanding of the issues and less opportunity to have their views brought to bear on these issues. This detracts from the technical competence of the solutions developed. In addition, people who do not control the selection and recall of their representatives have less awareness of the reasons for the decisions made and less understanding of the way they were made. This all but removes the possibility of social integration.

People do not become real representatives of a workplace interest group simply by virtue of their membership in the group. Instead, they tend to serve the interests of the people who place them in their positions on action or planning teams. If the people who place them in their positions and the people whose interests they are intended to serve are not one and the same, a conflict of interest results. Thus, both managers and union officers should resist the temptation to fill positions on action and planning teams by appointment. Appointments are legitimate only when the appointee is supposed to carry out the wishes of the appointer. Pressures of time (like the need to form a planning team quickly to address a pressing problem) and money (like the cost of an election where large numbers of constituents are involved) sometimes force union officers to compromise this principle by appointing members to action or planning teams. Such appointments should be kept to a minimum and should be made only by union officers who have themselves been elected by secret ballot. On the management side, since the numbers of middle manager and first-line supervisor constituents are relatively small, elections are always feasible. In general, where a team member is supposed to carry out the wishes of a group of constituents, he or she should be directly elected by these constituents.

Perhaps one of the greatest threats to true representation is the reluctance of small groups and work teams to conduct secret ballots. Often, people react negatively to the term "secret," thinking that it is somehow in conflict with the openness of joint management. Yet formal, secret ballots are crucial to true representation. Without the secret ballot, it is virtually impossible for the representatives to feel that they are accountable to their constituents. This is so for several reasons. First, elections by discussion or by show of hands can be easily manipulated by one or two members of the group or team. On countless occasions, I have seen people "go along" with nominations I knew they would have resisted if they could have done so without alienating a strong or popular member of the group. Further, when people decide not to "go along," it is divisive to the group. Elections by discussion or show of hands create a "no win" situation. Volunteerism is even less satisfactory. Most people will not volunteer unless encouraged to do so. They want to be sure that they are wanted and will be accepted if they do volunteer. For this reason, union and management leaders can easily control the membership of action and planning teams by giving a few words of encouragement to the people they would like to see serving on these teams.

These difficulties can be avoided by establishing a simple secret balloting procedure. Work teams and other workplace interest groups are given ballot boxes and standard ballots. In small groups, nominations are not necessary. Each voter enters two pieces of information on the ballot: whether he or she is willing to serve if elected, and the name of the group member he or she is voting for. Then someone from outside the group looks at the ballots and announces the name of the person (among those who were willing to serve) who got the most votes. Recall procedures should also be simple and nonthreatening to the voters. Recall elections that are difficult to bring about either do not happen or cause a great deal of unnecessary turmoil when they do happen. One excellent device (used by the Cadillac Detroit-Hamtramck plant) is to hold a confirmatory or recall vote three months after an individual has been elected.

It is not enough, however, to provide sound election and recall procedures. In addition, constituencies should be discrete and representation should be multiple for rank-and-file workers. A constituency is discrete when each constituent has only one representative on the team in question. Let us suppose, for example, that an election is being held in a work unit made up of sixteen members. Two participation stewards are being elected to sit on the unit action team. In order for the constituencies of these stewards to be discrete, the unit must be divided into two separate election "precincts," with each precinct returning its own representative. "At large" representation works well for stewards whose job it is to handle grievances. It gives workers a "choice of attorney." The job of participation steward, however, requires in-depth, two-way communication with constituents. As a practical matter, this just doesn't happen where two stewards have the same constituents.

Finally, representation should be multiple for rank-and-file workers. In distributive bargaining, it is necessary for workers to speak with one voice. In integrative bargaining, it is necessary that they speak with many voices. In integrative bargaining, the idea is to be creative, to get as many possible solutions discussed as possible. When workers are represented by only one participation steward, almost invariably he or she becomes an advocate of one point of view and downplays or even fails to mention other points of view held by the constituents. This is only natural. In addition, placing three participation stewards on each action team multiplies by three the number of workers who are directly involved in the bargaining process. It also reduces the size of their constituencies, thus allowing their constituents to become more involved in the bargaining process.

A Parallel Organization Should Be Self-Designed. The parallel organization is a means of providing all members of the workplace with access to its decision-making process. It is a basic assumption of the parallel organization that work methods and administrative rules, policies, procedures, and programs that have been developed by representatives of all the members of the organization work better than those that have been designed solely by managers and their staff assistants. The rules, policies, and procedures that govern the activities of the parallel organization itself must also be regarded in this light. In fact, since the parallel organization sets the ground rules for most other decision making, it is of overriding importance that the people who will use it design it.

Further, employees are likely to regard a proposed parallel organization as a management "scam." They have seen programs with labels such as job enrichment, quality circles, and human relations come and go and are often afraid to get their hopes up and then be disappointed by another program that seems, on the surface, to be similar. Of course, the fact that parallel organizations are jointly controlled by organized labor goes a long way toward softening this skepticism. And folding the participative system into the collective bargaining process goes an even longer way. But providing for people's input into the design of a parallel organization not only softens their skepticism, it creates a decision-making system that is tailored to their needs.

Self-design does not mean that every member of the organization sits on the action or planning team doing the designing. But it does mean that everyone has a representative on this team and that the team is formed according to the principle of "wholeness." It is important that the members of the team establish meaningful two-way communication with their constituents during the design process. The self-design principle also means that the team should present the results of its work to its constituents. A joint management system should include provisions under which members of the union can petition for a referendum to decide whether the system should be adopted and, subsequently, whether it should be continued.

While most joint management efforts adhere to the self-design principle in the initial design of the system, it is even more important to build in a self-redesign capability. Many of the people who originally designed the system are likely to be gone in a few years. The new organization members will have had no hand in designing the participative arrangements. Yet it is crucial that they assume ownership of these arrangements. Therefore, the original system design should include permanent planning teams responsible for continually evaluating the participative system and recommending changes.

Labor and Management Policies Must Be Adapted to Joint Management. The assumptions of joint management are diametrically opposed to those of scientific management. Yet many of the policies of traditionally managed workplaces have a strong scientific management bias. Further, the policies of their corresponding unions reflect this bias. The result is that many existing labor and management policies and procedures are in conflict with those of joint management systems and their parallel organizations. The parallel organization seeks to promote cooperation, sharing, and democratic values, and the primary organizations of both labor and management continue to reward competition, hoarding, and authoritarian values. In "greenfields sites," labor and management have a golden opportunity to start from scratch. In existing work-places that are converting to joint management, the adaptation principle is most crucial. It is also the most difficult to grasp, the most expensive to carry out—and the most often ignored.

For example, the Pima County government (described in Chapter Five) continues to maintain a merit pay system ten years after it converted to joint management. This system continues to promote individual competition, divisiveness, and hoarding behavior—while Pima County's parallel organization seeks to promote cooperation, skills sharing, and social integration. Even more striking, the Pima County attorney's office recently installed a piecework system of compensation for its lawyers—at the same time that it is seeking to promote teamwork within the office. Another example from Chapter Five is the use of an individual suggestion award system by the General Motors plant in Detroit-Hamtramck. This is even harder to understand than the Pima County case because the GM plant is a greenfields site.

Actually, none of these examples is difficult to understand. Both the Pima County system and the GM Detroit-Hamtramck system are management dominated. Management is oriented toward maintaining short-term external control over the behavior of employees. Merit pay, suggestion award systems, and piecework are time-honored methods of maintaining this kind of control. If I (or the chief steward of the union) were a manager in a similar situation, we would maintain or invent similar systems. To expect a manager to drop the need to exercise external controls over employees is unrealistic. It is labor's job to prevent these external controls from being maintained.

But it is equally necessary that labor adapt its policies to joint management. The union should review its bargaining and contract administration policies and adapt them to the needs of joint management. The only case described in this book (and, in fact, the only case I know of) where a union has made a serious attempt at adaptation is Shell-Sarnia. And even ECWU Local 800 has failed to extend bargaining to the lower levels of the organization and has not given union officer status to workers serving on integrative bargaining committees. Neither does Local 800 provide separate union training for these workers.

It is not a matter of blaming either labor or management for their failures to adapt. Joint management presents both parties with an extremely complex and difficult situation at a time when their hands are already full. Labor is in an especially difficult situation because it has very limited resources at the local level. Yet it must adapt its own policies, put the pressure on management to adapt its policies, and, on top of it all, participate in the review and adaptation of management's policies.

There is a recent trend, especially in greenfields sites, toward adapting management policies but leaving labor policies essentially untouched (see the descriptions of Saturn and Cadillac Detroit-Hamtramck in Chapter Five). This is dangerous in that it makes the participative system vulnerable to abuse. It opens the door to using the team concept, for example, as a tool for coercively speeding up production and busting unions. In some cases, the parallel organization appears to workers to be taking over many union functions and doing them better than the union can. However, joint management, while it can be a danger to labor if labor takes a passive role, can be a remarkable opportunity for labor if labor chooses to devote major resources to it. Joint management has the potential for becoming a win/win situation: good for both labor and management.

The adaptation of management and labor policies is key to the long-term success of joint management and is discussed in detail in Chapters Twenty-Three and Twenty-Four. These chapters both propose approaches to adaptation and provide checklists of specific policies that management and labor should review.

Process Principles

Process principles define the kinds of behavior appropriate in action teams, planning teams, and autonomous work teams. The work of these teams cannot be carried out effectively unless their members observe these principles. Where the members of work units, in their day-to-day and hour-to-hour relationships, fail to observe these process principles, a dissonance is created between their experiences in the action and planning teams and their experiences in their work units. This is true whether or not their work units have been converted to autonomous work teams. This section speaks primarily to the application of process principles in action and planning teams. It is the task of the action team at the work unit level to develop rules, policies, and procedures for the unit that promote the use of these principles on the worksite. In performing this task, the action team may or may not decide to convert the unit to an autonomous work team.

The process principles are more difficult to enforce than the design principles. They have to do with the underlying quality of human behavior. Violations, unless they are extreme, are often a matter of opinion. However, most people will observe sound process principles if the ideas behind them are introduced in a respectful way. This means, first, that organization members should be involved in formulating the specific principles to be observed. The design team can bring this involvement about through asking itself what behaviors might be appropriate to the system it is developing and through discussing these behaviors with its constituents. Second, the written rules, policies, and procedures governing the parallel organization should include a description of the process principles formulated by the design team. This means that, in a collective sense, the principles are agreed to by the primary organization when its members ratify the rules, policies, and procedures of the parallel organization.

Each organization formulates these principles in its own way. The formulations that appear below are based on "codes of behavior" developed by a number of different organizations. They describe six process principles: honesty, equality, consensus, trust, respect, and good faith.

Honesty. The nature of distributive bargaining requires "dishonesty" of its practitioners in the same sense that the nature of a poker game requires deceit of the players. For example, it would not make sense for a participant in distributive bargaining to reveal his or her final position early in the bargaining process.

The nature of the integrative bargaining that occurs in the action, planning, and autonomous work teams of the parallel organization requires a quite different kind of behavior. These teams cannot be effective unless the participants are open and honest about their thoughts and feelings. For example, if a manager were to withhold information about a problem, the action team could not deal with the problem effectively. Further, if the manager's dishonesty were discovered, it would damage his or her credibility with the rest of the team. The principle of honesty requires that members of action and planning teams speak "the truth, the whole truth, and nothing but the truth." Of course, this is not always possible in a literal sense. An employee representative's obligations to constituents or a manager's obligations to superiors may prevent the whole truth from being spoken. Accordingly, the principle may be stated in the following two parts:

> The whole truth should be spoken where this is possible
>   without compromising one's constituents or, in the case
>   of a manager, one's superiors.
> Where it is not possible to speak the whole truth, this fact
>   should be announced to the group.

Equality. In order to accomplish their ends, action and planning teams need to operate in protected environments. Members must feel free to speak their minds without the artificial constraints imposed by their positions in the hierarchy. This does *not* mean that people can treat each other with disrespect or lack of consideration. The opposite is true: people must treat each other with great respect in order for the parallel organization to function well. However, each member of a team should be listened to with equal respect, regardless of position in the primary organization. Members of these teams should relate as equals, as human beings whose opinions and feelings about the matters being discussed are of equal importance. It is only when an action team reaches a decision point that the views of the senior manager-member become worth more than the views of the other members. This is so because the senior manager-member's position makes him or her accountable for the decision.

There are extremely reliable signs that reveal whether or not the managers who sit on action teams are observing this principle. If they enter into the discussion yet do not dominate it, if they put forward their ideas yet carefully listen to the ideas of others, if they are secure enough to put forward an idea and later abandon it in favor of someone else's idea, they are observing this principle. The most common technique used by managers to disregard this principle is to say nothing until everyone else has expressed an opinion and then hand down a decision. This technique protects the insecure manager from threatening situations. It also robs parallel organizations of much of their value.

Consensus. The dictionary says that consensus is a "collective opinion or agreement." A more detailed definition is necessary in order to understand its application to the work of action and planning teams. When consensus is reached in one of these teams, it does not necessarily mean that, in the team's collective opinion, it is endorsing the best possible solution to a problem. Rather, it means that the members of the team agree that the course of action arrived at is better than no course of action. Some members of the team may feel that a far better solution could have been adopted. But they do not feel that the one reached is immoral or unethical and, since they are unable to persuade the rest of the team to agree with the solution they favor, they agree to the one that has the weight of the team behind it. Their agreement, however, is not passive. Once it is given, it means that all members of the team will actively support and work for the success of the decision just as though it were their own idea.

Two rules must be followed in order to square the principle of consensus with the accountability of the manager. (1) Where the accountable manager wishes to do something with which others in the group disagree, he or she has the final say. (2) Where the accountable manager does not wish to do something desired by others in the group, he or she has the final say.

In practice, managers rarely use their final say under these circumstances. In the first place, the principle of consensus forces such thorough discussions of issues that the various parties generally reconcile their differences. In the second place, it does not generally make good sense for a manager to veto a solution to a problem that has been agreed to by all the workplace interest groups in the organization.

Where the parallel organization is being used as an integrative bargaining mechanism, an additional rule must be followed to square it with the collective bargaining process. This rule can be stated as follows: "Where the accountable manager makes a decision in opposition to the other members of the action team, no job action will be contemplated by the union at that time. However, the matter may be labeled a distributive bargaining issue and referred to the union bargaining committee to be placed on the table during the next round of contract talks."

Trust. Trust is perhaps more a product of the parallel organization than a process principle. It is a principle, however, to the extent that the parties need to trust each other to some extent in order to observe the other process principles. Thus, in the early life of a parallel organization, trust is required as an act of faith. Then, as trust is earned, it becomes less provisional and can weather the inevitable storms that are bound to occur in all organizations. Trust should be easier to build where the parallel organization is used as a bargaining mechanism. People should be more inclined to keep their word voluntarily where the other parties to the process have a means of recourse if their word is not kept. In this way, performance should build trust.

Respect. When people fail to treat each other with respect, it is often due, at least in part, to their failure to fully understand each other. Since disrespect produces defensive behavior and defensive behavior prevents people from understanding each other, it is vital to the effective functioning of the parallel organization that the members of action and planning teams not get involved in this vicious circle. All parties must understand, before they become involved in teams, that people cannot be expected to relate to each other on the person-to-person basis required by the parallel organization unless they are treated with respect.

Good Faith. This principle is a repeat of the first (honesty) principle from a different perspective. This principle recognizes how easy it is for anyone who is a member of an action or planning team to pretend to observe the first five principles—and yet, in fact, sabotage the parallel organization. On the other hand, if the parties all make a good-faith attempt to observe the process principles (and if the parallel organization is well designed), it will almost certainly operate to the benefit of everyone concerned.

Chapter 3

The Structure of
the Parallel Organization

Chapter Two discusses the principles that are recommended for designing and operating parallel organizations. This chapter proposes a structure for translating these principles into reality. It discusses how the parallel organization can be charted; its purpose, authority, influence, membership, levels, and appeals system; and some rules for preventing it from competing with existing arrangements.

The parallel organization is a concrete part of the organizational structure. It can and should appear on the organizational chart. It gets its name from the fact that, where a parallel organization exists, the box representing each unit of the primary organization has at least one unit of the parallel organization sitting beside it—or parallel to it—on the chart. At the bargaining unit level, the parallel organization is also parallel to the collective bargaining structure. In considering Figure 1, it is useful to keep in mind that the parallel structure is occupied for only a few hours each month, while the primary structure functions continuously. The function of the parallel organization is to engage in integrative bargaining (that is, to develop and agree on plans for the social and technical design of the workplace). The function of the primary organization is to carry out these plans.

Figure 1. What a Parallel Organization Looks Like.

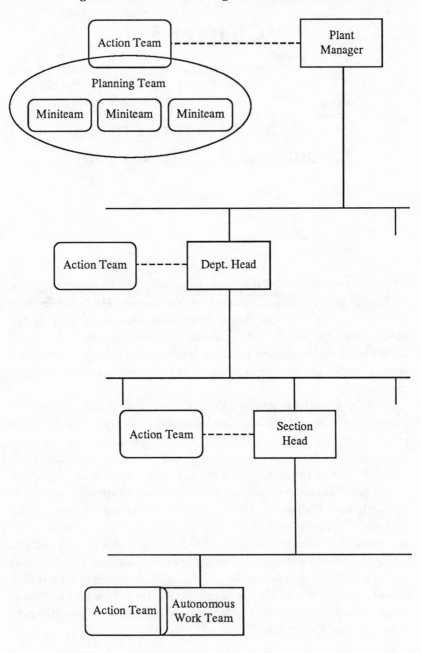

The action teams above the worksite level are not shown as overlapping with the units of the primary organization. However, the line manager involved (like the plant manager, department head, or section head) does sit on the action team parallel to his or her organizational unit. The action team at the worksite level is shown as overlapping. This is because it usually consists of the leader of the primary work unit (in this case, an autonomous work team) and two or three participation stewards elected by the members of the unit. Where a work unit is made up of fewer than ten employees, it often serves as both work unit and action team. That is, all unit members are also members of the action team. Action teams at higher levels often include union officers who are responsible for both the distributive and integrative bargaining relationships (that is, combined-function union officers) and elected representatives of subordinate manager groups (for example, first-line supervisors and middle managers). Planning teams are larger and include representatives from all of the various workplace interest groups in the organization being served. Planning teams are usually organized into sub- or miniteams of from five to seven members each.

Purpose of the Parallel Organization

Why do we need this additional organizational structure? What can it do that the primary organization cannot? How do we distinguish between the responsibilities of the two?

The purpose of the parallel organization is to produce rules, policies, procedures, programs, and work methods that are technically sound, tailored to the specific unit in which they will be used, designed to meet the needs of organization members, well understood by the people who must carry them out, and accepted by all the members of the primary organization. We need it because rules, policies, procedures, programs, and work methods that are developed solely by management are not always sound, are frequently misunderstood, do not always meet the needs of organization members, and are sometimes resisted by workers and by other levels of management. We also need the parallel organization because the traditional bargaining process is not equipped to produce solutions tailored to local conditions. In many organizations, the focus of management is on dealing with crises. Since a well-designed parallel organization helps to avoid these crises, it can be thought of as the part of the organizational structure that is specially designed for *preventive management.*

The parallel organization is responsible for identifying problems and for developing solutions to them in the form of rules, policies, procedures, programs, and work methods. It is a planning organization that seeks to solve existing problems and prevent potential problems from occurring in the future. The primary organization is responsible for carrying out, on a day-to-day and hour-to-hour basis, rules, policies, procedures, programs, and work methods; some are developed by the parallel organization and some are developed by the staff offices of the primary organization. In practice, the parallel organization often revises and fine-tunes rules, policies, and procedures developed by the staff offices of the primary organization when problems it identifies can be traced to these rules, policies, and procedures.

Authority of the Parallel Organization

Can the parallel organization decide what the primary organization should do? If it can, does this create chaos?

The action teams of the parallel organization do have the authority to make decisions. The planning teams do not. But we must remember that the authority of an action team flows from its senior manager-member, who is also the head of its corresponding unit in the primary organization. Further, the integrative bargaining process engaged in by action and planning teams is based on consensus. This means that the senior manager-member (along with the other members) must be convinced that something is desirable before the action team can reach a decision on it. Further, as we discuss later in this chapter, a guiding rule of the parallel organization is that the authority structure stays the same. Action teams cannot make decisions that do not have the approval of the senior manager-member. In other words, the integrative bargaining performed by the parallel organization is similar to traditional collective bargaining in that management has the right to make the final decision. The difference is that, in regular contract negotiations, labor can seek to change management's mind with a strike or the threat of a strike. This is not the case in integrative bargaining. If labor feels strongly that management has taken an unjustified position, its recourse is to refer the matter to the distributive bargaining committee. If consensus cannot be reached in integrative bargaining, for all practical purposes the problem being dealt with is not a problem at all, but an issue. And issues belong at the distributive bargaining table.

Influence

However, authority is only one component of power (see Chapter Seven). The other component is influence. While the parallel organization leaves the authority structure of an organization intact, it significantly changes its influence structure.

In a traditionally managed organization, management has all the authority and most of the day-to-day influence. Of course, organized labor exerts a major long-term influence through the regular collective bargaining process. The little day-to-day influence that is exerted by nonsupervisory personnel has two important characteristics. First, it is exerted through the informal organization. This means that everyone does not have an equal shot at it. Most of it is exerted by people with charisma and natural political ability. These people are the centers of the cliques that are the main channels for day-to-day influence in traditionally managed workplaces. Second, the influence exerted in these organizations tends to be reactive and negative. Frequently, the informal organization uses its influence after the fact. Management takes an action or considers taking an action and the informal organization is able to modify or prevent it.

In one sense, the parallel organization takes over the "influence" function of the informal organization. However, it carries on this function in very different ways than does the informal organization. It allows all organization members equal access to influence. It legitimizes the use of influence and defines the situations in which it is required. Most important, it applies influence in ways that are reconciling and healing rather than polarizing and divisive. It is able to do this, in large part, because it involves the democratically elected representatives of all workplace interest groups in the process through which it exerts its influence (that is, the integrative bargaining process).

The degree of influence exerted by organization members through the parallel organization is suggested by the fact that existing parallel organizations report an extremely high percentage of approved proposals. In many cases, 100 percent of the proposals submitted to the top-level action team are approved. It is generally unwise for a top manager to disapprove a proposal that has the support of all the organization's workplace interest groups. In addition, a well-designed parallel organization regards top management as a workplace interest group and ensures that its representatives participate in the actual planning/problem-solving process that produces proposals. If we were to increase these natural strengths of the parallel organization by folding it into the collective bargaining process, it is reasonable to suppose that its influence would be even more effectively exerted.

Membership

Action teams meet in plenary session; they do not usually organize themselves into subaction teams. This means that an action team cannot accommodate more than seven to nine members. Due to this size limitation, each member of a top-level action team often represents a "cluster" of workplace interest groups. This clustering is generally accomplished by grouping organizational units rather than levels of the hierarchy. That is, hierarchical interest groups, such as first-line supervisors and middle managers, still have their separate representatives. However, a participation steward sitting on an action team might represent five or six major organizational units. In contrast, most of the work of planning teams is accomplished in miniteams of five to seven members. Thus, the planning team itself can be quite large (for example, a planning team might consist of twenty members organized into four five-member miniteams). This allows the members of each major organizational unit served to have their own representative. However, planning teams occur only at an organization's higher levels.

Levels of the Parallel Organization

For the purposes of our discussion, we will classify the levels of the parallel organization as the executive level, the operating level, the intermediate level, and the worksite level.

The Executive Level. Quite often, this level is also the bargaining unit level. It has a number of fairly autonomous organizations reporting to it. For example, the top level of a corporation, a state, a school system, a city, or a county would fit this description. At this level, the main responsibilities of the action team are to sanction, support, and monitor the joint management system and to review and act on proposals from its planning team. The action team is normally made up of the chief executive officer, the heads of the unions involved, representatives of subordinate levels of management, and participation stewards who also serve on lower-level action teams.

In very large and geographically scattered organizations (like large corporations), the administrative policies and the policies giving guidance to lower levels of the parallel organization are so general that they can be developed by the action team itself. In these instances, no planning team is formed. For most organizations, however, the planning team at the executive level is an important tool for ensuring that administrative policies (including those that guide lower levels of parallel organization) are sound, well understood, and acceptable.

The Operating Level. This is the level occupied by fairly autonomous organizations made up of large numbers of interdependent units. For our purposes, the key criterion is that this is the lowest level that has the authority to design its own decision-making system. Examples of this level might be a General Motors assembly plant, a state correctional facility, and a county department of transportation. The functions of the parallel organization at this level differ from those at the executive level in a very important respect: it is at this level that the grass-roots procedures of the parallel organization are developed. At the executive level, the parallel organization defines institutional relationships. These relationships are insulated from the large majority of organizational members by a number of hierarchical levels. The planning work done at the executive levels is extremely important in that it establishes a policy framework that either facilitates or impedes interunit and interpersonal relationships at the grass-roots levels.

However, it is at the operational level that this policy framework is translated into the procedures that make it either meaningful or farcical. The thoughts and feelings of an organization's managers and workers focus on the operational level and look to the action and planning teams at this level to meet their needs. This is normally the lowest level at which a written agreement covers terms of office, election procedures, frequency of meetings, proposal formats, and so on. The average organization member has never seen a copy of the executive-level parallel agreement. By way of contrast, many people carry a copy of the operating-level agreement in their back pockets. This is the level where, as the saying goes, "the action is."

Since the bulk of the rules, procedures, and work methods that govern the day-to-day activities of both the parallel and primary organizations are promulgated at the operating level, this level should have a planning team. Planning teams at the operating level are often organized into miniteams, each dealing with a different planning area. For example, there might be a miniteam on education and training, one on personnel matters, one on procurement procedures, one on fiscal matters, another on work methods, and one to develop parallel organization procedures.

The Intermediate Levels. These are all the levels between the operating level and the work unit. For example, a plant might have a number of departments, each department having its sections and each section having its work units. The departments and sections would correspond to the intermediate levels of the plant's parallel organization. Intermediate levels rarely need planning groups, since most of their rules, policies, procedures, and programs are developed at the operating or executive levels. Action teams at this level are mainly responsible for coordinating the activities of the parallel organization with those of the primary organization and for sanctioning and supporting joint management in their jurisdictions.

The existence of this level of action teams ensures that each middle manager is included in the activities of the parallel organization that most closely affect him or her. It also gives the middle manager a key role in the functioning of the joint management system (that is, as the link between the parallel and primary organizations). An intermediate-level action team is made up of the senior manager-member, planning stewards from lower-level teams, and representatives of subordinate management groups.

In many cases, labor and management fail to create parallel structures at these intermediate levels. This is a serious error. The involvement of middle management is crucial to the success of any parallel organization. It is not enough to have middle managers represented on executive- and operating-level action and planning teams. The most meaningful kind of involvement for the middle manager is sitting on his or her own action team.

The Worksite Level. The worksite level of the parallel organization corresponds to the level of the primary organization where the work is actually done. At this level, the primary work unit (or autonomous work team) is generally made up of one first-line supervisor and from five to fifty workers, depending on the nature of the work being done. Occasionally, the first-line supervisor has an assistant. Action teams at the worksite level identify problems and, where they affect only that primary work unit, develop solutions to them. Where they affect other work units as well, the action team refers them to a higher level for solution. This ensures that members of the organization are always represented when a problem that affects them is being worked on. At the worksite level, the action team does its own problem solving; planning teams are almost never used.

Worksite-level action teams are normally made up of two or three participation stewards and the head of the primary work unit. At this level, the makeup of the action team is quite fluid. The participation stewards and the primary unit head (senior manager-member) are regarded as a "core group" that has accepted responsibility for meeting periodically and for identifying problems and working to solve them. However, all members of the primary work unit have the right to attend meetings and participate in the work of the action team if they so desire. Thus, core group meetings not infrequently include one or two members of the primary work unit who are not participation stewards. Where the work unit has fewer than ten members, all of these members often serve on the worksite-level action team.

At this level, problems with administrative policies and procedures often affect more than one work unit and so are often referred to higher-level planning teams for solution. The worksite-level action team often concentrates its problem-solving energy on problems involving work methods. This means that the work of these action teams has the potential for directly affecting the way the work of the primary unit is organized and the amount of hour-to-hour autonomy and participation its members experience. The action team at this level is in an excellent position to function as a design team for converting its primary work unit to an autonomous work team.

Rules for Parallel Organizations

There are a number of rules that labor and management have found useful for avoiding conflicts between the primary and parallel organization and between the parallel organization and the negotiation and administration of the basic labor contract. Some of these rules, however, do not apply in all cases. Where a rule is relevant only in certain contexts, this will be noted below.

Contractual Issues Must Not Be Discussed. During the 1970s, when parallel organizations were in their early experimental stage, it was considered crucial that matters covered by the basic labor contract not be discussed in parallel organization meetings. To do so might weaken the collective bargaining process and, by doing so, weaken the union. In addition, it is difficult to discuss win/lose issues in the same forum with win/win problems. Win/lose issues take priority, feelings run high, tempers get short, and the deviousness that is natural to adversary bargaining gets in the way of any constructive problem solving.

However, not all issues covered by the basic labor contract are win/lose issues. Despite the difficulties involved, what Walton and

McKersie (1965) termed "integrative bargaining" does take place during contract talks and the results appear in the contract. In addition, as the members of parallel organization teams develop feelings of trust for each other, these teams are capable of taking on issues that contain some win/lose elements. For these reasons, some industrial relations experts have recently advocated that the line between adversary collective bargaining and the parallel organization be drawn using process rather than content as the criterion (Ronchi and Morgan, 1983).

I support this view with certain qualifications. First, it is hard for me to conceive of circumstances where the bargaining of basic compensation would not interfere with the mainstream work of a parallel organization. Second, contractual matters should not be treated where workers attribute the accomplishments of the parallel organization to management rather than to the union. Where this is done, workers tend to question the need for their unions (Showalter and Yetman, 1983).

Where a union uses the parallel organization as a forum for extended bargaining, recognizes the workers who conduct this bargaining as legitimate union officers (for example, participation stewards), and enforces the rules, policies, and procedures produced in the same way it enforces the basic labor contract, there is little need to categorically place any issues off limits—except, perhaps, those involving basic compensation.

The Authority Structure Does Not Change. In this respect, integrative bargaining is no different from distributive bargaining. Management's role is to decide and the union's role is to seek to influence the decision. In distributive bargaining, the union seeks to influence management's decisions through the threat of job action. In integrative bargaining, it seeks to influence them through the use of information, discussion, and joint problem solving. These methods are highly effective in integrative bargaining because the problems being dealt with are common to both parties.

The rule (that the authority structure does not change) is necessary both to protect management's prerogatives and to preserve labor's integrity. The parallel organization gives management more and better information on which to base its decisions. It also tends to produce decisions that are more acceptable to labor. However, it accomplishes these things within the constraints of the existing authority structure. Neither participation stewards nor combined-function union officers are held accountable for the consequences of decisions. Accordingly, they are not given the authority to make them. Without this authority, unions stand on firm ground. They can continue to play the role of the "Monday morning quarterback," criticizing management decisions after they have had the opportunity to see their results. It would be hard for the union to play this necessary role if it had made the faulty decisions itself.

Communication Lines Should Follow Lines of Authority. It is crucial to the coordination of parallel organization activities that formal communications between its levels go through regular management channels. For example, where one action team wishes to refer a problem to a higher-level action team for study, the request should not be sent directly from one team to the other. It should be addressed from the senior manager-member of the lower-level team (in the capacity of line manager) to his or her immediate supervisor. This is not to say that the teams at various levels of the parallel organization should not exchange information. For example, it is highly desirable that action teams distribute their minutes to lower-level teams. It is also desirable that action teams have linked memberships (for example, the participation stewards on a given action team should be drawn from—and represent—all the participation stewards at the next lower level). Neither is it to say that participation stewards should not keep their union informed. Of course, they should. But administrative correspondence should be channelled through the primary organization. The managers of the primary organization cannot do their jobs if they are left out of the planning–problem solving–design communication loop. Of course, where certain levels of the primary organization are not held accountable for performance (as appears to be the case with the Saturn system described in Chapter Five), it may not be so crucial to include them in the communication loop. It is important to remember that the parallel organization is a planning, not an implementing, mechanism. Once a consensus has been reached, it is up to the senior manager-member to carry it out through the primary organization. The parallel organization limits itself to monitoring prog-ress—making sure that the senior manager-member sees to it that the consensus decision is implemented.

Participation Is Mandatory for Managers and Voluntary for Workers. Managers are obliged to carry out their responsibilities in the parallel organization. The development of rules, policies, proce-dures, and work methods is simply one of the functions for which managers are compensated. The management system used to carry out this function is determined by top management or—where this system is extended bargaining—negotiated by top management and labor.

Workers, on the other hand, do not function under an em-ployment contract that calls upon them to do managerial tasks. Accordingly, participation in the parallel organization is voluntary for workers. Having voluntarily accepted election as a participation steward, however, a worker is held accountable by the union and by constituents for the performance of parallel organization duties. Workers unwilling to perform these duties have the option of re-signing their positions as participation stewards. Should an orga-nization's job evaluation policies be adapted so that employees are appropriately compensated for their planning and problem-solving activities, it might then be feasible to make these activities mandatory.

Individual Grievances Are Not Discussed. The function of the parallel organization is to prevent problems, not to remedy them once they have occurred. It develops rules, policies, procedures, and programs, but does not administer them. This is the function of the primary organization. In addition, this rule is necessary from a practical standpoint. An individual who seeks to use a parallel or-ganization meeting to seek redress disrupts the meeting and wastes time that might otherwise be used in developing solutions to sys-temic problems. Fortunately, it is not difficult to enforce this rule. Team members almost always protest when one of their number seeks to use a team meeting to pursue a grievance.

Guarantees Are Necessary. Parallel organizations tend to in-crease productivity through the combined efforts of managers and workers. It would be unrealistic to expect managers to participate wholeheartedly or to expect workers to participate at all if they were made to suffer as a result of productivity gains. Since the nature of its job often makes top management subject to strong pressures (to reduce staff) when an organization experiences productivity gains, both subordinate managers and workers need protection. Subordinate managers must be content with assurances that they will neither lose their jobs nor suffer losses in compensation due to the activities of the parallel organization. Unions normally see that similar assurances for workers are translated into contractual provisions. These provisions are negotiated in the bargaining unit and are usually included in the parallel agreement at that level. Where a union is bargaining for the right to extended integrative bargaining, it may be obliged to guarantee against any decrease in labor productivity. It is worth noting that, under the "associational unionism" concept proposed by Heckscher (1988), the various levels of management would also be unionized and in a position to negotiate contractual assurances.

Enforcing the Parallel Organization and Its Products

For the sake of all the parties involved, the rules, policies, and procedures that govern a parallel organization must be enforceable. They are contained in written parallel agreements developed jointly at the executive and operating levels of the parallel organization. Where the parallel organization functions as an extended bargaining mechanism, both its parallel agreements and the policies and procedures it develops are subject to the same enforcement procedures as the basic labor contract.

There are five major reasons that parallel agreements should be enforceable: the tension between long- and short-term interests, the tendency for crises to dictate actions, personnel changes among managers, the growing pains in the early life of a joint management system, and the tendency of a nonenforceable system to weaken the union.

Unfortunately, many managers operate on a short time frame. They are evaluated on the basis of their short-term accomplishments. Accordingly, they choose courses of action with immediate payoffs. Of course, these courses of action are sometimes not productive over the long term. This general tendency to favor the short term is a problem for parallel organizations. For example, it makes sense from a long-term point of view to release workers to participate in the meetings of action and planning teams. Over the long term, these meetings will prevent problems from occurring and result in increased productivity. From a short-term point of view, however, it makes more sense to keep these workers on their jobs, dealing with the crises of the day. Parallel agreements, which provide for such matters as release time, must be enforceable in order to counter the tendency of organizations to favor short-term over long-term benefits.

Ironically, the parallel organization—which seeks to replace crisis management with preventive management—must protect itself against the pressures of crises. Whenever crises occur (and they are daily occurrences in many workplaces), they tend to take precedence over the activities of the parallel organization. While a crisis of major proportions should take precedence over, for example, an action team meeting, parallel agreements should define the term "major" in this context. In order for these definitions to influence day-to-day organizational life, however, they must be enforceable.

A new top or middle manager who takes over an organization often has a tendency to change whatever management system is being used. A new manager who takes over a jointly managed organization not only has this tendency; in all likelihood, he or she is not trained in the particular approaches to leadership (see Chapter Eleven) that are appropriate in a jointly managed organization. These factors can cause a great deal of conflict and can sometimes lead to the abandonment of joint management unless the parallel agreements that define the manager's responsibilities are enforceable.

Where a parallel organization has not been folded into the collective bargaining process, it may be resisted by some subordinate managers and some lower-level union officers. They are told that it will benefit them, but they are not convinced. Accordingly, they undermine and sabotage it. In this way, they make themselves into accurate prophets of doom. The system cannot benefit them unless they invest their energies in making it work. Yet they may choose to invest their energies in making sure it does not work. In a way, their resistance is quite rational. Why should they give up the known present for an unknown future? This situation can be dealt with by making it clearly in their immediate self-interest to follow the rules, policies, and procedures of the new system. Making these rules enforceable goes a long way toward accomplishing this. The power of this strategy is illustrated by the Shell-Sarnia case described in Chapter Five. Officers of ECWU Local 800 state that, before the rules were grievable, few people took the system seriously. Since the rules were made enforceable, managers have been careful to follow them.

Where a participative system is working reasonably well, workers often regard it as the place "where the action is." Then, if meetings are not held or if agreed-upon plans are not implemented, they wait to see what will happen. Where nothing happens or where the union is not involved in setting things right, they get a powerful message: "The participative system belongs to management." At this point workers begin to compare what they are accomplishing through the management-driven participative system and what they are accomplishing through the union-driven contract negotiation and administration system. They also begin to reflect on the fact that the participative system is free, but that the union is costing them their dues money. When local ECWU leaders at Shell-Sarnia faced this kind of situation, they went to the brink of strike to win enforceability. This convinced the members of Local 800 that their union, not management, should be given credit for the participative system.

Chapter 4

The Process of
Integrative Bargaining

Integrative bargaining is the process used by the parallel organization to carry out its work. In the context of the parallel organization, integrative bargaining has a number of special features. As
Walton and McKersie (1965) observed it in their seminal study, it
took place at the traditional bargaining table. This meant that it
was normally combined with distributive bargaining, that there
were only two points of view to consider, that the bargainers represented large numbers of constituents, that it took place under intense
time pressures, and that it dealt with problems that lent themselves
to uniform solutions that could be applied throughout the bargaining unit. Integrative bargaining, as it occurs in the parallel organization, is quite different. This chapter will discuss the special
features of integrative bargaining as it is (or can be) carried on in the
parallel organization.

Integrative Bargaining in the Parallel Organization

Its Separation from Distributive Bargaining

While some efforts have been made in the past to separate
distributive and integrative bargaining (for example, continuous

negotiations, open-ended bargaining), for the most part integrative bargaining has had to compete with distributive bargaining at the regular bargaining table. Much of the parallel organization's strength flows from the fact that it separates them cleanly, in terms of both space and time. It separates the two processes at the bargaining unit level and creates additional integrative bargaining mechanisms at every level and in every unit of the organization. Distributive bargaining is restricted to the bargaining unit level. This makes it unlikely that ill feelings generated by distributive bargaining will spill over into the integrative bargaining process. It also helps distinguish between the kinds of behaviors appropriate in distributive bargaining and the kinds appropriate in the parallel organization. As Walton and McKersie (1965) note, it is difficult for bargainers to shift from distributive to integrative tactics in the same bargaining session. Also, integrative tactics require special skills like solving problems and reaching consensus, and training is required for the development of these skills. Another factor that makes integrative bargaining difficult at the regular table is that, even if both sides desire a given outcome, neither side wishes to propose it. Each side waits for the other to propose it, hoping to gain concessions in other areas by "reluctantly" agreeing to something it wanted in the first place.

The Involvement of Additional Parties: Multilateral Bargaining

At the bargaining unit level, labor and management present themselves to each other as monoliths. Both sides seek to achieve unity within their parties before going to the table. While this is easier for management than for labor, it is considered necessary by both parties. Labor must be able to "deliver" its members and it is unthinkable for management bargaining team members to take different views of the issues being bargained.

The parallel organization, on the other hand, is specifically designed to recognize the fact that management and labor are not monoliths. The first design principle of the parallel organization is wholeness: the inclusion of all workplace interest groups. Middle managers are acknowledged to have somewhat different interests than first-line supervisors, and workers in one unit are acknowledged to have somewhat different interests than workers in another. The parallel organization brings representatives of all the interest groups together to discuss the similarities and differences in their points of view and to reconcile the differences.

Experience suggests that when these differences are not acknowledged and discussed they become exaggerated in people's minds and discourage them from even attempting to solve mutual problems. When these differences are discussed and made specific, however, people often find that they can be overcome and that mutually beneficial solutions can be developed. This finding of mutually beneficial solutions by all the workplace interest groups is termed "social integration." "Perhaps the most significant capability of the parallel organization is that it provides a means of achieving harmony within the social systems of complex organizations regarding decisions affecting both the social and technical systems. It achieves harmony regarding social system decisions by ensuring that each member of the organization is represented during the development of the rules, policies, and procedures governing his or her relationships with other organization members. It achieves harmony regarding technical system decisions by ensuring that each member is represented during the development of the rules, policies, and procedures governing his or her relationships with the technical system, during the acquisition of machines, tools, and conveyances, and during the development of the procedures that define the relationships among these machines, tools, and conveyances. This harmony within the social system is termed 'social integration,' whether it is brought to bear on social or on technical system decisions" (Herrick, 1985, p. 971). A key distinction between traditional integrative bargaining and integrative bargaining in the parallel organization flows out of the parallel organization's insistence on including all workplace interest groups. This distinction is that the parallel organization reaches its agreements through consensus. At the traditional table, even where integrative bargaining is being attempted, only two points of view need to be reconciled.

Smaller Numbers of Constituents

A union officer at the traditional bargaining table often represents hundreds or even thousands of constituents. This leads to "lowest common denominator" bargaining, where issues are pressed only if almost everyone in the bargaining unit has some interest in them. It also makes communication between the representative and his or her constituents a serious problem.

The parallel organization seeks to reduce the ratio of constituents to representatives in several ways. First, it decentralizes the bargaining process. For example, a representative of teachers may have 7,000 constituents at the bargaining unit level, 1,000 at the area level, 50 at the school level and 5 at the department level. Communication becomes both more intense and more feasible as the number of constituents decreases. Second, the parallel organization does not use "at large" representatives. That is, where there are two or more representatives on a given action or planning team, each one represents a different body of constituents. This also intensifies communication. Finally, at its higher levels the parallel organization includes as many as six or seven planning teams for every action team. For example, an organization of 3,500 employees may establish one action team with nine members and seven planning teams with five members each at the bargaining unit level. This means that, even at the bargaining unit level, the ratio of constituents to representatives would be only about 100 to 1—as opposed to 3,500 to 1 at the traditional bargaining table. This same organization might also have both action and planning teams at the departmental level with constituent-to-representative ratios of 10 or 12 to 1.

Easing of Time Pressures

Where integrative and distributive bargaining are mixed, there is usually a focus on reaching agreement on a contract by a given date. This creates time pressures that make integrative bargaining difficult. In order to be effective, integrative bargaining should follow a step-by-step problem-solving process. These steps take time. Further, they should extend over a number of meetings so that input can be gathered from constituents during the problem-solving process. Even without the other complicating factors (like disagreement on the wage issue), it would be difficult to solve more than one or two problems while negotiating a contract. And, in most organizations, there are more than one or two problems to solve.

The other side of this coin, of course, is that parallel organization requires spending a great deal of time in integrative bargaining. There are often many problems to solve at every level of the organization and solving each problem requires time. Without the parallel organization, these problems are solved unilaterally by management. This requires less time. However, the solutions are not likely to be as responsive as those developed through the parallel organization and they will certainly not be as well supported by the members of the organization.

Tailor-Made Solutions to Problems

Since traditional integrative bargaining occurs only at the bargaining unit level, it tends to produce solutions that are applied uniformly throughout the unit. However, something that is a problem in one part of the bargaining unit is not necessarily a problem thoughout the unit. Further, even where a problem exists throughout the unit, it may call for somewhat different solutions in different parts of the unit. The present collective bargaining system is not equipped to deal effectively with this situation. It is best equipped to produce uniform resolutions to both issues and problems.

The parallel organization, on the other hand, is specifically designed to produce "tailor-made" solutions for local problems. Each organizational unit has its action team and larger organizational units often have planning teams as well. The solutions that are developed apply only to the organizational unit that has the problem. Where these solutions are inconsistent with either management policy or the basic labor contract, waivers must be obtained from management or labor at the bargaining unit level before they can be implemented.

However, the fact that the parallel organization produces nonuniform solutions has not, in practice, created serious difficulties for the union. This is true for several reasons. First, most of the solutions developed in the parallel organization do not conflict with either management policy or the basic labor contract. They deal with special situations that were not anticipated by management or labor.

Second, where employees are familiar with the philosophy and purpose of the parallel organization, they do not object to most nonuniform solutions. Where they do object, there are probably good reasons for thinking about applying the solution more broadly or working out a number of local solutions addressing the same problem. For example, the employees in the Bolivar, Tennessee, mirror plant were unhappy when the "buff and polish" department employees worked out an arrangement under which they went home after meeting their production quota. The unhappiness of the other employees simply pointed to the desirability of either working out plantwide productivity gain-sharing arrangements or working out arrangements where each department could share in increased productivity in its own way.

Third, the formal structure of the parallel organization makes it possible for both labor and management to keep track of the solutions that are being developed, identify those that are potentially delicate, and ensure that they are not implemented in such a way as to cause institutional problems. Often, this can be done simply by announcing the solution to employees as an experiment that will be evaluated after a time and applied to other parts of the bargaining unit if appropriate.

The Bargaining of Mixed Items

In order to avoid conflicts with traditional collective bargaining, many parallel organizations avoid "conditions of employment" issues, even where these issues are "mixed" (that is, involve elements of both conflict and mutual gain). Where the parallel organization is folded into the collective bargaining process, the necessity for avoiding these mixed items no longer exists. The parallel organization becomes simply another part of the collective bargaining mechanism. It might be useful, therefore, to present a classification of bargaining items according to their bargainability under the National Labor Relations Act (NLRA) along with a classification according to their content.

Classification According to the NLRA. The NLRA's bargainability classification is also made up of three categories: mandatory items, illegal items, and voluntary items. Mandatory items are wages, hours, and other terms and conditions of employment. Employers and unions are required to bargain in good faith with regard to them. Illegal items are those that are specifically prohibited under the act, such as a proposal for a "closed shop." Voluntary items are poorly defined, but include such matters as a clause fixing the size and membership of the employer or union bargaining team (Anderson, 1975).

Classification According to Content. Items bargained in extended integrative bargaining will generally fall into one of the following three categories: conditions of employment, work methods, and the rules of the parallel organization. "Conditions of employment" items correspond to the NLRA's "mandatory" items. However, they usually deal with matters that are specific to individual divisions, departments, branches, or units of the organization. The "conditions of employment" items that find their way into the parallel organization tend to be of a "mixed" nature. "Work methods" items deal with production problems and tend to be integrative in nature. The rules of the road for the parallel organization come close to being "pure" integrative items. The test of whether a matter is appropriate for treatment by the parallel organization is simply "Can the parties reach consensus on a solution?" It is probable that many items concerning "work methods" and "rules of the parallel organization" will fall into the NLRA's voluntary category. This would mean that the employer and union would have to agree to bargain them.

The Classic Text on Integrative Bargaining

While integrative bargaining in the context of the parallel organization is different in some respects from integrative bargaining as it was observed by Walton and McKersie, there are many other respects in which it is the same. Managers and unionists involved in the administration of a parallel organization, or who are considering some form of joint management, would profit greatly from reading *A Behavioral Theory of Labor-Management Negotiations*. It remains for some future researchers to observe the operation of the parallel organization and to give us an analysis of extended integrative bargaining comparable to Walton and McKersie's analysis of collective bargaining in 1965.

Chapter 5

∾──◇──∾

Jointly Managed
Workplaces:
Four Examples

My purpose here is to give concrete examples of how some of the
ideas presented in this book play out in real life. The four workplaces described in this chapter are the Detroit-Hamtramck Cadillac
assembly plant; the Shell chemical plant in Sarnia, Ontario; the
Pima County, Arizona, government; and the Saturn assembly plant
in Spring Hill, Tennessee. All but the Pima County experiment are
"greenfields sites" (new organizations designed to be participative
from their inception).

I use two sets of criteria in discussing these participative
systems. The first set has to do with the design characteristics of
each system. Is it whole? Is it representative? Is it self-designed?
Have the administrative systems of labor and management been
adapted to joint management? The second set of criteria has to do
with the impact of the participative systems on human well-being,
productivity, and union-employee relations. Have they benefited
the employees? Have they increased productivity? How have they
affected workers' attitudes toward their unions? The answers to the
second set of questions are, of course, incomplete and—in some
cases—speculative.

79

Cadillac Detroit-Hamtramck Assembly Center

The factual information contained in the Background, Participative System, and Results sections of this writeup was gathered during interviews and discussions with managers, union officers, and workers at the Cadillac Detroit-Hamtramck plant. These interviews and discussions were held from February to July 1989. Every effort has been made to ensure the accuracy of this information, including providing drafts of these sections to officials at both the plant and corporate levels for their comments. The analysis contained in the Design Characteristics and Comment sections represents the opinion of the author.

Background

This plant began production in late 1985. Because it was a "greenfields" site, of course, installation of a participative system was much easier. The plant employs about 3,300 people, most of whom transferred in from other plants in the area. Some of these plants have since closed down. Cadillac Detroit-Hamtramck uses state-of-the-art technology, including robots, automated guide vehicles, computer-integrated manufacturing technology, and just-in-time scheduling. There are twenty-one miles of conveyor and, at full production, the plant produces sixty-three cars each hour. At this writing (mid 1989), the plant has a "Job Opportunity Bank" (J.O.B.) of 207 hourly employees. The GM J.O.B. program was created by the 1987 UAW/GM labor agreement. Under this program, employees are kept on the payroll when jobs are eliminated for any reason other than a change in the number of cars being produced. J.O.B. assignments are worked out by the UAW Local 22 Shop Committee and management. They include such widely different tasks as serving on plantwide problem-solving teams, acting as spokespersons at auto shows, serving as tour guides in the plant, filling in on the line, and working at divisional headquarters.

The Participative System

The system has five components. First is a plantwide Labor-Management Planning Committee, which plans and oversees the system. Second, there are a large number of plant-level problem-solving teams. A total of eighty-one hourly workers spend full time on these teams, among which are the world-class quality council, the electrical team, the Hydramatic/Cadillac team, and the damage team. The team members were selected by the Labor-Management Planning Committee according to seniority from a pool of applicants who met the job requirements. The teams deal solely with production problems.

The third system component is made up of sixty-five part-time product development and improvement teams (PDITs). A typical PDIT is made up of about five members (for example, an hourly employee, a salaried employee, a release engineer, a product engineer, and a financial analyst). The PDITs normally meet for about two hours a week to discuss ways in which parts can be designed to better fit with the production process. The sixty-five PDITs correspond to sixty-five areas of the car, like transmission and throttle control. PDIT members are selected by the appropriate vehicle system management team (VSMT). These teams are made up of the managers who are responsible for the PDIT's area of the car.

The fourth component, the Assembly Line Effectiveness Center (ALEC), consists of a simulated assembly area used by PDITs and work teams in cooperation with salaried engineers. It and the sixty-five PDITs get the "voice of the assembler" into the design and engineering process with the aim of developing a car that can be built more easily.

The fifth component consists of about 370 production teams. Each team is made up of five to eight workers and is led by an elected team leader who makes an additional $.50 per hour in addition to the standard wage that is paid all other hourly noncraft employees (about $15 per hour in 1989). There is a salaried team manager for each six to seven production teams. The team leader is authorized to deal with all matters except discipline. Each team decides how it will function. Some teams function like traditional work units and their leaders simply act as lead workers. Other teams rotate jobs, control the work process, and function with only very general supervision from their team manager. Figure 2 charts the Cadillac Detroit-Hamtramck participative system.

Figure 2. The Detroit-Hamtramck Assembly Center Participative System.

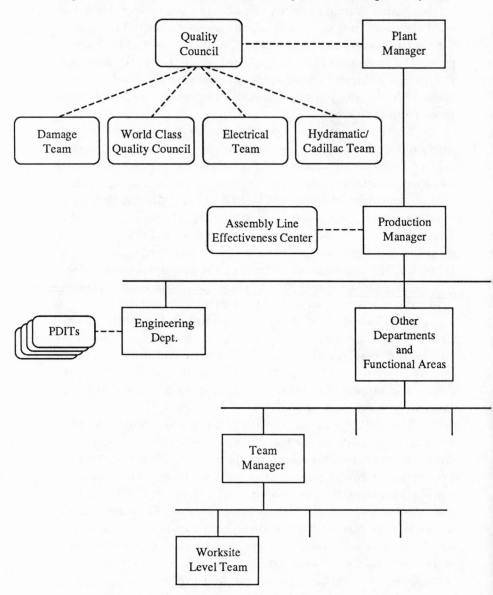

Note: There are 14 functional areas, 7 departments, 65 PDITs, 55 team managers, and 370 worksite-level teams.

Results

Human Well-being. There are no survey data available to shed light on matters such as job satisfaction. Certainly, the eighty-one hourly employees who work full-time on problem-solving teams are satisfied. One such employee said, "At Fleetwood, I didn't want to come to work; I hated it. But now I am learning things and making a difference. Now there is respect for me." I sat down with a group of hourly employees in the cafeteria and asked one of them how things were. He said, "It's sure better than Fleetwood!" The other workers at the table nodded their heads in agreement. On the other hand, another worker told me, "It bothers me a lot that we're always told we have to do better because we're competing with Lake Orion [another assembly plant] for the second shift. But when they get the production where they want it, they don't give us back the second shift—they cut jobs. And what if we did get it back? Then what about the brothers and sisters at Lake Orion?"

Productivity. It is difficult to assess the impact of the participative system on productivity because the basic system has been in place since the beginning. However, productivity changes since the plant began operating in September 1985 are attributed, in part (by some plant employees), to the fact that the participative system has been constantly expanded and improved. One of these changes reduced defects from an average of 12 per car in 1986 to an average of 3.6 in June 1989 (2.0 is considered "world class"). Another piece of evidence that productivity has improved comes from an hourly worker who said, "Management told my work team they wanted everything checked. They wanted quality up so we could compete. So we got all excited. We bought into it. Then, when quality got up where they wanted it, they eliminated half the jobs in the team."

It should be noted that the elimination of jobs does not mean that workers are laid off. They are instead assigned to the Job Opportunity Bank. The Cadillac Detroit-Hamtramck plant manager commented on the long-term impact of the participative system on productivity: "There are frustrations. Jointness slows you down while you're waiting for everyone to agree on a solution to a problem or on a program. But, once everyone does agree, you can really get things done! Take ALEC [the Assembly Line Effectiveness Center], for example. Management couldn't have put that together alone and, just in the month or so it's been going, it's been working great."

Union-Employee Relations. A member of one of the full-time problem-solving teams said, "In joint process, people talk a lot about the union not being involved, but I seldom hear people criticize the management side." Another full-time problem-solving team member said, "When bad-guy managers don't work participatively with people here, they get laid off." This comment suggests that workers see the participative system as being enforced by management, not by their union. Another worker commented, "It is difficult for the union because, when we improve the process, we eventually lose jobs." Most of the hourly workers I talked to (who were not on full-time problem-solving teams) volunteered comments critical of the union. The most common one was "We don't get much for $30 a month" (the union dues). People said they would call a committee person and not receive a visit for three weeks. Others said that the leadership would keep coming to agreements with management and then get blasted by members and have to go back and get a different agreement. "They don't know what we want" was a common complaint.

Late in the spring of 1989 (several months after the interviews that produced these comments about the union), elections were held for new Local 22 officers and for plant delegates to the UAW convention. New Directions candidates, who were seen by workers as being "anti–team concept" and "antijointness," won both elections. They swept the seven delegate positions. It is important to note, however, that the newly elected chairperson of the Local 22 Detroit-Hamtramck Shop Committee does not see himself as being anti–team concept or antijointness. He says, "I'm New Directions, but I'm not anti–team concept or antijointness. I'm against joint programs that don't work, that pit worker against worker. The union has common goals with management and it has goals that are in conflict. The point is that labor has to keep its own identity. We need to work on the common goals together and negotiate the goals that are in conflict."

Design Characteristics

These comments are geared to the four design principles described in Chapter Two.

Wholeness. The plant-level Labor-Management Planning Committee is not whole. While it includes top management and labor, it does not include middle or first-line management or office workers. The structure itself is not whole, since managers at the three lower levels of the organization do not have action or planning teams to advise them and to solve problems. The problem-solving teams that operate at the plantwide level are not whole. They are made up mainly of hourly workers. However, two of the problem-solving teams are made up of one representative from each of the plant's ten departments. This makes them whole in one sense: they include all departmental points of view. Office workers do not have the option of functioning as members of autonomous work teams and are not represented on plantwide problem-solving teams.

Representation. The people who represent constituencies on the plantwide planning committee (the union leaders) are elected. First-level managers (team leaders) are elected and subject to a strong recall system. The members of the PDITs and the full-time problem-solving teams are appointed.

Self-design. The various components of the system were worked out in the Labor-Management Planning Committee. The production teams are said to be free to design their own day-to-day participative arrangements. In theory, these teams are given the freedom to decide how much autonomy they wish to exercise and how they wish to distribute tasks within their teams. There is, of course, some disagreement about the amount of freedom actually allowed. One hourly worker told me, "For a while, the foreman said we had to rotate. We complained to the plant manager and he said we didn't have to. Then, for a while, we had to again. Now you can't rotate even if you want to."

Adaptation. Management has made an effort to adapt its policies to the participative system. For example, team leaders are elected, and management made an unsuccessful effort to install a "pay for skills" system. The two most obvious "failures to adapt" (on the part of management) are the use of an individual suggestion award system and the failure of the attempt to pay workers according to the number of skills they master. The union leadership prior to the 1989 elections, on the other hand, appears to have taken no adaptive steps other than sitting on the plantwide Labor-Management Planning Committee and seeking to defend labor values such as seniority. The union has not created new union offices for the workers who sit on PDITS or problem-solving teams. Neither is it providing training for these workers so that they can maintain their solidarity and represent union interests as they function on these teams. The participative system has not been folded into the collective bargaining process. It deals almost solely with production problems—not working conditions. No written parallel agreements define the system. Due to the "production" nature of the problems being dealt with, the enforceability issue has not arisen. It should be noted, however, that—as of this writing—the new local union officers have been in office for only a short period of time. It is possible that they may take some of these adaptive steps.

Comment

The Detroit-Hamtramck participative system appears to have had a marked success in improving productivity and some successes in improving human well-being (especially among full-time members of problem-solving teams). It is perhaps the most sophisticated and effective of our four examples at "closing the technical loop." That is, it is well equipped to bring maximum insights and knowledge to bear on solutions to technical (production) problems. The system's major weaknesses, on the other hand, are (1) it cannot reconcile the different points of view of the various workplace interest groups, (2) it is not designed to deal with "conditions of employment" problems, and (3) it does not help the union build the loyalty of its members. The results of the recent UAW elections suggest that some adjustments will need to be made to regain the support of the workers and continue the productivity improvements. Modifications in the system, making it more whole and representative, should help. Adaptations of the management and union administrative structures are even more important. It appears from the unwillingness of some employees to "buy in" to the need for ever increasing productivity that these adaptations might well include some mechanism for productivity gain sharing (see Chapter Twenty). A major long-term problem of the Cadillac Detroit-Hamtramck system is that it is inequitable. It pays a great many people hourly wages to do management work. This is not causing difficulties at present because of the high hourly pay and the fact that jobs in the auto industry are threatened. Another problem involves the plant-level full-time problem-solving teams. Should some or all of these teams be made regular units in the staffing pattern, they would cease to be parts of the participative system. At that point, they would simply be additional units of industrial engineers staffed by former hourly employees.

Shell Chemical Plant, Sarnia, Ontario

The factual information contained in the Background, Participative System, and Results sections of this writeup was gathered during interviews and discussions with managers and union officers at the Shell-Sarnia plant and from published sources. These interviews and discussions were held during the spring and summer of 1989. Every effort has been made to ensure the accuracy of this information, including providing drafts of these sections to labor and management officials at the plant level for their comments. The analysis contained in the Design Characteristics and Results sections represents the opinion of the author.

Background

Like Cadillac Detroit-Hamtramck, this joint management effort between Local 800 of the Energy and Chemical Workers Union (ECWU) and Shell Canada was a "greenfields site." That is, it was designed as a participative plant from its beginning in 1978. This plant, which employs about 200 people (131 of whom are members of Local 800), operates continuously around the clock 365 days a year. It produces fifty grades of polypropylene and two grades of isopropyl alcohol.

The Participative System

The participation system has four components: the Union-Management Committee, the permanent and ad hoc committees, the *Good Work Practices Handbook (GWPH)*, and the seven work teams that make up the plant's operating and maintenance departments. The Union-Management Committee is made up of the six-member Local 800 executive body, the plant manager, representatives from the other two levels of management, and human resources staff. The administrative and engineering employees are not represented on this committee and are therefore inadequately represented on permanent and ad hoc committees. The Union-Management Committee determines the composition of the permanent and ad hoc committees, facilitates their work, and acts on their recommendations. A representative of the plant manager and at least one member of the union executive body sit on each of the permanent and ad hoc committees. These committees continually develop ways to organize and accomplish work (for example, to introduce new technology, redesign the warehouse function, achieve team autonomy, and define the role of the team coordinator and relate this role to team autonomy). These matters legally "belong" to management, but are bargained voluntarily with efforts to reach consensus.

The *GWPH* is a collection of flexible rules that are continually developed and modified (Rankin and Mansell, 1986). These rules concern issues that, in traditional plants, are normally bargained periodically and included in the basic labor contract (like shift hours, parking, the progression system, overtime distribution, and so forth). These rules also govern the operation of the participative system. There is no set structure for bargaining the *GWPH*. Any manager, union official, member, or group of members can request through the team, the steward, the local executive, or a coordinator that a rule be changed. The procedures for agreeing on the changes depend on the nature of the issue or problem. In the case of overtime distribution, a task force was formed to develop the solution. While problem identification can occur at any level, the actual bargaining is done at the plant level.

The fourth component (the seven work teams) consists of six process teams working twelve-hour shifts and one craft team working days only. All the teams are semiautonomous. All members of the six process teams are trained to operate most parts of the production process, and each worker is skilled in one support function (for example, scheduling, laboratory work, warehousing, and maintenance). The teams assign work, provide or arrange for technical training, authorize overtime, and schedule vacations. Each team has a coordinator who provides facilitative supervision (see Chapters Eleven and Fifteen) and represents the interests of management. Shell-Sarnia has only three levels of management, where a traditional plant of its kind might have four or five. Before the plant opened, this structure was developed by a task force that included the then president of Local 800. The union participated with the understanding that it would be a "full partner" and maintain "a high profile" (Halpern, 1984). The structure includes three permanent committees: the joint health and safety committee, the training advisory board, and the team norm review board. The eleven-member team norm review board continually redesigns the participative system (Halpern, 1985). Figure 3 is a chart of the Shell-Sarnia participative system.

Results

The productivity and human well-being results are impressive. According to Local 800 president Roger Jenkins and chief steward Judy McKibbon, the participative system had some slack years from 1985 to 1988. However, Jenkins and McKibbon believe it is now back on track.

Productivity. Product development and quality are excellent and continue to improve. Throughput and on-stream time are substantially above design. According to plant manager William Thomas, for example, the plant was designed to produce 70,000 tonnes of polypropylene each year, but produced 145,000 tonnes in 1988. Safety figures are average for this kind of plant. Absenteeism was

Figure 3. The Shell-Sarnia Participative System.

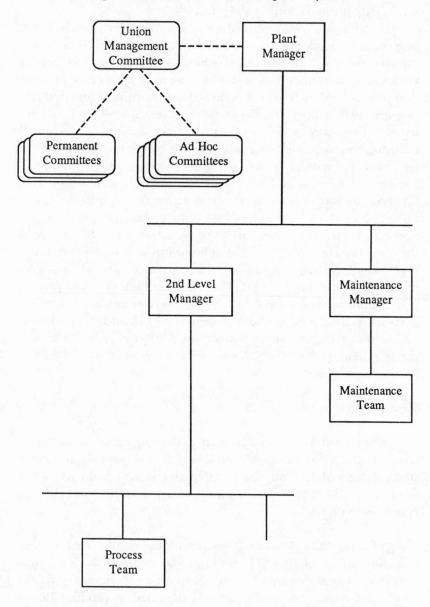

There are seven process teams.

lower than in any other Shell Canada operating facility during the initial years (Halpern, 1985). Local 800 president Jenkins points out, however, that it is now marginally higher than in other Shell production locations.

Human Well-being. While no survey results on human well-being are available, interviews with union officers suggest that the system is now serving the needs of the workers. Over its first six years, the plant had only 11 formal grievances. This compared with 150 in a nearby traditional plant (Halpern, 1985). Jenkins says, "The number of members participating in committee activities is higher now than it ever has been. People are more willing to participate now because they are seeing some results. For example, in May 1989, a committee proposal to reduce the number of coordinators [facilitative supervisors] in each work team from two to one was approved and implemented. There is an air of cautious optimism in the plant."

Union-Employee Relations. McKibbon has commented, "When you are sharing responsibility all the time, it's hard for the union to get the credit for achievements. That's a real problem" (Forum, 1984). Local 800 found one answer to this problem in 1988. The plant manager had not been strict with his subordinate managers about living by the rules of the participative system. The result was that the system had fallen into disrepair. Middle and first-line managers stopped holding problem-solving meetings and began to gather more and more power back into their own hands. There were instances of *GWPH* rules being shrugged off by managers. In the fall of 1987, a new plant manager came in. In 1988, Local 800 made worker participation the focus of its contract negotiations. Jenkins and McKibbon say, "Our lawyer gave us language to make the *GWPH* enforceable. We went to the brink of striking two times to get that language." According to Jenkins, "Since we got the language making the *GWPH* grievable, the task forces have begun meeting again and our members are enthusiastic." McKibbon believes that Local 800 members now give the union credit for the participative system because they witnessed an adversary action by the union that made management live up to its promises to participate.

Management is in general agreement with these views. However, Keith Howell, coordinator of the maintenance team, adds, "I don't think that it was a deliberate attempt at a power grab by management. If you aren't having participation meetings, you still have to get the job done and so you tend to slide away from being participative." The plant manager, William Thomas, has this to say: "In addition to the enforceability language in the contract—and I'm not disputing its significance—the hiring of an organizational effectiveness adviser and the joint development of a teamwork renewal program were also important."

Design Characteristics

Wholeness. The major weakness of the Shell-Sarnia system is its lack of wholeness. First, there is no parallel structure at the second level of management. Thus, according to Jenkins and McKibbon, the "management only" meetings held at this level are regarded by workers with some suspicion. This lack of a parallel structure at the second level of management would be even more serious if Shell-Sarnia were a larger plant. In a small plant such as Shell-Sarnia, a large percentage of employees are involved in the problem-solving process even though it is centralized at the plant level. Second, there is no parallel structure at the work team level. This lack of an action team at the work team level would be fine if the teams consisted of six to seven workers each. But, at Shell-Sarnia, each team consists of about twenty workers. This makes it difficult to do a disciplined and thorough job of problem solving using the entire team. Finally, administrative and engineering employees are not organized in autonomous work teams and are rarely represented on permanent and ad hoc committees. Because of this, they seem to have difficulty understanding the concept that underlies the operation of the plant. Jenkins believes that the inadequate representation of the engineering group presents a special problem because of the need to integrate the plant's social and technical systems.

Representation. People volunteer to serve on Shell-Sarnia's permanent and ad hoc committees. Any volunteer system of representation is vulnerable to manipulation. Further, people tend to form a stronger concept of themselves as representatives if they are elected (and subject to recall) by the people they are representing.

Self-design. The system was originally designed by a task force that included the president of Local 800. The seven teams and the ad hoc and permanent committees continually negotiate issues such as the relation between the team and its coordinator (Rankin and Mansell, 1986). The participative arrangements at the worksite level meet the self-design criterion to a high degree. Further, workers have the opportunity to approach their local union officers, the members of the permanent and ad hoc committees, and management with suggestions for structural changes. The self-design principle seems to be well established.

Adaptation. Management policies are well adapted to joint management principles. For example, the work organization is based on team tasks, multiskilled workers, facilitative supervision, fewer levels of management, shared information, pay for knowledge, and one job classification. Union policies have been adapted to a greater extent than in any other workplace with which I am familiar. The 1988 contract includes language that makes the *GWPH* enforceable. In this respect, Shell-Sarnia is a path-breaking organization. However, worker representatives on permanent and ad hoc committees do not act in the capacity of union officers. The labor contract states that "the company agrees to recognize one steward from each shift team and in addition one steward from the craft team" (Halpern, 1984). It would serve to further strengthen the system if this language were changed to read "the company agrees to recognize one contract administration steward from each shift team, one contract administration steward from the craft team, and as many participation stewards as are required to fill the worker slots on the permanent and ad hoc committees." Further, the local union does not provide separate training for members serving on problem-solving teams. This training is necessary in order to inform these members of their responsibilities to the union and to their immediate constituents as they participate in the problem-solving process. Finally, the union has not extended the integrative bargaining function to lower organizational levels. This, however, is not as serious as it would be in a larger plant.

Comment

Shell-Sarnia has created a parallel organization that comes closer to meeting the four design principles set forth in Chapter Two than any other organization with which I am familiar. It is not perfectly consistent with these principles—but it is so close that it is in a league by itself. Its most outstanding strength lies in the enforceability of the participative system and its products. This was a brilliant and decisive move by ECWU Local 800. The system's most serious weakness is that integrative bargaining at Shell-Sarnia is not extended to lower levels of the organization. Since the parallel organization is not vertically whole, lower-level managers do not have their own action teams. In order to become directly involved in formal integrative bargaining, workers must be selected for membership on plantwide permanent or ad hoc committees. The Shell-Sarnia experience is of the greatest importance because it demonstrates the feasibility of folding a participative system into the collective bargaining process.

Pima County, Arizona

The factual information contained in the Background, Participative System, and Results sections of this writeup was gathered during interviews and discussions with managers, union officers, and workers in Pima County, Arizona, and from published sources. These interviews and discussions were held while consulting with Pima County and its unions from 1979 to 1983 and while visiting the county during the spring of 1989. Every effort has been made to ensure the accuracy of this information, including providing drafts of these sections to the chair of the top-level county labor-management committee. The analysis contained in the Design Characteristics and Comment sections represents the opinion of the author.

Background

The government of Pima County, located in southern Arizona (a "right to work" state), has about 5,000 employees. These employees maintain the roads, operate a hospital, enforce the law, administer the courts, and provide water and many other services to the residents of the county. In 1977, Pima County joined with one of its unions, Local 449 of the American Federation of State, County, and Municipal Employees (AFSCME), to participate in "Project Network," an experimental two-year labor-management cooperation program sponsored by the federal government. In mid 1989, thirteen of the county's thirty-four departments had "QWL" (that is, employee participation) systems. These thirteen departments employ 75 percent of the county's employees.

The Participative System

Each line manager, from the county manager down to the work unit head, sits on his or her own labor-management action team (the terminology used for action teams, planning teams, and so on varies from department to department). At the county and department levels, these action teams are served by planning teams. These planning teams develop policies, procedures, and programs aimed at solving existing or anticipated problems. The teams deal with both conditions of employment and production problems. When the members of a planning team have reached consensus on the solution to a problem they put it in the form of a proposal and submit it to their action team for approval. Action teams that are not served by planning teams (action teams below the departmental level) do their own problem solving. All members of action and planning teams (except those members who represent top management) are elected. Each action and planning team includes representation from all interested workplace interest groups. The action and planning teams at the county level designed and continually modify the participative system at that level, and the teams in each of the county's thirteen participative departments design and modify their departmental systems. Only a few departments have made any effort to convert their work units to autonomous work teams. Since only about 460 of the county's employees belong to the two participating unions (AFSCME Local 449 and the Pima Corrections Association), nonmembers are frequently elected to represent their fellow workers on action and planning teams. The county's parallel agreements and the policies, procedures, and programs developed by its parallel organization are nonenforceable. Figure 4 is a chart of the Pima County participative system. This chart is not accurate for all departments, however. For example, Kino Hospital (which has very few unionized employees since the demise of the Pima County Nurses Association) does not use the parallel organization. There is not even a top-level labor-management steering committee. Its participative system consists of autonomous work teams serviced by a staff office.

Results

Pima County has not placed a high priority on keeping track of results. However, the scattered information available suggests a reasonable level of success.

Human Well-being. In "before and after" questionnaires administered in the transportation department and at the county health care facility (Posada del Sol), employees reported that they were treated more fairly, trusted their superiors more, and were experiencing more job satisfaction. Interviews with employees were also impressive. For example, Jerry Robles, a heavy equipment operator, said that QWL had improved his opinion of himself. "Since the QWL came in, I've seen a lot of my ideas get put into proposals and accepted. Now, every day I see the county being run in ways that have my ideas in them. I have a better opinion of myself now and it's rubbed off on my friends in the neighborhood. Now they come to me when they want advice. About what? I won't tell you. It's confidential" (Herrick, 1983–84, p. 62).

In other departments and at the county level, things are not going quite so smoothly. Interviews conducted in the spring of 1989 with members of five county departments, AFSCME and PCA officers, and members and staff of the countywide planning team produced many negative comments. Here are a few examples.

Figure 4. The Pima County Government Participative System.

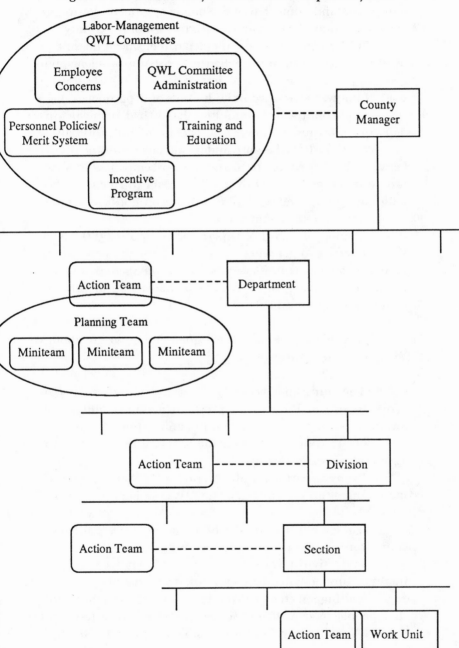

The trouble with QWL is that some departments have bought in and some haven't. Some department heads are elected and don't have to move with the rest of the county.

In departments where the department head doesn't sit on the top-level committee when it is solving problems, but gets proposals from the committee instead, QWL doesn't work. I know. I've worked in both kinds of departments.

The county-level committee has a bad name in this department because we never hear back from our proposals.

QWL is dying because middle management [the people between the department head and the workers] know they can ignore it and get away with it. They aren't threatened. They laugh at QWL because they know it hasn't got top management support in the county.

I think the board of supervisors supports QWL. Now the problem is to get whoever they pick for the new county manager to support it. [Several weeks before these interviews, Pima County had lost its county manager and an interim county manager was in charge.]

However, employees also had some good things to say about the QWL system. Here are a few examples.

The thing that keeps QWL going is the Quality of Work Incentives Program [a program making annual cash awards for group effort, cooperation, and self-development].

QWL would be great for the county if the county manager made managers use it.

In my department, all the problems that come up in management are put through the QWL system. This works smoothly.

If the eight department head vacancies were filled on condition that the people hired would use the QWL system and if productivity measures were installed to prove that QWL increases productivity, then we would have something!

The biggest change QWL brought to this department is that people used to blame someone else when things went wrong. Now they say, "I'm responsible for what goes on."

Productivity. Pima County has no overall productivity measurement system. However, there is an almost universal opinion among employees in the QWL departments that it has increased their productivity. In addition, there are some areas in which "before and after" measurements have been made. For example, in the transportation department, road-grading efficiency was tracked from the early years of the program. During the first three years, the efficiency index rose from 0.14 to 1.19 to produce a total savings of $12,222,000. At that point, the index was revised, and comparable data for the last six years are not available. Public works manager Martin Lujan had this to say: "The efficiency increase has been mainly due to QWL. First, it got people more involved and working smarter. On top of that, the QWL committees have come up with some good recommendations for training programs. Management has implemented these programs and, as a result, people have become much more competent in their jobs" (Herrick, 1983–84, p. 63).

Union-Employee Relations. Unions in Pima County were weak when the participative program began in 1977 and were still weak in 1989. Arizona's right-to-work law prohibits unions from bargaining for union membership as a condition of employment. The percentages of potential employees organized by Pima County unions suggest that the participative system has neither helped nor hurt their appeal to members. In order to be recognized by the county, a union must have 200 members. AFSCME Local 449 has hovered around this figure for years. The newly organized Pima Corrections Association (PCA) now has 230 out of a possible 430 members.

Design Characteristics

Of our four examples, Pima County's system comes closest to being whole, representative, and self-designed. However, virtually no steps have been taken to adapt the policies and practices of either management or labor to joint management principles.

Wholeness. In 1986, the county manager was changed from an ex officio member of the action team to a full "consensus" member. This was done because the team had been bogged down by the necessity of proposing solutions to the county manager that he had not participated in developing. The new structure has not helped, however, because the county manager rarely attends action team meetings. In the thirteen (of thirty-four) county departments having parallel organizations, the action teams and planning teams are generally whole. In addition, these departments are whole in the sense that they have action teams at all levels—down to and including the worksite level. However, most departments lack wholeness in the sense that they have not converted their work units to autonomous work teams.

Representation. The elective principle is fairly well observed. The secret ballot is used in county and department-level elections and most departments have provisions for recall. "At large" representation is avoided. An exception to this general rule is that managers are elected to the county-level planning team by constituencies that consist of both employees and managers. Workers have multiple representation on most action and planning teams.

Self-design. The system was originally designed by representative design teams at all levels and is now continually redesigned by the action and planning teams of the parallel organization. Until 1986, the county-level action and planning teams went on two retreats each year and made any needed adjustments in their structure and procedures at these retreats. In 1987 and 1988, however (during the period when there was no outside consultant), no retreats were held. Some flaws that have crept into the planning team structure (for example, the lack of top management representatives and the mixed constituencies of middle and lower-level managers) have—according to a number of those interviewed—seriously hampered its effectiveness.

Adaptation. The failure of labor and management to adapt their policies to the principles of joint management is the biggest problem with the Pima County participative system. On the management side, some progress has been made. For example, the county now gives financial awards to the work units showing the most teamwork and cooperation. However, it also continues to award merit raises to individual employees on the recommendations of their supervisors. This practice, of course, tends to "set employees at each other's throats" and gets in the way of teamwork and cooperation. The county attorney's office presents another example of working with one hand to create a participative system and with the other hand to destroy it. In this office, the attorneys were put on a "piecework" bonus system after the QWL system was installed. According to some county employees, the piecework bonus system not only inhibits cooperation among attorneys, but—since the bonus system does not include support staff—also inhibits cooperation between support staff and attorneys. On the union side, AFSCME Local 449 was the driving force behind starting the QWL system in 1977 and decentralizing it to the departmental level in 1980. It also insisted on hiring a new outside consultant in 1988 to replace the one who left in mid 1987. However, AFSCME has not been strong enough to adapt itself in the ways suggested in Chapter Twenty-Four. It has not, therefore, been able to identify itself enough with QWL in the minds of county employees to use the participative system as an organizing tool. As Judy McKibbon of ECWU Local 800 says, "It's hard for the union to get credit for [employee participation] achievements" (Forum, 1984).

Comment

It is important to recognize that the dynamics of public-sector organizations do not favor participative management. In order for meaningful participation to exist, top management must make it in the interests of middle and lower levels of management to share power. In the private sector, top management has a motive for doing this. Over the past seventeen years, top management in many companies has become convinced that participative management increases productivity. Since it needs increased productivity in order to compete in the marketplace, it requires middle and lower-level managers to manage participatively. For example, in the Cadillac Detroit-Hamtramck plant, employees report that "bad-guy, non-participative managers" are fired. In the public sector, on the other hand, increased productivity is often a disincentive for managers. A department head who increases productivity one year is likely to receive a reduced budget the following year. Of course, top management might have another potential motive for forcing lower levels of management to share power: union pressure. In Pima County the unions exert this pressure to the best of their ability, but they are too weak to get top management's attention. Thus, the major weakness of the Pima County participative system is that, while it espouses sound design and process principles, it does not translate these principles into action.

Saturn

The factual information contained in the Background, Participative System, and Results sections of this writeup was gathered from telephone discussions with labor and management representatives of the UAW and Saturn and from published and unpublished written materials. These telephone discussions were held during the spring of 1989. Every effort has been made to ensure the accuracy of this information, including providing drafts of these sections to the labor and management representatives for their comments. The analysis contained in the Design Characteristics and Comment sections represents the opinion of the author.

Background

In 1983, General Motors (GM) invited the UAW to take part in the planning of a small-car auto plant capable of competing with foreign makes (Fisher, 1985). The parties established a joint study center to explore innovative approaches to staffing and operating the new plant. In July 1985, the Saturn Corporation (a wholly owned GM subsidiary) and the UAW signed a memorandum of agreement outlining Saturn's philosophy, organization, and relationships with the union. Spring Hill, Tennessee, was selected as the site for the new plant, and 1991 model Saturn vehicles should be introduced in the fall of 1990. As of mid 1989, the Spring Hill facility was not yet complete.

The Participative System

The Saturn participative system, as described in the agreement (Memorandum of Agreement Between Saturn Corporation and UAW, 1985) and in the Saturn material titled "Work Unit Module Advisor Job Information," is aimed at providing a consensus decision-making process at the various levels of the organization. In addition, the Saturn labor contract replaces hourly pay with a salary tied to profits (Levin, 1989). At the top of the five-level participative structure is a Saturn Action Council (SAC). This council, which includes an elected union officer (the UAW vice-president who is also director of the GM Department), is concerned with the long-range goals and health of Saturn. It provides the resources and creates the environment that enables Saturn members to do their jobs.

The remainder of this description focuses on the participative structure for the manufacturing and assembly complex at Spring Hill, Tennessee. The top unit of the Spring Hill parallel organization is the Manufacturing Action Council (MAC). The MAC, which also has an elected UAW member (the president of the local), implements Saturn philosophy and provides resources to the next lower level—the business unit level. The UAW MAC adviser represents the UAW on the MAC consensus decision-making body and is the highest local administrator of the agreement. The business unit is a group of work unit modules representing a common area (like body panels, assembly, and power train). The business unit is the lowest organizational unit with an administrative head. Each business unit also has an elected UAW adviser (a vice-president of the local), who administers the agreement in the unit on behalf of the union and sits on the Business Team Ring, the consensus-reaching body at the business unit level. The Business Team Ring is made up of all the module advisers from the next lower organizational level. The next lower level is the work unit module (WUM). This is a grouping of three to ten work units with six to fifteen employees in each unit. Each WUM is serviced by two module advisers, one from the UAW and one from management. These module advisers are selected by the MAC Adviser Team and act as resources (not supervisors) to the work units that are assigned to them. The first level in the Saturn structure is the work unit level. The work unit is a group of about six to fifteen employees who are initially led by a charter team member (the first working member of the unit to be selected by the business team). As soon as a work unit becomes able to manage its own affairs without a formal leadership position, its charter team member position will be abolished and a UAW counselor (that is, steward) will be elected. Figure 5 charts the Saturn participative system.

Results

No results will be available until Saturn begins production.

Design Characteristics

Wholeness. There are no problem-solving teams at the first or second levels of the organization. Workers are represented on the third-, fourth- and fifth-level consensus-making teams by a single elected union officer. The various levels of management (charter team members, module advisers, and so forth) are not represented on fourth- and fifth-level consensus-making teams. Nonunion (office) employees are not represented in the participative system. At the first or worksite level, the work teams are small enough to act as "committees of the whole."

Representation. The UAW advisers are elected by union members. However, there is only one such adviser on each consensus-making body. Charter team members are not elected but are appointed by the Business Team, which includes a union officer. Module advisers are not elected but are appointed by the MAC, which includes a union officer. The design does not appear to provide for broad participation in integrative bargaining. Influence is shared with the union, but relatively few union members are in a position to participate directly. The major weakness of the system with regard to this criterion is that it fails to provide for multiple representation of workers. That is, each problem-solving team has only one worker representative (a combined-function union officer).

Figure 5. The Saturn Participative System.

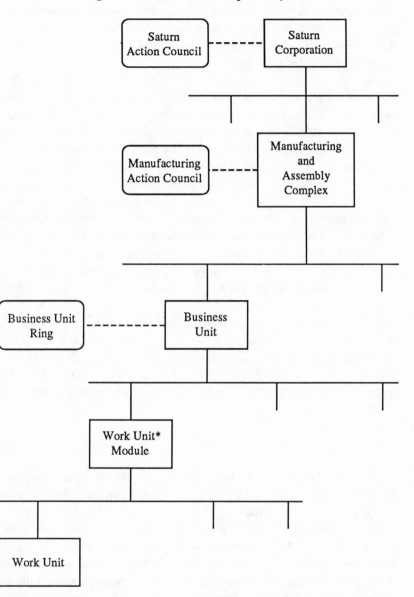

Note: The work unit module consists of two coequal advisers to the work units: one from the UAW and one from management.

Self-design. The Saturn structure is being designed by the joint UAW-GM Study Center. Thus, the union has been a full partner in the initial design. However, given the limited participative structure, most employees are likely to have little influence over the continuing redesign process.

Adaptation. Management policies are well adapted to joint management. The compensation, training, and career ladder provisions of the 1985 agreement suggest management policies and programs that are highly consistent with self-development, cooperation, and teamwork. While I would prefer productivity gain sharing rather than profit sharing (see Chapter Twenty), the replacement of hourly pay with a salary tied to profits is noteworthy. The union has integrated its administrative structure with the participative system, but has not adapted this structure so as to be consistent with the principles of joint management. The top levels of the union are involved in the deliberations of the consensus-making bodies. However, the decisions of the consensus-making bodies are not enforceable. Unlike at Shell-Sarnia, the parallel organization has not been folded into the collective bargaining process. While it has not altered its approach to collective bargaining, the UAW has made one major departure from traditional union thinking. It has made the union representative (the UAW module adviser) coequal with the management representative in the performance of facilitative management functions.

Comment

The Saturn participative system is highly centralized and keeps the power in the hands of top management and labor officers. There is little decentralization of the integrative bargaining process. The only integrative bargaining (other than that which would occur in SAC and MAC) would focus on day-to-day production problems and would occur among work unit members and between work unit members and their charter team member. Saturn relies on arrangements within the work unit to provide opportunities for worker participation. Participation in the development of rules, policies, procedures, and programs (whether involving conditions of employment or production) is limited to managers and top union officers. Thus, Saturn takes a quite different approach than the one suggested in this book. The traditional collective bargaining process remains unchanged. Whether this system will work well in terms of human well-being, productivity, and worker-union relations remains to be seen. It does seem clear that it is not aimed at involving large numbers of employees in directly influencing their conditions of employment. Saturn appears to be a highly sophisticated system aimed at increasing productivity and providing good working conditions within the context of advanced management concepts and generally traditional union ideas.

These advanced management concepts are highly unusual. For example, there does not appear to be any managerial accountability at the work unit or work unit module levels. There is no module manager. After the charter team member position is eliminated, there will be no team leader. This means that, in traditional terms, the business unit head will be the first-level supervisor for as many as 150 workers. Another radical feature of the design is that a manager and a union representative will be coequals in providing services and advice to each work unit module (grouping of three to ten work units). It does not appear that either position will be accountable for the performance of the teams. To the extent that the two positions do perform management functions, however, the union representative will be jointly responsible for these functions. This, of course, is not a traditional union idea.

Conclusions

The Cadillac Detroit-Hamtramck participative system provides an extremely well-thought-through means of gaining broad employee input into technical design problems. It fails to address either labor's need to decentralize its influence over conditions of employment or management's need to reconcile conflicting interests within the workplace. Shell-Sarnia provides for broad employee input into both technical problems and conditions of employment. Of the four examples, the Shell-Sarnia participative system is by far the most consistent with the design principles proposed in Chapter Two. The Pima County system is handicapped by problems special to the public sector. It is strong with regard to the wholeness, representation, and self-design principles, but is ineffective in practice because neither management nor labor has adapted its policies to be consistent with joint management. The Saturn system appears to be a highly sophisticated integration of traditional union ideas with advanced management concepts. Since it focuses on the institutional labor-management relationship, however, it does not appear to be designed so as to address the need for broad employee input into social and technical concerns. Neither is it designed to reconcile the views of the various interest groups within the workplace.

Workers and Their Unions. Using ECWU chief steward Judy McKibbon's words, if the unions do not "get the credit for the achievements" of employee participation systems as these systems become more common, workers' loyalties are likely to become more and more identified with their companies and less and less identifed with their unions. Each of the unions that figures in the examples described above has made some effort to adapt its policies so that they are consistent with the employee participation system. However, these efforts should be measured against this question: "Do the employees thank the union for benefits achieved through the employee participation system or do they thank management?" With regard to Saturn, this question has yet to be answered. However, I believe that a participative system should be whole, representative, and self-designed, and that labor and management policies should be adapted to the principles of joint management in order to best meet the needs of management and the institutional and personal needs of unionized workers. Considered in the light of these criteria, the Cadillac, Pima County, and Saturn designs are seriously flawed, each in different ways. The ECWU at Shell-Sarnia has done the best job of adaptation.

Productivity. In a speech before an American Federation of Labor-Congress of Industrial Organizations (AFL-CIO) conference televised by C-Span on April 18, 1989, Secretary of Labor Elizabeth Dole stated that worker participation programs invariably increase productivity. If we assume that smoothly operating programs increase productivity more than troubled programs, these histories of jointly managed organizations have some important things to say to labor and management. The Cadillac Detroit-Hamtramck system is moderately integrated with management policies but ranks low on wholeness, representation, and self-design and is not tied to mainstream bargaining. In March 1989, Detroit-Hamtramck union members voted out their incumbent officers and voted in a slate that many workers perceived as being antiparticipation. Our "closest to ideal" participative system, Shell-Sarnia, was in trouble until ECWU Local 800 went to the brink of strike to make its procedures and products enforceable. Now, according to Local 800 officers, the plant and the system are doing well. The Pima County system is sadly lacking in adaptation. While it ranks high in wholeness, representation, and self-design, it cannot be said to be running smoothly—witness the many negative comments made by employees. While the Saturn system appears to be flawed with regard to wholeness, representation, and the adaptation of labor policies to joint management principles, it cannot be properly assessed until the plant is producing automobiles. There is much to be learned from studying these four examples. Each design feature has implications, not only for the short-term success of the system in terms of human well-being and productivity but also for the long-term impact of the system on human well-being, productivity, and organized labor.

Part II

The Dynamics of
Jointly Managed
Organizations

In this part we will consider how planning, controlling, exercising power, and engaging in conflict are affected by the presence of a joint management system. Of course, the extent to which a joint management system affects these functions depends on the nature of the system. For example, a participative system that is neither whole nor representative nor self-designed and that is dominated by management might not result in employees who are self-controlled. Instead, it might substitute a more subtle and manipulative form of external control. A system that ranks high on all four design criteria, on the other hand, should give different meanings to the traditional concepts of control, planning, power, and conflict. The chapters of this part discuss these different meanings based on experience with existing participative systems that rank relatively high on the four design criteria. Planning under these systems differs from planning in traditionally managed organizations in that the process includes all the interested parties. The basic means of control shifts from external supervision to internal discipline. Power becomes more evenly distributed. In addition, there are means of resolving conflicts before they are repressed and become deeply embedded in the organization's culture.

Chapter 6

Redesigning Processes for Planning and Controlling

One dictionary says that a plan is "a detailed scheme or method for the accomplishment of an object." It also says that to control is "to exercise a regulating influence over: to direct." Using these definitions, there is no clear separation between the planning and controlling functions in an organization. "Detailed schemes and methods" exercise a strong influence over the work that is then done to accomplish their object. Thus, the planning function is merged with the controlling function. In a jointly managed workplace, where the people who do the planning also do the work, the two functions are merged in the same person. This arrangement enables people to be internally, rather than externally, controlled. They become inner-directed workers.

However, it is useful to separate the two functions in describing how they are carried out in organizations. Therefore, we will define planning as the development of rules, policies, procedures, and programs for later use in attaining an object. We will define controlling as the monitoring of these rules, policies, and so on in order (1) to be certain that they are being followed and (2) to ensure that they are—in fact—accomplishing their object. Using these definitions, a well-designed parallel organization can transform planning into a collective process that reconciles the views of the parties involved. At the same time, it (and the autonomous work team) can transform certain aspects of controlling into an individual process (internal control) made possible, in large part, because the individual employee's views have been taken into account during the planning process.

These definitions view planning as a process that is engaged in before the actual work begins in order to give that work a better chance of attaining its object. They view controlling as a real-time process with two paradoxical aspects. First, it ensures that the work activity follows the plan to produce the desired quantity and quality of product or service. Second, it ensures that variations from the plan are made when they are necessary in order to accomplish the object.

Planning

Dwight Eisenhower once said, "Plans are nothing; planning is everything." By this, I think he meant that the planning process "is everything" because it forces the planners to think the problem through. The resultant plans "are nothing" because they are subject to change as circumstances change. Having thought the problem through, however, the originators of the plans are able to change them effectively as the situation changes.

In traditional organizations, the planning process is rarely designed in accordance with the former president's aphorism. Most organizations use staff specialists to do the bulk of their planning. As Webber, Morgan, and Browne (1985) remark, "The wrong people do the planning." The line managers responsible for carrying out plans (and modifying them as necessary) do not have the benefit of the process that Eisenhower called "everything." They have only the benefit of the plans, which the former president called "nothing."

Further, even if Webber's recommendations were heeded and line managers were included in the planning process, only a small portion of the planning benefits would be realized. All the members of an organization—not just its managers—are engaged in carrying out its plans. The more these organization members are involved in the planning process, the more they will understand the reasons for the plans and the better they will be equipped to modify them as appropriate. In addition, people who are involved in the planning process tend to become more committed to accomplishing its objectives and to be more fulfilled through their work.

The parallel organization and the autonomous work team are both planning mechanisms. The parallel organization is essentially an intermediate-range planning mechanism. When it is folded into the collective bargaining process, its plans become enforceable. The autonomous work team carries out a combination of short-range planning and real-time production activities. The differences between the real-time production activities of the autonomous work team and those of the traditional work unit are discussed in the next part of this chapter. Joint management has two kinds of implications for the planning function: those concerned with planning as it is done in the parallel organization and those concerned with planning as it is performed in the autonomous work team.

Planning in the Parallel Organization. Both the primary and the parallel organizations have planning functions. Where do those of the primary organization leave off and those of the parallel organization begin?

The answer is simplified by the way the parallel organization is structured. That is, the manager who is responsible for the primary organizational unit is also the senior manager-member of that unit's action team. Further, that same manager (or his or her superior manager) retains the authority to approve plans developed by the parallel organization. Where the primary organizational unit is large enough to warrant a planning team, the line manager may not be a member of that team. Nevertheless, he or she is represented on the planning team and sits on the action team that reviews the planning team's proposals and has the authority to approve, disapprove, or return them for modification. Thus the jurisdiction of the parallel organization coincides with that of the primary organization. It can develop plans in any area in which the head of the primary organization is authorized to develop plans. Where a manager is responsible for strategic planning, the parallel organization at his or her level should be involved in this planning. The parallel organization can be regarded as a planning tool that is available to help the manager carry out planning responsibilities. It can also be regarded, of course, as a forum in which the union can bargain conditions of employment and work methods.

The essence of planning is that it is preventive. Milne's Christopher Robin provides an apt definition of planning when Pooh asks him what "getting organized" means. He says it is "what you do before you do something, so that when you do it, it's not all mixed up" (Webber, Morgan, and Browne, 1985). One of the virtues of the parallel organization is that it disciplines managers to spend more of their time preventing things from being "all mixed up" and less time untangling them. Typically, managers give a great deal of attention to untangling foul-ups (crisis management) and very little time to arranging things so that fewer crises occur (preventive management).

It might be helpful to consider the activities of the parallel organization in the contexts of long-, intermediate-, and short-range planning. Webber, Morgan, and Browne (1985) describe long-range planning as determining organization strategy and mission, inter-mediate-range planning as determining quantity and quality of outputs, and short-range planning as scheduling activities. The time frames involved vary with the nature of the work. For example, an automobile company might think of long-term planning in terms of eight to ten years, while a maker of ladies' garments might think of it in terms of ten months. In practice, parallel organiza-tions spend little time on either long- or short-range planning. The autonomous work team, on the other hand, focuses on short-range planning.

There is no reason, other than the required time and energy, that action and planning teams at all levels of the parallel organiza-tion should not engage in long-range, strategic planning. Top management could profitably ask these teams to develop and sub-mit their ideas on what the organization's mission should be and how it might change its structure to accomplish this mission. By the same token, any middle manager asked for input into the long-range planning process would be wise to ask his or her planning team for its views. At present, however, this is rarely done.

In practice, middle and upper levels of the parallel organiza-tion usually concern themselves with two kinds of intermediate-range planning. First, they develop rules, policies, and procedures. This process tends to be stimulated by situations in which things are "all mixed up." The rules, policies, and procedures are designed to straighten these things out and to avoid similar mix-ups in the future. Because it focuses on situations that are "all mixed up," the parallel organization makes extensive use of formal problem-solving processes. In the context of the parallel organization, planning and problem solving are one and the same. Where the parallel organization is functioning as an extended bargaining mechanism, planning, problem solving, and integrative bargaining are all one and the same. In these cases, plans dealing with conditions of employment are subject to the grievance procedure. Plans dealing with work methods may or may not be grievable, depending on whether the union has successfully bargained the right to bargain them.

Second, middle- and upper-level planning teams design programs or projects they believe will have beneficial effects on productivity or on the quality of working life. For example, a planning team might design a tuition reimbursement program aimed at enabling nurse assistants and licensed practical nurses to become registered nurses. In this example, the planning team might be addressing an anticipated, rather than an immediate, problem. In these ways, the parallel organization contributes both to the quantity and quality of outputs and to the quality of working life experienced by organization members.

The initiative for involving the parallel organization in either short- or long-range planning is most likely to come from management. The priorities of nonsupervisory employees naturally lie with straightening out "mixed up" situations. Except at the worksite level, this tends to fall within the purview of intermediate-range planning. However, it is likely that planning teams above the work unit level will become more involved in short-range planning and that all planning teams will become more involved in long-range planning as management recognizes the contributions they can make and as unions adopt policies aimed at obtaining fuller participatory rights for their members.

Before moving on to consider the role of the autonomous work team in planning, a few words about the worksite-level action team should be helpful. This action team is the link between the parallel organization and the autonomous work team. Where a jointly managed enterprise has a parallel organization, but has not converted its primary work units to autonomous work teams, the worksite-level action team is the link between the parallel organization and the traditional primary work unit.

Where a work unit has ten or more members, the worksite-level action team usually consists of two or three participation stewards and the first-line supervisor. While meetings are open to the other members of the work unit or autonomous work team, these three people do the lion's share of the intermediate-level planning. This planning generally focuses on two areas—modifications in work methods and modifications in governance procedures—where these work methods and governance procedures are within the control of the first-line supervisor.

Planning in the Autonomous Work Team. The lines between the worksite-level action team and its autonomous work team are blurred. The members of the action team are also members of the autonomous work team. The other members of the autonomous work team both participate in the planning process through their participation stewards and, where a problem is of special interest to them, attend the planning meetings themselves. Where an autonomous work team has only a few members, they are all members of the corresponding action team. However, it is helpful to distinguish between the intermediate-range planning done by employees as members of the action team and the short-range planning they do as members of the autonomous work team.

The work methods and governance procedures designed by a worksite-level action team set the stage for both the planning and controlling activities of its autonomous work team. For example, an action team might design a procedure that calls for all the members of the autonomous work team to meet each morning to decide which member will carry out which work assignment. In designing this procedure, the action team is performing intermediate-range planning. When the action team members actually meet with the rest of the work unit (or autonomous work team) to participate in deciding the day's work assignments, they are engaging in short-term planning. The specific short-term planning activities performed by each autonomous work team vary with the desires of its members and the nature of the task being performed. One of the advantages of the procedures arrived at through integrative bargaining is their flexibility. They are detailed, but they can be changed quickly to meet new conditions.

Controlling

Eric Trist (1981) describes the "old paradigm" organization as using external controls and the "new paradigm" organization as using internal controls. External controls include close supervision and specialist staffs. Internal controls reside within the employees themselves. Where employees are trained in multiple skills and are involved in the management process, there is less need for external controls to ensure that they meet production standards and react appropriately to variances (that is, changed circumstances).

The Parallel Organization. This aspect of Trist's new paradigm is central to the parallel organization. Rules, policies, and procedures produced by the parallel organization require fewer external controls than do those produced by staff offices. This is true for two reasons. First, they are more likely to meet the needs of the employees and of the organization. They are not developed on the basis of personnel surveys interpreted by staff employees. Instead, all employees are given the opportunity to participate in their design. This eliminates the potential errors that arise when staff people guess other employees' feelings about their working conditions on the basis of their answers to survey questions—and then guess the implications of the supposed feelings for administrative rules, policies, and procedures. The parallel organization eliminates these guessing games and thus produces end products that are more appropriate to the circumstances.

In addition, people are more likely to follow a rule, procedure, or policy that they have developed themselves than one that is imposed on them by someone else. Where the rule is made externally, it must be controlled externally. Where it is made (or accepted) by the people affected, its control can be left largely to them.

Finally, the discussion that accompanies the production of

rules, policies, and procedures by the parallel organization creates an understanding of them that is lacking when they are produced by staff people. This understanding is not limited to the employees and managers who are members of the planning teams that develop them or the action teams that review and approve them. Where the participation stewards communicate effectively with their constituents, the entire organization is involved in the debate and discussion. Thus, organization members understand the nature of the decision that is finally made and the reasons it is made. This has an extremely important result: since employees understand the purpose of the rule, policy, or procedure, they are able to interpret it in such a way as to take account of changing circumstances. This makes for a more flexible and adaptable organization. Not only are fewer external controls required to ensure that employees follow the organization's procedures; fewer external controls are required to ensure that they do not follow "the letter of the law" when to do so would be unproductive.

The Autonomous Work Team. Trist's concept of internal control is also central to the autonomous work team. This, of course, is not surprising, since he has been influential in shaping recent team theory. The force of internal control is probably the strongest as it applies to the short-range planning of the autonomous work team. There is usually little need to check up on the daily activities of autonomous work team members. This is so because they participate in its planning activities on a day-to-day and hour-to-hour basis and because they do so directly, rather than through representatives.

The force of internal control is almost as strong as it applies to the intermediate-range planning done by the work unit action team. The participation stewards on these action teams normally serve no more than five to twelve constituents each and are therefore able to involve them in planning debates and discussions far more effectively than is possible at higher levels, where participation stewards have many more constituents. The rules, policies, and procedures developed to guide the operations and governance of the autonomous work team also tend to be fine-tuned to the situation. They are tested against reality every day and changed when they fail to pass this test. Normally, they are designed on the principle of "minimum critical specification." This means that they leave as much discretion as possible in the hands of the individual employee. In this way, joint management can collectivize planning and individualize controlling.

Internal Control and the Role of the Supervisor. Where employees exercise internal control (that is, where they take upon themselves whatever actions are necessary to produce the desired quantity and quality of good or service), the role of the supervisor changes. He or she spends less time checking the work of subordinates, making decisions for them, and dealing with disciplinary problems. This frees time that can be spent making sure that employees have the tools, raw materials, skills, knowledge, and motivation to get the job done. Thus the supervisor's role becomes one of negotiating with other units (boundary maintenance), planning, and ensuring that employees are well trained and informed. As operational and personnel crises (like grievances) decrease, middle managers can also shift their emphasis from crisis management to planning.

Staff Functions and the Parallel Organization

Without careful planning, friction will probably occur between the parallel organization and an organization's staff offices. The task of the parallel organization is to plan. At the worksite level, this planning may duplicate or conflict with the work of staff industrial engineers. At higher levels, the parallel organization often produces policies and procedures in the areas of personnel, budget, finance, and procurement. This may cause staff personnel to feel resentful and threatened. Unless steps are taken to reconcile the interests of staff people with those of the parallel organization, the two may waste time and energy seeking to impede and obstruct each other. For example, personnel offices are frequently "too busy" to respond to a planning team's requests for information. Since many planning team projects cannot be accomplished without information from the personnel office, this can sabotage the work of a parallel organization and discredit it in the eyes of other organization members. Another common difficulty with many existing parallel organizations is that staff people assume they are representing top management when they attend planning team meetings. Top managers are typically reluctant to tell them that their role is to serve the planning team rather than to supervise it.

These difficulties should be lessened where the parallel organization has been folded into the collective bargaining process. Staff people in unionized workplaces understand that collective bargaining is "serious" and that requests for information from the management bargaining team should receive their prompt attention. Conferring official union officer status (like that of participation steward) on all employees sitting on action and planning teams and making the products of the parallel organization enforceable should also help staff specialists to understand their "serving" role.

Even where the parallel organization engages in enforceable bargaining, however, the reward system for staff specialists should be modified to make it in their best interests to provide quality service to action and planning teams. This reward system should provide both tangible and intangible benefits. For example, responsibilities for assisting the parallel organization should be reflected by key job evaluation criteria in the position descriptions for each position in each staff office. In addition, the performance evaluation system should be amended so that the effectiveness of each staff person in carrying out these responsibilities is evaluated by the cochairs of the action or planning teams served and becomes a major criterion in the staff specialist's overall performance rating. These modifications in the job evaluation and performance evaluation systems are especially important as they relate to the organization's key staff officials. The chief executive officer should make it clear that these officials will receive major credit if the parallel organization is successful and major blame if it is not.

This arrangement is feasible only if the chief executive officer personally sits on the organization's top action team. Further, staff personnel must be in the same staff relationship to its planning teams as they are to the chief executive officer. That is, they cannot direct and control the work of these planning teams—as they will certainly attempt to do if the chief executive officer does not make it clear that the planning teams are acting in his or her place and should be provided the same kind of staff services. If the parallel organization is provided quality staff services, quality planning is likely to result. If quality planning does result, the responsible staff officers should receive credit, and this credit should be reflected in their job and performance evaluations as well as in the thanks of the chief executive officer and of the appropriate action and planning teams.

Chapter 7

Gaining Power by
Giving Up Control

Under extended bargaining (and autonomous work teams), the planning function (at all levels of the organization) and the controlling function (at the work unit level) are restructured in a way that substantially alters the power relationships of the organization. This does not mean, however, that management loses power and that the union and its members gain this lost power. To the contrary, both management and the union gain power as institutions and both managers and employees gain power as people. A foreman in one joint management experiment said, "Since I started giving it [power] away, I've never had so much" (Maccoby, 1981, p. 75). I think this foreman meant that when he started letting go of his control over people, he began increasing his ability to get things done.

This chapter will first present a definition of the term "power." It will then develop the idea that both labor and management can gain power through the use of joint management practices. After setting the stage in this way, it will discuss the impact of joint management on various factors in the power equation.

Power as Authority and Influence

For our purposes here, we will adopt the view set forth by Bacharach and Lawler (1981) that power has two aspects: authority and influence. Authority is the formal ability to make a decision. It is often vested in positions by laws, regulations, or other official documents such as articles of incorporation. At lower levels, the authority to make a certain decision or type of decision is frequently a matter of tacit understanding between superior and subordinate. People are held accountable on the basis of their authority to make decisions.

Influence is the ability to affect the nature of the decisions made by those in authority. It is often exerted by making proposals and giving advice. The probability that such proposals and advice will be accepted depends on a great many factors ranging from their intrinsic worth to the penalties that the proposer is willing and able to impose on the decision maker should the proposal be disapproved. For example, a union that is willing and able to strike can sometimes exert a great deal of influence. Neither authority nor influence act by themselves. Power is exercised and events are controlled by the interaction between the two.

In collective bargaining (whether distributive or integrative), management exercises the authority. The union seeks to maximize its influence over the resultant decisions. This is true whether an organization is traditionally or jointly managed. Distributive bargaining provides an effective structure for dealing with win/lose matters, where a decision favorable to one side is necessarily unfavorable to the other. It does not work well, however, in dealing with matters that can be resolved to the mutual benefit of the parties. These matters require a different kind of interaction between authority and influence. This different interaction (integrative bargaining) is based on the idea that the more influence is brought to bear on a decision, the better will be the result.

Influence as an Unlimited Resource

Tannenbaum (1962) has shown that the total amount of influence in an organization can be increased or decreased. Others (McMahon and Perritt, 1973; Ivancevich, 1970) have confirmed his findings. Further, these researchers found that organizations in which larger amounts of influence are exerted are more effective than those in which smaller amounts are brought to bear. These findings can be readily understood in the context of joint management. Let us contrast the amount of influence exerted over the development of a personnel procedure in a traditionally managed organization with the amount that might be exerted under joint management. In the traditional organization, this kind of task is usually given to a personnel technician. The technician consults books and articles on the subject and may, depending on the nature of the procedure being written, administer a questionnaire to some or all of the organization's employees. The procedure is then drafted, cleared with the heads of the organization's major departments, and submitted to the chief executive officer for approval. In this case, influence is exerted on the procedure by the personnel technician, the authors of the books and articles consulted, the staff assistants to the department heads, the department heads themselves, and the chief executive officer. It is also possible that some of the questionnaire results might influence the work of the personnel technician.

In the parallel organization, the developmental work is often done by an executive-level planning miniteam, with staff assistance from a personnel technician. This group first asks for input from the operations-level planning teams. The members of the operations-level teams consult their constituents and provide the input. The procedure is written and, depending on its importance and on the nature of the input received, is either placed on a referendum ballot to be voted on by all employees or is simply forwarded to the chief executive officer for action, along with the comments of the personnel officer. Assuming that the representatives on the planning teams do a good job in communicating with their constituents, every member of the organization has had the opportunity to influence the procedure. If the procedure is important, a large number of these members may take advantage of this opportunity.

In the first case, only a handful of people exert influence on the development of the personnel procedure. In addition, none of this influence is exerted on behalf of either the union or its members. Neither is it exerted on behalf of such other constituencies as first-line supervisors and middle managers. Thus, the amount of influence exerted is small. Its quality is also suspect, since it is exerted by proxy. That is, people are not exerting it on their own behalf and that of their own interest groups. Instead, they are guessing at the kind of influence other people (workers, first-line supervisors, middle managers, and so on) might exert if they had the chance. In addition, they often modify their guesses so that the results are acceptable to themselves and to their bosses.

In the well-designed parallel organization, the amount of influence exerted is great and its quality is high. As many as two-thirds or more of the organization's members might bring their influence to bear. In addition, they exert it on their own behalf. This means that influence in jointly managed organizations is politicized. It is associated with rewards and sanctions.

The authority component of power is much the same in a jointly managed organization as in one that is traditionally managed. The same people make the final decisions and are held accountable for them. The amount and nature of the influence brought to bear on these decisions, however, are very different—as are the content and quality of the decisions themselves.

The Faces of Power Under Joint Management

The dynamics of power vary with different management styles and systems. This section comments on some of the bases, tactics, and personal characteristics associated with power from a joint management point of view.

The Bases of Power. French and Raven (1959) and Raven (1974) suggest six bases of power: rewards, punishments, legitimacy, expertise, referent power, and information.

The parallel organization strengthens the ability of rewards to influence behavior. It does this by providing all organization members the opportunity to help design the organization's reward system. Thus the rewards offered are likely to be both valued and attainable.

Punishments become a far less important way of exercising power on a day-to-day basis. People working under an effective joint management system tend to exercise internal control over their actions. However, the union may need to use the threat of punishment in order to convince management that a parallel organization and autonomous work groups should be designed and installed and administered in accordance with the parallel agreement. For example, ECWU Local 800 took Shell-Sarnia to the brink of strike in order to get contract language that made the plant's *Good Work Practices Handbook* grievable.

Legitimacy is the "organizationally sanctioned ability to control others" (Steers, Ungson, and Mowday, 1985, p. 433). Management texts usually associate legitimacy with authority and give, as an example, the ability of the supervisor to control the worker. In the parallel organization, the term "legitimacy" acquires a broader meaning. Not only does the organization sanction the ability of managers at all levels to make decisions (that is, provide them the authority to do so); it also sanctions the ability of all organization members (including managers) to influence the development of its rules, policies, and procedures. These rules, policies, and procedures often move in the direction of allowing each employee greater control over his or her own actions. In this way, the organization sanctions its members' ability to control their own actions, rather than those of other people.

It is crucial to the success of the parallel organization that its rules, policies, and procedures be legitimized. Where the parallel organization itself is bargained and where the parallel agreement and its products become (by extension) parts of the basic labor contract, this condition is fully met. Most existing parallel organizations, because they are not legitimate in this sense, experience very serious problems. Management, which has responsibility for the day-to-day administration of the system, often places the activities of the parallel organization at the bottom of the priority list (for example, it fails to hold meetings or implement agreed-upon programs). For this reason, many parallel organizations have failed to live up to their potential.

Expertise is the exercise of power through the possession of specialized skills or knowledge. The parallel organization tends to decrease the uniqueness of the expert power held by staff specialists and increase the expert power held by other members of the organization. This occurs in three ways. First, the integrative bargaining process requires the sharing of information. As the members of action and planning teams obtain information bearing on such matters as the budget, operating statements, administrative procedures, and so forth, they are better able to exert influence on these matters. Second, in order to operate the parallel organization, all organization members must be trained in problem-solving skills and educated in management ideas and principles. This gives them the ability and the confidence to question staff specialists until they understand the matters under discussion. Finally, the parallel organization places the staff specialist in a clearly defined service relationship to its planning and action teams. If the top manager fails to make this clear (that the staff specialist stands in the same service relationship to these teams as to the top manager), it is difficult for these teams to cope with the staff specialist's greater access to information. Perhaps even more crucial is the need for the top manager to make it in the self-interest of each staff specialist to accept the service role and work hard at it. This can best be accomplished through redesigning roles, performance evaluation procedures, and reward systems.

Extended bargaining and autonomous work teams increase the total amount of expertise available in an organization. In this sense, expert power becomes more important. In another sense, it becomes less important because it becomes extremely difficult for organization members to gain power by withholding scarce information and skills from others. This does not mean that the role of the staff specialist becomes less important under decentralized bargaining. To the contrary, the staff specialist becomes more powerful (in the sense of producing better results) by being able to contribute to rules, policies, and procedures that are both more appropriate and more accepted by organization members. Competent staff people are still needed to provide a depth of knowledge and a degree of skill that the action or planning team member cannot expect to acquire on a part-time basis. However, the action or planning team being serviced—not the staff specialist—must decide the nature of the rule, policy, procedure, or program being proposed. The key procedural point is that the planning teams of the parallel organization should listen to the advice of staff experts, but need not be bound by this advice.

Referent power is "the ability to influence others because they identify with you or want to be like you" (Steers, Ungson, and

Mowday, 1985, p. 433). For example, senior managers who are admired by junior managers may exercise referent power with regard to them. The "natural leaders" among an organization's employees exercise referent power over their fellows. In addition, first-line supervisors who are admired for their personal and professional qualities can supplement their legitimate power with referent power. However, the amount of referent power exercised by managers over workers and by workers over managers in traditionally managed firms is somewhat limited. The two groups see themselves as having different interests and do not often interact on a personal basis.

In organizations using the parallel organization, however, referent power is more available for use *between* members of labor and management. This is so for two main reasons. First, the two groups have identified areas where they have interests in common and are working toward mutual goals. This makes it more feasible for a member of one group to "identify" with a member of the other. In addition, the parallel organization brings representatives of the two groups into frequent contact in situations where they can observe each other's personal and professional qualities at first hand. As a result, managers often develop feelings of admiration and respect for workers and vice versa. This is another of the dynamics that make it possible for a larger total amount of influence to be exercised in jointly managed than in traditional organizations.

Power is often exercised by people through the control of information. Information is so vital to the functioning of an organization that the mere possibility of its being withheld or delayed places considerable power in the hands of its possessors. To deny a group of people information about a matter is to prevent them from influencing it. However, in a jointly managed organization the object is to increase, rather than decrease, the total amount of influence. It follows that the more open both labor and management are to sharing their information, the more effective the joint management system will be. Put another way, the task of the parallel organization is to solve problems to the mutual advantage of the parties. This can best be done where all the available information about the problems is in the hands of action, planning, and autonomous work teams.

Managers often find it extremely difficult to overcome their fear of sharing information. For example, managers frequently withhold information regarding their plans because they are afraid of raising employees' expectations and then—if the plans do not materialize—having to deal with the employees' disappointment. In addition, managers who share information make themselves vulnerable to being second-guessed by their employees. A manager who shares information demystifies his or her job.

It is clear both that a great deal depends on sharing information in joint management and that there are powerful forces at work to discourage it. This issue should be treated in depth when managers and employees are being trained to assume duties under an integrative bargaining system.

The Tactics of Power. Pfeffer (1981) identifies a number of tactics that can be used to obtain power. I will treat Pfeffer's first four tactics together (providing resources, creating dependence, coping with uncertainty, and being irreplaceable) since they are closely related, especially in the context of joint management. In essence, they suggest that one can secure power by gaining control over resources needed by others, then increase this power by eliminating other sources for the resources one controls. The dependence relationship will be intensified if one can come to the rescue with these resources in a crisis. The impression of being irreplaceable makes power complete.

The jointly managed organization seeks to eliminate these tactics. It operates on the theory that there should be multiple sources for each resource, that crises can be avoided if single-source dependencies are kept to a minimum, and that no one should be irreplaceable—even for an hour or for a shift. Thus, the jointly managed organization promotes the common holding of information regarding when, where, and how resources can be obtained. It also trains employees in multiple skills. One of the advantages of multiskill competence is that it prevents people from applying power by being the only ones who are capable of coping with an unexpected situation. If all the employees of a work unit are trained in all the tasks that unit is called upon to perform, neither the absence of a particular employee nor a rapid shift in the outputs required of the unit will create a crisis.

Of course, this very feature of multiskilling can weaken the position of the union; it becomes more difficult to create a crisis. The best way for unions to deal with this issue, in my view, is to make multiskilling (and other, similar problems) the subject of extended integrative bargaining. In this way, the specific features of each multiskilling proposal can be examined carefully and resolved in a way that does not work to the disadvantage of the employees.

The rules, policies, and procedures governing the parallel organization make up the organization's decision process for intermediate-range planning. The work methods produced by the parallel organization at the worksite level control the decision-making process of the autonomous work team. To the extent that the design of the parallel organization itself is influenced by the members of the organization, they share in the power that comes from controlling decision-making processes.

In the traditionally managed organization, consensus needs to be developed only among an elite group of managers. Under extended integrative bargaining, it needs to be developed in every planning and action team. Since these teams are made up of people from different interest groups, the task is difficult. People must understand that they do not need to agree that they have arrived at the best possible plan in order to reach consensus on it. They also need to recognize that total consensus can almost never be reached among all the members of the organization. It is usually feasible only in relatively small groups where issues can be discussed in depth and at length.

The parallel organization is a political mechanism and political skills are needed by those who operate it. It is different from the traditional organization in that the political process is both open to all organization members and open in its practices and processes. This means that the political skills it requires are different from those of the traditional organization. They must be based on openness, credibility, trust, and honesty—whereas the skills used in many organizations are secretive, devious, and manipulative.

Personal Characteristics and the Possession of Power. Wofford (1982) lists some personal characteristics that determine the amount of power a person is likely to gain. We will consider several of these characteristics: Machiavellianism, trustworthiness, and credibility.

Christie and Geis (1970) developed a scale that measures people according to the value they place on manipulating other people for personal gain as opposed to the value they place on being emotionally involved with others. The former were labeled "high Machs" and the latter "low Machs." Low Machs were found to be at a disadvantage because they valued honesty, justice, and honor. People who rated extremely low on the Mach scale were found to make poor administrators because their attachments to their subordinates affected their ability to make cold, objective decisions.

This view of character may be correct as it relates to the traditional organization. However, the arrangements for interaction in the parallel organization are different and place a negative premium on manipulation and dishonesty. The business of the parallel organization is done in open meetings. The problem-solving process (integrative bargaining) that occurs in these meetings is successful only to the extent that the participants are open and honest with each other. Further, the frequent and continuing nature of these meetings makes it difficult to be dishonest and get away with it. For example, a manager who withholds information that is material to a problem under discussion will probably be found out. If and when the information becomes common knowledge, the manager will have to answer the question "Did you know this when we were discussing such-and-such a problem?"

This is not to say that no manipulation for personal gain occurs in parallel organizations, but manipulation, secrecy, and dishonesty are less functional and therefore tend to decrease relative to other, more open modes of behavior.

Wofford (1982, p. 222) says that trustworthiness and credibility "are not only significant for the manager who is attempting to persuade his subordinates to follow a new policy, but also for the participative manager whose subordinates must believe that their involvement is not a subtle guise for manipulating them to adopt a predetermined decision. The effective manipulator must convince his Targets that their response will benefit them."

In the integrative bargaining process, all parties involved should strive to avoid manipulation like the plague. The point is not to give an appearance of trustworthiness and create an image of credibility in order to enhance one's ability to manipulate. It is rather to live up to one's word and to "tell the whole truth and nothing but the truth." This releases the productive energies of the people who are involved in the process. Managers will not devote their full energies to the process unless they believe in the dependability and honesty of their labor colleagues and vice versa. When a system is first installed, this mutual trust is likely to be tentative and conditional. It is then either confirmed or destroyed by the behavior of the participants over time. For example, a manager who approves a joint proposal but does not promptly implement it cannot expect to enjoy the trust of his or her associates. Trust must be earned and continually reaffirmed.

Chapter 8

Dealing with Conflict
and Competition

Most us wish, on the one hand, to domineer, feel superior to, and maintain a distance between ourselves and our fellows and, on the other hand, to love, be loved by, and be at one with them. We have tendencies that lead us in both directions and our behavior reflects our ambivalence. We are concerned here with the ways in which joint management affects these tendencies and the ways in which competition, conflict, and cooperation can be managed by the parallel organization. This chapter first defines the terms "competition," "conflict," and "cooperation." Next it comments on the positive and negative aspects of competition, conflict, and cooperation in the context of joint management. Finally, it discusses some ways to maximize their positive and minimize their negative aspects.

Competition, Conflict, and Cooperation

To compete is to strive for something that cannot be shared or that one is not willing to share. A runner competes with other runners for first place in a race. A junior manager may compete with other junior managers for a senior managerial position. A research scientist may compete with other scientists for the glory and recognition that goes with an important discovery. Two research institutes may compete with each other for a federal grant. In all these cases, a scarce resource is desired by more than one person or organization. Even if there were no scarce material resources in the world, people might still compete with each other to dominate and to feel superior. By their very nature, domination and superiority are always in limited supply. Competition can be destructive in two major ways. First, it stands in the way of helpful, loving relationships—people or organizations in competition with each other are not likely to go out of their way to help each other or to provide emotional support. Second, it may lead to hurtful, destructive relationships—people in competition may harm or obstruct (that is, be in conflict with) each other. However, competition is not necessarily destructive. For example, two departments in competition may be so physically and functionally separate from each other that they have no potential for developing either helpful or destructive relationships. Thus, competition can neither prevent them from giving active assistance nor lead them to indulge in obstructive behavior. Further, competition is an energizer. It motivates people and organizations to be active and productive. The task is not to eliminate competition but to so arrange things that its benefits are maximized and its harmful aspects minimized.

The term "conflict" will be used here to describe a situation where people or organizations are inflicting damage on each other. Competition can exist without conflict, but this is usually the case only where it is either impossible or unwise for the parties to hurt each other. For example, let us suppose that a personnel department and an industrial relations department are in competition for the glory and recognition of being the more important staff arm of the chief executive officer. As long as each department works to achieve this objective only by seeking to excel in its own sphere, competition exists without conflict. But the moment one department head speaks disparagingly of the other (or any other member of a department takes a hostile action), the two departments are in conflict. Since, in this and in many other cases, slowness to respond to a request for information qualifies as a hostile action, it would be very difficult in this case to keep competition from developing into conflict.

Cooperation, on the other hand, occurs when people or organizations assist each other in working toward a common goal. It is difficult to overestimate the far-reaching effects of cooperation on the workings of an organization and on the psychological health of its members. The most powerful and ubiquitous effects of cooperation lie in its amazing ability to free up positive actions. In the course of each day's work, there are countless small and large actions that persons or organizations can either take or not take to assist each other. Where a state of cooperation exists, people are free to take these actions. Where a state of conflict or competition exists, people do not feel free either to volunteer help or even to ask for it. For example, almost everyone who has ever worked in an office knows how painful it is to pick up the phone and call another office for information when that other office is not in a cooperative relationship with one's own. More often than not, such calls for information are not made and the work of the organization suffers.

Is Conflict Ever Good?

The notion that conflict has its "up" side is becoming ever more popular among academic writers. Since the claims of joint management rest in considerable part on its ability to reconcile divergent views and avoid conflict, it should be useful to look at the positive outcomes that are claimed for conflict and see how they fit with the philosophy and practice of joint management. Steers, Ungson, and Mowday (1985, p. 419) have drawn on the work of Miles (1980) and Thomas (1976) to compile a list of these outcomes. This list is summarized below.

1. Conflict between divergent views often results in better decisions or solutions to problems.
2. Conflict is stimulating and provides a chance to test ideas.
3. Conflict can highlight problems and lead to their solution.
4. Conflict is a sign that people are motivated.
5. Conflict among groups increases the internal cohesiveness of each group.

The existence of divergent views and the willingness of people to present and defend these views in the face of prevailing organizational opinion are certainly positive outcomes, for both economic and human reasons. However, they are most positive as outcomes of trust rather than as outcomes of conflict. While conflict sometimes culminates in a contest between two polarized views, trust enables a variety of views to be debated on their merits and the best features to be drawn from each. People desirous of blocking or impeding each other tend to hide their disagreements for fear of "tipping the opposition off." They express their substantive differences only when the right tactical moment arrives. People who trust and who are in a cooperative relationship with each other, on the other hand, tend to express and explain their substantive disagreements openly. The proposition that conflict is stimulating may arise from some confusion of the term "conflict" with the term "disagreement." Conflict is almost always defined in management texts as involving blocking (Miles, 1980), thwarting (Baron, 1983), impeding (Wofford, 1982), or interfering (Webber, Morgan, and Browne, 1985). We have only to consult our experience to confirm the idea that open disagreement is stimulating. However, blocking, thwarting, and so on do not create the feelings of trust that are conducive to open disagreement. It is true that blocking, thwarting, and so forth can lead to the identification and resolution of problems. However, the problems resolved are most often the very blocking and thwarting we are asked to credit for their resolution.

The claim that conflict is positive because it can be a *sign* that people are motivated does not hold water. If it could be demonstrated that conflict motivates people, that would be worthy of discussion. The proposition that conflict among groups promotes cohesiveness within the groups, however, appears to be valid. There can be little doubt that conflict is threatening and the notion that groups become more cohesive when threatened from the outside is consistent with both empirical research (Sherif and others, 1961) and experience. Cohesive groups are more highly motivated to attain group goals (Wofford, 1982). Thus, assuming group and organizational goals to be the same, an argument can be made that attempts by one group to block or thwart another group might, in some cases, result in higher productivity.

However, it does not necessarily follow that conflict is the most desirable way to increase group cohesiveness. It is likely that a sufficient threat can be created by competition, and the harmful effects of blocking and thwarting avoided. The challenge here lies in so arranging things that the groups in question find it impossible or unfeasible to block, thwart, impede, or interfere with each other.

Ways to Prevent Conflict

Some conflict is no doubt inevitable in organizational life. For example, it is probably a necessary part of distributive bargaining. A later section will propose some ways to deal with the conflicts that do inevitably arise. This section, however, will suggest a number of techniques to prevent them from occurring in the first place: an emphasis on common goals, the use of the political process to reconcile, decentralization, and system design.

Common Goals. A common goal is one that the parties potentially (or even actually) in conflict accept as being mutually advantageous. The difficulty in creating common goals is to link a clearly defined end product to the mutual advantage of the parties in a way that is easily understandable and indisputable. Thus, the task of creating a common goal divides itself into two components: arranging the work process so that the parties potentially in conflict are jointly engaged in producing the same end product, and arranging the rewards system so that it is to their mutual advantage to do so. These matters are appropriate for consideration by action and planning teams at all levels.

One of the necessary steps in forming an autonomous work team is for the team to define what Susman (1979) calls its "primary task." This primary task is the essential end product that the team is responsible for producing and against which the team is measured. It becomes the team's common goal. One of its virtues is that, to the extent it is accepted, it moderates conflict and promotes cooperation. The work process can also be arranged at higher levels of the organization so that groups or organizational units that are potentially in conflict can be assigned common goals. For example, the chief executive officer might assign the personnel office and the executive-level planning team the common goal of developing a job classification system that pays on the basis of skills learned rather than on the basis of tasks performed. In this example, it would be necessary to carefully define the roles and accountability of the two groups. The act of cooperating to produce a clearly defined end product creates feelings of satisfaction that, in themselves, constitute a reward system. At the organizational level, however, it is desirable to reinforce psychological rewards with economic rewards. As it applies to basic compensation systems, this kind of reinforcement is discussed in Part Six of this book. For example, the common goal of a total organization can be operationalized by a carefully constructed gain-sharing plan.

Common goals, such as the development of a job classification system by the personnel office and a planning team, can be reinforced by the promise of rewards that are noncompetitive. For example, the planning team and its staff assistants from the personnel office could share in an achievement award, the personnel staffers could receive high performance ratings, and the personnel director might be given membership on a high-status advisory board. In other words, common goals do not need to be reinforced by common rewards. The rewards may be tailored to the needs of the different parties involved as long as they are given for achieving the same common goal.

Use of a Political System. Two of the functions of any political system are to prevent and manage conflict. Totalitarian political systems use force and repression in carrying out these functions, while democracies use a complex system of reconciliation through representation. Despite the difficulties presented by the large numbers of constituents represented by each elected official, democratic systems have been remarkably successful in reconciling the many opposing interests that make up modern political jurisdictions. Democratic principles can be expected to be even more effective at the organizational level, where the number of constituents per representative can often be counted on the fingers of both hands.

Until the early 1970s, collective bargaining was the major political system used to manage conflict in North American workplaces. When specific organizations or industries were threatened from the outside, they typically reacted by supplementing collective bargaining with some form of labor-management cooperation. The closest thing to a comprehensive conflict management system was the Scanlon Plan. More recently, many work organizations have recognized the increasing importance of solving mutual problems and the inappropriateness of the traditional collective bargaining process for this purpose. This recognition has led to the evolution of the parallel organization. We will next discuss the role of the parallel organization in conflict resolution and contrast it with the evolving role of the collective bargaining system.

The parallel organization is less a means of resolving conflict than a means of preventing it. It solves existing problems, not by mediating among the parties, but by redesigning the rules, policies, and procedures that caused the problems. In this way, similar kinds of problems are prevented from arising in the future. Many of these problems are not common to the whole bargaining unit. They are peculiar to smaller organizational units. The parallel organization, with its planning or action teams at every level of the organization, is ideally suited to produce solutions that are tailored to these problems. In effect, the parallel organization tends to decentralize integrative bargaining to the appropriate organizational level. The difficulty with most existing parallel organizations is that they are management driven. While they may resolve and prevent conflicts in the short run, in effect they constitute "company unions" in unionized workplaces and are likely to lead to major conflicts in the long run. This book's thesis is that long-term conflicts can be avoided by acknowledging that the parallel organization is a bargaining mechanism and by folding it into the collective bargaining process.

Parallel organizations prevent short-term conflict by finding solutions to problems that are both technically sound and accepted by the people who must live with them. A great deal of the conflict in traditionally managed organizations is created by solutions that, because they are developed by staff people instead of by a representative group, do not take into account all the relevant information that is available and are not "owned" by organization members. Much of this unnecessary conflict can be avoided through the use of parallel organizations.

Distributive bargaining is also an effective means of preventing conflict. It places issues on which there are many conflicting views, even among union members, in a political forum where resolutions can be at least minimally acceptable to all. Since employees elect their negotiators, empower them to negotiate, and ratify the resultant contract, they have an obligation to live by it. In this way, the political process tends to limit conflict to questions regarding whether or not the contract is being observed. In the past, since collective bargaining has dealt with both issues and problems, labor contracts have been lengthy, cumbersome, and difficult to enforce. Should integrative bargaining be developed by unions and folded into the collective bargaining process, basic labor contracts should become more focused and easier to enforce. Many of the more detailed provisions would be bargained at lower levels in the organization and, since they would have been arrived at through consensus, should require little enforcement effort.

Decentralization. The optimal degree of decentralization for a given organization must depend on the natures of that organization's social and technical systems. No one formula can be applied in all instances. There are, however, general characteristics of decentralization that it is well to keep in mind. One of these characteristics is the tendency of decentralization to decrease conflict within organizational units, between line and staff units, and between the levels of the hierarchy. When lower-level units are provided with control of their own resources, they do not need to compete for these resources with other lower-level units. When they have the authority to act independently, they are less likely to be at odds with their superior units over delays in getting their recommendations approved. This tendency is relevant to our discussion, since authority in jointly managed organizations tends, over time, to be delegated to lower levels of the organization. There are two main reasons for this. First, action teams at lower levels become frustrated when they reach agreement with the head of their primary organization unit on solutions to problems but the unit head is not authorized to act on the solutions. This creates a pressure on higher-level managers to delegate more authority. Second, the additional technical and management skills acquired by workers and first-line supervisors in a joint management situation make them capable of assuming more authority.

Many of the conflicts that occur within primary work units are caused because the first-line supervisor is unable or unwilling to make certain decisions. For example, a unit might need an additional tool of a certain kind, but be unable to obtain it because the supervisor lacks the authority. This results in conflict between the workers who must share the existing tools and between the workers and the supervisor who seeks to mediate their quarrels. This kind of conflict can be reduced by delegating additional procurement authority to the supervisor.

Centralized authority is often exercised by managers through staff units (for example, personnel, budget, or procurement). Subordinate managers are held accountable for the production of goods or services, but do not control the resources necessary to get the job done. This creates conflicts between the subordinate line managers and the staff units. It is sometimes feasible to eliminate these conflicts by decentralizing the staff functions to the subordinate managers. This is not feasible, however, without taking steps to ensure that the subordinate managers possess the resources and the will to carry them out.

Where people are not given the authority they need to do their jobs well, both internal and external conflicts are created. A conflict is created within the people doing the jobs because they cannot meet either their own expectations or the expectations of others. Conflicts are also created between levels of the hierarchy. Subordinates will occasionally obstruct the plans of their superiors in order to demonstrate their need for more authority. It is not unheard of, for example, for people to (perversely) carry out instructions they know will have unpleasant results. These conflicts can sometimes be avoided by additional delegations of authority.

System Design to Remove the Causes of Conflict. The planning teams of the parallel organization can be used as mechanisms for systematically redesigning the administrative structure to eliminate causes for conflict. Some of the major causes of conflict that the planning team should consider have already been discussed (conflicting goals, inappropriate political systems, and excessive cen-

tralization). In addition, this section briefly comments on task interdependence, jurisdictional ambiguity, lack of communication, and
competition for resources.

Tasks are interdependent where one person or unit depends
on the work of another person or unit to get the job done well and
on time. One approach to reducing the conflict this situation sometimes creates has already been discussed: the development of common goals. Another approach is to reduce the interdependence. For
example, the primary task of a unit might be redefined to exclude
results that are outside its control. Or a unit that is dependent on
another unit for staff services might be assigned these staff functions
itself.

Top managers sometimes keep accountability ambiguous
simply because sorting it out is a difficult and sensitive job. Yet it is
also difficult for people to avoid conflict, whether they are rank-
and-file workers or managers, when the lines between their jobs and
the jobs of others are not well understood. This does not mean that
jobs should be separate. In fact, autonomous work teams often assign everyone but the team leader the same job and rely on common
goals and other factors to prevent conflict. It does mean, however,
that everyone should have a clear understanding of the jurisdictional lines. They should be clear and well understood. Planning
teams are in an ideal position to consider jurisdictional problem
areas and recommend solutions to their action teams, since they
include representatives from the jurisdictions involved.

The parallel organization is itself a communications mechanism and often breaks down stereotypes and reduces conflicts between groups simply by bringing them together to solve common
problems. Sometimes, however, these benefits are limited to the
participation stewards who actually sit on the planning and action
teams. It might be well to emphasize here that a parallel organization will not be fully successful unless the people who sit on action
and planning teams, whether they are union participation stewards
or represent first-line supervisors, middle managers, or other nonunion personnel, are in constant two-way communication with
their constituents.

Competition for resources is a prime source of conflict. Units
that are interested in doing a good job will, as a matter of course,

impede and obstruct other units in order to gain access to scarce resources. Much of this conflict can be prevented by making resource decisions on an annual rather than on a daily basis and by providing an open forum in which these decisions can be debated. Making resource decisions within a long time frame, of course, implies some form of decentralization. For example, a unit might be provided an annual budget for the purchase of tools instead of being required to obtain approval for each tool separately. The general principle is that resource control should be decentralized to the lowest-level unit that has a common goal and will therefore not fight for resources within itself. Again, the level at which resources might best be located is a matter that planning teams are well positioned to consider.

Managing Conflict

The line between preventing and managing conflict is sometimes difficult to draw. Here we will consider under conflict management only actual conflicts that arise and require resolution in order for either the primary or the parallel organization to continue functioning optimally. The three kinds of conflict we will discuss are operational conflict, conflict over the content of plans, and conflict over the planning process.

Operational Conflict. This is conflict between units or people in the primary organization over day-to-day operations. For example, one manager might request the loan of a piece of equipment from another manager and be refused. This kind of conflict can be decided only by the manager to whom these subordinate managers report.

Conflict Over the Content of Plans. Final decisions on the policies, plans, and procedures developed in planning or action teams are made by management within the existing authority structure. This is true whether or not the parallel organization has been folded into the collective bargaining process. The approval or disapproval of a plan or policy is an operational decision and solely within the province of management. In practice, it is almost always unwise and untenable for a manager to disapprove a plan that has been jointly developed and concurred in by representatives of all the workplace interest groups (including subordinate managers) that make up the organization. In addition, planning teams are so structured that the top manager is also represented in the development process.

Conflicts Over the Planning Process. These conflicts are of two kinds. First, there are conflicts over whether the rules, policies, and procedures that govern the parallel organization itself are being followed. For example, a parallel agreement might specify that plans of a certain sort must be implemented within two weeks of the date they are approved. In this situation, a group of employees might be in conflict with a manager because they feel that a plan developed by their planning team has not been so implemented. Second, there may be conflicts over the adequacy of the rules, policies, and procedures contained in the parallel agreement. For example, planning team members may have proposed a certain procedure, been overruled by the responsible manager, and—after operating for a time under the manager's decision—decide that they cannot accept it.

Where the parallel organization has been folded into the collective bargaining process, the first kind of conflict (over whether the rules, policies, and procedures of joint management are being followed) is resolved by the grievance procedure.

The second kind of conflict is resolved by converting the rule, policy, or procedure involved from a "problem" into an "issue." That is, the matter is referred to the union bargaining committee to be taken up in the collective bargaining process. A joint management system with rules, policies, and procedures that have been jointly developed and mutually agreed to is highly desirable. Where an adequate rule, policy, or procedure cannot be arrived at in this way, however, and where it is vital to the operation of the system, the only recourse is to negotiate it in the distributive bargaining arena. This can be done by waiting until contract talks or by calling a special distributive bargaining session.

Part III

Individuals in
Jointly Managed
Organizations

This part discusses some of the theories that bear on the way individuals function in organizations. The value of these theories does not lie so much in their correctness or incorrectness as in their ability to stimulate our thinking. Part Three seeks to focus this "ability to stimulate" by relating each theory to the philosophy and practices of joint management. The theories apply in different ways to the different workplace interest groups. The different situations and different vested interests of managers, for example, separate them in certain ways from nonsupervisory employees. The first step in reconciling these differences is to acknowledge them.

Chapter Nine deals with human needs, attitudes, and behavior. It discusses such questions as "What needs does joint management seek to satisfy and what behaviors does it encourage?" Chapter Ten presents some motivational ideas consistent with the principles and practice of joint management. Chapter Eleven describes the kind of leader who functions most effectively in a jointly managed organization and relates this "ideal" leader to various leadership theories. The discussion in these chapters assumes a joint management system that is designed and operated according to the principles set forth in Chapter Two. Many of the benefits described cannot be gotten through a management-dominated system.

Chapter 9

Individual Needs, Attitudes, and Behaviors

The term "need" is used here to describe a state in which something desirable is lacking but is not absolutely required. Neither is the something that is lacking always desired by the person who lacks it. This definition, of course, makes it necessary that we adopt some system of values to distinguish between those things that are desirable and those that are not. The system of values used in this chapter is Maslow's "hierarchy of needs" (1968). Our attitudes toward things, people, and conditions generally have both intellectual and emotional components. In practice, we usually combine these components when we measure our attitudes and make a single judgment on a positive-negative scale. For example, we might be asked on a questionnaire whether we are "very satisfied," "somewhat satisfied," "not so satisfied," or "not at all satisfied" with our jobs. Or we might be asked the same question with regard to a specific aspect of our jobs (like pay). Thus, the term "attitude" is often used to describe the sum of how we think and feel about a given thing, person, or condition (or an aspect of the person, thing, or condition) along a positive-negative scale. This chapter discusses needs, attitudes, and behavior separately—each in the context of joint management. Chapter Ten discusses the relationships among needs, attitudes, behavior, and management systems.

Needs

Maslow suggested that there is a general tendency in human beings to wish to satisfy certain needs. He arranged these needs into five ascending categories: physiological, safety, social, esteem, and self-actualization. Maslow's hierarchy of needs theory assumes that people turn their attention to higher-order needs only after they have succeeded in satisfying (at least to some extent) their lower-order needs. Physiological needs must be met in order to survive. They include such things as food, shelter, and water. Safety needs must be met in order to be safe from physical harm and the fear of physical harm. Social needs have to do with being loved and accepted by others. Esteem needs consist of our needs to respect ourselves and receive the respect of others. Self-actualization is development of one's potentials to the fullest extent possible.

Figure 6. Maslow's Hierarchy of Needs.

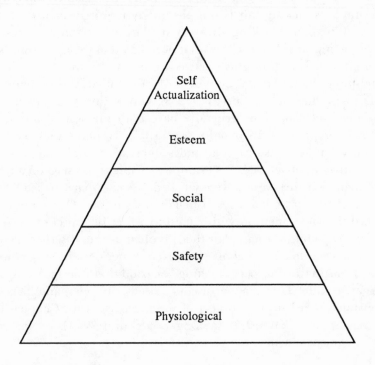

Maslow's ideas have been used both to affirm and to deny the desirability of providing greater opportunities for autonomy and participation in the workplace. Some people have argued that the higher-order needs (which involve autonomy and participation) should be satisfied in order to increase both productivity and job satisfaction. Others have countered by saying that, since the higher-order needs cannot be activated until the lower-order needs are satisfied, we should concentrate on eliminating poverty rather than dealing with matters as frivolous as higher-order needs. These arguments notwithstanding, the necessity for increasing American productivity has led to an increasing emphasis in the workplace on efforts to provide people with opportunities to satisfy their needs for belonging, esteem, and self-actualization. The reason for this emphasis is that the same actions that satisfy these needs have also been found to increase productivity (Kanter, 1983; Pasmore, Francis, Haldeman, and Shani, 1982; Nicholas, 1982).

Further, the notion that lower-order needs must be satisfied before higher-order needs are activated has undergone some revision. A survey of research compiled by Wahba and Birdwell (1976) found little support for this part of Maslow's theory. However, it seems unlikely that Maslow meant his theory to be taken literally. A less rigid interpretation would not require that a lower-order need be *completely* met before the next, higher-order need is activated. The lower-order need might be only *partially* met and still free up energy that could become involved with higher-order needs.

Physiological and Security Needs. In the long term, joint management may have a significant impact on the effectiveness with which we—as a society—are able to meet our physiological and security needs. There are also several ways in which jointly managed workplaces give short-term attention to these needs. First, joint management may help an enterprise stay in business and thus save jobs. Second, workplaces that follow the suggestions made in Part Six of this book with regard to pay and other economic rewards may provide their members with a generally higher standard of living. Finally, parallel organizations are sometimes effective in reducing occupational safety and health hazards.

Needs to Belong. Joint management is a conscious attempt to so structure organizations that people can not only meet both their needs to belong and their individual needs but can meet them in ways that are mutually supportive. In a traditionally managed workplace, union members may have a strong sense of belonging and solidarity with their brothers and sisters. However, this sense of belonging flows in large part from the threat presented by management and is nurtured by the hostility between supervisory and nonsupervisory personnel.

When joint management is based on extended integrative bargaining and when the other design principles discussed in Chapter Three are followed, it retains the solidarity of union members and continues to base this solidarity on the bona fide conflicts of interest that exist between labor and management. However, it aims at breaking down the day-to-day barriers that often separate supervisory and nonsupervisory personnel. Conflict is confined to those areas where it is appropriate and is dealt with through the distributive bargaining process. This enables both workers and managers to belong, not only to their occupational groups but also to their autonomous work teams, action teams, planning teams, and the organization as a whole. This has a profound psychological value: it enables people to group together around common organizational goals. Where the matters on which conflict is appropriate are not separated from those on which cooperation is appropriate, this kind of "belonging" is impossible. The second principle of joint management (the promotion of cooperation through group rewards) is specifically aimed at reinforcing people's ability to meet their needs for belonging. Both group rewards and the cooperation they promote tend to create cohesive groups that provide their members strong senses of belonging.

A parallel organization that closely adheres to the four design principles offers workers the opportunity to participate in an effective planning process *as union stewards*. It strengthens their loyalties to their union. On the other hand, a parallel organization that is not whole, representative, and self-designed, and that has to deal with labor and management policies that have not been adapted to joint management, can very easily be dominated by management and used as a "company union."

Esteem Needs. One way that joint management integrates people's needs to belong with their needs to be separate (and even unique) is to give them opportunities to engage in activities that both strengthen their self-esteem and earn the gratitude, rather than the envy, of their fellows. This important point can be illustrated by contrasting a typical situation under traditional management practices with a typical situation under joint management.

Let us suppose that a worker in a traditionally managed maintenance unit submits a suggestion under an individual suggestion awards program. The suggestion proposes a better way to assign job orders. It is approved and turns out well, both in terms of productivity and worker satisfaction. The worker gets a cash award. The worker has not only submitted this and other suggestions, but is also highly productive on the job. She is one of the 10 percent in her unit who receive a merit raise later that year.

Contrast this with the following actual situation from a jointly managed workplace. A maintenance worker is elected to serve as a participation steward on his worksite-level action team. He proposes, among other things, a better way to assign job orders. It is discussed and modified in minor ways within the action team and discussed by the team's participation stewards with the other members of the work unit. The supervisor approves it in the next action team meeting and it turns out well, both in terms of productivity and worker satisfaction. This work unit has a record of innovation and high productivity and is one of the 10 percent of units in the organization that receive a cash award to be divided equally among its members later that year.

In the first case, the worker's self-esteem would probably have been both helped and harmed. She received recognition from management for her contribution and competence. But it is not unlikely that her fellow workers regarded her with envy and with a certain amount of contempt. It is not unusual for those who are singled out for rewards by management to pay a price for these rewards in terms of their relationships with their coworkers. This price, when it is exacted, affects people's needs to belong as well as their needs for esteem. The worker in this story would certainly not have enhanced her sense of belonging to her work unit. In the second case, the worker would have enhanced the esteem in which he was held by management, the esteem in which he was held by his fellows, and his own self-esteem. Further, he would have strengthened his already strong sense of belonging to his work unit. Probably, he would be recognized by his fellows as a contributor to their common welfare.

Self-Actualization Needs. Meeting one's needs for self-actualization involves taking advantage of opportunities to increase one's skills, knowledge, and wisdom. In a traditionally managed workplace, these opportunities are often restricted. The first, third, and fourth principles of joint management, on the other hand, are aimed at ensuring that these opportunities are available to everyone in the organization (that is, let the worker help decide how best to do the job, hire people who can take responsibility and train them to do so, and let workers combine thinking and doing). A well-designed parallel organization provides opportunities for meeting esteem and self-actualization needs in such a way that people can take advantage of them without jeopardizing their needs for belonging.

Attitudes

Prior to the early 1970s, there were few structural efforts to improve organizational attitudes. Such efforts, while generally successful, were—for the most part—limited to the several hundred organizations that used Scanlon plans. For a variety of reasons, most attempts to improve organizational attitudes used an interpersonal approach. The interpersonal approach contrasts with the structured approach (for example, the parallel organization) used by joint management in the assumptions the two approaches make about attitudes.

The interpersonal approach assumes that attitudes can be changed through experiential training techniques. It also assumes that the attitude changes will then lead to behavioral changes and that the behavioral changes will lead to increased organizational effectiveness. The interpersonal approach uses such techniques as sensitivity training, team building, grid organizational development, role playing, and confrontation exercises.

The structural approach comes at the problem from a quite different perspective. It assumes that any attitude changes that might occur will be temporary if they are inconsistent with the culture and the administrative systems of the organizations in which the "changed" people work. It also assumes that attitude changes are more realistically viewed as a product of changed behavior rather than its cause. The structural approach uses such techniques as the parallel organization, the autonomous work team, productivity gain sharing, and worker ownership. This is not to say that the structural approach either discounts the importance of attitudes or fails to use interpersonal techniques. To the contrary, it regards attitudes that embrace cooperative behavior, the assumption of responsibility, and democratic values as necessary to the health of a joint management system. Further, it uses interpersonal techniques such as team building and role playing exercises to train people to function in parallel organizations and autonomous work teams. However, these techniques are used by joint management systems only to change attitudes temporarily so that the systems can begin to function. The changed behaviors that the system requires and the rewards that are provided for these changed behaviors are relied upon to produce lasting attitude changes. These lasting attitude changes then contribute both to the more effective operation of the organization and to the well-being of the organization members.

It is important to note that the attitudes changed by joint management systems do not all have to do with the work situation. For example, when Conrad Yrigolla, a senior heavy equipment operator in a jointly managed public-sector organization, was asked if he had noticed any changes, he answered, "I believe myself that the taxpayers are getting more work for their money than they did in years past—a whole lot of work more! And I've got a change in attitude from it. I've done a lot more reading than I used to do a couple of years back before QWL [the joint management system]. Actually, as soon as I got out of high school I just put down those books and didn't want to know nothing from nothing. But now I do a lot more reading. I even read the newspapers . . . just for the hell of knowing what's going on. At first my wife was a little bent out of shape. I sort of neglected her when I was doing a lot of reading and writing trying to get QWL set up. But I explained to her 'this is what I want to do.' Now she realizes what's going on and it's ok with her" (Herrick, 1983–84, p. 61).

Henry Ullman, a supervisor in the same organization, gave an example of how his changed attitudes had affected his behavior off the job. "When the QWL came in, right away I put 2 and 2 together. I noticed that communications at work had been real bad and got better with the QWL. Then I put this together with the communications gap we had at home. Well, I sat down one evening and talked to my wife and my boys. I said, 'we got this program at work' and explained it to them. My wife and biggest boy, Eric, asked me, 'why are you saying these things?' 'Well,' I said, 'It has helped at work and I don't see why it wouldn't help us here at home.' So we started on what we call our QHL [Quality of Home Life] meetings at dinner every night and after a week or so we began to communicate. That was two years ago. My home life is much better now that we have the QHL and my whole family will tell you the same thing" (Herrick, 1983–84, p. 62). The parallel organization and the autonomous work team reinforce positive attitudes toward change, openness, creativity, cooperation, honesty, and activity.

Behavior

Well-designed joint management systems tend to reinforce positive attitudes toward positive behaviors. They also provide forums in which people can practice behavior that is consistent with joint management and receive benefits from this behavior. And it is a good thing that they do: in order to make joint management work well, organization members need to strongly embrace the kinds of behavior that are consistent with positive attitudes toward change, openness, creativity, cooperation, honesty, and activity. Further, organization members need to embrace these kinds of behavior at some minimal level in order for a joint management system to survive its first few months. This presents an apparent "Catch-22" problem. On one hand, a functioning joint management system is needed to reinforce the attitudes and provide the forums that create the needed kinds of behavior. On the other hand, the behaviors are needed in order for the joint management system to function at all.

This Catch-22 problem can be solved by getting provisional

agreement from the organization members to adopt the desired kinds of behavior on a "trial" basis, usually for a one-year period. Assuming that all the parties adopt the behavior in good faith (especially the keystone behavior, trustworthiness), the system will work well and, by working well, will reinforce the required behaviors. Figure 7 is an example of a "behavioral" agreement reached prior to the adoption of joint management by one organization. Where a parallel organization is folded into the collective bargaining process, the newly required behaviors are taken more seriously and the problem is much simplified. Even in this case, however, the new behaviors must be defined, discussed, and agreed to. The kinds of behavior required by joint management can be grouped under the following headings for purposes of discussion: supportive behavior, creative behavior, constructive behavior, and honest behavior. At first glance, it might seem unnecessary to draw attention to the need for these behaviors in jointly managed organizations. After all, are they not needed in all organizations?

The answer to this is somewhat complicated. It might be desirable on ethical grounds, for example, that people behave honestly in all organizations. However, our definition of honesty includes openness and it is generally not feasible to behave openly in competitive situations where other people are behaving secretively. It might also be desirable from a humanitarian point of view that people cooperate with each other in all organizations. However, it is often not practical to cooperate with someone who is competing with you for scarce resources. As a practical matter, experience has shown that traditional organizations cannot convert to joint management without conducting extensive training aimed at persuading people to make tentative changes in their behaviors. This training must be followed by experiences in day-to-day situations where the new behaviors yield positive results.

Supportive Behavior. This is behavior that supports the goals, self-images, and dignity of the other members of the organization (whether workers or managers) and assists them in meeting both their lower-order and higher-order needs. Supportive behavior means treating one's fellow workers with respect and listening re-

Figure 7. An Illustrative Code of Behavior.

POSADA DEL SOL
QWL CODE

---

1. I will act openly and in good faith in the QWL relationship and will treat others involved with me in this relationship with respect and good will. I will not be devious or indirect in my dealings with them.

2. I will treat QWL business as a priority, part of my regular job responsibilities and attend all QWL meetings unless a work crisis makes it clearly impossible for me to do so.

3. I will not use the QWL relationship or confidential information learned in it to the disadvantage of others.

4. I will not use the QWL meetings as gripe sessions or to vent my feelings on others. I will be especially careful not to use these meetings to air personal grievances or to try to gain personal ends.

5. I will always guide my actions in the QWL relationship by the twin goals of attempting to improve services to the public and increase work satisfaction. When a matter has no bearing on either of these goals, I will not push it in QWL discussions.

6. I will not use my participation and cooperation in QWL as a means of gaining ends which are not to the benefit of all parties. For example, I will not withdraw or threaten to withdraw my active cooperation in QWL activities in order to force another party to my way of thinking in any matter.

7. If I am a representative of an employee group, I will join the other employee group(s) to further our mutual interest in improving productivity and increasing work satisfaction and will not use QWL as a forum for discussing matters which are not to our mutual benefit.

8. If I am a supervisor, I will not retaliate or hold it against employees for making suggestions and/or speaking their minds on matters since this is their duty under QWL. If I am a non-supervisory employee, I will not take advantage of this by being disrespectful or offensive in the way I make suggestions and/or speak my mind. QWL MEANS TREATING OTHERS WITH MORE RESPECT, NOT LESS.

9. I recognize the reasons for disagreement in the adversary labor-management relationship, but will not act in contentious or deceitful ways in the QWL relationship.

Note: Reprinted from Pocket Guide to the Posada Del Sol/ AFSCNB/PCMA QWL Management System by permission of The Pima County, Arizona, Management and AFSCME Local 449.

spectfully to their opinions and contributions in problem-solving sessions. It also means working cooperatively with others, whether they are in your immediate work unit or in another unit with which you have contact. For example, if your unit has equipment that is not in use and another unit is being held up for lack of equipment, supportive behavior means volunteering your assistance. To behave supportively is to "go the extra mile." Where you see that a fellow worker can use your help, go out of your way to offer it. Where another unit needs information, give as much energy to gathering it as though you needed it personally. Supportive behavior means following the "golden rule," "Do unto others as you would have them do unto you."

Creative Behavior. Joint management is, among other things, a mechanism for adapting to a changing world. Therefore, it requires the ability to change. But this does not mean passively accepting change. It means constantly creating new solutions to new problems. This is what is meant by creative behavior. The problems are of many kinds. Some of them have to do with work methods, some with operating policies, some with administrative matters, and still others with the rules, policies, and procedures that govern the joint management system itself. All these matters are in a continual state of change. The solution that was a stroke of genius last year may not be working well this year. In a jointly managed organization, developing solutions to new problems is everybody's business. Therefore, everybody needs to be actively creative. Passive behavior may be appropriate in workplaces where only managers are given the opportunity to bring about constructive change on a day-to-day basis. Active behavior is needed in joint management.

Constructive Behavior. Members of jointly managed organizations tend to say "yes" more frequently than "no." Of course, it is necessary sometimes to say no. Where, after careful consideration, we disagree with another person's opinion or feel it is inappropriate to do what another person wishes us to, we must say no. However, a negative mind-set and negative behavior do not work well where work is done cooperatively and people are highly interdependent. It is particularly harmful when people adopt behavior that reflects their negative attitudes toward joint management itself. For example, some people attend unit meetings and sit silently in the back of the room with their caps pulled down over their sunglasses and their chairs leaned back against the wall. This kind of behavior is not constructive (assuming that the parallel organization is well designed) because it resists any involvement in controlling their environment. Another example of nonconstructive behavior is retaliation against people who contribute their ideas in problem-solving meetings. It is only human nature for a manager to be upset the first few times a subordinate expresses views that are contrary to his or her own. However, it is neither natural nor defensible for the manager to retaliate against the subordinate. Since retaliation is extremely difficult to prove, behaving constructively also means behaving in good faith. Managers are also sometimes tempted to sit back silently in a meeting and wait until their subordinates have discussed a problem and worked out a solution. Then the manager will step in and make a decision. This way he or she avoids becoming vulnerable and perhaps having his or her ideas rejected. The problem is that this kind of behavior also avoids either contributing to the solution or developing a feeling of personal commitment to it. Participants in joint management, whether they are managers, workers, or union officers, should continually ask themselves, "Is the line of behavior I am about to pursue constructive or destructive?" If the behavior impedes the common goals of joint management (or the steps that must be taken to achieve these goals), it is destructive and should be avoided.

Honest Behavior. In the context of joint management, to be honest is to tell the truth in a direct, helpful, friendly, open, nonmanipulative way. It is not honest to hurt people by telling them what you believe is a truth about themselves unless it is crystal clear to you that they will be helped more than hurt by your statement. It is not honest to reveal matters told you in confidence, nor is it honest to mislead by telling half-truths or to say things (whether they are true or not) in order to manipulate or cause harm.

It is honest to be direct. This means that honesty requires the courage to be vulnerable. When we are direct, we cannot retreat from our words and pretend to have meant something else. It is honest to state our motives correctly. If these motives are sometimes selfish, this is only natural and will be accepted by others. But if we pretend motives we do not have, we will only be teaching others to be cynical. To be honest is to be as good as one's word. An honest person honors his or her agreements, whether to be at a meeting at a given time or to prepare a draft proposal for review by a certain date. To be honest is to keep one's commitments and to avoid deceiving others about one's motives or actions.

Honest behavior in a joint management system can have spectacular results. At first, people do not expect honesty and react with surprise. For example, the first important proposal submitted by a planning team tests the honesty of top management. If management gives credit to the planning team instead of saying, "Oh, we were going to do that anyway," it is being honest. If, after approving the proposal, management implements it according to an agreed-upon schedule, it is being honest. This kind of honesty encourages union officers and workers to trust the system and to invest their energies in supporting it with active, creative behavior. Honest behavior will be met with honest behavior.

On the other hand, if any of the parties are dishonest, the others are likely to react by being dishonest themselves. If a participation steward supports a plan in action team meetings but disparages it to his or her constituents, management will probably respond by being dishonest too. Another example of dishonest behavior that is especially damaging in a joint management situation is the withholding of information when it is relevant to a problem-solving discussion. Management sometimes justifies this dishonesty on the grounds that it was given the information in confidence by higher levels of management. This is no excuse. Under these circumstances, managers should state that they have relevant information but hold it in confidence. Then they should make a point of revealing it as soon as possible. Efforts to be honest are appreciated just as much as dishonest behavior is resented.

Chapter 10

Motivating Managers
and Workers

To motivate is to stimulate to action; to provide with an incentive. The action that managers seek to stimulate is, of course, productive work. The incentives they provide in order to stimulate productive work vary. They may use implied threats against job security. Or they may subscribe to more humanistic assumptions about human nature and use techniques such as job enrichment. Or they may believe that money is the real motivator. Whatever incentives they use, traditional managers arrive at these incentives through a kind of guessing game. The usual recipe is a dash of theory, a pound or two of results from employee questionnaires, and a dollop of assumptions about human nature. These ingredients are mixed and cooked in the personnel office. The meal is then approved by top management and served up to the employees.

Using a well-designed parallel organization, the process is quite different. Motivational theories are used by action and planning teams, not as bases for taking action but to stimulate discussions of what the members of the organization actually want in the way of incentives. Labor and management divide incentive matters into issues (those matters on which interests conflict; for example, amount of compensation) and problems (those matters that can be resolved to the mutual benefit of the parties). They then seek to

162

resolve the issues through collective bargaining and the problems through joint management. This provides organization members with the influence they need to solve incentives problems. They use the parallel organization to develop incentive programs and policies that are right for their particular needs and attitudes. In this way, guesswork gives way to political reality. Both managers and workers become, in a new and powerful sense, self-motivated. The members of action or planning teams may discuss a needed procedure for hours. Then someone describes the problem from a different point of view or adds an additional piece of information. The different point of view or the new piece of information sparks an idea from another group member and the needed procedure quickly takes shape and is agreed to. Through their involvement in this process, the participation stewards understand the matter so thoroughly that they are able to explain it satisfactorily to their constituents and get their input.

This chapter first discusses several motivational theories and comments on their relevance to joint management practice. Then it describes some features of joint management systems that are especially important if these systems are to play an effective role in motivating the managers and workers of the organization.

Motivational Theories

Jointly managed organizations need management theories. But the number of people who use these theories increases greatly and the way they are used changes. The members of planning teams, along with the staff specialists who are assigned to serve these teams, have the deepest involvement with theory. However, to the extent the planning team communicates effectively with its constituents, all organization members become familiar with those theories that are relevant to the problems under consideration. In addition, while the members of an autonomous work team may have less opportunity to discuss theory than the members of a planning team, they do have a use for it in their day-to-day activities. For example, goal-setting theory is relevant to daily work scheduling activities.

A jointly managed organization does not rely heavily on theory as a basis for developing and recommending policy. Instead, it is used as a context in which the members of the organization can think about and discuss alternatives. It is especially useful in stimulating creative ideas and in helping people speculate about their probable reactions to possibilities outside their previous experience. This section discusses the following motivational theories: equity theory, expectancy theory, goal theory, and reinforcement theory.

Equity Theory. This theory, proposed by Adams (1965), assumes that people form a ratio in their minds between the amount they contribute to their jobs and the payoff they receive. Contributions include whatever seems significant to the person making the calculation. They could be anything from intelligence to faithful attendance at work. Similarly, the payoffs could be anything from salary to the size of the person's office.

Having established their ratios, people then compare them with the ratios of others. One who finds that his or her ratio is greater will experience overpayment inequity and will try to contribute more or in some other way restore the balance. If the ratio is less, the person will experience underpayment inequity and will reduce contributions (for example, stay home "sick"). I have witnessed this latter phenomenon in organizations with merit pay systems. For every one or two people who receive a merit raise, there are usually eight or nine who do not. It is not uncommon to hear members of the group who did not get raises say openly (to an outsider, at any rate), "If they think they can give that s.o.b. Jones a merit raise and still expect to get a day's work out of me, they've got another think coming!"

To overcompensate one employee or group of employees, in order to produce feelings of guilt and a greater effort to lessen these feelings, seems to be a hare-brained—or at best questionable—strategy. Among other shortcomings, it would be likely to produce at least as many sufferers from underpayment as beneficiaries from overpayment. Research shows a general tendency among us to significantly overestimate both our contributions and other people's pay (Lawler, 1981).

The more desirable situation is one where all employees see themselves as being treated equitably. At least one study suggests that joint management systems do tend to increase people's feelings of equity (Herrick, 1983). They do this in a variety of ways; one of the most important is the identification of equity problems and the revision of personnel rules, policies, procedures, and programs to moderate these problems. The autonomous work team can also play an important role in increasing feelings of equity. The members jointly develop the group's rules governing contributions (like task assignments and shift assignments). This gives each individual the opportunity to influence his or her equity ratio in a legitimate and sanctioned way.

Some inequity problems are so major in their scope and impact that they cannot be corrected by modifying one or two local procedures or by "developing a program." They are often a mixture of problems and issues—they should be discussed in an executive-level planning or action team and a study should be undertaken to resolve them. For example, at some point a jointly managed organization should revise its job classification system to give credit for participation in the management process. A project of this magnitude might require a year's one-quarter time work on the part of the incentives miniteam of the planning team.

Expectancy Theory. This theory (Vroom, 1964; Porter and Lawler, 1968) assumes that workers make conscious judgments about whether they are capable of meeting management's requirements for a particular reward, how much they want the reward, and what the probability is that they will—in fact—get it once they have kept their part of the bargain.

Academics sometimes translate these judgments into numerical terms in order to compare the levels of motivation that would result from different situations. For example, if a worker figured there was a 50/50 chance he or she could perform well enough to meet the criteria for a bonus, the first expectancy would receive a .5. If, on a scale of one to ten, he or she thought the reward being offered was an 8, a .8 would be assigned to factor two. If the worker trusted management enough to think there was a 90 percent chance it would, in fact, give the reward for meeting the requirements, a .9 would be assigned to the third factor. The factors would then be multiplied together to arrive at a motivation score (that is, $.5 \times .8 \times .9$

= .36). It might help a planning team that is considering alternative incentive plans to "try out" this formula on each alternative plan and compare the results. The main benefit from this approach would, of course, come from the discussions this process would stimulate among team members.

Expectancy theory maintains that there are four determinants of performance, of which motivation is only one. The others are abilities and traits, role clarity, and opportunity to perform. The emphasis that joint management places on education and training improves people's abilities. The ongoing discussions of task assignments that occur in autonomous work teams help clarify roles. The development of incentive systems by planning teams tends to improve people's opportunity to perform in the sense that planning teams are unlikely to set unrealistic requirements for rewards. The joint setting of objectives and goals by autonomous work teams helps give people a realistic "opportunity to perform" in carrying out their day-to-day tasks.

Goal Theory. Goal theory (Locke, 1968) is generally consistent with equity, expectancy, and reinforcement theories of motivation, but focuses on a specific means of increasing motivation: goal setting. Research on goal theory has suggested a number of conclusions that should be considered by action and planning teams. First, goals "that are difficult and challenging for the worker and that clearly specify what is to be accomplished bring about the highest level of performance" (Wofford, 1982, p. 65). Nonspecific goals such as "do your best" result in the lowest performance. Where specific (but low) goals are set, it is unlikely that they will be exceeded by much. Yet the setting of high, specific, and realistic goals has been shown to increase performance markedly. In one study (Latham and Baldes, 1975), a group of loggers who were loading their trucks at 60 percent of maximum load were given a goal of 94 percent. Their performance rose to 94 percent in seven months and then leveled off at about 90 percent. Of course, other factors influence the effectiveness of goal setting. For example, people have to trust management not to raise the goals if they are met and not to punish people if they are not met. In the case of the loggers, there was a sharp decline in productivity for a period of several weeks while the loggers were testing management's promise not to punish them if they failed to meet the new standard. Goals are of little use if they are not accepted.

A second major conclusion is that goals should be set participatively. In fact, one study found that participation influenced performance positively only when it included participation in goal setting (Sorcher and Danzig, 1969). These findings suggest that action and planning teams should make it their business to be involved in goal setting at all levels of the organization and should be specific, challenging, and realistic in setting goals. At higher levels in the organization, goal setting may be connected with the development of incentive plans. In the action team at the worksite level, it may be connected with the development of a quarterly operating plan. In the autonomous work team it may be connected with scheduling each day's work. At all these levels, people should be alert to the importance of participating in goal setting. They should set themselves the task of learning, through both reading and experience, the kinds of goals and the goal-setting processes that work best in their organization.

Reinforcement Theory. This theory is based on people's ability to learn the relationship between cause and effect and to adopt the behavior that causes the desired effect. Because reinforcement theory was originally developed by researchers, such as B. F. Skinner, who based their conclusions on experiments using animals, its use is often regarded as manipulative. It is seen as operating on people's unconscious minds, rather than as giving them the opportunity to make rational choices. Skinner, for example, experimented with pigeons. The pigeons would randomly peck in a box until they hit a lever that caused food to drop out. After a few accidental "hits," the pigeons learned the relationship between cause and effect.

Where reinforcement theory is applied in the workplace, however, the activity is not random, the hits are not accidental, and learning the cause-effect relationship is not unconscious. All these facts tend to make the application of reinforcement theory less manipulative than the theory itself. This is not to say that reinforcement theory is never applied in a manipulative manner. Often it is, like most other management theories. But the answer to the question of whether it is manipulative in any given situation depends on the manner in which it is applied, not on the theory. As we shall see, the conscious application of reinforcement theory to the design of incentive systems can hardly be called manipulative when it is done jointly by all the members of the organization.

Reinforcement theory suggests that four kinds of consequences can affect behavior. First, a desired behavior can be rewarded by providing a new benefit. This is called positive reinforcement. Second, the failure to behave in a desired way can be punished until the desired behavior is forthcoming. This is negative reinforcement. Next, an undesired behavior can be punished. Finally, an undesired behavior can be discouraged by ignoring it. This is termed extinction. One of the important things to remember about reinforcement theory is that rewards are far more effective than punishments. Another important thing is that the rewards should be closely linked to the behaviors and should follow them as soon as possible. These criteria are not based on any mystical workings of the unconscious mind. They are based on common sense. If people are unaware of the specific ways in which their efforts are linked to a group bonus, for example, they will assume that the linkage has been left purposefully vague so that, if funds are urgently required elsewhere at the end of the bonus period, they can be diverted. If a bonus is scheduled to occur once a year, to use another example, people will reason that there is "many a slip twixt the cup and the lip" and that a slip at the end of the year will cost twelve times as much as one at the end of the first month. Before considering the relevance of reinforcement theory to joint management, we should note that, under most circumstances, extinction is preferable to punishment. Punishment sometimes reinforces undesirable behavior. At the least, it gains attention for the offender. Sometimes it earns the sympathy of others.

Specific Implications

Each of the several theories discussed above can help us in the design and operation of joint management systems. Some of the major implications of these theories for these systems are considered below.

Design Implications. Perhaps the most important application of reinforcement theory to joint management should occur when the joint management system is being designed. It is not too difficult for the action team designing the parallel organization to develop rules, policies, and procedures that, if followed, would increase the influence of all members of the organization. It is, however, difficult to design a system that makes sense to all the organizational interest groups (for example, middle managers, first-line supervisors, top management, workers, local union officers, international union officers, stewards). In order for the system to make sense to them, the rules, policies, and procedures that govern its activities, taken as a whole, must serve their interests. The challenge is to design rules, policies, and procedures that take into account these interests and to design rewards that effectively reinforce adherence to these rules, policies, and procedures. Motivational theories can help us meet this challenge. The members of the action team that is designing the system should ask themselves and their constituents what rewards they feel are appropriate in return for behavior that supports both the letter and the spirit of joint management. Let us suppose that we are members of such an action team. What lessons might we draw from the four motivational theories discussed above?

First, our system should give worksite-level action teams as much freedom as possible to devise their own arrangements governing task assignments and rewards. Further, when we are designing our executive and operating-level planning teams, we should be sure to establish a miniteam and give it the task of reviewing existing reward systems and developing new ones. Equity theory suggests that, where an individual's contribution/reward ratio is not in harmony with the ratios of other organization members, both the individual's inner peace and productivity suffer. Allowing work unit members to significantly influence their task assignments (contributions) and their rewards makes it more probable that they will see their contribution/reward ratios as equitable.

Of course, there needs to be some uniformity throughout the

organization regarding the basic compensation system. While methods of distributing group bonuses within the primary work unit, for example, might be left to its members, the basic job classification plan should cover all employees. It would be the task of the rewards miniteam of the executive-level planning team to review the existing classification plan and recommend changes making it more consistent with the joint management system (for example, paying for the number of skills a person learns rather than for the duties the person actually performs).

A second theoretical proposition that should catch our collective eye is contained in expectancy theory. This is the idea that people are not likely to be motivated unless they feel reasonably certain that the promised reward will, in fact, be forthcoming. Imagine the motivation levels of the employees of Nassau County in New York when they bought into a productivity gain-sharing plan and, at the end of the first year, discovered that the county and the union had decided not to pay bonuses after all (Hayes, 1977). If, as seems likely, they then estimated the chances of any future promises being kept at zero, expectancy theory tells us that their motivation to improve performance was also zero.

This suggests that rewards for behaviors supportive to a joint management system should be both enforceable and enforced. That is, the procedures for rewarding behaviors supportive to the system, along with the rules, policies, and procedures that govern the system itself, should be an enforceable part of the labor contract. This would provide a grievance procedure to handle complaints when these rules, policies, or procedures are violated. The existence of such a grievance procedure would benefit all parties by forcing them to avoid the long-term consequences of actions harmful to the joint management system.

Goal theory tells us that, in order to be effective, goals should be challenging, specific, and developed by the people who must meet them. As members of the action team that is designing the system, we must propose functions for the action teams and planning teams of our organization's joint management system. It would appear desirable to specify among these functions the development of operational goals at every level of the organization. The parallel organization is designed as a mechanism for participation. If goal setting is one of the management functions that benefits most from participation, we should not leave its inclusion to chance. Action teams at a level high enough to warrant the use of planning teams should, of course, rely on them to develop and propose a set of goals.

We should also specify in our rules, policies, and procedures positive and prompt reinforcement for behaviors supportive to the joint management system. In order to do so, we need to carefully consider two questions. First, what are the specific supportive behaviors that each interest group (middle managers, first-line supervisors, planning stewards, and so on) should exhibit and how can each group's and each individual's performance regarding them best be evaluated? Second, what are the rewards most desired by each group and how can their desires best be met? We should take care to consult the views of our constituents on these questions. Even where the parallel organization has been folded into the collective bargaining process, incentives should be developed to reward good integrative bargaining behaviors.

Operational Implications. Motivational theories are relevant not only to the designers but also to the operators of joint management systems. Let us imagine that our system has been designed and is now in operation. We are members of a planning team and are making up our annual work plan. Reinforcement theory suggests that we assign one of our miniteams the task of considering gain-sharing and worker ownership approaches and reporting to the planning team on their feasibility. Equity theory suggests that another miniteam should undertake the job of reviewing and recommending changes in the organization's job classification system. Still another miniteam could devise a special incentives program aimed at rewarding people from all interest groups for behaviors supportive to the joint management system. But perhaps the most important item on our work plan would be the development of a revised managerial evaluation plan that would base a significant portion of each manager's and first-line supervisor's performance evaluation on the extent to which he or she utilized and supported the joint management system. It is true that, in the long run, the tie between productivity and joint management should produce supportive behavior on the part of managers. Reinforcement theory, however, suggests that rewards that are not provided promptly are ineffective. The revision of the managerial evaluation plan could provide for prompt rewards.

Chapter 11

⌒〜〜〜✧〜〜〜⌒

Leaders Who Empower People

Leadership in a jointly managed organization bears little resemblance to leadership in a traditionally managed workplace. It is different in terms of the numbers of people who act in leadership roles, in terms of the traits that leaders should have, in terms of the behavior expected of leaders, and in terms of the duties and results for which they are held accountable. In a well-designed joint management system, everyone is involved—to some extent—in certain aspects of the management function. If the organization uses autonomous work teams, even the rank-and-file employee who holds no union office participates in planning, coordinating, and scheduling the group's day-to-day work. A parallel organization that is well designed in terms of "wholeness" greatly increases the number of leaders in the workplace. For example, let us suppose that a workplace has one participation steward for every eight employees. If the participation stewards' terms of office are six months, over the course of three years perhaps two-thirds of the organization's nonsupervisory personnel will have held positions of leadership. Surface traits, such as charisma, become less important in a jointly managed organization. Traits linked to caring and dependable behavior become more important. Competitive behaviors become dysfunctional. The duties of leaders also change. In a parallel organization, for example, participation stewards are responsible for communication, problem solving, and persuasion. They bring the ideas of their constituents to meetings, keep their constituents informed of what happens in these meetings, and participate with the other members of their action and planning teams in solving problems. They must then persuade their constituents to actively support the solutions to these problems that have won consensus within their team as both technically and politically feasible.

They must do this even when they may not themselves believe that a given solution is the best that could possibly be developed. Their task as leaders is to work toward consensus. But consensus does not mean agreeing that a solution is the best in absolute terms. It means agreeing to support the best solution that is politically feasible. Since problems often involve four or five workplace interest groups (top management, middle management, first-line supervision, local union officers, rank-and-file workers, and so on), leading one's constituents toward a position that is acceptable to all these groups is often difficult. While consensus in a literal sense is virtually impossible where large numbers of people are involved, jointly managed organizations require a much closer approach to it than do traditional ones. This means that both participation stewards and the representatives of the other workplace interest groups must exercise high levels of leadership. In joint management systems, managers become teachers and educators. They develop the skills and competencies of their subordinates so that the subordinates can perform independently, whereas traditional leaders control and coordinate other people's work. This means that managers must be judged on the basis of the results produced by the organizational units for which they are responsible rather than, as is often the case in traditional organizations, on the basis of their own individual efforts. While outstanding subordinates are sometimes threats to managers in traditional situations, in a jointly managed workplace they prove the manager's competence. This chapter seeks to clarify the kinds of leadership needed under joint management, in two ways. First, it describes three general theories of leadership and relates them to joint management. Second, it summarizes the views of three theorists on the nature of leadership in democratically managed organizations.

Theories of Leadership

Until the twentieth century, management theorists supposed that "leaders were born, not made." It was assumed that some people possessed traits that made them natural leaders, while others did not. These assumptions, however, did not hold up well when tested by organizational researchers. Stogdill (1948) found that only three traits (height, intelligence, and initiative) had much to do with leadership ability. He also found that even these traits did not hold up in all cases. Instead, different kinds of leaders were required for different kinds of situations. Stogdill's findings led to a body of research focusing on leadership behaviors rather than leadership traits. This research identified two main kinds of behavior: relationship-oriented behavior and task-oriented behavior. The former involves such activities as helping subordinates, doing favors for them and looking after their welfare, being friendly, being sociable, and being generally available. The latter involves controlling and coordinating their work. Traditional leadership theories are *situational* in nature. That is, they identify different management situations and propose leadership behaviors appropriate for each such situation. Three of these theories are discussed below: Fiedler's contingency theory, Vroom and Yetton's normative theory, and House's path-goal theory.

The Contingency Theory of Leadership. This theory (Fiedler, 1967) maintains that a group's performance is determined by the way the leader's behavior fits (or does not fit) the work situation. Leadership behavior is classified as either relationship oriented or task oriented. The work situation is classified according to three factors: leader-member relations, task structure, and position power. It is high in leader-member relations if the leader is accepted, trusted, and respected by the group. It is high in task structure if the goals, duties, and roles of the group members are unambiguous and clearly understood. It is high in position power if the leader's position is strong (for example, if the leader has the resources to reward and punish).

Fiedler tested his theory in a series of laboratory experiments. He concluded that task-oriented leaders were superior in work situations rated either "very favorable" or "very unfavorable" according to the three factors described above. Relationship-oriented leaders were the better performers in work situations rated in the middle ("moderately favorable" or "moderately unfavorable"). These results are said to suggest that, in highly favorable work situations, leaders have little to do but "take charge and give direction" and that, in highly unfavorable situations, a strong leader is required to win the "battle of wills" with subordinates (Steers, Ungson, and Mowday, 1985).

It is instructive to comment on these results from the point of view of joint management. First, we might ask ourselves whether we would wish a leader in a jointly managed organization to be relationship oriented or task oriented. While it might be pleasant if our leader were sociable and friendly and inclined to do favors for subordinates, these behaviors are certainly not crucial. If carried to extremes, the egalitarian workers in our jointly managed workplace might even consider them to be patronizing. Neither do we want our leader to spend a great deal of time helping subordinates get their work done. While a good leader pitches in when needed, our leader should have arranged things so he or she rarely needs to pitch in.

If the relationship-oriented leader does not seem to fit our needs, how about the task-oriented leader? The task-oriented leader, the reader will recall, is a coordinator and controller. But these are the functions performed by the nonsupervisory employees in our autonomous work teams! As Susman tells us in a later section of this chapter, the leader of an autonomous work team is not responsible for coordination within the group. The reader will also recall from the introduction to this book that joint management relies on workers being internally, not externally, controlled. It appears that Fiedler's theory has little to offer us as members of jointly managed organizations—other than to help us by making it clear that the old assumptions about leadership types do not apply to our situation.

The Normative Theory of Leadership. It is important for us to discuss Vroom and Yetton's normative theory of leadership, since it appears to challenge the fourth principle of joint management. The fourth principle reads: "Let workers combine thinking and doing; let workers and managers think together." Vroom and Yetton (1973) propose that the extent to which workers and managers think together should depend on the matter being thought about (that is, the nature of the specific decision being made). They describe five decision-making styles, ranging from the manager's making the decision without talking to subordinates about it to the manager's allowing the subordinates to make the decision. For each decision, the manager determines the appropriate decision-making style by considering a number of questions (Is the quality of the decision important? Do my subordinates need to be committed to this decision? Will they accept an autocratic decision on this matter?). For example, suppose you are the leader of a group that maintains the grounds of a large estate. You need to decide what brand of tools to order for the coming year. The different brands are about equal in price and quality. Here is how you could use the Vroom-Yetton decision tree to arrive at a decision-making strategy. First, you would ask yourself if the problem possesses a quality requirement. That is, will the brand selected have much impact on the performance of the group? You decide that the answer is no. Then you ask yourself, "Is acceptance of the decision by subordinates important for effective implementation?" You reason that your subordinates are going to perform as well with one brand as with another. At this point, the Vroom-Yetton guide informs you that it makes little difference which decision style you select. Any of the five is feasible. This discussion of the Vroom-Yetton normative theory of leadership underscores an important way in which the assumptions of joint management differ from those of traditional management. The Vroom-Yetton model assumes that the commitment of subordinates to an organization's goals has nothing to do with their involvement or lack of involvement in solving its problems. It assumes that workers have very limited thought processes: that while they will become committed to a specific decision if they are involved in making it, their involvement in the making of decisions as a general thing will not lead them to become committed to overall organizational goals. Certainly Vroom and Yetton would involve employees in setting organizational goals. However, once this has been done, Vroom and Yetton seem to assume that their commitment to the goals will have been secured. Therefore, management can base the involvement of employees in operational decisions on other criteria. Given these assumptions, their approach makes sense. Joint management, on the other hand, assumes that members of an organization will share its goals only if they are consistently involved in the decision-making process—from goal setting to day-to-day operational decisions.

The decision tree also assumes that the acceptance (or lack of acceptance) of a given decision has little effect on the acceptance of subsequent decisions. Each decision is treated as though it were a separate problem. Joint management makes different assumptions on this point as well. It assumes that, when employees are not given an opportunity to express their agreement or disagreement with a given decision, this disagreement will affect the implementation of future decisions. Given this assumption, it makes little sense to ask, "Is acceptance of the decision by subordinates important for effective implementation?" Joint management takes a synergistic view of workplace events. Each event is related to many other events and can either be "out of sync" or can act in concert with them to produce powerful results.

Substitutes for Leadership. A line of thought pursued by Kerr and Jermier (1978) appears to have a closer application to the practice of joint management. They argue that certain characteristics of the subordinate, the task, and the organization tend to neutralize leadership behavior of managers. For example, competent, experienced, and trained subordinates tend to make task-oriented leadership behavior unnecessary. Routine tasks that provide their own feedback also tend to neutralize task-oriented leadership behavior. Intrinsically satisfying tasks and closely knit work groups tend to lessen the need for relationship-oriented leadership behavior.

So far, these ideas—regarded in a somewhat different light—can be made consistent with joint management practice. Instead of regarding the subordinate, task, and organization characteristics as neutralizing leadership behavior or as making it irrelevant, however, joint management regards the creation of these characteristics as the essence of the leadership function. According to joint management ideas, leaders who spend their energies on either relationship-oriented or task-oriented behaviors are not doing their jobs.

Their main function is to ensure that the subordinates, the tasks, and the organization possess characteristics that promote "self-leadership" by all organization members. Thus, the task of leadership in a jointly managed organization is to create a comprehensive set of what Kerr and Jermier call "substitutes for leadership."

Not all of Kerr and Jermier's "substitutes" can be treated in this manner. For example, they describe the "indifference" of some subordinates "toward organizational rewards" as a substitute for both relationship-oriented and task-oriented leadership behavior. Here they appear to be mixing apples and oranges (that is, mixing characteristics that substitute for leadership and characteristics that make it difficult for leaders to exert influence). The principles of joint management certainly do not advocate creating an indifference to organizational rewards. To the contrary, the second principle of joint management is to promote cooperation through group and organizational rewards. One of the functions of the leader is to support a participative structure (like the parallel organization) in which organization members design their own reward systems.

Leadership in Democratically Managed Workplaces

Fortunately, the past decade has produced some theorists whose ideas have been developed in large part through their experience as consultants to labor-management "quality of working life" experiments in the United States. Much of their experience has been with participative systems in unionized workplaces.

Maccoby's Long-Term Leader. On the basis of more than a decade's first-hand experience with joint management, Michael Maccoby (1981) concludes, among other things, that the present tighter economy makes the short-term, exploitative leader dysfunctional. However, our systems for selecting, evaluating, and promoting leaders are still geared to quick success rather than to long-term development. Thus, we are perpetuating a brand of leadership that does not serve the economic interests of either individual firms or the country.

Maccoby, an anthropologist and psychoanalyst, says that the long-term leader does not lead by domination or manipulation and

is not especially charismatic. Three qualities are of critical importance to the long-term leader's self-development. First is a "caring,
responsible, and respectful attitude" (p. 221). Long-term leaders are
concerned about the well-being of people. This concern translates
into actions that tend to develop and strengthen their subordinates'
capabilities. Second is flexibility. Long-term leaders continually
reassess the structure, policies, and procedures of their organizations
and are willing to sponsor change. Third, long-term managers are
participative. They are willing to share their power because they
realize that the more they share the more they have. They involve
subordinates in the planning process. This takes more time initially, but leads to greater efficiency and effectiveness in the long
run. Having given up their tight control over the mechanics of the
work process, long-term leaders need moral gyroscopes to guide
them in their new educative roles. This means they should be educated in the humanities "first of all in clear writing and speaking,
but also in religion, ethical philosophy, depth psychology, and history" (p. 231).

Bernstein's Democratic Power-Holder. Bernstein (1976)
points out that, even in democratized firms, managers and elected
worker representatives make up a special group, simply because
they wield more power in the organization. The most important
attribute of this special group is that its members must be educators.
Democratic power-holders must have the desire and capability of
teaching their subordinates or constituents how to use power themselves and thus reduce their dependence on the power-holders. This
attribute is important because, without it, power-holders will tend
to use their power to preserve and further their own interests. Of
course, democratic systems cannot rely solely upon personal attrib-
utes to guard against this tendency. They must have built-in protective mechanisms (for example, election procedures).

The educative mind-set should be a major consideration in
selecting power-holders. It can be recognized by a number of specific criteria against which candidates for leadership should be evaluated. These criteria are shown under the column titled "Fosters or
Facilitates Democratization" in Figure 8.

Figure 8. Additional Traits Required of Power-Holders.

Discourages or Prevents Democratization		Fosters or Facilitates Democratization
1. Desire to maintain exclusive prerogatives	⊢—⊢—⊢	Egalitarian values
2. Paternalism	⊢—⊢—⊢	Reciprocity
3. Belief that leader must set example by appearing infallible (tries to hide all mistakes)	⊢—⊢—⊢	Awareness of own fallibility; admits errors to managed
4. Governing from position of formal power	⊢—⊢—⊢	Governing by merit, explanation, and consent of governed
5. Mistrustful, feels all others need "close watching"— hence: intense supervisions, limits freedom of subordinates	⊢—⊢—⊢	Confidence in others—hence: willingness to listen and to delegate responsibility
6. Proclivity to secrecy, holding back information	⊢—⊢—⊢	Policy of educating the managed; open access to information

Source: Reprinted by permission of Transaction Publishers, from *Workplace Democratization: Its Internal Dynamics,* by Paul Bernstein. Copyright © 1979 by Transaction Publishers.

The values that prevent democratization are safe, easy, and protected. Those that facilitate it are difficult and place the leader in a vulnerable position. When leaders maintain exclusive prerogatives (like limousines), they build walls between themselves and their followers. When they reject the value of reciprocity, they cannot benefit from the gifts of wisdom and emotional support that they might otherwise receive from their subordinates. The need to appear infallible often prevents leaders from offering their ideas *during* the problem-solving process. Democratic leaders must govern by persuasion and must have confidence in the abilities of their subordinates to get the job done independently. Above all, democratic leaders must be educators. This means that their primary task is to educate and train and their obligation is to share whatever information they possess.

Leaders who lack any one of these traits are liable to fail as democratic managers. Taken as a whole, the traits represent a system of values. Where one or more of them is lacking, the leader may be unable to establish credibility with his or her followers. However, it is also true that leaders who exhibit some of these traits in a tentative way sometimes elicit positive responses from their subordinates. These positive responses encourage the leaders to be less tentative in their democratic behavior. For example, Martin Lujan, a public works manager in a joint management experiment, reported the following experience. "Before QWL [a participative management system] many of us in management didn't realize how innovative employees could be in carrying out their duties. Now we've seen it demonstrated that there's a lot of creativity there. This has given us the confidence it takes to let loose and give employees more freedom in deciding how to go about getting things done" (Herrick, 1983–84).

Susman's Team Leader. Susman (1979, Chapter Eight) addresses himself specifically to leadership in the autonomous work team. He maintains that the traits and behaviors described by Maccoby and Bernstein are unlikely to manifest themselves unless the total management system has been designed to include the "conditions" that support these traits and behaviors. Susman's point can be illustrated by discussing two behaviors that the leader of an autonomous work team should not engage in: controlling and coordinating the activities of the team. The team leader cannot avoid these behaviors unless the members of the work team are capable of controlling and coordinating their own activities. In order for them to have this capability, at least two conditions must be met. The team must have a clear "primary task" and it must be organized around the "redundancy of functions" principle. One function of the team leader is to help the team members define for themselves the primary task of the team. The primary task is the team's goal: the results for which it is held accountable by higher levels of the organization. The team must take care to define its primary task in terms of results, not in terms of procedures and steps. The reason for this is that, once the members have the results desired by the team clearly in mind, they can alter their procedures and steps as circumstances dictate and still attain the needed results. This alteration of procedures and steps to meet changed circumstances is the essence of the team's controlling and coordinating activity. The members' clear understanding of the team's primary task is the first condition that must be met before the team leader can delegate this activity to the members.

The second necessary condition is conformity to the "redundancy of functions" principle (Emery and Trist, 1973). In brief, this principle requires that all the members of the work team be capable of performing all (or many) of the tasks required of the team. Thus the team, at any given time, has "redundant" skills (that is, more skills than it is using at that time). When considered over the long term, however, these skills are not redundant. Team members cannot alter their procedures and steps to meet changed circumstances unless they are capable of performing the different procedures and steps that the changed circumstances require.

Once the controlling and coordinating functions have been assumed by the team members, Susman sees the leader's main responsibility to be mediating between the work team and its environment. He terms this function "boundary maintenance." The leader's boundary maintenance function has two aspects: dealing with the technical world and dealing with the phenomenal world. Technical boundary control involves making sure that the team has the raw materials and other resources it requires from the outside world where and when it needs them. Phenomenal boundary maintenance involves making sure the team has the psychological resources and supplies it requires. For example, it is the leader's responsibility to ensure that team members receive rewards and recognition for their accomplishments.

The Empowering Leader

The picture that emerges from the experiences and writings of Maccoby, Bernstein, and Susman seems to stand our previous notions of leadership on their heads. Instead of exerting power, the democratic leader bestows power. Instead of controlling and coordinating activities, the democratic leader trains subordinates so that they can control and coordinate themselves. Instead of directing people to do specific tasks, the leader serves them by making sure they have the raw materials and resources to carry out the tasks they have already decided upon among themselves. This new role reduces the leader's petty power to impose his or her will on other people. However, it calls upon the leader to assume a much greater and more serious power: the power to assist others in their self-development. This is the helping power exercised by the best of our educators. Unlike the power of dominance, it is rewarded by love and respect rather than by dislike and resentment. It is the power of the creator, rather than the power of the tyrant.

However, it is unrealistic to expect anyone to be an empowering leader unless his or her boss and followers change their ways as well. Empowering leaders get better results and develop quality subordinates. In order to do this, they must stay in the background and maintain low profiles. For example, an empowering leader (Jones) might, after careful coaching, give a subordinate (White) the job of running a highly visible meeting. Let's suppose that the meeting is a great success. In a traditional organization, the natural reactions of the leader's boss (Smith) and subordinate (White) would go something like this:

BOSS: I'm worried about Jones. He doesn't seem to be much of a leader. White seems to be in charge, not him. I noticed that the people at the meeting were ignoring him and asking White questions. Just what I need. Another problem!

SUBORDINATE: Did you see the way I handled that meeting? Let's face it, old Jonesy is OK behind the scenes—but he isn't a take-charge guy and he's got no charisma. So he gets cold feet and has me run the show. I wonder how long it'll be before old Smitty gives me his job.

Is it any wonder that empowering leaders are rare in traditional organizations? What sane person would go out of his or her way to invite this kind of reaction? If it expects to develop empowering leaders, the jointly managed workplace must reward, not penalize, behavior like that of "old Jonesy" (see Chapter Nineteen).

Conclusions

The leadership characteristics and behaviors that are considered desirable in traditionally managed organizations are not necessarily those that are needed in joint management. Yet many jointly managed organizations continue to evaluate their managers using traditional criteria. Planning teams in jointly managed workplaces would do well to develop new performance evaluation criteria for managers based on the work of theorists such as Maccoby, Bernstein, and Susman.

Part IV

⎯⎯⎯⎯✦⎯⎯⎯⎯

Groups in
Jointly Managed
Organizations

Perhaps the most important structural difference between traditional management and a well-designed joint management system is that the former relies mainly on individuals to plan and carry out its work. The latter relies mainly on groups. Of course, traditional management uses work units to produce its goods or services. However, each member of a work unit is typically controlled by a supervisor, who also coordinates the member's work with the work of other members. Thus, the emphasis is on hierarchical rather than group relationships. The members of an autonomous work team, on the other hand, are largely self-controlled and coordinate their work with each other.

Part Four of this book deals with groups in two different ways. First, Chapter Twelve discusses the general dynamics of groups and shows how these dynamics affect groups in joint management. Second, Chapters Thirteen, Fourteen, and Fifteen talk specifically about the features of the three groups used in joint management: the action team, the planning team, and the autonomous work team. It is important to note that these features may not necessarily be typical of action, planning, and autonomous work teams in the "real world." The features described are those I consider, as a general thing, to be desirable. They are consistent with well-designed parallel organizations and with the use of the parallel organization as a mechanism for extended integrative bargaining. Since very little research has been done on the design features that are most effective in joint management (Herrick, 1985), these features are based on experience rather than on systematic research.

Chapter 12

How Groups Become Teams

Joint management uses groups to a far greater extent than does traditional management. At the worksite level, it uses both the autonomous work team and the action team. At executive and operating levels, it uses both the action and the planning team. We should keep in mind that—even in jointly managed organizations—mid- and high-level operational functions generally continue to be the province of individuals operating through the primary organization. The primary organization is responsible for operations, while the parallel organization occupies itself mainly with integrative bargaining aimed at producing intermediate-range plans. At the work unit level, groups do become involved in operations. The leader of the autonomous work team is responsible for boundary maintenance, while the team itself performs a combination of operational and planning functions. It both controls and coordinates its internal operations and performs short-range planning (for example, scheduling) functions. The action team at the work unit level normally does the autonomous work team's intermediate-range planning. Since the team is so central to joint management, this chapter devotes considerable space to a discussion of group dynamics. It then emphasizes some points that are especially relevant to the use of teams in joint management systems.

Group Dynamics

A group is three or more people who interact with one another in such a way that each member influences every other member (Wofford, 1982). We call groups in joint management "teams" because their members are—we hope—not only interacting with each other but interacting with each other in a positive way. A team is a group of people who are working together in a cooperative way to achieve common goals. The groups used in joint management (action teams, planning teams, and autonomous work teams) are formal. That is, they are assigned specific organizational tasks, often of a continuing nature. While they are formal, it is true that they often assume some of the functions that, in traditionally managed organizations, are carried out by informal groups. For example, informal groups within an organizational unit sometimes exert a strong influence over the unit head's policies and procedures. This kind of influence tends to decrease in jointly managed organizations. If informal groups wish to influence the unit head, they must do it through the parallel organization or risk criticism from other employees for undermining the democratic process. Thus, joint management tends to integrate the formal and the informal organizations.

The remainder of this section discusses the following characteristics that apply to groups in general: membership, size, cohesiveness, goals, rewards, and stages of development.

Membership. The character traits, interpersonal needs, and abilities of a group's members will affect their productivity and the way they get along together. For example, people with authoritarian traits, when they are placed in positions of power, tend to become demanding and controlling. On the other hand, when they are placed in subordinate positions they are submissive and compliant (Nadler, 1959). People who are empathetic and sociable tend to seek and attain leadership in groups (Cattell and Stice, 1960) and groups made up of self-reliant, dependable, responsible members are more effective and better satisfied than other groups (Shaw, 1976).

Since autonomous work teams, action teams, and planning teams are structured to minimize either controlling or compliant behavior, people with strongly authoritarian personalities might be uncomfortable—at least initially—in jointly managed situations. On the other hand, people who possess qualities such as empathy and dependability are likely to perform well in almost any situation. However, in my experience, most people—whatever their character traits—respond positively to membership in joint management teams.

Where group members are elected (as in action and planning teams), organization members can consider their own and their co-workers' character traits as they cast their ballots and as they decide whether to stand for office themselves. Where group members are organizationally assigned (as in most autonomous work teams), alternative assignments should be found for people who do not wish to become group members. This is not usually necessary, however, since a unanimous vote is generally required before a primary work unit converts to an autonomous work team.

Size. Small groups are generally more effective than larger ones. Larger groups experience communications difficulties and often break up into small cliques (Tichy, 1973). However, there is some disagreement about the optimum size for group effectiveness. One researcher (Steiner, 1972) sets it at four, while another (Manners, 1975) found problem-solving effectiveness to be highest in groups of eleven.

This difference of opinion is understandable. Where group members have no vested interest in the problem to be solved and therefore regard solving it as an intellectual exercise, it might be feasible to bring the knowledge and experience of eleven people to bear on it. Where solving a problem means reconciling different interests, however, the process is more emotional than intellectual. Each group member must come to an understanding, not only of the objective facts but of the feelings and motivations of the other members. This might be possible in a group of eleven, but it would require more time and planning (for example, a two- or three-day retreat) than is generally feasible. It is more feasible to attain this deeper understanding in a smaller group where each member can ask and respond to questions at length.

Since the work of groups in joint management—especially

that of action and planning teams—does involve the reconciliation of conflicting interests, it is best to keep them as small as possible. Of course, it is also necessary to ensure that all employees affected by a problem are represented on the team that is dealing with it. For these reasons, the composition of higher-level action teams often reflects a compromise between the need to keep the group small and the need to ensure that all affected organization members are represented. The tension between these conflicting needs can be resolved by separating the "review and approval" function from the development of proposals. This can be done by establishing a larger planning team to act as staff to a small action team. While planning teams rarely have fewer than fifteen members, their actual planning/problem-solving/integrative bargaining work is done in miniteams of perhaps four to six members each.

Cohesiveness. The members of a cohesive group stick together by keeping the group together over time, by cooperating with each other in their work, and by defending each other to outsiders. It is frequently pointed out that cohesiveness can be a problem. Where group goals are not consistent with organizational goals, it can result in low productivity (Seashore, 1954). That is, a cohesive group that decides its interests are best served by limiting output can be a painful thorn in management's side. On the other hand, where its goals are consistent with the goals of the organization, a cohesive group is highly effective. Here is a list of five factors that tend to create cohesion in groups: small size, success, time, agreement on goals, and status.

1. *Small Size.* We have already noted that small groups tend to be more effective than larger ones. One reason for this is that small groups tend to be more cohesive.

2. *Success.* There is nothing like success to create esprit de corps in a small group, especially if everyone in the group plays a part in producing the success. Conversely, failure—especially an early failure—can destroy a group's cohesiveness. This is especially true as it applies to action and planning teams in joint management. For example, a planning team's first proposal is often regarded by its members as "testing the system." If this proposal is not promptly approved by the action team and implemented by the

responsible manager, the planning team is likely to be demoralized. Members stop attending meetings regularly and cohesion is delayed or prevented.

3. *Time.* Cohesiveness depends in large part on group members coming to know and understand each other. This takes time. Thus, frequent turnover can be a major obstacle to cohesiveness in a primary work unit or autonomous work team. Time plays an even greater role in creating or destroying cohesiveness in action and planning teams. Action teams might meet for only an hour and one-half every other week, and planning teams might be allocated as little as thirteen to fifteen hours a month for their activities. This means that people must work very hard at knowing and understanding each other in the little time they have available. Every absence of a group member from a scheduled meeting is a serious threat to the group's chances of becoming cohesive. Every time a group meeting is cancelled—especially during its early life—its chances of becoming cohesive diminish.

4. *Agreement on Goals.* Since teams in joint management are made up of representatives from different workplace interest groups, it is natural that their members should have some goals that conflict. If these teams are to become cohesive, therefore, they must restrict their activities to those goals they hold in common, first, by making issues such as wages and fringes off limits and, second, by defining specific goals that all group members can share.

5. *High Status.* Members of groups with high status tend to identify with these groups and to "stick together" with their fellow members. Nonmembers are eager to join high-status groups. This is important in joint management, where the success of the participative system depends, in part, on the willingness of rank-and-file workers to serve on action and planning teams. Whether a joint management team has high or low status depends, in large part, on its success in solving problems. Thus, the efforts of team members can strongly affect the status of their team. However, the efforts of team members cannot guarantee success. The actions (or lack of actions) of top managers and union officers who do not belong to it can also affect a team's success. For example, a planning team may develop a quality solution to a problem, but—if its action team fails

to approve and implement the solution—other organization members will consider it unsuccessful.

Rewards. Where group members work cooperatively together, their groups tend to be substantially more productive than groups with members who work individually or in competition with each other (Johnson and others, 1981). Productivity can be negatively affected by adding even a small element of competition to a basically cooperative situation. One group of researchers found that distributing 80 percent of the available rewards on a group basis and assigning the remaining 20 percent to the most productive worker in the group resulted in significantly lower productivity than distributing all the rewards on a group basis (Rosenbaum and others, 1980).

It is true that, where workers do not depend on each other at all (for example, some salespeople who operate within clear geographical boundaries), competition can be beneficial to productivity. Where people work in groups, however, this is rarely the case. Certainly, group members who are engaged in planning and in solving problems together are highly interdependent.

The methods used to reward people strongly influence the extent to which they cooperate with one another (see Part Six). Group payment methods tend to promote cooperation among group members. However, since these same methods tend to promote competition among groups, we must be careful in applying them.

Action and planning teams present special problems. Since their members are often subject to great pressures from their constituents to produce results (and, sometimes, from their supervisors to spend less time at meetings), it is desirable to provide them with all the rewards possible, both psychological and material. It is not generally wise, however, to single out individuals for special recognition. One possibility for rewarding nonsupervisory members is to make participation in action or planning team activities a criterion in job evaluation. In addition, both supervisory and nonsupervisory personnel who have served on highly effective action and planning teams could be given both psychological and material rewards. For example, the top-level action team serving the employees of Pima

County, Arizona, makes annual cash awards to the action teams, planning teams, and primary work units that it judges were most effective during the year. Since these cash awards are made at a formal ceremony and presented by elected officials of the county, they provide both psychological and material benefits. These rewards do not appear to have led to any conflict between or among teams. This may be due to the fact that a very small percentage of eligible teams receive them. While the members of a team might feel hurt and angry if their team were the only one not to receive a reward, they do not seem to have negative reactions when nineteen of every twenty teams fail to get rewards and theirs is one of the nineteen.

Group Development. It is helpful to the members of newly formed groups to have some familiarity with the idea that groups pass through definite stages of development. This familiarity helps them keep from becoming too discouraged when their groups fail to produce immediate results. It is even more important for top management and union officials to be familiar with this idea. If they do not take specific actions to facilitate group development, it is probable that most groups will get "stuck" at one of the lower stages of development and fail to become productive. The three-stage model of group development summarized below draws on Bales and Strodtbeck (1951), Bennis and Shepard (1965), and Tuckman (1965).

Stage I, *Setting Ground Rules:* The development process can be greatly enhanced by a thorough orientation at the time a group is formed. This orientation should include not only information regarding the tasks the group is expected to perform and training in the skills required to perform them well, but also information regarding the behavior that is expected of group members, the procedures the group is expected to follow, and the roles individual group members are expected to play. Groups that are poorly oriented will have difficulty progressing to Stage II. In addition, when they do arrive at Stage II they will have developed their own ideas as to tasks, behavior, procedures, and roles. Frequently, these ideas will not be consistent with the needs of the organization. Yet they will be almost impossible to change. Organizations are very often "penny wise and pound foolish" in their neglect of the orientation stage of group development.

Stage II, *Forming the Team:* While the matters over which most Stage II confrontation takes place ostensibly have to do with the tasks the group is working on, the nature of this stage is basically emotional. The members are seeking their places in the group. Questions of authority, influence, and specific work roles are being worked out among group members. A key point to remember about Stage II is that confrontation is necessary and desirable. Members of a group cannot generally assume their roles and be comfortable with themselves and with the other group members until they have openly discussed the problems and feelings involved. Two other points are equally important. First, to confront an issue or feeling means to discuss it openly. It does not mean to discuss it in a hostile or aggressive manner. Quite the contrary. In order to be effective, confrontation should be caring and, above all, respectful. Second, we do not confront each other easily and naturally. If left to their own devices, the members of a group are likely to avoid confronting an issue until it has become so magnified that the confrontation—when it comes—is hostile and to no avail.

The organization's top managers and union leaders should help its groups with this problem. They should make sure that the groups' orientation stage covers the need for *caring* confrontation and they should provide facilitation services to groups that need them during Stage II.

Stage III, *Getting Things Done:* Some tasks may be accomplished by groups during Stage II. Indeed, if nothing is accomplished during the confrontation stage it is unlikely that the group will ever progress to Stage III. Remember that success is one of the main sources of cohesion. Once a group has reached Stage III, its members function well without direction. They understand and accept the goals of the group and their roles in attaining these goals. They take the initiative in coordinating their work with that of other group members. They are ready to become a team.

Cohesive action and planning teams begin to devote most of their energies to identifying and analyzing problems and proposing rules, procedures, policies, and programs that deal with these problems. However, care must be taken to ensure that cohesive teams remain cohesive. This means that top managers and union leaders should take steps to ensure that the conditions of size, success, time, agreement on goals, and status continue to be favorable to cohesion as time goes on.

Implications for Joint Management

The above section points out a number of specific ways in which group dynamics relate to joint management. This section identifies and amplifies a few general points that are particularly important.

Reconciliation: The Essence. The essential feature of joint management is not that action and planning teams provide quality solutions to problems. Neither is it that autonomous work teams are highly productive. Its essential feature is that it reconciles the various and divergent interests of organization members. This essential feature leads to quality solutions and high productivity. It also frees organization members to develop their skills and their capacities for mature, self-reliant, caring, responsible behavior. There are other ways to produce quality solutions to problems and to increase the productivity of work teams (quality circles, job enrichment, and so on). The essential features and goals of these other ways differ from those of joint management. Joint management strives primarily for human goals and accepts economic goals as highly desirable by-products. The fact that the parallel organization's essential feature is reconciliation has practical implications. For example, a design team guided by this essential feature is unlikely to set up problem-solving teams made up of volunteers. Neither is a planning or action team that operates by this principle likely to engage in hostile confrontation. If the members of an organization are guided by the principle of reconciliation as they design and operate their joint management system, the details will fall into place more readily.

Design: The Means. There is little doubt that most people are capable of acting in responsible, constructive, and caring ways. They will adopt this kind of behavior, however, only if it makes sense. That is, people will not be open and trusting with their fellow team members if it seems probable that they will be taken advantage of. Neither will they share their skills with others if this kind of sharing seems likely to reduce the size of their paychecks. This means that the members of design teams must carefully consider every detail when they are establishing the characteristics of action, planning, and autonomous work teams and the processes through which these teams will be established. A careful balance should be struck between specifying characteristics and leaving them to be specified by the teams themselves.

Commitment: The Energy. Even if action, planning, and autonomous work teams are designed and operated according to the principle of reconciliation, they may still be unsuccessful. Another ingredient is necessary: commitment. It is not enough, for example, to design an adequate orientation period for newly formed groups. If top management and union officials fail to commit the time and resources to carry out the orientation competently and energetically, the teams will fail to produce. This is only one of countless illustrations that could be used to make the point that, without commitment from top union and management officials, well-designed teams and dedicated team members are not enough. When a set of teams fails to produce, it is by no means evidence that "teams don't work." Rather, it is an indication either that they were poorly designed or that top management and union officers failed to see that they received the time and other resources necessary for success—or both. This book takes the position that the best way of ensuring the commitment of top management and union officers is to make the activities of action and planning teams an integral part of the collective bargaining process.

Chapter 13

Action Teams:
Linking Planning
and Implementation

Joint management uses three kinds of teams: the action team, the planning team, and the autonomous work team. The action and planning teams make up the parallel organization, which acts in concert with the primary organization at all levels of the hierarchy. The main task that the parallel and the primary organization work together to accomplish is to nurture the organization's autonomous work teams. If the members of the autonomous work teams are supplied with the resources and capabilities to work together toward personal and organizational goals, and if the organization's procedures, policies, plans, and programs (especially those having to do with rewards) make it rational for them to do so, the parallel and primary organizations are doing their job well. The more the parallel organization is used as a mechanism for extended bargaining, the more effective it can be in supporting and protecting the autonomous work teams.

It must be recognized, of course, that the conversion of an organization's primary work units to autonomous work teams cannot be accomplished overnight. In addition, some workplaces have parallel organizations but do not make any conscious effort to convert to autonomous work teams. For these reasons, the parallel and primary organizations sometimes nurture traditional work units in addition to or instead of autonomous work teams. The presence of the parallel organization may influence first-line supervisors to manage these units more participatively, but there is no clear redefinition of the first-line supervisory role from controller and coordinator to boundary maintainer and educator. It appears that joint management can function effectively over the short term using the parallel organization only. Whether the systematic reorganization of the primary work unit can be postponed indefinitely is not so clear. At any rate, to postpone this reorganization does not seem desirable. The different levels of the organization can be more supportive of each other if they operate according to the same principles. In addition, the action team at the work unit level is a natural and ready-made mechanism through which the reorganization of the work unit can be accomplished.

While it may be feasible for parallel organizations to carry on extended integrative bargaining without converting the work units of the organization to autonomous work teams, it is not recommended that autonomous work teams be used without parallel organizations. Parallel organizations are an effective means of ensuring that the team concept is not used as a coercive "speed-up" device or as a means of weakening the union. Some workplaces use parallel organizations without autonomous work teams. Others attempt to integrate autonomous work teams into the regular management structure. This book presents them as interdependent parts of a total joint management system. It assumes that each needs the other for long-term survival.

This chapter describes the purpose, composition, functions, and formation of action teams. It also distinguishes among the roles of action team members. Differences among action teams at the different levels of the organization (executive, operations, intermediate, and worksite levels) are pointed out. The comments in this chapter are made in the context of the third design principle: self-design. That is, the members of each organization must consider their own special situation and their own priorities in making each specific design decision. For example, one organization might decide on three-month terms of office because it wishes to directly involve a large number of workers in the integrative bargaining process. Another organization might opt for nine-month terms of office because it wishes to have the same people work on complex problems from beginning to end.

Purpose

The general purpose of any action team is to support cooperation among—and participation and self-development by—all the members of its corresponding primary organizational unit. The action team is in a position to accomplish this purpose because it links the planning function (carried out by the parallel organization) with the implementation function (carried out by the primary organization). It lies between the shadow (the plan) and the rock (reality) and links the two together. The linking pin is the senior manager-member, since he or she manages the unit of the primary organization served by the action team. One of the most common complaints of employees in workplaces that now have parallel organizations is that the senior manager-member is lax in making sure that approved plans get carried out. He or she fails to link the shadow to the rock. Should the parallel organization be fully integrated into the collective bargaining process, it would be in an even stronger position to link itself with the primary organization. Then the senior manager-member would be obliged to give priority attention to implementing agreed-upon plans—or be subject to the filing of grievances.

Composition of Action Teams

Higher-level action teams are often linked to lower-level action teams (for example, where a department-level action team has three participation stewards, they are often elected from among the fifteen or so participation stewards serving on action teams at the next lower level). Therefore, a discussion of action team composition should begin with the worksite level. At this level, the action team generally consists of the first-line supervisor (or team leader) and two or three participation stewards. The number of participation stewards varies with the size of the work unit. One steward normally represents from four to twelve constituents. Where a work team consists of nine or fewer members (including the team leader), typically all of them sit on the action team. In this case, one or two participation stewards would still be elected to represent the work unit on higher-level action teams.

Intermediate-level action teams are made up of the manager who heads the corresponding primary organizational unit (called the senior manager-member) along with participation stewards and subordinate managers from the next lower level of the parallel organization. The participation stewards and subordinate managers often serve on a rotating basis. For example, if there were a total of twelve participation stewards at the next lower level of the parallel organization, they might organize themselves into four groups of three each. Then each group of three might serve on the action team for three months of the year. Usually, every level of subordinate managers is represented on an action team. Where an organization is extremely "tall" (that is, has many hierarchical levels), this may not be feasible. In this case, it might be well for the organization's planning team to study its primary organization with an eye toward the possibility of eliminating some of its levels. Intermediate-level action teams rarely have more than seven members.

Executive- and operations-level action teams are formed using the same general principles used in forming action teams at the intermediate level. However, at these levels it often is not feasible to include a representative from every level of management. A membership of more than seven to nine people tends to restrict and inhibit the kind of detailed discussion that is necessary before people can reach a deep and mutual understanding of each other and of the problems being considered. However, action teams at these levels are able to deal with this constraint by ensuring that their planning teams include representation from all levels of management.

Executive- and operations-level action teams also differ from intermediate-level teams in that they normally include combined-function union officers (officers whose responsibilities include both distributive and integrative bargaining) in addition to participation stewards. Thus, presidents or business agents of locals often sit on executive-level action teams and chief stewards or committee members often sit on operations-level teams. In general, wherever a single union officer has the same jurisdiction as an action team, he or she sits on that action team. This applies to intermediate-level teams as well as to those at the executive and operations levels.

Functions

The six functions of the action team occur at the executive, operational, intermediate, and worksite levels (see Chapter Three for a description of these levels). They are to sanction and support the joint management system, to initiate studies and request advice, to review and act on requests for studies, to review and act on proposals, to monitor the implementation of proposals, and to solve problems. When these functions (and the policies, procedures, and programs they produce) are enforceable and when they are carried on (for labor) by recognized union officers, they constitute extended integrative bargaining.

The six functions are carried out in different ways at different levels. For example, the executive and operational levels are normally served by planning teams and, for this reason, spend very little time going through the formal problem-solving steps. They occasionally identify problems but leave the rest of the problem-solving process to their planning teams. Action teams at the worksite level, on the other hand, spend very little time reviewing and acting upon proposals submitted by others. Occasionally, they may review and comment on proposals from other worksite-level teams or requests for advice from higher-level action teams. For the most part, however, action teams at the worksite level spend their time planning and solving problems. All members of the work unit are invited to participate in this process when they wish. Therefore, they have little need to prepare proposals and submit them to the action team for review. The six action team functions are discussed below as they apply to the various organizational levels.

Sanctioning and Supporting Joint Management. This function is important at all levels, but is essential at the executive level. The reason is that the other levels normally follow the lead of the executive level. If the executive-level action team gives off signals that it is not serious about joint management, lower-level teams tend to follow suit. The most effective way for labor and management to sanction a joint management system is for them to fold it into the collective bargaining process.

Of course, much of the sanction and support provided by action teams, regardless of level, is given by the management members of these groups in the performance of their regular duties in the primary organization. For example, one of the most powerful steps a manager can take in support of joint management is to promote a subordinate manager who manages according to joint management principles. Another powerful step is to pass over a subordinate manager who fails to do so. Of course, managing according to joint management principles cannot be the only criterion for promotion. However, it should be an important one and, during the early life of a joint management system, when some middle managers are resisting the change and others are supporting it, a strong case can be made for making it the overriding consideration.

Even when the sanction and support is given by the action team itself, rather than by managers in their regular capacities, it is dependent on the approval of the senior manager serving on the team. For example, an action team may have before it a proposal to modify the organization's job evaluation system so as to include membership on action and planning teams as an evaluation criterion. The authority to approve this proposal lies solely with the senior manager.

Nevertheless, the subordinate managers and union officers who serve on an action team are in a strong position to influence the senior manager's use of his or her authority to sanction and support joint management. Indeed, they are responsible to their constituents for doing so. Where the senior manager-member of an action team fails to provide sanction and support, the other members have two responsibilities. First, they should attempt to persuade the senior manager to take the steps they believe are required. Second, if their attempts to persuade are unsuccessful, it is their responsibility to file a grievance.

It would be difficult to list all the specific steps that action teams should take to sanction and support joint management. However, it is not difficult to name an essential element that should be a part of all these steps. This element is promptness. It is also helpful to consider the following general categories into which these steps fall.

First is adequate resources—a joint management system costs money. It is an investment that is expected to produce a high return by increasing organizational efficiency and effectiveness. But it cannot produce this high return if adequate resources are not allocated to it. These resources include such items as funds to pay for an awards system, funds to underwrite training and education programs, funds to pay for additional positions to coordinate the system, and the release of organization members from their primary organization duties for enough time to effectively operate the parallel organization.

Second is consistent administrative actions. Joint management espouses a change in values from competition and authoritarianism to cooperation and participation. Organization members must place enough faith in this change to risk acting cooperatively and participatively. Their faith in the change can be greatly strengthened by administrative actions consistent with the new values. It can be destroyed by administrative actions that are not. Yet, when faced with a crisis, managers sometimes forget both the values of joint management and even the fact that they are involved in a joint management system. Nonsupervisory employees, on the other hand, while they may be ignorant of the crisis, are acutely sensitive to any actions that are inconsistent with the new values. For example, rewarding a subordinate manager who opposes these values may assist a top manager in resolving a crisis. Other organization members, however, are probably unaware of the crisis and will certainly be disillusioned by the action. Another administrative action that tends to destroy faith in the reality of the new values is the failure of the senior manager-member of an action team to promptly implement a proposal the team has approved. This failure is sometimes due to the press of other business and sometimes due to management's failure to earmark and protect the resources necessary for implementing the proposal. Whatever the reasons, inconsistent administrative actions such as these are costly in the long run. They may assist in resolving crises, but they perpetuate a system that is geared to manage crises rather than prevent them.

Third is consistent administrative policies. Traditionally

managed organizations operate according to a set of administrative policies that are consistent with competition and authoritarianism. It is the responsibility of action teams at all levels to review and revise those policies they are authorized to change and to ask higher-level action teams to review and revise those that they are not. Action teams often fail to carry out this responsibility because the problems caused by inconsistent administrative policies are not always obvious. For example, the usual response of action teams to complaints about merit pay systems is to work on the performance evaluation criteria and selection procedures of these systems. The deeper problem (that there is a fundamental conflict between merit pay and the values of joint management) is both more difficult to recognize and more difficult to correct. The necessity for revising an organization's administrative policies as one means of "adapting" the primary organization to joint management is treated in more detail in Chapter Twenty-Three.

Initiating Studies and Requesting Advice. These two activities are closely related because they tend to place the levels of the parallel organization on a more equal footing. Just as the senior manager-member of an action team is sometimes tempted to play a passive role in order to maintain control, so do action teams themselves sometimes treat the joint management system as though it existed solely for the benefit of nonsupervisory employees. This is a major mistake for two reasons. First, it is patronizing and irritates people at lower levels. Second, it ignores the substantial benefits that can be gained by using the parallel organization to address management concerns.

Members of executive- and operations-level action teams are in an excellent position to initiate studies of problems, since they are normally served by planning teams. Because they are familiar with the total organization, they are sometimes able to identify problems for study that have escaped the notice of people at lower levels in the organization. For example, an executive-level action team might recognize the need to review and modify the organization's job classification system to take account of joint management activities. People at lower levels might not realize that such a review is possible, or may be more concerned with short-term problems.

Higher-level action teams, especially the senior manager-members of these groups, can profitably use the parallel organization as a means of obtaining advice. Often senior managers hear about a problem from subordinate managers and jump quickly to conclusions about the solution that should be applied. They then issue instructions that may or may not be appropriate. An alternative course of action is for the senior manager to define the problem in a memorandum addressed to all the action teams under his or her jurisdiction and ask for their advice on how to solve it. In this way, the senior manager can come to a far deeper understanding of the problem and is less likely to have the solution "blow up" in his or her face.

Reviewing and Acting on Requests for Studies. At the worksite level, this is called the problem identification process. While the specific steps of this process vary from worksite to worksite, a typical process might go something like this. A meeting of all the members of the primary work unit or autonomous work team is led by the members of the worksite-level action team. Each person present is asked to name the two problems he or she would most like the action team to work on. The chair of the action team leads a discussion of the problems named, in order to arrive at a fairly short, coherent, and mutually exclusive list. The chair manages the discussion so that each problem on the list is considered from two points of view: first, its importance, and, second, the likelihood that the action team can resolve it. Then a vote is taken to rank the problems in priority order. The action team then draws up a six-month work plan based on this ranking. Problems that also affect other primary work units are described in writing and forwarded up the parallel organization with requests that they be studied at the appropriate level.

Intermediate-level action teams receive these requests for studies and review them to determine whether or not they affect units outside the jurisdiction of the team. If they do, the team forwards them up the primary organization until they reach a level representing all affected units. It is at this level that the study (problem solving) should be accomplished. If the action team that should carry out the study is not served by a permanent planning team, it may form an ad hoc planning team. This is usually done by the appointment of people who already hold elective positions in lower-level action teams.

Operations- and executive-level action teams consider requests for studies and, where the studies appear justified, refer them to their planning teams. Where an action team decides that a study should not be done, it sends the request back down the line along with an explanation. Any request that is referred to a planning team should be accompanied by a priority rating and a target date by which the action team expects a completed proposal.

Reviewing and Acting on Proposals. Intermediate- and worksite-level action teams do not receive many proposals. Once in a great while, one of these action teams will attempt to solve a problem that extends beyond its own jurisdiction by developing a proposal and sending it to the other affected action teams for comment. For the most part, however, this kind of problem is handled when a higher- (that is, intermediate) level action team forms an ad hoc planning team. However, higher-level action teams do sometimes refer problems to the lower-level action teams within their jurisdiction and ask for suggested solutions. These referrals are made by the concerned action team but submitted through regular primary organization lines.

Executive- and operations-level action teams spend a substantial proportion of their time reviewing and acting on proposals developed by their planning teams. Each such proposal is usually presented by the planning miniteam that actually prepared it. Theoretically, the action team may approve, disapprove, or return a proposal for more work. In practice, proposals are virtually never disapproved. This is because the senior manager-member of the action team has been kept informed of the nature of the proposal by his or her representative on the planning team and has participated in the developmental process through this representative. The practical problem that does often arise is that proposals are approved, but either are not implemented or are delayed in their implementation. The senior manager-member fails to do the job of making "rocks out of shadows." This is perhaps the major problem with action teams and is dealt with at greater length in the next section.

Monitoring the Implementation of Proposals. If we include the solutions arrived at informally by worksite-level action teams in our definition of the term "proposal," we can say that action teams at all levels are in the most danger of falling down on the job after a proposal has been approved and the time has come to implement it. It sometimes seems that one crisis after another jumps into line ahead of the proposal and receives the attention and resources that might have been devoted to implementing it. The consequences of this are serious. First, the crises that the proposal was designed to prevent are not prevented and the problem is compounded. Second, the organization members interpret the delay as a signal that the old values of competition and authoritarianism have been reinstated. These two consequences lead to undermining the joint management system. The most effective step that can be taken to avoid this situation is to fold the activities of the parallel organization into the collective bargaining process.

Action team members can take several other steps to avoid this situation. First, they should be careful not to pressure the senior manager-member to approve a proposal that he or she will probably be unable to implement. It is far better to approve a more modest proposal that can surely be implemented. Second, they should consider writing provisions into the joint management system itself that raise approved proposals to crisis status. That is, the consequences to the senior manager-member for failing to implement a proposal should be made comparably unpleasant to the consequences of failing to deal with a crisis. Third, the union officer members should shoulder the responsibility for keeping constant track of each approved proposal and performing the admittedly unpleasant task of bringing to the attention of the senior manager-member all the proposals that are behind in their implementation schedule. This should be a regular agenda item for every meeting.

Problem Solving. The only action teams that spend virtually all of their time engaged in the formal problem-solving process are those at the worksite level. Executive-level and operations-level action teams generally have planning teams that perform this function for them. When an intermediate-level action team identifies a problem that affects more than one of the organizational units within its jurisdiction, it tends to form an ad hoc planning team rather than devote its own time to problem solving.

This is not to say that higher-level action teams do not solve problems. They usually solve them, however, by reviewing the information gathered and the analyses performed by other people rather than gathering and analyzing data themselves. Where all the data required to solve a problem are readily at hand and no extensive analysis is required, higher-level action teams sometimes solve problems quickly and informally through discussion. There is no reason higher-level action teams should not engage in the formal problem-solving process. In fact, it would probably be to everyone's advantage if they did take an occasional problem through the formal process themselves. The fact that they do not is simply a matter of logistics: they spend less time in meetings than planning teams and lower-level action teams and the time they do spend is used on other functions.

The problems that are most sensibly addressed by the worksite-level action team are those that the first-line supervisor (or, in the case of the autonomous work team, the team leader) has the authority to resolve. Since most of the team leader's authority tends to deal with work methods, the worksite-level action team tends to focus on work-methods problems. After the action team has identified a problem and gone through the problem-solving steps described in Chapter Seventeen, it often finds that these steps have led naturally to a consensus solution. At that point, the team leader simply acknowledges the consensus and agrees to implement the solution. If the team leader lacks the authority to implement a solution, a written proposal summarizing the action team's analysis may be submitted through primary organizational channels.

Formation

Participation stewards are elected by (and subject to recall by) discrete groups of constituents at the worksite level. Each group of four to twelve members of the organization elects one, and only one, participation steward. This makes it possible to hold each participation steward accountable for two-way communication with a specific group of organization members. If an organization member fails to "get the word" on an item, the participation steward responsible for the lapse can be readily identified. Each participation steward carries a list of the names of his or her constituents and checks off the names on this list before and after every action team meeting. Participation stewards can be selected for membership on higher-level action teams in a variety of ways. The important thing is that the stewards being represented have the right to decide the method of selecting their representative. In all cases, however, there should be a clear line of accountability from top to bottom. That is, participation stewards serving on higher-level committees should also have discrete groups of constituents. For example, if three participation stewards serving on an intermediate-level action group represent twelve other stewards at the next lower level, each of the three stewards should be responsible for communicating with only four of the twelve. If each of the three stewards is held generally responsible for communicating with all twelve constituents, experience has shown that very little communication takes place.

Representatives of team leaders, middle managers, and other constituencies are also held accountable for communicating with discrete constituencies. Managers generally serve on intermediate-level action teams according to some system of rotation. For example, if an action team has six action teams at the next lower level, each of the six unit heads involved would probably serve a two-month term each year on the higher-level action team. Action teams at the executive and operating levels generally draw their manager-members from the planning teams that serve them, since managers are normally elected to planning teams by their peers.

Senior manager-members, of course, serve on action teams by virtue of their positions in the primary organization. The term of office of subordinate managers generally depends on the method used by their peers to place them on the team. Participation stewards serving on action teams usually serve terms of from six to twelve months. Many organizations find that participation stewards tend to "burn out" after six months or so.

Roles of Members

There are four general categories of action team members: the senior manager-member, subordinate managers, participation stewards, and other union officers. In addition, each action team usually elects a chairperson. All organization members should have a clear understanding of these five roles.

The Senior Manager-Member. The senior manager-member acts as the link between the parallel and the primary organizations. Therefore, he or she has two roles. During the formal problem-solving process and during the discussions that occur during the review of proposals and requests for studies, it is important that the senior manager-member interact with the other members of the team as an equal, *not* as a superior. Only the most personally secure senior managers are able to do this easily. For most, it takes hard work and discipline. Two common ways in which managers avoid equal interaction are, first, dominating the problem-solving process and, second, not participating in it at all. The latter method is the easiest and most destructive. Senior managers who attempt to dominate the process eventually encounter resistance from the other team members. This brings the problem to a head so that it can be solved. Senior managers who keep themselves detached from the process until the time arrives when a decision is appropriate present a more difficult problem. When asked by other members, "Why don't you say what you think?" they answer, "Oh, I don't want to dominate the process." This carries the implicit message that the senior manager possesses tremendous powers. Yet, on the surface, it appears to be a benevolent statement and is therefore difficult to cope with. Of course, most senior managers are not comfortable joining in the discussions of the group as equal members. To express their ideas (as opposed to their authoritative positions) during the problem-solving process makes them vulnerable. Often other team members turn out to have better ideas and the senior manager is brought face-to-face with his or her fallibility. While in the long run this may be beneficial to the senior manager's character, in the short run it can be painful.

During the time matters are being discussed, all members of the action team are equal and should be listened to with equal respect. This is based on the probability that each member can contribute an equal amount to the discussion if he or she is not inhibited. When the discussion is over and the time has come to make a decision, however, the role of the senior manager-member changes. Then senior managers take off their "equal" hats and assume their roles as heads of units in the primary organization. Where the discussion has produced a consensus in which they share, they simply acknowledge the consensus and make appropriate commitments regarding implementation. Where there is no consensus, the senior manager must make a decision. This decision may be to gather more information or to pursue one or the other of various alternatives discussed. But a decision must be made and the senior manager must make it.

Subordinate Managers. The role of subordinate managers can also be difficult if it is not clearly understood by the senior manager-member. The natural inclination of the senior manager is to view subordinate managers as extensions of himself or herself. This is an appropriate and necessary view as it applies to the activities of the primary organization. In the parallel organization, however, the role of the subordinate manager is to represent the views and interests of other subordinate managers and not those of the senior manager.

The parallel organization depends for its success on its ability to reconcile conflicting views. If the subordinate manager fails to represent the views of constituents, they cannot be reconciled with other views and the parallel organization fails to accomplish its purpose. For example, suppose that the autonomous work team leaders of an organization feel that they need the authority to make a certain kind of decision in order to better accomplish the goals of the organization. It is the task of their representative on the action team that is considering the matter to defend their position to the best of his or her ability. If the senior manager-member of the action team disagrees with their position, the team leader representative must be willing to disagree (and argue with) the "boss." Even if the team leader representative is personally lukewarm on the idea, he or she must defend it in opposition to the senior manager-member.

Subordinate managers who are members of action teams normally represent other subordinate managers at a given level in the organization. For example, one may represent a group of team leaders, another may represent a group of division or department heads, and so on. While sitting in team meetings, the subordinate manager-representative is responsible for representing the views of constituents. This makes it crucial to communicate with these constituents between meetings. In order to perform effectively, the subordinate manager-member must be sure that each and every constituent understands the problems under consideration by the action team and knows the status of these problems. Further, the representative must understand the views of each constituent regarding each problem. Members of planning teams represent so many constituents that this kind of communication is impossible. In action teams it is both feasible and necessary.

Participation Stewards. Like the subordinate manager-member of an action team, the participation steward represents the views and interests of constituents. Participation stewards speak as equals to all other team members and are listened to with equal respect. They must establish two-way communication with their constituents in the same way that subordinate manager-members do with theirs.

It is important to emphasize, however, that members of action teams do not function in an adversary mode. While they must represent the views of their constituents and, on occasion, must disagree with other members of the team, their object is not to impose their views on the other members but to discover and develop solutions that meet the needs of all the organization members represented on the action team. Where this kind of solution cannot be developed, the matter should be either dropped or referred to the bargaining committee so that it can be dealt with through the distributive bargaining process.

On the rare occasion where the senior manager-member makes a decision contrary to the interests of the participation stewards, they must decide whether to accept the decision (in return for past—or possible future—decisions that are favorable to their interests) or to label the problem an "issue" and refer it to the distributive bargaining process. They should also review the way in which the decision was made to see if the decision-making process was consistent with the provisions of the parallel agreement. If not, the decision would be subject to the filing of a grievance. If the decision raises a question of principle, the participation stewards should seriously consider grieving it or referring it to distributive bargaining. Of course, where the parallel organization has not been folded into the collective bargaining process, these options may not be available to the participation steward. It is paradoxical that, where the system is grievable (as at Shell-Sarnia—see Chapter Five), there are few occasions for grievances to be filed, and where it is not grievable, there are many.

Combined-Function Union Officers. Participation stewards are concerned only with the activities of the parallel organization. The local presidents, business agents, chief stewards, and so on who sit on action teams are concerned with both the integrative and the distributive sides of the relationship. Thus, one of their major roles on action teams is to coordinate the union's integrative and distributive bargaining activities. The most obvious way in which they do this is to keep track of the issues that exist on the distributive side of the relationship and the problems that are being jointly solved on the integrative side. This enables them to recognize instances where an issue should be reclassified as a problem and moved from the bargaining committee to the parallel organization and vice versa. This and other ways in which organized labor's integrative and distributive bargaining activities can be coordinated are discussed in detail in Chapter Twenty-Four. This coordinative role of combined-function union officers is similar to the role of manager-members in linking the parallel and primary organizations. They act as "linking pins" between the parallel organization and their primary organization (that is, the administrative structure of the union).

Their second major role is to monitor the operation of the parallel organization to ensure that its rules, policies, and procedures are being followed by all the parties involved. For example, if a subordinate manager (within the jurisdiction of the action team's senior manager-member) is subverting the joint management system by failing to hold meetings, it is the responsibility of the combined-function union officers to take appropriate action. They might first try to negotiate corrective action with the subordinate manager or with the senior manager-member of their action group.

If these informal negotiations fail, they would file a grievance—assuming that the parallel organization had been folded into the collective bargaining process.

Their third major role is to monitor the rules, policies, procedures, and programs on which agreement has been reached to ensure that they are being followed or, in the case of programs, promptly implemented. Again, where the parallel organization is being used as an extended bargaining mechanism, the combined-function union officer would file and pursue grievances where appropriate. Where this is not the case, the union officer seeks to bring the primary organization into conformity through whatever means are available.

In addition to these institutional roles, combined-function union officers participate fully as equal members of their action team in all its functions. Like the senior manager-members, they are sometimes tempted to sit back in silence until the creative problem-solving discussion is over and then to tell the team why the solution won't work. They should resist this temptation. While joining in the problem-solving process as an equal requires a great deal of inner strength, it pays dividends both for the organization and for the personal development of the individual.

Action Team Chairs. Action teams generally alternate the chair between labor and management. The tenure of the team chairperson varies; six months is a typical term of office. At the executive level, some joint management systems use cochairs, one from management and one from labor. The team chairperson's role, of course, has to do only with the activities of the team itself. Implementing the team's proposals is a function of the primary organization and is the responsibility of the senior manager-member. The team chair schedules the meeting, prepares the agenda, and facilitates the discussion. He or she is responsible for making sure that the team carries out all of its five functions. In short, the team chair is in charge, but only during the time that the meeting is taking place. He or she is not in a position to link the team with either the primary organization or the union structure. These linkages must be maintained by the senior manager-member and the combined-function union officer(s).

In facilitating meetings, the team chair should strive to arrange things so that all the team members participate on an equal basis. Where a senior manager-member or a combined-function union officer are not participating as equals, it is the team chair's job to correct the situation. Where a participation steward is not being listened to with respect, the team chair should intervene. Where any team member is for any reason inhibited from expressing a view, it is the team chair's job to set things right. Setting things right, of course, does not always mean intervening while the meeting is going on. Individual counseling sessions are sometimes in order. In short, the team chair is usually the facilitator and should receive formal training in facilitator skills.

At the worksite level, action teams spend a great deal of time engaged in formal problem solving. At this level, perhaps the most important task of the team chair is to make sure that the problem solving is—in fact—formal. The natural inclinations of action team members often lead them to define problems in terms of solutions, fail to gather more information than is already at hand, fail to seriously consider alternative solutions, and so on. The best way to cope with these natural inclinations is to insist on rigorous adherence to the formal problem-solving steps. This is the job of the team chairperson.

It is generally best that the senior manager-member not be the team chair. This leaves him or her free to participate fully in the discussion without being tempted to dominate it.

Chapter 14

Planning Teams:
Reconciling
Workplace Interest Groups

Rules, policies, procedures, and programs developed by staff offices in traditional organizations are often "dogs that won't hunt." They frequently fail because they do not take into account the politics of the situation and are not accepted by the members of the organization. The main function of the planning team is to develop "dogs that will hunt."

At a given level in any parallel organization, the size, complexity, and autonomy of the primary organizational unit make it difficult for the action team to function effectively by itself. There are so many different workplace interest groups that they cannot all be represented on an action team of seven to nine members. There are so many problems to be solved through integrative bargaining that the seven to nine members of the action team do not have the time to deal with them. Yet to substantially increase the size of the action team would prevent its members from reaching the deep understanding of each other that is necessary to their success. In addition, it is not usually possible to secure the time of the organization's top managers and union officers for the fifteen to twenty hours per month that are needed to carry out the actual problem solving (planning) process. Therefore, the action team needs a staff arm to work on problems that affect all or most of the subunits of its primary organization. Yet it cannot rely on the staff arms of the primary organization for this purpose. If it did this, it would fail to capitalize on the major strength of the parallel organization: its ability to solve problems in ways that reconcile the views of the organization's many workplace interest groups. The formation of a planning team can solve these difficulties. It can be made as large as is necessary to represent all the workplace interest groups. It is within the authority of the action team's senior manager-member to release these representatives from their regular duties for the time they need to spend on planning team activities. Further, the members of a planning team can be organized into a number of miniteams that are appropriately sized to do problem-solving/planning work.

Yet the planning team is not a true staff arm to its action team. It is subject to the administrative direction of the action team, but its members are responsible only to their constituents for "substance." That is, a planning team may work hard to produce a proposal on a subject requested by its action team and to meet the action team's deadlines. With regard to the substance of the proposal, however, the planning team is responsible only to its constituents. Of course, every member of the organization—including its top manager—is a constituent of the planning team. Thus, the planning team's task of producing proposals that reconcile the views of all its constituents also produces proposals that meet the needs of the organization.

Purpose

The purpose of the planning team is to perform the staff work needed by its action team in such a way that its proposals reconcile the views of the various workplace interest groups of the organization. There is a great deal of information available to the planning team. It has access to the information kept by the staff offices of the primary organization as well as the information in the possession of its many constituents. This enables it to produce proposals with high technical quality. The political nature of the planning team enables it to produce proposals that meet the needs of organization members and have the support of these members.

Relationship to Staff Offices

The major problem that must be faced in creating and operating planning teams arises from the fact that their functions duplicate some of the functions of the primary organization's staff offices. They often run into "turf" problems with the personnel, labor relations, purchasing, accounting, administrative services, budget, finance, procurement, strategic planning, and other staff functions.

This duplication occurs because one of the functions of each staff office is to develop rules, policies, procedures, and programs in its area of responsibility. At the same time, one of the functions of the planning team is to identify problems that are interfering with either human well-being or productivity and to develop proposals for solving these problems. Since the solutions to these problems often involve developing new rules, policies, procedures, and programs, the planning team constantly finds itself treading on the turf of one of the staff offices. If this problem is not dealt with in a decisive manner, it is almost certain to cripple the planning team. Staff offices are likely to "drag their feet" when asked for information by the planning team. They may also work behind the scenes to divert resources allocated to the planning team to other purposes. If asked to review and clear rules, policies, procedures, and programs developed by the planning team, they may raise petty objections rather than make constructive suggestions. If asked to attend planning team meetings in a staff capacity, they may seek to "take over" the team—using their greater knowledge to rule out the team's ideas as unrealistic.

The crippling effect of these problems on the work of planning teams can be greatly reduced by folding the activities of the parallel organization into the collective bargaining process. Staff offices are accustomed to take collective bargaining seriously and to provide management with the staff support needed to engage in it successfully. These problems should be virtually eliminated if, in addition to folding the activities of the parallel organization into the collective bargaining process, specific steps are taken to make it in the interests of the staff specialists to cooperate with the planning teams. The top manager can define the relationships of the staff offices to the planning team in such a way as to make cooperation, rather than conflict, serve their interests. The staff offices should be officially assigned the task of providing staff services to the planning team and should be rewarded when this task is performed well. Some specific ways of assigning this task and of rewarding the staff offices for performing it are discussed in Chapter Twenty-Three. This difficult question is also analyzed at length in Pelle Ehn's excellent book, *Work-Oriented Design of Computer Artifacts* (1988).

Composition

We have already touched on the composition of the planning team in Chapter Three. The guiding principle that governs its composition is simple: it should include a member for each of the major workplace interest groups that compose the organization.

Translating this principle into action, however, is far from simple. The first difficulty lies in defining the term "major." Clearly, the term cannot mean the same thing when applied at the executive level and at the worksite level. Some "grouping of groups" must occur at higher levels in order to keep the planning team to a manageable size. Generally, the term is defined pragmatically. That is, it is given a definition that appears workable. This definition is a product of a realistic number of planning team members, the average number of constituents each member would serve, and the total number of workplace interest groups.

For example, one organization set the "realistic" number of executive-level planning team members at thirty because this was the number that could be accommodated by the only available conference room. This produced an average of about two hundred constituents for each participation steward. Thus, the organizational workplace interest groups needed to be aggregated at a level of the primary organization that had about two hundred members. Where units at that level had far fewer members (for example, thirty to one hundred), they were grouped with other smaller units and represented by one participation steward.

Figure 9 illustrates the way an executive-level parallel organization might be structured in a hypothetical county government.

At the operating level, it is sometimes feasible to represent almost every primary work unit on the planning team. For exam-

**Figure 9. Action and Planning Teams at the Executive Level:
A County Government.**

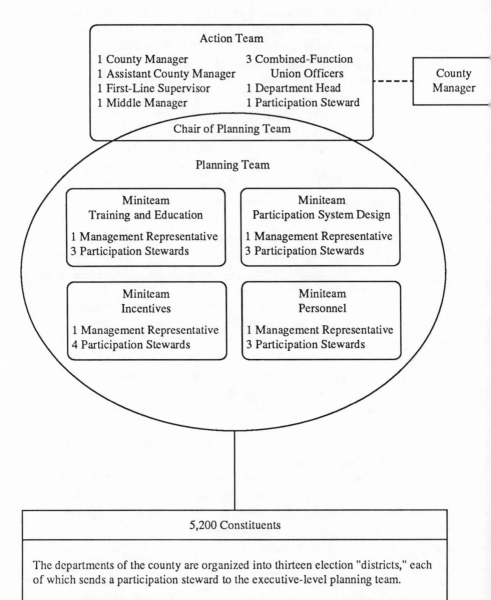

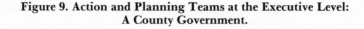

ple, Figure 10 charts an operations-level parallel organization for a
health care center (with three wards and 220 employees). The action
team has eight members and the planning team has sixteen: nine
nurse assistants (NAs), one from each shift of each ward; one representative each from top and first-line management; three registered
nurses (RNs); a licensed practical nurse (LPN); and a representative
from support staff. In this example, the combined-function union
officers sit only on the action team. The top management representative is appointed by the facility administrator, sits on both the
action team and the planning team, and meets with all three planning miniteams.

Figure 11 charts an operating-level parallel organization for
a hypothetical manufacturing plant with 3,200 employees. It should
be noted that this chart shows only the operating level. Each department, section, branch, and work team in the plant would also have
its action team.

Organization

The planning team seeks to reconcile the views of many
workplace interest groups and to translate these reconciled views
into organizational rules, policies, procedures, and programs. In
accomplishing this aim, however, it faces a dilemma. That is, problem solving that is combined with reconciliation is best done in
groups of no more than four to six members. Yet almost every
organization that is large, complex, and autonomous enough to
warrant a planning group has at least fifteen to twenty-five workplace interest groups that require representation. This dilemma is
usually resolved by an organizational compromise. That is, while
the planning team itself may have as many as thirty members, the
actual planning is done in miniteams of four to six members. The
results of this planning are presented at meetings (usually monthly)
of the total planning team. Constituencies not represented on a
particular problem during the actual planning process are represented during this monthly review process. Their representatives
must use the review process as a forum for raising their concerns.
Most planning teams require a consensus before a proposal is forwarded to its action team.

Figure 10. Action and Planning Teams at the Operating Level: A Health Care Center.

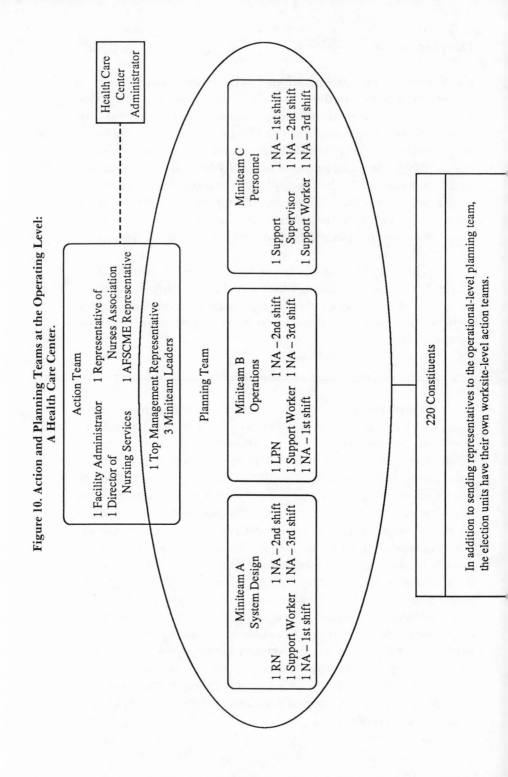

Health Care Center Administrator

Action Team

1 Facility Administrator   1 Representative of
1 Director of   Nurses Association
  Nursing Services   1 AFSCME Representative

1 Top Management Representative
3 Miniteam Leaders

Planning Team

Miniteam A
System Design

1 RN   1 NA – 2nd shift
1 Support Worker 1 NA – 3rd shift
1 NA – 1st shift

Miniteam B
Operations

1 LPN   1 NA – 2nd shift
1 Support Worker 1 NA – 3rd shift
1 NA – 1st shift

Miniteam C
Personnel

1 Support   1 NA – 1st shift
  Supervisor   1 NA – 2nd shift
1 Support Worker 1 NA – 3rd shift

220 Constituents

In addition to sending representatives to the operational-level planning team, the election units have their own worksite-level action teams.

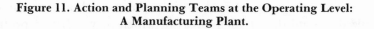

**Figure 11. Action and Planning Teams at the Operating Level:
A Manufacturing Plant.**

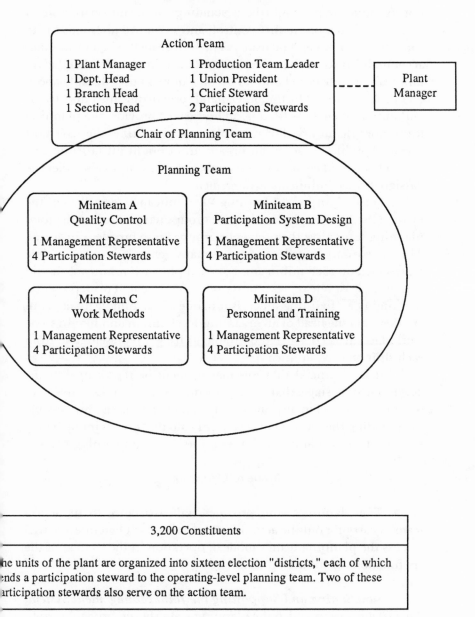

The units of the plant are organized into sixteen election "districts," each of which sends a participation steward to the operating-level planning team. Two of these participation stewards also serve on the action team.

The miniteams of four to six members each are usually organized around the problem areas in which they will be working. For example, there might be a standing miniteam on personnel policies, another on quality control, and so on. An alternative is to constitute them as ad hoc teams. The former method tends to place accountability for each problem area at the miniteam level and gives miniteam members a chance to become more knowledgeable about one problem area. On the other hand, organizing into miniteams without assigned areas (that is, ad hoc teams) provides the planning team more flexibility. For example, at a given time the five most pressing problems facing an organization might all fall into one area. This would create a serious imbalance of workloads under the "assigned area" miniteam arrangement.

For the purpose of forming the miniteams, regardless of the method used, the workplace interest groups represented on the total planning team must themselves be grouped into broader categories. This is necessary in order to have as many general views as possible represented on each miniteam. For example, each miniteam should include at least one representative of management. This representative might be a first-line supervisor in one case, a middle manager in another, and the head of an operating-level unit in another. In some workplaces it is considered desirable to have a representative from each shift on each miniteam.

It is so crucial that top management be represented at the developmental stage that its representative or representatives are often not assigned to any one miniteam, but are instead responsible for attending the meeting of each miniteam that occurs immediately prior to its presentation of a proposal to the total planning team.

Mode of Operation

The planning team provides staff assistance to its action team in carrying out the action team's functions. Therefore, we will discuss the planning team's mode of operation in the context of the six functions of the action team.

Sanctioning and Supporting the Joint Management System.
This is one area in which the planning team should probably estab-

lish a standing miniteam, rather than give "sanctioning and supporting" assignments to an ad hoc miniteam. Just as the primary organization needs a mechanism to make it adaptable to change, so does the joint management system itself need some means of ensuring that it adapts to change. One way to meet this need is to establish a miniteam with the sole and continuing task of evaluating the effectiveness of the joint management system and developing whatever changes are needed in its rules, policies, and procedures for the total planning team to recommend to its action team. If no such miniteam is established, the planning team should develop some other mechanism for ensuring that evaluations are performed and changes recommended.

System Evaluation. Criteria should be developed in at least three areas: system operation, system accomplishments, and constituent satisfaction. The specific criteria used and the ways they are measured will vary, depending on the nature of the organization and whether the evaluation is being done at the executive or the operations level. The area of system operating deals with such matters as whether the required meetings are being held, whether the meetings are producing solutions to problems, whether teams that engage in problem solving are following the prescribed steps, and whether the written proposals being submitted represent completed staff work. The area of system accomplishments has to do with the end results achieved by the system. For example, how many dollars has it saved? How much has productivity improved? How much has employee well-being improved? The area of constituent satisfaction addresses such questions as "How satisfied are the members of the organization with the joint management system and with its various components?" and "What changes would organization members like to have made in the system's rules, policies, and procedures?"

A reporting system should be developed to provide information on which to base the evaluation of "system operations" and "system accomplishments." An excellent way to measure constituent satisfaction is to have each member of the planning team conduct structured interviews with at least two constituents each month. This both provides evaluation data and ensures that representatives stay in touch with the views of their constituents.

Recommendations for Change. The rules, policies, and procedures that define a joint management system are incorporated into the parallel agreement upon which the system is based. Therefore, changes in these rules, policies, and procedures must be reflected in the agreement. Most such agreements, while they are for one-year periods, can be changed by mutual consent any time during the one-year period. Especially at the executive level, they often include provisions for annual retreats at which the action and planning teams meet together to modify their parallel agreement and to develop work plans for the following year. Whatever the level, it is the task of the planning team to make recommendations for changes at least annually. At the executive level, these recommendations usually deal with the composition, organization, and procedures of the action and planning teams themselves. For example, a planning team that had previously delegated the formulation of its budget to its principal staff assistant might recommend procedures through which the members of the team itself would be involved in budget formulation. Another example can be drawn from the experience at Shell-Sarnia. The Shell-Sarnia committee responsible for proposing design changes in its joint management system might well consider the impact on the system of the "secret sessions" being held by the coordinating group at the second management level. These sessions are perceived by workers as "secret" because there is no parallel structure at the second level of management.

At the operating level, these recommendations also cover the intermediate- and worksite-level action teams and the autonomous work teams. The rules, policies, and procedures governing these teams are of great concern to the members of the organizational unit involved. In addition, the participation stewards, since they may serve as few as a dozen constituents, are far more available to the members of the organization. These factors tend to promote a great deal of desirable debate and discussion around the planning team's recommendations. The joint management system at the operating level has a substantial effect on people's hour-to-hour and day-to-day lives and is taken very seriously by everyone concerned.

Initiating Studies and Requesting Advice. Through their work on organizationwide problems, the members of planning teams often acquire a broad and long-term view of matters. This view enables them to recognize problems that have not yet become crises and recommend to their action teams that these problems be studied. In addition, a major concern of planning team members is to make sure that they are acting in accordance with the views of their constituents. Since a planning team member at the executive level may have hundreds of constituents, it is not always easy to stay in touch with their views. For this reason, planning teams often find it useful to formally request their constituents' advice on problems they are studying and solutions they have developed. Brief opinion polls are sometimes used to guide the planning team as it analyzes a problem. These polls can be accomplished through either interviews or written questionnaires. After a planning team has developed a particularly important and controversial proposal, it may hold a ratification vote on the proposal itself. While such ratification votes are not binding on the senior manager-member of the action team, they do give an accurate idea of the degree to which the proposal is accepted by the members of the organization.

Reviewing and Acting on Requests for Studies. Requests for studies are often originated by planning teams. They define the problem in writing and explain the reasons they think it should be studied. They then submit the request to their action team to be forwarded up the line through the primary organization until it reaches an action team that can deal with it. This action team will often refer it to its own planning team for that team's recommendations on whether or not the study should be done. Action and planning teams can gain a great deal of credibility by responding energetically to requests for studies. On the other hand, they can create cynicism and apathy at lower levels of the organization by failing to respond promptly to such requests.

Reviewing and Acting on Proposals. The planning team cannot, of course, approve a proposal for implementation. It does, however, meet "as a whole" and review the proposals prepared by its miniteams. The only actions it can take on these proposals are to approve them and forward them to the action team, to disapprove them, or to return them to the miniteam for more work. Normally, a planning team reaches consensus on a proposal before forwarding it to its action team. This review function is important because it is often the only opportunity that members who did not participate in the development of a proposal have to express their views on it. Ideally, miniteams should give interim presentations at which this kind of discussion could occur. Time pressures, however, often prevent this from happening.

Implementing and Monitoring Proposals. As a general rule, the action team itself has little to do with implementing proposals. After the action team reaches consensus on a proposal (which, in effect, means that the senior manager-member has approved it and that everyone else agrees with that approval), the senior manager-member assumes his or her role as head of the corresponding unit of the primary organization and, in that role, implements the proposal. This is usually accomplished by assigning its implementation to a subordinate manager. While the primary organization has its own mechanisms for ensuring that assignments get carried out, the combined-function union officers play a major role in monitoring assignments that involve proposals approved by the action team. With regard to these assignments, they should check before each action team meeting to learn the implementation status of these proposals and, where necessary, bring this status to the attention of the senior manager-member. The members of the planning team are not generally responsible for monitoring proposals. When their constituents complain to them that an approved proposal is not being implemented by the responsible subordinate manager, they simply bring this to the attention of their combined-function union officer who sits on the action team.

Problem Solving. This function (the actual problem-solving process) is usually delegated to the planning team by its action team and occupies most of the planning team's time. It is not performed by the planning team as a whole, but rather by its miniteams. These miniteams of four to six members meet perhaps once a week to solve problems. In addition, the members of each miniteam often gather information and prepare draft materials between meetings. Planning miniteams should be careful to avoid general, undisciplined discussions. They should be aware of where they are in the problem-solving process at all times and stick to the business at hand. It is natural for people engaged in problem solving to wish to jump quickly from the problem to a solution without doing the hard work of gathering information and thinking through the implications of alternative solutions. The best way to avoid this temptation is to structure each meeting around a specific work objective (defining the problem, identifying needed information and its sources, and so on) and to stick to that objective until it is accomplished to everyone's satisfaction. Chapter Seventeen discusses the problem-solving process in detail.

Formation of Planning Teams

Several issues must be considered with regard to the formation of planning teams: how members are selected, how planning teams "link" with other teams, and what terms of office are appropriate.

Selection. Normally, all members of the planning team except those members who represent top management are elected by their constituencies. Representatives of top management are appointed by the top manager. Representatives of groups such as middle managers sometimes serve rotational terms on action teams. This works well, since they rarely represent more than four to six constituents. A first-line supervisor on a planning team, however, normally represents at least a dozen other supervisors. This makes rotation unfeasible. Accordingly, secret-ballot elections are usually held for all planning team slots except those that represent top management and those that can be filled through rotation.

Linking with Other Teams. In some organizations it is possible to select planning team members from among members of action and planning teams at lower levels. This tends to improve coordination among the teams on different levels. It is often feasible at the operating level in organizations that have no more than twenty or so primary work units. At the executive level, however, "linking" with other levels sometimes presents difficulties. During the time that an executive-level organization is converting to joint management, for example, not all of its components have action or planning teams from which to draw. Even after the conversion is complete, it is sometimes more disruptive to the work of the organization to have the same person serving on action or planning teams at five or six levels of the organization than to make membership on the executive-level planning team a separate matter.

Terms of Office. At the operating level, terms of office are generally the same on the planning team as on action teams, since some planning team members serve by virtue of their membership on lower-level action teams. The term of office at this level is most often six months or a year. This is based on the fact that most of the planning projects undertaken at this level are resolved in three to six months. In addition, the pressures from constituents can be intense and many planning team members tend to "burn out" after six to nine months. At the executive level, the time between initiating and completing a planning project may be as much as twelve to eighteen months, and terms of office often run to two years.

Roles of Members

The essential task of each planning team member is to represent the interests of the constituent(s) who appointed or elected him or her to the group. The different members carry out this task in different ways.

Representatives of the Top Manager. By "top manager" we mean the senior manager-member of the action team (who is also the head of its corresponding unit in the primary organization). Depending on the size of the planning team and its level in the organization, the top manager may appoint one, two, or three representatives. It is in everybody's interest that enough representatives are appointed to ensure that the top manager's views are taken into account in the actual problem-solving process before the proposal is formalized. A representative of the top manager should have discussed every major proposal with the responsible miniteam before the proposal is presented to the total planning team. The second factor that either makes or breaks these representatives is whether they are able to keep in close contact with the top manager. If they are not, proposals reach the action team without having been negotiated to the top manager's satisfaction. This does not mean that the top manager has the ability to arbitrarily veto an idea while it is being developed. However, the top manager may have knowledge of some circumstance (for example, a corporate plan to shift a supplier) that makes the idea unfeasible. The action team would then either disapprove the unfeasible proposal or return it for revision, and the planning team's credibility and morale would be damaged. The best way to avoid this situation is to secure the top manager's agreement—at the time the joint management system is first designed—to be regularly available to his or her representatives. Where the procedures of the parallel organization are enforceable, behaviors such as not granting ready access to representatives can be grieved. In these instances, people tend to take the procedures of the parallel organization much more seriously.

Representatives of Other Management Groups. The task is the same for these people as for the representatives of the top manager: to provide good representation. However, the steps they must take to carry it out are different. A middle management representative at the executive level may have two hundred constituent middle managers scattered throughout the organization. The task of these representatives is twofold: first, to communicate with their constituents, and, second, to represent their constituents in the development and review of proposals. The means for them to accomplish the second part of their task are built into the problem-solving and review process of the planning team. The means of communicating with constituents vary with such factors as the number of constituents and whether or not they are geographically dispersed. Whether the means are newsletters or periodic meetings, the task cannot be ignored without damaging the effectiveness of the planning team.

Participation Stewards. Again, the participation steward's most difficult and—at the same time—most important task is to communicate with constituents. One partial method, which can also be tied into the evaluation function, is to interview one or two constituents each month. This is not sufficient in itself, however. Another method is for the participation steward to be available to constituents at a regular time and place each month. The lunch hour often works well for this.

Combined-Function Union Officers. Where combined-function union officers serve on planning teams, their special role is to represent the views of all their members. Each participation steward necessarily represents the views of a limited constituency.

The Chairperson or Cochairs. Some planning teams operate with cochairs, one from labor and one from management. Others have only one chairperson, with labor and management taking turns at holding the job. The term of office of a planning team chair might be six months or a year, depending on factors such as whether the team is at the executive or the operations level. Operating with cochairs provides a mechanism for reconciling the views of labor and management on a day-to-day basis. However, since the cochairs are located out in the organization, doing their regular jobs, there is a tendency for support staff to perform this reconciling function. Staff personnel, because they are full time, are the first to learn of the need for a decision. They then call the cochairs to advise them of this need. The natural tendency of the first cochair contacted is to agree with or propose a given course of action and ask the staff person to clear it with the other cochair. This often serves to intensify what is already a problem with many planning teams: the tendency of power to gravitate into the hands of staff personnel.

The role of the planning team chair is very different from that of the action team chair. The responsibility of the action team chair, as a general rule, begins when the meeting begins and ends when the meeting ends. Between meetings, the senior manager-member "runs the show." The planning team, however, has no senior manager-member. In addition, the planning team is larger and has a great deal of work of its own to do. In effect, it is comparable to a major staff unit of the primary organization. This places an administrative burden on the chairperson. For this reason, the chairperson of an executive-level planning team may be released from his or her regular duties for one-half time to carry this burden.

Where the chairperson is not given sufficient release time, the real control of the planning team may pass, in large part, to its staff. Thus, the first role of the planning team chair is that of team leader. He or she must ensure that the team members are provided the time, space, resources, and rewards they need in order to perform well. Like other leaders in joint management situations, the chair is an educator and a maintainer of boundaries (see Chapter Eleven for a discussion of the leadership role under joint management).

The chair also has another special role: to skillfully lead meetings of a particular kind. These meetings involve from fifteen to thirty people and their object is to reach consensus on a variety of matters. These characteristics make these meetings extremely difficult to lead. In fact, the key to leading such a meeting is to recognize that an informed consensus is impossible unless the team members understand the problems being discussed before the meeting begins. One method for bringing about this understanding is to have planning team support staff phone each member before each meeting to discuss the agenda.

In facilitating the meeting itself, the chair should keep one guiding principle in mind: to watch for signs that members either do not understand a problem or disagree with a solution, and to find ways to encourage them to declare their misunderstandings and disagreements. Time constraints will tempt the chair to dominate the meeting, but he or she should resist this temptation. In a small team of four to six that meets once a week, attempts to dominate may—in the long run—be constructive. In such a situation, it is probable that the team will confront and resolve the situation. In a large team that meets less frequently, the dynamics are more political than interpersonal. The members tend to manipulate situations (like the situation presented by a dominating leader) rather than confront them.

Miniteam Leaders. Due to the fact that the actual planning process occurs in the miniteams, these positions are central to the success of the planning team. As soon as a person is selected by a miniteam to be its leader, the planning team chair should ensure that he or she receives substantial training in the responsibilities of the job and in the skills necessary to carry out these responsibilities.

Even if the planning team is ideally constituted in all other respects, the failure to provide miniteam leaders with formal training may limit its effectiveness. This is a classic case illustrating what Robert Burton (1577–1640) meant by the saying "penny wise, pound foolish." The miniteam leader should be skilled in communication, problem solving, proposal writing, and leadership. The specific responsibilities of the job vary from organization to organization. In general, the miniteam leader has two roles: to be responsible for education and boundary maintenance, and to lead and participate in the problem-solving process. One key responsibility of all miniteam leaders is to ensure that the formal problem-solving steps are followed—that the process does not degenerate into a series of general discussions based on insufficient data.

Support Staff. There are two kinds of support staff to be considered here: those who provide administrative support and those who provide technical assistance. The former raise problems of both control and cooperation. With regard to the latter, the problem is mainly one of inducing them to provide quality technical assistance to the planning team.

The planning team must have a "home" in the primary organization. Meetings must be arranged, agendas must be typed, budgets must be prepared, supplies must be obtained, and so on. A major difficulty that faces every joint management system is the natural tendency of the administrative support staff to seek to control, rather than to serve, the planning team. If they are successful in their attempts, the planning team loses its credibility and its effectiveness.

Several factors favor these staff attempts to gain control. First, it is easier for the top manager to exercise control through primary organization channels than to build a new relationship each year with the chairperson of the planning team. It is easier logistically because the heads of the staff offices can be summoned at any time and will appear promptly in the office of the top manager. It is easier psychologically because the top manager has no need to reconcile his or her views with those of subordinates. It is in their self-interest to agree. Second, the staff office "has the horses." It has the knowledge, skills, and time to do the detailed work involved in such key areas as fiscal management and budget preparation. It is tempting for the planning team members, who do not possess the same knowledge and skills and have limited time to spend on planning team activities, to accept what the staff produces without asking the hard questions. Third, especially where the chairperson is not given substantial release time from regular duties, the top manager sometimes actually gives the head of the staff office formal decision-making authority with regard to administrative matters, such as approving expenditures and budgets. Fourth, the head of the staff office is sometimes appointed to the planning team itself by top management. This is a serious mistake. It effectively removes any possibility that the staff office might assume a serving relationship to the team. Finally, if the staff office does not control the planning team, it tends to compete with it. Giving it the control it desires is often seen as the only way of resolving this built-in conflict.

None the less, if the planning team is to be effective, steps should be taken to ensure that it is self-controlled. The most effective such step would be to make the activities an integral part of the collective bargaining process. This would place the personnel or industrial relations officer in the same relationship to the planning team as to the regular bargaining structure. In addition, the top manager could formally assign the head of the personnel or labor relations office the task of providing services to the planning team. Further, the top manager should require the chair of the planning team to make periodic written evaluations of the staff officer responsible for administrative support. These evaluations should be prepared by the chair in consultation with the leaders of the miniteams. In addition, the top manager should schedule weekly or biweekly meetings *alone* with the planning team chair. This would enable a relationship of trust to develop between the two. Next, the chair should be released from regular duties for at least one-half time and should be provided with office space and a staff assistant. Finally, the chair should be delegated the specific budget, finance, and other authorities needed to administer the planning team. The top manager should then hold him or her accountable for exercising these authorities effectively. Needless to say, the organization's job evaluation system would need to take account of these steps in setting the compensation of the chair.

Technical assistance and information is mainly needed at the miniteam level. Unless special steps are taken, it tends to be poor in quality or nonexistent. This is so because the miniteam, on any given problem, needs technical assistance from the very staff office (budget, personnel, procurement, and so on) whose turf it is invading. This competitive factor, when combined with the large workloads of staff offices and miniteams' lack of "clout," means that they do their planning at a serious disadvantage.

Several of the steps above should also be taken to ensure adequate technical assistance for planning miniteams. The heads of the organization's staff offices should be assigned the task of providing the planning team with technical assistance and information and should be evaluated by the top manager on their performance of this function. The staff offices should recognize that the planning team does not add to their workload; rather, it helps do the work. Staff specialists should be assigned to miniteams by their office heads on the request of the planning team chair. The quality of the assistance they provide should have a major influence on their performance evaluations. One key to ensuring that quality technical assistance is provided is to establish a system that gives the staff office heads major credit for plans developed by the planning team. Another key, of course, would be to fold the activities of the parallel organization into the collective bargaining process—the central recommendation of this book.

Chapter 15

⟡⟶⟡

Autonomous Work Teams: Merging the Parallel and the Primary Organizations

Like the parallel organization, the autonomous work team is used in unionized workplaces to increase productivity and improve the quality of working life. Unlike the parallel organization, the autonomous work team has also been used extensively in nonunion organizations without being found to be in violation of the National Labor Relations Act.

The "team concept" has recently been attacked by groups within organized labor. Mike Parker and Jane Slaughter (1988) charge that the team concept is being used by management to exploit workers. They say that the team concept is not bad in and of itself, but that it is being used to impose Tayloristic work methods, to speed up production, and to weaken the labor movement. However, the team concept has much in it that is of potential benefit to employees. It can add interest and meaning to their work lives. The problem, then, is one of figuring out how to avoid "throwing the baby out with the bathwater." How can the team concept be used in a way that benefits both labor and management? How can things be so arranged that employees get the psychological benefits of working in teams and participating in hour-to-hour problem solving— without being economically exploited and having their unions weakened? How can management (and the union) get the economic benefits of the team concept without being tempted to abuse it and so "kill the goose that lays the golden eggs"?

I believe that the benefits of the team concept to both labor and management can be not only protected but increased, through the use of the parallel organization as an extended bargaining mechanism. They can be protected by including the general team concept arrangements in parallel agreements at the higher levels of the organization and the specific arrangements for each autonomous work team in the parallel agreement for its work unit. Since these parallel agreements would be monitored by the local union and would be enforceable parts of the labor contract, employees and their unions would be in a strong position to prevent abuses. The general guidelines would have been reached through integrative bargaining at higher levels of the organization. The specific working arrangements for each team would have been reached through consensus by the team leader and members. Where a mistake is made in setting up these general and specific arrangements, it can be treated as simply another problem to be solved by the appropriate action or planning team. After this team has reached consensus, the agreement can be modified. Through the use of the parallel organization, team concept arrangements and activities can be kept out in the open and constantly monitored so that they continue to benefit both labor and management. The sharing of increased productivity achieved through the team concept is discussed in Part Six.

The benefits of the team concept can be increased through tying it to the parallel organization. As Pasmore, Francis, Haldeman, and Shani (1982, p. 1195) point out, in most cases autonomous work team and other similar experiments have been "conducted in small departments . . . it may have been difficult or impossible for the designers to arrange for changes in company policies, rules and procedures for the sake of supporting the experimental changes." Without such changes, the general management principles that govern autonomous work teams are so different from those that govern their parent organizations that they find it difficult to survive.

Arranging for constructive changes in company policies, rules, and procedures is, of course, the strong suit of the parallel organization. As its lowest-level action teams convert their primary work units to autonomous work teams, the higher-level action and planning teams of the parallel organization can develop policies, rules, and procedures that support this new form of work organization. If a workplace were to use the parallel organization as a bargaining mechanism, the nature of the team concept and the continuation or noncontinuation of autonomous work teams would be strongly influenced by the workers and their union.

The autonomous work team technique is not a prefabricated solution that can be taken off the shelf and imposed on a primary work unit. The idea is not that every primary work unit can function best if it is given the maximum amount of autonomy. Rather, there is an optimum level for each work unit that can be determined only by an analysis of the requirements of the unit's social and technical systems (Emery and Trist, 1969). Action teams at the worksite level are ideally suited to perform this kind of analysis. They are representative, already constituted and recognized as legitimate, and can be integrated into the administrative systems of labor and management. Further, they are permanent teams. They can, therefore, not only provide the initial design for the autonomous work teams, but continuously adapt these teams as conditions change. Since all of the members of a worksite-level action team are also members of the corresponding autonomous work team (or work unit), this is the level where the primary and parallel organizations merge.

The autonomous work team is rarely, if ever, completely free from supervision. For this reason, many people prefer the term "semiautonomous work team." For reasons of brevity, however, this book uses the shorter phrase "autonomous work team."

Purposes of the Autonomous Work Team

The autonomous work team can be used to maximize both productivity and the psychological benefits that people derive from work. Many forms of work organization first design work procedures and then expect the workers to adjust to these procedures. The autonomous work team achieves its purposes by allowing workers a great deal of discretion in choosing their own administrative procedures and the work methods they will use in each given situation.

One of the ways in which this policy tends to increase productivity is that it makes the autonomous work team adaptable: that is, its procedures and methods are not "cast in concrete." They can be changed as circumstances change.

Theory

This set of ideas is part of what the British theorist Eric Trist terms "sociotechnical systems theory" (Trist and Bamforth, 1951; Trist, Higgin, Murray, and Pollock, 1963). The main assumption of sociotechnical systems design is that "any work site contains two systems, a technical system and a social system" (Trist, Susman, and Brown, 1977). The technical system (machines, administrative procedures, data systems, tools, conveyances, and so forth) and the social system (people's attitudes, beliefs, and feelings) should be designed at the same time so that the total system can express the best match between them. "Joint optimization" (Emery, 1959) is a key concept of sociotechnical systems theory. It states that the total organization will function optimally only if each of its two systems is designed to fit the requirements of the other. Since human beliefs, attitudes, and feelings cannot be designed in the same sense that this term is applied to machines, tools, and conveyances, the term "social system" has come to include the rules, policies, and procedures that arrange relationships among people (that is, the governance subsystem). Table 2 (Herrick, 1985) lists the components of the social and technical systems.

When a primary work unit's social and technical systems are analyzed together, with the intent of jointly optimizing them, the result is often some form of autonomous work team. However, this is not always the case. Either the social or technical system (or both) may require some other form of work organization. For example, the beliefs, attitudes, and feelings of the workers involved may be opposed to the idea of teamwork and the prospect of assuming greater individual responsibilities. Another example occurs in advanced technology industries where there is limited overlap between member skills and these skills are too complex for all to learn. In this situation, "matrix"-type groups may be appropriate (Herbst, 1976).

Table 2. Components of the Social and Technical Systems.

Social System	Technical System
Work methods	Machines, tools, and conveyances
Personnel policies and procedures	Policies and procedures governing machines and so forth
Decision-making policies and procedures	Budget, financial, procurement polices and procedures

Source: Herrick, 1985, p. 973. Reprinted by permission of publisher.

General Principles

The general principles upon which autonomous work teams are based are suggested by Trist's table contrasting the characteristics of what he calls the old and new organizational paradigms (1981, p. 1195).

Old Paradigm	New Paradigm
The technological imperative	Joint optimization
Man as an extension of the machine	Man as complementary to the machine
Man as an expendable spare part	Man as a resource to be developed
Maximum task breakdown, simple narrow skills	Optimum task grouping, multiple broad skills
External controls (supervisors, specialist staffs, procedures)	Internal controls (self-regulating subsystems)
Tall organization chart, autocratic style	Flat organization chart, participative style
Competition, gamesmanship	Collaboration, collegiality
Organization's purposes only	Members and society's purposes also
Alienation	Commitment
Low risk taking	Innovation

Trist's new-paradigm characteristics are consistent with, and indeed one of the sources of, the four general principles of joint management set forth in the introduction to this book. The first five characteristics can be regarded as the general principles that underlie the autonomous work team concept.

Design Principles

The following four principles, which draw heavily on Susman's description (1979) of his work with Trist and Brown in an underground coal mine, should be useful to any work unit action team interested in converting its work unit to an autonomous work team.

Consistent Primary Task. The action team should define the primary task of its work unit in a way that is consistent with the capabilities of the technical system and acceptable to the members of the work unit. A well-defined primary task frees the members of an autonomous work team to be innovative and resourceful. Without a well-defined and well-understood primary task, members of a work unit can only follow accepted procedures and hope for the best. Once everyone has a clear idea of what the total team is trying to accomplish, however, people are able not only to be more flexible in their actions, but also to be more helpful to their fellow team members.

Constructive Performance Measurement. The primary task should be expressed in terms of the results expected. If this expression is not meaningful, the results produced by the team may not be meaningful. Performance should be measured according to results that are within the control of the team yet are also central to the goals of the total organization. Reconciling these two needs is often difficult. For example, we often measure the performance of regulatory officers by the number of inspections they make, since this result is clearly within their control. Yet it is often unclear whether making large numbers of inspections is the best way to further the compliance goals of the total organization. It may be the accepted way simply because the work unit has not clearly defined its primary task or developed effective performance measurements. As Susman points out, the performance of work units (or autonomous work teams) that are highly interdependent should be measured in the aggregate. For example, if shifts in an underground coal mine are measured separately, each shift will engage in competitive strategies that maximize its own production at the expense of the other shifts. This leads to lower aggregate productivity.

Redundant Functions. Ideally, the autonomous work team should be designed so that all of its members possess all of the skills required to perform the primary task of the team. This design principle, which is based on the redundancy of functions rather than of parts (Emery, 1967), enables a number of team members to deal effectively with an unforeseen situation (for example, a large order for a certain machine part, or the absence of a team member). An organization that followed the "redundancy of parts" principle might save in training costs by organizing work so that each worker needs to master only one simple operation. It would, however, be handicapped in its attempts to deal with variations in such factors as workload and the availability of personnel. As Susman (1979) comments, "minimal pay and status differences" between members will facilitate the learning of multiple skills. Higher-level action and planning teams might also wish to consider compensation policies that base workers' pay on the number of skills they possess, rather than on the specific duties they perform on a regular basis.

Facilitative Supervision. The supervisor's role in an autonomous work team changes radically. The traditional supervisor is responsible for discipline, for showing team members how to do their jobs on an hour-to-hour basis, and for checking up on them to see that quantity and quality are maintained. The autonomous work team leader is responsible for seeing that team members are ready, willing, and able to get the job done. The team members are responsible for doing it. This means that the supervisor handles relationships with other units (for example, to ensure that tools and raw materials are delivered and that end products are picked up), ensures that the team has a safe and healthful workplace, and trains team members so that they can acquire all the skills necessary to achieve the team's primary task.

Design Steps

The general principles and the design principles discussed above should be helpful in analyzing an organization's social and technical systems. The specific design features of the autonomous work team (or whatever organizational arrangement best matches the social and technical systems) are products of this analysis. A nine-step analytical procedure formulated by Emery (1967)) is adapted for work unit use and summarized below.

1. The worksite-level action team develops an initial description of the work unit's social and technical systems.
2. The operations of the work unit (that is, all the changes it makes in its raw material) are identified, whether they are made by people or by machines.
3. The key variances (in raw materials, demand for product or services, personnel, instructions from higher levels, and so on) are identified. A variance is key if it significantly affects either the quantity or quality of production or the operating or social costs of production.
4. A table of variance control is drawn up to determine the extent to which the key variances are controlled by the members of the work unit, including the supervisor.
5. The members of the work unit discuss their roles under existing arrangements, possible changes in these roles, and the obstacles to implementing these changes.
6. The action team then considers the interdependencies of its work unit with other work units, with staff units, and with higher levels of the organization.
7. It then focuses on the sources from which its work unit receives its materials, supplies, cases, information, and so forth and on the organizations to which it delivers its product(s).
8. The action unit then considers the impact (on its work team and on the immediate neighbors of its work unit) of the parent organization's social and technical policies.
9. The action team produces a design proposal for new working arrangements in its work unit. If necessary, it returns to any one of the preceding steps for more work. The proposal should

include, if necessary, the implications of the new working arrangements for neighboring units.

Normally, work units need some staff assistance from higher levels in performing their sociotechnical systems analyses and implementing their new working arrangements. Since the members of planning teams have often acquired a basic knowledge of this subject along with some analytical skills, they can often be trained to provide this assistance. Using planning team members instead of staff personnel also reinforces the fourth and fifth general principles set forth by Trist (1981) (multiple skills and internal controls).

Structure

The specific rules, policies, and procedures that govern the activities of autonomous work teams depend on the social and technical systems involved. However, it is worth noting that they should be kept to a minimum. The concept of "minimum critical specification" (Herbst, 1974) points out that detailed procedures impede the flexibility of response that should characterize the autonomous work team. Rules, policies, and procedures should be developed, however, to clarify for all members of the autonomous work team what their roles and responsibilities are. They should also provide a clear charter for the team's methods as well as authority for its self-governance.

Part V

Special Skills for Implementing Joint Management

In a jointly managed workplace, managers need to improve their interpersonal and communication skills. Workers need to improve their interpersonal and communications skills and develop skills in problem solving and proposal writing. In addition, the nature of the communications and problem-solving skills required is different. This is true whether or not the parallel organization is folded into the collective bargaining process. In a traditionally managed workplace, the emphasis is on individual problem solving. Staff specialists gather information, analyze it, and prepare written reports and proposals.

In a jointly managed workplace, the problem-solving process is a team effort. This places a high premium on oral communication skills. It also places a high premium on the skills necessary for effective group work. This is not to downplay the importance of written communication skills in joint management. Not infrequently, the problem-solving/planning process proceeds smoothly until the time comes to prepare a written proposal; then it falls to the ground. Often, nonsupervisory employees have had little occasion to hone their written communication skills and find the writing of proposals to be very hard work. Extensive training of all employees in communications, problem solving, and proposal writing is needed in jointly managed organizations. The chapters in this part should help meet this need.

Chapter 16

Interpersonal and
Communication Skills

When workers and managers are asked what they believe to be the most valuable change brought about by joint management, they often answer "better communication." There is some truth in the idea that joint management is a set of structures (the parallel organization and the autonomous work team) that result in improved communication. However, good communication is not an end in itself. It is only the first step toward reconciling conflicting views and taking actions consistent with these reconciled views. The process that can be used to reconcile these conflicting views is extended integrative bargaining. Communication comes into the picture in two ways. First, communication skills are essential to the members of the action and planning teams that are doing the bargaining. Second, when effective integrative bargaining is carried on at all levels of the organization, its members tend to be extremely well informed on the organization's plans, programs, and status.

The term "communication" comes from the Latin *communicare*, "to make common." What needs to be made common in a joint management situation? The answer to this question is that, if reconciliation is to occur and if patterns of influence are to change, not only objective information but also feelings must be made common. This definition of the term "communicate" has important design implications for joint management systems. First, it means that while these systems can rely on the written word to be precise and to serve as a record of understandings reached, they must rely on face-to-face contact in order to accomplish the kind of communication that leads to genuine understanding. When feelings are expressed in memoranda, the result is often caricature, not understanding. For example, memoranda that tell how strongly employees object to management decisions tend to caricature employees' feelings and produce anger and rigidity on the part of management. When employees make their objections face-to-face in a labor-management team that has learned the art of communication, on the other hand, their feelings are more accurately communicated and understood. For their part, they are more likely to acknowledge the basic humanity of managers if they have the chance to carry on a conversation with them.

Of course, understanding is not achieved just by forming a labor-management team and holding meetings. The team must first learn the art of communicating in a joint management situation. This chapter first discusses some communication concepts as they apply specifically to joint management. Then it describes a number of communication problems that occur in joint management systems and suggests approaches to dealing with these problems.

Communication Concepts

One study estimates that supervisors spend 59 percent and managers spend 80 percent of their time communicating (Mintzberg, 1973). In joint management systems, all employees have the opportunity to play a part in the management process. In order to take advantage of this opportunity, they need to be aware of the following communication concepts.

Status. Status differences are obstacles to communication (Halperin, Snyer, Shenkkel, and Houston, 1976). People with lower status are sometimes reluctant to express negative feelings to people with higher status. For example, an employee who has just been complaining bitterly to his fellows is asked by the boss how things are going. He responds, "Fine, just fine," and the boss's misconceptions about the morale of her unit are reinforced. In joint management systems, employees often develop a trust in their bosses that makes them less inhibited about expressing their feelings. The greater the status differences between employees and managers, however, the more difficult it is for a joint management system to function effectively. The reason for this is not only that the employees are inhibited in expressing their ideas but also that the high-status managers are inhibited in accepting them. Since the deliberations of action and planning teams depend on everyone's opinions being given equal weight, the system falls to the ground when managers cannot bring themselves to accept the notion that they can benefit from employees' ideas. This often occurs where the manager holds professional credentials and the need for credentials blocks the career path from employee to manager. For example, it is difficult for some doctors to give equal weight to nurses' opinions and for some nurses to benefit from the ideas of nurse assistants. One approach to this problem is for the organization's planning team to develop programs under which employees are given opportunities to become credentialed.

Listening. People cannot understand each other unless they listen carefully to each other's words and tones of voice. This would seem to be easy enough, but the fact is that most of us need to give conscious attention to developing our listening skills. These skills are especially important in action and planning teams. There is no way that conflicting interests can be reconciled until the people involved have a clear understanding of what each other's interests are. Such understanding requires careful, disciplined listening. This kind of listening is especially difficult in large groups—where the members have to compete for "air time." In large groups, people know that—if they go with the flow of the conversation—they are unlikely to get a chance to express their own special ideas. Therefore, while one person is speaking the others are often preparing their own remarks instead of listening. It is a good idea to limit action teams to no more than seven to nine members, whenever possible, in order to avoid this problem. Since planning teams do their developmental work in miniteams of four to six, there is adequate time for the "give and take" necessary for real understanding to occur. When the whole planning team meets in plenary session, it takes a highly skilled team leader to facilitate an acceptable level of understanding.

Openness. Most managers are "guarded" themselves and discourage the open expression of ideas and feelings by their subordinates (Argyris, 1966). This traditional management attitude presents a problem in joint management, which cannot reconcile conflicting ideas and feelings if these ideas and feelings are not openly expressed. Openness, as a new cultural value in most organizations, needs to be thoroughly discussed by both managers and employees prior to the initiation of a joint management system. But discussion is not enough by itself. There are valid reasons for not being open in traditional management situations. Employees cannot be open for fear of retaliation. Managers cannot be open because they fear that employees may use the information or feelings they disclose against them. In a traditional management situation, this fear is often justified. Employees may mistake openness for weakness and meet it with disrespect. This illustrates the danger of changing one aspect of a management system and leaving the other aspects intact. In order for openness to work, the whole system must be redesigned in accordance with joint management principles (see Introduction and Chapter Two).

Self-Confidence. Self-confident managers have the easiest time in adapting to joint management. It takes self-confidence to discuss plans for the future with subordinates. They will almost certainly see flaws in the plans and make suggestions to improve them. This may result in better plans, but it takes a self-confident, secure manager with a strong self-concept to accept the ideas of others in a face-to-face situation. Any manager can accept an idea if he or she is insulated from its originator by a suggestion box. But only a self-confident manager can take a position and then modify it in "real time." Insecurity leads some managers to inhibit communication in team meetings. They either dominate the conversation—thus discouraging their subordinates from participating in the problem-solving process—or remain silent, thus protecting themselves from the pain of discovering that someone else has a better grasp of the situation than they do. If they remain silent and do not join in the problem-solving process, they can make a decision after the other team members have revealed their thoughts. In this way, they avoid becoming vulnerable. Fortunately, however, both managers and workers tend to become more self-confident the more they participate in the joint management process. As they find that they can trust each other, their self-confidence and self-esteem tend to increase. This leads to personal fulfillment as well as to improved organizational effectiveness.

Nonverbal Communication. Mehrabian (1970) tells us that only 7 percent of attitude change is produced by the verbal content of messages. The rest comes from body language, spatial arrangements, and sounds other than words. For example, employees are often skeptical during the early stages of initiating a parallel organization. In an orientation meeting, the most hostile and skeptical employees can be found in the back of the room (spatial arrangements) with their chairs leaned back against the wall (body language), whispering and laughing among themselves (sounds other than words). In this way they produce negative attitudes in both their fellow employees and the people who are giving the orientation. Another example of nonverbal communication sometimes occurs in action team meetings. The senior manager-member maintains a polite, but reserved and distant, expression on her face. The other members of the action team interpret her expression to mean that she is participating in the parallel organization against her will and has no intention of allowing it to develop the rules, policies, and procedures of her unit. Accordingly, they fail to give the planning/problem-solving process the work and energy it requires and the action team never becomes productive.

Defensiveness. When a person is put down or pressured to change his or her opinion, the chances are that the person—whether manager or worker—will become defensive. When one party to a conversation becomes defensive, effective communication ceases. Therefore, in a system that depends on communication for its lifeblood, it is important to learn ways of expressing one's ideas that neither put down nor pressure other people. One such way is to preface statements with phrases like "I feel . . . ," "I don't understand . . . ," and "I would like. . . ." This informs others of your opinions, frustrations, and disappointments without blaming them or pressuring them to change their views. If it is necessary to take issue with the views of others, we should be sure to take issue with their views and not with them as human beings.

Trust. Trust among the members of an organization increases the flow and effectiveness of communication (Zand, 1972). Parallel organizations have been shown to increase the level of trust in an organization (Herrick, 1983–84). They do this by structuring a situation in which it is feasible for people to meet each other's expectations. In other words, trust must be earned. However, there is a time—when joint management is just being initiated—when trust is an act of faith. The parties, in effect, decide to trust each other conditionally. Then they wait and see. It is especially important at this time that all parties involved be very careful to keep their agreements, whether these agreements are explicit or implied. One broken word or instance of hurtful behavior can be costly.

Feedback. The use of feedback can both clarify meanings and increase the flow of communication. At the interpersonal level, reflective listening is an excellent technique for providing feedback. This technique has three steps.

1. Listen to what the other person is saying. Listen not only to the content of the words but also to the feeling behind the words.
2. Tell the person, in your own words, what you understand their thoughts and feelings to be.
3. Wait for the person to agree or disagree with you! Don't give advice or analysis. Allow the person time to vent his or her feelings.

Another aspect of feedback that is crucial to parallel organizations is feedback from management on written proposals made to higher levels. If management does not act promptly on such proposals and explain its actions fully to the group that initiated them, workers and lower-level managers will lose faith in the system and stop investing the kind of energy required for its success.

Architecture. The design of buildings and the layout of existing space can have a significant impact on communication. This has been recognized by firms such as Intel, which "designed its new buildings with many small conference rooms to encourage managers to get together for informal meetings" (Steers, Ungson, and Mowday, 1985, p. 379). Other firms, such as the Ford Motor Company, have experimented with "open space," where offices are separated only by partitions (Baron, 1983). The unilateral adoption of such "solutions" by management is not, however, appropriate in a joint management situation. Joint management calls for the kind of "participative design" advocated and practiced by Swedish architects Jan Ahlin (1974), Jan Åke Granath (1986), and Jan Henriksson (1983). The parallel organization can be used as a forum in which proposals are participatively developed for the design of new buildings and the utilization of old space.

Communication Problems

This section focuses on the main problems that occur in joint management systems.

Within Action and Planning Teams. Perhaps the three most serious communication problems that occur within action and planning teams are "fear of retaliation," the "nonparticipating manager," and the "short circuit." Initially, employees are almost always fearful that, if they suggest ways of doing things that are different from the status quo, the boss will take their suggestions as criticism and retaliate against them. This is an especially difficult problem, since retaliation can be so easily disguised and denied. Employees generally hold back until the manager gives some clear signal that he or she will not retaliate. This signal cannot be given, however, until an employee makes the first move. In Posada del Sol, an Arizona health care center that was adopting a parallel organization, employee representatives were at first careful to keep their real thoughts and feelings concealed. Then Irene Boyiddle, a social worker, took sharp issue with some opinions expressed by the director of nursing. After several weeks had gone by and no retaliation had been made against Boyiddle, the other employees on her action team felt safe in expressing themselves and communication in the team went from poor to excellent (Herrick and Mazany, 1982).

The second main problem, the nonparticipating manager, is mentioned briefly in the previous discussion of the role self-confidence plays in communication. The effectiveness of the parallel organization depends, in part, on the principle that everyone is equal in a team meeting. This does not mean that everyone has the same decision-making authority. The head of the primary organizational unit (the senior manager-member) is the one who has this authority. But it does mean that, in the problem-solving process, everyone's ideas should receive the same consideration and should be judged on their merit rather than according to their source. When it is put into practice, this principle can be very threatening to managers. They may be accustomed to having their opinions listened to with great respect while the opinions of others are dismissed without consideration. When everyone's ideas are given equal consideration, managers may discover that some of their subordinates have ideas that are brighter and opinions that are sounder than their own. Some managers have such high self-esteem that they are able to accept this. Others avoid the discomfort by dominating the problem-solving process. Still others use a "sit back and wait" tactic, saying little until the others have revealed their ideas. Then the manager sits in judgment of all the ideas that have been revealed and makes a decision. This is the old game of "labor proposes and management disposes" and can destroy the effectiveness of an action team. The remedy for this problem lies largely in the hands of the employees. If they earn the manager's trust in the ways outlined in the section on communication concepts (above), the manager is likely to gain in self-confidence and begin to participate in problem-solving discussions.

The third main communication problem in action and planning teams, the "short circuit," is created by both employees and managers. Both groups tend to define problems in terms of possible solutions. For example, action and planning teams often define one of their problems as "not having enough staff" rather than "being unable to get our work done." This way of defining the problem short circuits the problem-solving process. Instead of brainstorming ways to get the work done, the team that has defined its problem as not having enough staff will brainstorm ways to lever more staff out of higher-level management. Of course, this may be a possible solution to the problem. But defining the problem in this way closes the door to many other possible solutions. It is the responsibility of the team leader/facilitator to make sure that problems are not defined in terms of possible solutions.

Between and Among Action and Planning Teams. Two of the top communication problems between and among these teams are lack of feedback and poor staff work. Lower-level managers and workers often work extremely hard on their action and planning teams. They invest their time and energy and, more important, they invest their emotions. The managers take the personal risks involved in bona fide participation in the problem-solving process. The workers risk making fools of themselves in the eyes of their fellow workers for "falling for another management scam."

In these ways, both groups entrust themselves to the tender mercies of higher-level decision makers. If higher-level managers do not make prompt and fair decisions on proposals and communicate, in person, their decisions and the reasons for them to the members of the teams that developed them, these members will feel betrayed. They will then stop investing their energies in the joint management system. No matter what the other demands on their time, it makes little sense for higher-level managers to invest the resources of their organization in creating a joint management system and then let it self-destruct while they are dealing with the crises it was created to help prevent. This difficulty is minimized in an organization that has folded the parallel organization into its collective bargaining process. Managers in these organizations must deal promptly with proposals generated by the parallel organization or they will have to deal with grievances instead.

Lower-level managers and workers, for their part, frequently make it difficult for higher-level managers to consider their proposals. They create this difficulty by failing to do good staff work. In order to be acted on, a proposal must contain all the information required for a decision—along with a logical argument placing this information in context. It is sad but true that this requirement is often imperfectly understood by lower-level managers and workers. The solution to this problem is, of course, for the union and higher levels of management to provide the needed training in problem solving and proposal writing to the members of all action and planning teams.

With Constituents. The members of action and planning teams must give priority attention to establishing good two-way communication with their constituents. Representatives on action teams at the work unit level normally have no more than four to twelve constituents. Each such representative should make it an ironclad rule to carry a list of constituents in his or her pocket and to talk with each person on the list before and after every team meeting. At intermediate and higher levels, the constituents of action team representatives are generally representatives themselves and should, in turn, meet with their constituents to convey the information down the line. It is important to remember that first-line supervisors and middle managers who sit on mid- and higher-level action teams also have constituencies with whom they must communicate.

The members of planning teams have larger constituencies and, therefore, larger communications duties. A member of a higher-level planning team, for example, may have hundreds, or even thousands, of constituents. The ways these representatives communicate with their constituents vary with the circumstances. It may be by newsletter or it may be by making themselves available to their constituents at designated places during certain lunch hours. Each planning team should consider its communication responsibilities and develop innovative ways to fulfill them.

In Autonomous Work Teams. Because the members of autonomous work teams take up the slack for each other in the case of absences from work and help each other deal with larger than normal workloads, it is vital that each member be constantly aware of each other member's situation. This means that each member must, on a continuing basis, think through what each other member needs to know about his or her situation and take whatever steps are necessary to communicate the needed information. Communication within autonomous work teams is largely a matter of individual responsibility. The team leader is, of course, responsible for communicating with other units and teams and for holding periodic meetings. The communication requirements within autonomous work teams are so extensive, however, that they can be met effectively only if each member constantly assesses them and acts on his or her own initiative.

Chapter 17

Problem-Solving Skills

In the context of joint management, problem solving almost always involves planning. That is, while an action or planning team may be seeking a solution to a problem that is currently causing difficulties, the solution will probably be put in the form of a rule, policy, procedure, or program and used to prevent the problem from arising again and causing further difficulties. If a joint management system were to use extended integrative bargaining, both the rules governing the integrative bargaining (that is, problem-solving) process itself and the rules, policies, procedures, and programs it produced would be enforceable. Each role in the problem-solving process (senior manager-member, facilitator, team chair, team memory, group member, and so on) requires a specific set of skills. Further, all the members of an action or planning team should be familiar with these roles, with the problem-solving steps, and with the techniques that the team can use to successfully complete these steps. This chapter comments first on the roles played by the various parties to the problem-solving process. Then it outlines the basic problem-solving steps and describes a few problem-solving techniques. All members of action and planning and autonomous work teams should receive intensive training in problem-solving skills. This chapter can be used as a source in the development of problem-solving training materials. It should be supplemented, however, with more detailed source material on how to conduct problem-solving meetings. One book containing this kind of material is *How to Make Meetings Work* (Doyle and Straus, 1976).

Roles of the Parties

Part Four contains some general information on the roles of the various members of action, planning, and autonomous work teams. Here we are concerned with the specific roles these members play before, during, and after the actual problem-solving process.

The Senior Manager-Member. Planning teams do not, of course, have senior manager-members. Further, action teams above the worksite level do not spend a great deal of time going through the formal problem-solving steps. Instead, they review and act on proposals that reflect the problem-solving activities of planning teams and worksite-level action teams. However, for our purposes here we will regard the review of a proposal as being a problem itself and include higher-level managers in our discussion.

The worksite-level action team may solve problems with only its core members present or with all the members of the autonomous work team in attendance. This depends on the nature of the problem, the press of work, the desires of the work team members, and the number of people in the work team. Before each meeting, the senior manager-member (the leader of the autonomous work team) contributes to the agenda, makes sure each member of the work team knows what is on the agenda, and makes the necessary scheduling and space arrangements so that the meeting can be held. While problems are being defined, researched, and analyzed and while alternatives are being formulated and evaluated, the senior manager-member plays the same role as the nonmanagerial members of the team. He or she simply contributes ideas to the topics under discussion. Once the team has reached a consensus, the senior manager-member informs the rest of the team that he or she is going to change roles for a moment and then articulates the decision that has been made and makes a commitment to implement it. Before the discussion of the next agenda item begins, the senior manager-member announces a return to nonleadership status.

In general, both leaders of autonomous work teams and senior manager-members of higher-level action teams play similar roles with regard to the six other action team functions (see Chapter Thirteen). They do not run the meetings. Instead, they participate in discussions on an equal level with the other team members. When the time comes to formalize a decision, the senior manager-member announces that he or she is "putting on a different hat," states the nature of the decision as he or she understands it, makes a commitment to implement it, and returns to nonleader status. Perhaps the most important task of the senior manager-member with regard to team problem solving is to make sure that decisions get carried out promptly and vigorously. Where this does not occur, the members of the organization soon lose faith in the joint management system.

The Facilitator. The facilitator is the person who is "in charge" during the meeting and responsible for moving the group through the problem-solving process. In order to do this effectively, the facilitator must maintain a strict neutrality regarding the content of the meeting. He or she is not allowed to express opinions on the nature of the problems being considering or on how they might be solved. The facilitator's job has to do with process, not content. Some organizations maintain pools of trained facilitators. These facilitators serve action and planning teams when particularly important problems are being discussed or when a team is having a hard time solving a problem on its own. In cases like these, where facilitators do not belong to the teams they serve, there is no difficulty about remaining neutral. In most cases, however, facilitators are members of the teams they serve and are responsible for representing their constituents' views on the problems being discussed. In these cases, the facilitator—at some point in the discussion—simply asks another team member to act as facilitator while he or she presents those views. The crucial point here is that the facilitator must formally step out of the role as facilitator before expressing an opinion on content. A facilitator who fails to observe this rule will quickly lose effectiveness. Facilitators guide the problem-solving process in a number of ways.

1. They focus the attention of the team on the problem and, more specifically, on the particular problem-solving step being addressed (definition, information gathering, and so forth).
2. They "referee" the game, making sure everyone plays by the rules. For example, one of the most important rules of joint management meetings is that members must treat each other and each other's ideas with respect. If someone calls an idea "stupid" or in any other way violates this rule, the facilitator must call "foul."
3. They make sure everyone gets the chance to participate. When people know that the rules will be enforced, they tend to be more willing to participate. In addition to enforcing the rules, however, the facilitator needs to make sure all members get the "air time" they need. This means finding tactful ways to limit the time taken by long-winded and repetitious team members and encouraging the more reserved team members to contribute their opinions.
4. They keep the team moving through the problem-solving steps until a consensus decision is reached. Without a skilled facilitator, problem-solving meetings tend to degenerate into lengthy and unproductive discussions of the problem. Extended general discussions are not fruitful. Disciplined thinking is what is required.
5. They act as the "team memory" (Doyle and Straus, 1976, Chapter Seven). Using either flip chart sheets or pieces of paper taped to the wall, the facilitator writes down the key ideas and information discussed. In larger teams, it is sometimes a good idea to have someone other than the facilitator act as recorder. This makes the team memory less obtrusive. In teams of fewer than seven, however, this is usually not feasible. Since both the facilitator and the team memory functions require neutrality, separating them would result in the "loss" of two team members.

Many of the most important skills needed by facilitators involve dealing with "problem people." Each individual member of a team can prevent the team from being productive unless he or she is effectively dealt with by the facilitator. Sometimes the problem person is intentionally disruptive (for example, a team member who launches personal attacks on other members or on the facilitator). Sometimes the problem may arise mainly from the team member's own personality difficulties (like a team member who is habitually late or habitually negative or habitually whispers). Sometimes, a special situation may cause a normally constructive team member to create problems (for example, a team member who is so upset by a particular aspect of a problem that he or she cannot stop talking about it). In any event, one thing facilitators can be sure of is that they will have to deal with these kinds of problems. It is not within the scope of this book to discuss them in detail or to describe the techniques available to deal with them. It should be noted, however, that effective techniques are available (see Doyle and Straus, 1976, Chapter Six) and that the success of the facilitator rests, in large part, on the ability to use them.

The Team Member. The role of the team members, including the senior manager-member, is to address themselves to the content of the problem being solved. Unless the facilitator is clearly "off base," they should leave the process to him or her. The role of the team members is to think and to share their thoughts. First, they think about the nature of the problem. Then they think about what information is needed in order to solve it. Then they think about what possible solutions are available. Then they think about the pros and cons of each solution. Finally, they think about what solution—on balance—is the best. After doing all this thinking, they have another responsibility. They must make a determined effort to reach consensus. In all their thinking and consensus reaching, team members are guided by the "golden rule" of the representative: "Do in this meeting as your constituents would have you do." Every participation steward and every representative of first-line management, middle management, or any other workplace interest group must think not only about the technical aspects of the problem but also about the needs and desires of his or her constituents. This constant need to balance the objective and the subjective aspects of problems makes membership on an action or planning team a difficult and demanding task. However, team members can look to a number of guidelines to help them perform well at this task.

1. Above all, be respectful of others. The team cannot be productive unless its members feel secure from personal abuse of any kind.
2. Do not, under any circumstances, whisper. If someone begins to whisper to you, simply change your seat. When members whisper, the energy escapes from a team like air escaping from a leaky balloon.
3. When you have an idea, express it. Assume that your ideas will be treated with respect.
4. Do not leave meetings early. This "pulls the plug" on the group's energy and virtually ensures that the meeting will be a failure.
5. Be positive. If you are negative by nature, this is a great opportunity for personal growth. Resolve to behave positively and you may be surprised to find that your feelings become more positive too. Instead of shaking your head, making groaning noises, looking dour, "putting down" ideas, and sitting outside the team semicircle, nod your head, make approving noises, smile, find positive things to say about people's ideas, and join the team physically. This kind of behavior can pay off, both for the team and for you personally.
6. Do not interrupt, speak for others, or instruct. Be calm, let people say what they have to say in their own words, and let people discover what they want to do in their own time. In the final analysis, you will save time this way.

The Participation Steward. During meetings the participation steward plays the role of team member, always representing the interests and ideas of constituents. Once the team has reached consensus, it is the participation steward's extremely difficult and delicate task to explain the consensus to his or her constituents and gain their acceptance of the rule, policy, procedure, or program. *This is perhaps the most important step in the integrative bargaining process.* The participation steward must lay the groundwork for this crucial step by maintaining close two-way communication with constituents during the period when the solution is being developed. Before every team meeting and after every team meeting the participation steward should talk with each constituent. The participation steward should make it a point to have a list of constituents at the meeting, with a check mark beside each name (showing that the steward had touched base with each constituent before the meeting) and notes of each constituent's views on the problem being discussed.

First-Level Supervisor and Middle-Manager Representatives. In addition to playing the role of team member during meetings, these people represent their constituencies in the same way that participation stewards represent theirs. They are responsible to their boss for showing up at meetings and for participating constructively in these meetings. When it comes to the positions they take on problems, however, they are responsible only to their constituents. That is, with regard to substance their role is the same as that of the participation steward.

The Chair and Cochair. Where an action or planning team has both a chair and cochair, the cochair assists the chair as requested. The chair is responsible for facilitating the meeting. He or she may either play the role of facilitator or arrange for someone else to play this role. Between meetings, the chair is responsible for preparing an agenda (in consultation with the team members), for scheduling meetings, for following up on any team business that came up at the last meeting, and for taking care of any team business that comes up between meetings. It should be emphasized here that, once consensus has been reached on a rule, policy, procedure, or program, it is no longer team business. It is then the task of the senior manager-member to implement it. It continues to be team business only in the sense that the other members of the team monitor the status of its implementation for their constituents. This is normally done by scheduling an "implementation status report" as the first item on an action team's agenda.

The Steps Used to Solve Problems

There are many ways to organize and label the problem-solving process. The important thing is not that it be organized and labeled in any specific way, but simply that it be organized and labeled. Action and planning teams need to know where they are in the problem-solving process in order to achieve the necessary focus. This means that some sequence of steps must be agreed upon and that these steps should have names and definitions. Without this sequence of steps, the facilitator would find it almost impossible to channel the energy of the team so as to reach a solution. One possible sequence of steps is described below. This sequence has six steps and culminates in consensus on a solution or course of action. After consensus is reached, it is the task of the senior manager-member to translate the decision into instructions to subordinates and to make sure these instructions are carried out. The participation stewards and combined-function union officers, of course, are responsible to their constituencies for monitoring the implementation of decisions and calling any difficulties to the attention of the senior manager-member. The six steps listed below cannot be followed in strict sequence. There is a good deal of "back and forth" required. For example, a team might find that it cannot fully analyze a problem until it has gone out and gathered additional information. It might even find that it cannot even define the problem on the basis of information already known to team members. Certainly, problem definitions often change as more information is gathered. Nevertheless, it is important that all team members, at any given time, focus their efforts on the same step of the process.

Step 1, Defining the Problem. The team should make a "first cut" at defining the problem. The facilitator might ask each team member to give his or her constituency's perception of the problem. This should lead to a team consensus on a working definition. As the team progresses through the five remaining steps of the process, the working definition may change. Problem definition is a key step and deserves a great deal of time and attention. A poor problem definition (for example, one that defines the problem in terms of a possible solution, such as "we need more staff") can lead to weeks, or even months, of wheel spinning and fruitless discussion.

Step 2, Analyzing the Problem. To analyze a problem is simply to break it down into its component parts. The old saying "No matter how you slice it, it's still bologna" does not apply to problem solving. It makes a great deal of difference how a problem is sliced. A good general rule is that problems should be broken down along lines that reflect their most salient features. For example, suppose we are members of a planning team that learns that its primary organization has received an unusually large number of grievances during the past quarter. We have tentatively defined the problem in terms of poor supervision. Now we need to test our definition with some analysis. Our first analytical step would probably be to divide the grievances by subunit of the primary organization. We might find that most of them come from the same subunit. This might lead us to redefine the problem as "poor supervision in subunit A." Now we can divide the problem into its component parts in a different way: we can classify the grievances according to content. If that fails to shed any light on the matter, we can classify them by demographics (the griever's race, sex, age, and so on). If, for example, subunit A is only one-half female but all of the grievances are from women, we might be led to a problem definition that includes possible sex discrimination.

Different problems need to be "sliced" or broken down in different ways. If we were analyzing a problem involving the tardy payment of claims, for example, we would probably break it down by learning how many days it takes to accomplish each step of the claims process even before we broke it down according to the type of claim involved. The point is that we cannot understand a problem until we have broken it down into its parts.

Step 3, Gathering Information. Of course, simply breaking a problem down into its parts does not enable us to understand it. We must then gather information that tells us something about the nature of each part. In a sense, problem analysis can be viewed as deciding what kinds of information are needed. Then we go out and gather the information (for example, find out how many of the grievances have been filed by women). While information gathering could be viewed as part of the problem-analysis step, we have chosen to look at it as a separate step for a practical reason: perhaps the most common sin committed by action and planning teams is their failure to do the hard work of going out between meetings and gathering information. This leads to a very destructive and embarrassing situation. The action team that is authorized to act on the proposal submitted to resolve the problem finds it cannot do so. It does not have the required information. Of course, this sin is not the sole property of groups in joint management. It is called incomplete staff work and is a problem throughout business, the military, and government. The reason is that to do complete staff work requires hard thinking and a great deal of energy and determination. The temptation is always to say, "Hey, we know what the problem (solution) is. It should be obvious to anyone with half a brain. We don't need any more facts." Unfortunately, problems and solutions are rarely obvious.

Step 4, Developing Alternatives. All team members should—during the first four steps of problem solving—try to keep their minds open to a wide range of alternative solutions. If a conscious effort is not made in this direction, there is a natural tendency for people to take hard and fast positions in favor of a particular alternative early in the problem-solving process. This can lead to undesirable outcomes. If all team members take an early position in favor of the same alternative, the team is unlikely to consider new and innovative possibilities. Neither is it likely to put in the effort required to produce completed staff work. This is the dreaded "groupthink" phenomenon. If, on the other hand, the team members take early positions in favor of different alternatives, the prospect for consensus is diminished. It is useful to record alternatives on the "team memory" early in the problem-solving process, but the facilitator should establish a ground rule preventing team members from defending or attacking any alternative until the team agrees that enough work has been done on the first four steps to make it desirable to enter Step 5.

One way to begin Step 4 is for the facilitator/recorder to recapture from the team memory all the alternatives that were stored there during the first three steps. Then the team can brainstorm additional alternatives. The rules of brainstorming, of course, prohibit the discussion or evaluation of alternatives. Only after all team members have exhausted their supplies of alternatives does the facilitator allow the problem-solving process to move to Step 5.

Step 5, Evaluating Alternatives. Just as a problem-solving team can move back and forth among Steps 1 through 4 without ill effects, so can a problem-solving team move back and forth between evaluating alternatives and reaching a consensus. However, if Step 5 is successfully completed, a solid basis for consensus will probably have evolved. It is a good idea to start Step 5 by discussing what constitutes a good solution. This gives the team a set of criteria against which each alternative can be evaluated. By agreeing to such a set of criteria before it begins to sort through the alternatives, the team smooths the way for an eventual consensus. If people begin to evaluate alternatives before they know what they are measuring them against, they are likely to take positions on the basis of the criterion that is most important to their constituencies and stick to it without giving any weight at all to other critiera. Of course, political acceptability is an important criterion. It is not the only one, however, and people are less likely to treat it as though it were if they have thought through all the criteria before they begin making judgments about the alternatives. Step 5 usually begins by shortening the long list of alternatives produced during Step 4 to a manageable length. This is done more through combining and synthesizing alternatives than through eliminating them. The most far-out and unlikely alternative may inspire an idea that adds significantly to the value of a more conventional solution. The shortened list should contain a manageable number of true alternatives, each of which represents a different approach to solving the problem. The first task of the team during the evaluation step is to discuss each alternative on the long list produced in Step 4 in a positive way and to find a means of saving any virtue it may possess. This may be done by selecting it as a true alternative or by adding some of its features to a core alternative. The second task is to produce a list of true alternatives. Since an alternative is a choice between two or more possibilities, this means that the list must offer the decision maker a real choice.

This insistence on producing a list of true alternatives may seem to interfere with laying the foundation for consensus. The temptation is to find a solution that is acceptable to everyone and to go with it. That is, a political solution is constructed without any real consideration of the choices that exist. This is far more likely to occur in joint management, where the context is political and the basic thrust is toward reconciliation, than it is in a traditional situation, where the context is less political and the main thrust is toward producing a technically sound solution. For this reason, facilitators and senior manager-members should take joint responsibility for ensuring that the group searches for true alternatives and avoids straw alternatives (alternatives that are clearly unfeasible, but that are presented to give an illusion of choice). When the proposed solution must be presented to a higher-level action team, there is an even more pressing need to develop true alternatives. The higher-level team will not have gone through the emotional process that produced consensus in the team that developed the solution. It will give some weight to the fact that a consensus has been reached, but will also ask itself, "Might a consensus also have been reached on an alternative solution?" It is far better to have considered all the true alternatives and to have rejected them on rational grounds than to have a higher-level action team reject a proposed solution because the proposal fails to consider such-and-such an alternative.

Step 6, Reaching Consensus. If the first five steps have been skillfully performed by all the members of a team and if the political situation is favorable, there may be no need for Step 6. Consensus will already have been reached. However, this is often not the case. One or all of the parties to the process (the facilitator, the senior manager-member, and the other members) may have failed to carry out their responsibilities or violated the rules governing their behavior. It may even be that the parties have all performed admirably, but the nature of the problem has prevented a consensus from evolving. Where the alternatives have been evaluated and the parties are at odds about the one to be selected, the facilitator can use a number of techniques in attempting to reach consensus. One such technique consists of these three steps.

1. *Conduct a negative vote.* Team members are asked to vote against those alternatives with which their constituencies "cannot live." If any alternatives remain, they are modified and reevaluated. It is likely that a consensus will emerge around one of them.

2. *Go back to the hustings.* If a consensus does not emerge, the team agrees on a statement describing both the issues that stand in the way of consensus and the unsuccessful proposals that have been made to break the impasse. The members then use this statement as the basis for obtaining their constituents' ideas on how to achieve consensus.

3. *Consider new possibilities.* At the next meeting, each member presents at least three ideas for reaching consensus that he or she gathered from his or her constituents. The facilitator, who will have established a ground rule prohibiting negative comments on the ideas until he or she has reacted to them, then suggests ways in which the team can use the constituent ideas to achieve consensus.

An essential point to keep in mind when trying to reach consensus is that, except in the case of an autonomous work team, all members of the team must satisfy not only themselves but their constituencies. It does no good at all for members to reach a consensus that will not be accepted by their constituencies. Therefore, when a team thinks it has a consensus, whether this point occurs in Step 5 or Step 6, each member must consider: "How is this going to play in Peoria?" This question should be answered not by speculation but by an active inquiry. Of course, the members of the team will have been in constant two-way communication with their constituents during each step of the problem-solving process. It may be that the required inquiry will have already been accomplished when consensus is reached within the team. In any event, problem-solving teams in jointly managed organizations must keep in mind the fact that they must create two kinds of agreement: consensus within the team and acceptance among the team's constituencies.

It is sometimes possible to find a consensus solution (one that will be agreed to and actively supported by everyone involved) when the people involved are the seven to fifteen or so members of a cohesive autonomous work team. It is rarely possible to find such a solution at the next higher level in the organization, where there may be thirty-five to fifty or more individuals involved. It is almost inevitable that some of these individuals are going to be dissatisfied with any solution, however finely crafted it may be. The object at higher levels is to develop a solution that is politically acceptable. It is unrealistic to expect true consensus.

Techniques

There are myriad techniques for use by problem-solving teams. Some of these techniques, such as brainstorming and negative voting, have been mentioned above. There are many others (the fishbone diagram, the Pareto diagram, force field analysis, and so on), each of which is extremely helpful in dealing with a particular kind of problem. Jointly managed organizations should make sure that the people who are facilitating their action and planning teams are trained in the use of these techniques.

Assignment of Roles

It is generally not a good idea to allow the senior manager-member to also assume a chair or cochair role on action teams. It does often work well to combine the facilitator/team memory role and assign it to the team chair or one of the cochairs.

Problems with Problem Solving

Perhaps the two most common difficulties that arise in problem solving involve acceptance and implementation. Difficulties with acceptance arise when members of teams fail to maintain constant two-way communication with their constituents. This failure sometimes causes constituents to reject the solutions their representatives produce. Difficulties with implementation arise when senior manager-members fail to follow up to ensure that their commitments to the team are translated into prompt and effective action. It is not that senior manager-members fail to see the desirability of following up. It is more that they fail to fully understand its importance. Organization members will lose faith in a joint management system if it does not produce results. When they lose faith, they are likely to stop devoting the time and energy to the system that it needs. Where the joint management system consists of a parallel organization folded into the collective bargaining process, senior manager-members are far more likely to understand the importance of promptly and effectively implementing team solutions.

Perhaps the most common problem with the process itself is the tendency of teams to resist the discipline of focusing on one step at a time. It is not unusual for meetings to deteriorate into aimless and unproductive discussions. Another necessary step that is often resisted by problem-solving teams is the gathering of information. Teams will sometimes be willing to agree to a solution but unwilling to do the legwork necessary to determine whether the solution is reasonable and workable. Another, related problem is the tendency of some teams to jump to conclusions. They define the problem in terms of one possible solution (for example, "We need more staff!") and resist discussing it from any other viewpoint. The most effective answer to these problems is training, training, and more training. Everyone should receive training in the basic roles and steps of problem solving. Facilitators should receive more intensive training in the skills and techniques that are needed to guide teams through the problem-solving process.

Chapter 18

Proposal-Writing Skills

Proficiency in writing proposals is perhaps the scarcest of the skills required by joint management. It is certainly the most difficult to teach or to learn. Yet, without this skill, the full potential of the parallel organization cannot be realized. It is not necessary to write a proposal in order to change a rule, policy, or procedure at the work-site level. However, many of the rules, policies, procedures, and programs that make up the administrative subsystems of the organization cannot be changed at the worksite level. They must be decided at the intermediate, operating, or executive levels. Most often, they are decided on the basis of proposals developed by planning teams and submitted to action teams. Further, the initial conversion of a production subsystem (work unit) to an autonomous work team involves a large number of interrelated changes. These changes often need to be submitted to higher levels for approval and always need to be recorded. In addition, a parallel organization should modify the administrative and production subsystems of the organization (for example, promotion policies, performance evaluation criteria, and organization of the work unit) so that they are consistent with its principles and practices. Then it should continually review and revise these subsystems in order to adapt them to changes in the organization and in its environment. A strength of the parallel organization is this ability to continually reconcile the views of the organization's workplace interest groups and continually adjust its administrative and production subsystems so that they are in harmony with these reconciled views. Only a portion of this strength (the portion that concerns minor adjustments in production subsystems) can be exerted without the use of the written proposal. This chapter discusses the purpose of proposals, their characteristics, the roles team members play with regard to them, and the procedures and problems often associated with them.

The Purpose of the Proposal

From the point of view of the action team that reviews the proposal, its purpose is to provide the facts and the logic that the members of the team need in order to reach consensus on a given course of action. From the point of view of the planning team (or, in some cases, the lower-level action team) that prepares the proposal, its purpose is to persuade the higher-level action team to agree with the course of action proposed. Written proposals are necessary when the solution to a problem must be approved at a higher level. Written proposals are necessary whether the parallel organization is used to create unenforceable rules, policies, procedures, and programs, or whether it has been folded into the collective bargaining process. When problems and solutions are complex, written proposals can help people fully understand the matters on which they are trying to reach consensus.

Characteristics of Written Proposals

This section describes the characteristics of proposals in terms of the classic questions: What? Why? When? and Who?

What Is a Proposal? A proposal is a written record of the problem-solving process. It normally contains six sections, one for each of the six problem-solving steps. For example, a proposal starts with a section defining the problem. This section usually includes a brief statement of the problem and a somewhat longer explanation of why the team chose to define the problem in the way it did. The next section contains all the information needed by the action team reviewing the proposal in order to understand the problem and evaluate the proposed solution. The third section analyzes the problem. It breaks the problem down into its component parts and relates the information contained in the second section to these component parts. The fourth section lists the "true" or feasible alternatives and gives the reasons for selecting them. These reasons generally explain the sense in which each alternative is, in fact, feasible. This section does not correspond exactly to Step 4, since Step 4 of the problem-solving process consists of listing all conceivable alternatives, whether they are feasible or not. Section 5 of the proposal evaluates the true alternatives. It presents the criteria against which the alternatives are being assessed and discusses each alternative in the light of each criterion. Section 6 recommends a solution.

Often, the most important part of a proposal is not included in these six sections. It is attached to the proposal proper and consists of the papers needed to translate the recommended solution into reality. A good general rule for proposal writers is this: after the action team to which the proposal is submitted has reached consensus on it, the senior manager-member should be able to implement the proposal simply by signing it. For example, if the recommended solution is to change a given set of personnel procedures, the proposal writers should identify the paragraphs of the organization's personnel manual that need to be rewritten, rewrite them, and attach the rewritten paragraphs to their proposal. In addition, the proposal should include a memorandum for the signature of the senior manager-member transmitting the revised paragraphs to the personnel officer with instructions to issue them by a given date.

Sometimes, of course, it is not feasible for the planning team to develop its solution to this point. However, it is always feasible for this team to decide exactly what action it wishes the senior manager-member of the action team to take. It then carries its own work to the point where that action can be taken by one stroke of the senior manager-member's pen. For example, a planning or lower-level action team may decide that it is not in a position to rewrite the relevant paragraphs of the personnel manual itself. Instead, it wants the personnel office to rewrite them and the senior manager-member of the action team to send them to the planning team for review. The principle remains the same. In this case, the planning team writes a memorandum for the senior manager member's signature, instructing the personnel office to rewrite the paragraphs. The action it desires can then be taken with one stroke of the senior manager's pen.

In general, the proposals of planning teams are far more complete than those submitted by lower-level action teams. That is, planning team proposals tend to "include the rewritten paragraphs of the personnel manual" while proposals from lower-level action teams tend to recommend that a top manager instruct someone else (often the planning team at his or her level) to rewrite the paragraphs. Indeed, lower-level action teams rarely possess enough information about organizationwide problems even to recommend that paragraphs be rewritten. Usually, they are in a position where they can only recommend that the senior manager-member instruct the planning team at his or her level to look into a problem. Occasionally, however, lower-level action teams want actions taken that affect only their primary organizational unit, but that their senior manager-member is not authorized to take (for example, purchase of a certain piece of equipment). In these cases they submit complete proposals containing all the information required to refer the problem to the manager at the next higher level.

Why Write a Proposal? There are two main reasons for writing proposals. First, where the person who must make the decision has not participated in the problem-solving process, some way must be found to communicate the results of that process to him or her before a decision can be made. The relevant facts and the logic of the process can best be communicated by a well-written proposal. Of course, the emotional component of the process cannot be effectively communicated in writing. The team that developed the proposal should back it up with a brief oral presentation in order to give the action team concerned an idea of the emotional energy that attaches to it. The second reason for writing proposals is that the process of writing and reviewing them serves both to stimulate the team's thinking and to keep it on track. It stimulates the team's thinking by clarifying ideas and inspiring reactions to them. Upon reviewing a draft proposal, team members will often say, "Hey, just a minute! I didn't think we'd agreed to anything like this. But it does give me an idea of something we could do." Sometimes very bad ideas can be presented orally by articulate and persuasive people in a way that convinces other people of their value. When reduced to writing, these same ideas are found to be empty and lacking in merit. Thus the written proposal is a means of quality control.

When Should a Proposal Be Written? Almost without exception, any solution, rule, policy, procedure, or plan developed by a planning team should be put in the form of a proposal or attached to a proposal. The level at which the planning team operates and the fact that it does not include the decision maker among its members makes this necessary. Two situations call for proposals to be written by action teams. The first arises when an action team is dealing with a problem that affects units of the primary organization in addition to its own. In this situation, the proposal should be that the action or planning team at the appropriate level should make an effort to solve the problem. For example, if a problem affects all the subunits of a department but does not affect any other departments, it should be dealt with at the departmental level. If it affects other departments, it should be dealt with at the next higher level above the department. If an action or planning team attempts to deal with a problem that affects other organizational units at the same level, it violates the principle of wholeness: all the affected parties are not involved in the problem-solving process. The second situation arises when an action team is dealing with a problem that affects only its own primary organizational unit but cannot be resolved by the senior manager-member. For example, an action team may decide that the most cost-effective way to solve a production problem is to buy a certain piece of equipment. However, the senior manager-member is authorized to approve equipment purchases only up to $1,000 and the needed equipment costs $1,500. In such cases, proposals are usually written and submitted to the next higher level of the primary organization.

Who Writes the Proposal? Proposal writing is, as a general rule, a one-person job. To require two or more people to collaborate on a proposal is to add an unnecessary step to the process. The unneccessary step arises out of the fact that the two or more people will need to reconcile their views on how the proposal should be worded and written before they can produce a draft. This step is unnecessary because the entire team's views on these matters will subsequently need to be reconciled in a team meeting. One person, working alone, can probably draft the proposal more quickly. The "one-person drafter" approach is also more democratic in that it gives the nondrafting members of the group more control over the content. If two or three people have been involved in drafting a proposal and have reconciled their own differences regarding it, they are likely to—in effect—form a natural coalition to resist any changes desired by other team members.

There are also practical reasons for making proposal writing a one-person job. First, it is unlikely that any team of five to seven people will include more than one member who has the talent and writing skills to draft a good proposal. The work of this person would only be slowed down and made more difficult if he or she were required to work with another, less skilled writer. This does not preclude giving everyone the opportunity to develop writing skills. Team members wishing to do so can volunteer to assist the team's proposal writer by doing legwork and research in return for the chance to improve their writing skills. It should be made clear, however, that these volunteers are acting as apprentices rather than as collaborators in the writing process. A second reason for not making a collaborative effort out of proposal writing is that the task is not easily fragmented. For example, dividing the task by asking one person to write three sections of the proposal and another person to write the remaining three sections generally results in an uncoordinated and inconsistent proposal. Since the six sections are closely interrelated and proceed from the same assumptions, they are best drafted by a single person. If a team contains two people who are skilled in proposal writing there is, of course, no objection to their working separately on different proposals.

Roles of Team Members in Proposal Writing

If possible, different people should play the roles of team facilitator and team proposal writer. The reason is that, when a proposal is being reviewed by the team, the proposal writer must explain and defend it. He or she cannot do this and still remain neutral regarding content. Yet remaining neutral regarding content is exactly what the facilitator must do. Therefore, while the facilitator may, on occasion, write a proposal, someone else should act as facilitator when it is being reviewed. It is also true that the proposal writer occupies a position of power. He or she interprets the oral agreements reached by the team and finds ways to resolve any flaws in the team's logic. This suggests the desirability of separating the role of proposal writer from other roles that wield power (like the facilitator and the senior manager-member).

Do's and Don'ts of Proposal Writing

As the six sections of a proposal are written, the proposal writer might profitably consider the following rules, which I have adapted from a training program developed by Pima County, Arizona (Pima County, 1984). These rules can also serve as criteria against which the originating group can evaluate its proposals before submitting them for approval and action.

1. *Don't* state the problem in terms of symptoms or solutions. Try to get to its heart. For example, it is often more fruitful to regard absenteeism as a symptom than as a problem. Identify the underlying problem that is causing the absenteeism and use it as the basis for the proposal. A possible solution that is often described as "the problem" is "We need more staff!" Instead of defining the problem in this way, identify the problems that have led you to believe that more staff members are needed.
2. *Do* describe the context and history of the problem. When did it start? Who is affected? Where does it occur? Why is it being given priority? Give the action team that is being asked to approve your solution a feel for the problem.
3. *Don't* give the approving action team any reason to say, "How can we tell whether or not we think this should be approved? The proposal doesn't contain all the relevant facts." This is called incomplete staff work. The proposal should be complete in itself. The approving action team should not be expected to

gather information. Don't assume it knows anything about the problem.

4. *Do* include information about people's feelings. For example, if a survey shows that 90 percent of the employees involved consider this to be their number one problem, and if 95 percent agree with the proposed solution, this information is highly relevant and should be included.

5. *Do* break the problem down into its component parts. This is not easy to do, but it pays large dividends. Make it a rule to start a sentence, "The component parts of the problem are" and then apply yourself to identifying the breakdown that was most useful to your group in solving the problem.

6. *Don't* leave out any viable alternatives and don't include any "straw men." It is unpleasant to have a proposal returned to your group with the question "Why did you not consider such-and-such an alternative?" especially if there is no good reason for not having done so.

7. *Do* relate your solution to your analysis of the problem. Your analysis should lead, in an orderly and logical way, to your solution.

8. *Do* include all the implementing papers that the senior manager-member of the approving action team will need to make your proposed solution happen. If a manual section is needed, make sure you have drafted it and attached it to your proposal. If the budget officer is the logical person to implement your solution, make sure your proposal includes a memorandum instructing him or her to do so. In addition, make sure these instructions include deadlines and reporting requirements.

9. *Don't* assume that your proposal will work. Include some built-in means of evaluating its results. For example, if the budget officer is the person who will be implementing it, your memorandum might require that he or she provide the senior manager-member of the action team a report evaluating the proposal after it has been in operation for six months.

Problems with Proposals

Inadequate written proposals are common in joint management systems and constitute one of their more serious problems.

The problem of inadequate proposals springs from two causes: (1) the raw material needed to write the proposal is often lacking, and (2) the members of the planning or action team are often lacking in proposal-writing skills. The first cause is discussed in Chapter Seventeen. It is difficult to write an adequate proposal based on an inadequate job of problem solving. However, it is not difficult to train facilitators, team members, and senior manager-members so that they are able to do an adequate jot of problem solving. It is only necessary to devote sufficient time and resources to their training. Thus, the second cause, the scarcity of skilled proposal writers, is the major problem that faces most organizations when it comes to translating their problem-solving activity into action. It is hard to maintain a sufficient number of people who are adequately trained and motivated to take on the difficult job of writing proposals. First, let us consider what constitutes a sufficient number. While a few proposals are written by lower-level action teams in the normal course of business, most are written either by planning miniteams or by worksite-level action teams engaged in the conversion from work unit to autonomous work team. Since a planning miniteam at the operating level services 50 to 150 employees and a similar miniteam at the executive level may service 1,000 or more people, the task—as it applies to planning teams—involves providing about a dozen proposal writers for every 1,000 employees. As it applies to worksite-level action teams, the task is to get about fifty to seventy-five conversion proposals (proposals to convert from work unit to autonomous work team) written and to provide for the writing of an occasional miscellaneous proposal by a lower-level action team.

In accomplishing these tasks, the following considerations should be kept in mind:

1. There are disadvantages to having the senior manager-member of an action team serve as its proposal writer (planning teams do not have senior manager-members).
2. There are disadvantages to having facilitators act as proposal writers.
3. Any time a nonmember serves as a proposal writer, the team has surrendered a portion of its power.
4. Proposal writing is hard work. The problem is not only find-

ing and developing writing skills, it is also giving people the incentive to use these skills.

This analysis leads us to several possible ideas for improving the quality of the proposals produced by a joint management system: providing recognition, providing financial rewards, creating a proposal-writing pool, and establishing a training program for proposal writers.

Recognition. An annual set of "golden pen" awards might be established. Each operating-level unit could make such an award, and all winners of operating-level awards could be considered for the executive-level "golden pen." The golden pen awards might or might not carry cash awards with them.

Compensation. Writing conversion proposals is a one-time job. Miscellaneous proposals by action teams are also rare. However, writing the proposals for a planning subteam might take fifteen to thirty hours a month. Since some of this time is likely to to be off the clock and all of it is likely to be spent above the writer's normal pay classification, a quarterly honorarium would not be amiss. Even a small sum such as $50 a quarter would be significant in terms of recognizing the function.

A Proposal-Writers' Pool. We have noted that to use a proposal writer who is not a member of the team has its dangers. In addition, it should certainly be possible in most cases to assign the members of a planning team to their miniteams so as to provide each miniteam a member who has the potential to become a skilled proposal writer. Nevertheless, it might be desirable and feasible to maintain a pool of skilled proposal writers to help lower-level action teams write an especially difficult proposal (for example, proposals converting work units to autonomous work teams).

Training. In an organization with 5,000 members, perhaps 25 to 35 people would need to be trained in proposal writing each year. The exact number would depend on such factors as the terms of office of planning team members and whether or not the organization maintains a proposal-writers' pool. The 25 to 35 people would receive at least ten hours of training in what higher-level action teams look for in proposals and how their needs can be satisfied. In addition, they could be reimbursed their tuition for any courses on writing they wished to take at local colleges or universities. However, people vary widely in the writing skills they already possess. The action teams that make decisions on who should receive this training should select people who have the potential to become highly skilled in a short period of time.

Part VI

⟞⟝⟞

Creating Equity and Incentives

Some of the greatest difficulties and opportunities presented by joint management lie in the area of economic rewards. One such difficulty/ opportunity lies in the fact that traditional compensation and award systems often promote competition and discourage cooperation. This interferes with the functioning of parallel organizations and autonomous work teams, since they need cooperative behavior in order to work well. Another difficulty/opportunity arises from the fact that, in joint management systems, rank-and-file employees perform management functions. Since management functions are generally more highly compensated than the other tasks performed by these employees, their compensation must be increased if equitable pay structures are to be maintained. Put another way, a joint management system tends to spread highly paid management functions more evenly among the members of an organization. In order to maintain compensation equity, pay must also be spread more evenly. Still another difficulty/opportunity lies in the tendency of joint management systems to increase productivity. This raises the question of how the economic benefits from this increased productivity should be distributed among labor, management, and stockholders.

Chapter Nineteen discusses some of the implications of joint management for wages, salaries, and economic awards. Chapter

Twenty describes several approaches to productivity gain sharing. These approaches can be used both to narrow the gap between managerial and nonmanagerial compensation and to distribute the benefits from increased productivity. Chapter Twenty-One suggests a more basic solution to the difficulties raised by both the redistribution of management functions and the tendency of joint management to result in productivity increases: the transfer of ownership to the members of the organization. It is important to note that the parallel organization is well fitted to develop compensation systems, productivity gain-sharing plans, and plans for transferring ownership to the members of the organization. These difficulties/opportunities can often be solved in ways that benefit both parties. Where the actual division of a finite amount of money is involved, distributive bargaining is appropriate. Where the problem is to develop a plan or system for distributing money, integrative bargaining works well.

Chapter 19

~~~~~~~~~~

Job and Performance
Evaluation Systems

Job evaluation, performance evaluation, and awards systems can be either serious obstacles or strong supports to the effectiveness of parallel organizations and autonomous work teams. Whether they are obstacles or supports depends on the processes used to design them and on their nature.

As a general rule, traditional job evaluation, performance evaluation, and awards systems are designed by staff specialists. Normally, they reward competitive behavior by organization members. They do not usually provide extra compensation for low-paid employees when they engage in management activities such as problem solving. These systems work well in organizations where the thinking function is assigned to one group of employees (management) and the acting function to another (labor). They do not work as well in organizations where workers are heavily involved in thinking as well as in doing.

Jointly managed organizations work best when everyone is involved in designing the compensation systems and when these systems reward cooperative behavior and problem-solving activities. Therefore, the conversion of existing organizations to joint management usually necessitates major changes in their compensation systems and in the processes used to design these systems. This chapter deals with some of the built-in conflicts that are often found between joint management practices and traditional job evaluation, performance evaluation, and awards systems. It also discusses ways in which integrative bargaining and the parallel organization can be used to reconcile these conflicts.

It is important to keep in mind, while reading this chapter and Chapters Twenty to Twenty-One, that the conflicts between traditional compensation systems and joint management arise from three major sources: the inequity created by the performance of higher-paid tasks by lower-paid employees, the need to equitably distribute any productivity gains realized by the joint systems, and the changed behaviors that are necessary to the functioning of joint management systems. It is not enough to remove the features of traditional compensation systems that discourage individual growth and cooperative behavior; alternative features need to be developed to positively reinforce the cooperative behaviors needed by joint management.

Job Evaluation

Most organizations seek to establish fair rates of pay for their jobs in two ways. First, they try to pay rates that are competitive with those paid for comparable jobs by other employers in the labor market area. Second, they try to set a rate for each job that reflects its worth to the organization. This second step is usually accomplished using criteria similar to those established by the War Labor Board during World War II: responsibility, required skill, required effort, and working conditions (Wallace and Fay, 1983). It produces a hierarchy or hierarchies of jobs arranged and paid according to the extent to which they meet these criteria.

The establishment of a parallel organization or autonomous work teams increases and rearranges the skills and levels of effort needed by many nonsupervisory employees. It also changes the nature of the skills and kinds of effort required of management positions. These changes raise a number of difficulties. The specific criteria used in job evaluation and the procedures for applying these criteria are often inappropriate for evaluating jobs after they are changed by joint management practices. Further, the development and application of new criteria are major undertakings and pose a threat to middle and lower-level managers. First, we will discuss some of the ways in which changes in job skills and levels of effort under joint management can make the specific criteria and procedures used in traditional job evaluation systems inappropriate. Then we will discuss the difficulties involved in changing these criteria and procedures.

Changes in Skills and Levels of Effort. Some of the major characteristics of jointly managed organizations that tend to change the job skills and levels of effort required of their members are rejection of the strict division-of-labor principle, reliance on the discretion of the worker, emphasis on team activity, tendency to seek flexibility, and the notion of the supervisor as facilitator and teacher.

I have already mentioned the fourth principle of scientific management: that the thinking and doing functions should be separate (Taylor, 1911). The fourth principle of joint management, on the other hand, combines these functions. Job evaluation plans have little difficulty with organizations that concentrate thinking in one set of jobs and doing in another. They simply instruct their compensation analysts to classify a job at the level of its "highest" task, as long as the job requires a substantial percentage of time to be spent at this task. In a jointly managed organization, many rank-and-file employees spend some—but not a substantial portion—of their time developing policies, procedures, and work methods. Few job evaluation schemes are equipped to take account of the fact that rank-and-file employees are now performing this high-level function. The matter has been dealt with in most jointly managed organizations, for the time being at any rate, by failing to compensate this high-level function on the grounds that it is being performed voluntarily.

Members of autonomous work teams often make minute-to-minute and hour-to-hour decisions that, in traditional organizations, would be made by their immediate supervisors. Job evaluation procedures that have been written to give credit for these decisions only to supervisory positions are inappropriate for evaluating jobs in autonomous work teams.

Both autonomous work teams and the parallel organization

depend heavily on team approaches to both problem solving and "nuts and bolts" work. Traditional job evaluation criteria, on the other hand, assume that each task is the sole property of a single job. They also tend to assume that the credit for making most decisions should go to supervisory positions. In joint management, while managers may make the final decisions in action and planning teams, rank-and-file employees participate in laying the groundwork for these decisions. As Jones (1983, p. 24) comments in describing joint management in the Canadian Federal Public Service, "the senior employee is credited with making the decision regardless of any actual contribution [by rank-and-file employees]."

In order to increase its ability to adapt to changing conditions, the jointly managed organization often trains its members to perform a variety of tasks requiring a variety of skills. Employees are encouraged to learn as many relevant skills as they can and are paid, not according to the work they usually do, but according to the number of skills they have mastered. This allows the organization to adapt easily to fluctuations in the availability of raw materials and in the demand for finished products or services. It also introduces a criterion that cannot be handled by most job evaluation systems, which are designed to measure the performance of tasks rather than the possession of skills. While "pay for skill" compensation systems can be mutually beneficial to labor and management where their specific features have been integratively bargained, they can also reduce labor's power by making it extremely difficult to organize a job action aimed at withholding a specific skill or group of skills.

Job evaluation systems often evaluate supervisors according to the kinds of decisions they make. Under joint management, supervisors tend to delegate many more operating decisions to their subordinates and to spend their own time making sure that their subordinates have the necessary tools and resources, providing training and advice, and handling relationships with other units of the organization. Therefore, job evaluation systems need to be revised to reward this kind of facilitative supervision.

Difficulty of Changing Job Evaluation Practices. The first difficulty lies in the simple magnitude of the task. Job evaluation criteria and procedures are, for the most part, included in the labor contract. Those procedures that are not in the contract are often included in official management documents. Thus, the revision of job evaluation policies and procedures requires a major joint effort by labor and management.

The second difficulty lies in the complexity and sensitivity of the questions to be decided. For example, is the facilitative supervision described above to be regarded as more or less valuable to the organization than the controlling supervision it replaces? Are all rank-and-file employees involved in autonomous work teams or in the parallel organization to be given pay raises? These questions lead to other sensitive issues. For example, does a jointly managed organization require as many facilitative supervisors as a traditionally managed organization requires controlling supervisors?

It is crucial, however, to overcome these difficulties. Organizations that attempt to combine the practices of joint management with the job evaluation systems of traditional management find themselves building parallel organizations and autonomous work teams with one hand and tearing them down with the other. Since job evaluation systems in unionized organizations are, for the most part, the product of collective bargaining, it might be constructive for unions to take the initiative in adapting them to joint management practices.

Performance Evaluation

The first section of this chapter addresses the problems that arise when traditional ways of linking compensation to *tasks performed* are applied in nontraditional joint management systems. This section discusses the problems that arise when traditional ways of linking compensation and promotion to the *quality of performance* are applied in these systems.

Compensation. Since pay is most commonly linked to performance at the individual level, and since Chapters Twenty and Twenty-One describe performance-based pay systems at the group and organizational levels, this section is limited to the issue of performance-based pay for individuals. That is, we will talk here about the practice of distinguishing among different people doing similar work by compensating them at different levels.

These distinctions are most commonly made either on the basis of the subjective opinion of the supervisor or on the basis of some objective measurement of work accomplished. Systems of the former type are generally termed "merit pay," while systems of the latter type are called "piecework."

Distinctions in pay among individuals doing the same work, as Lawler (1981) notes, work best in large organizations where jobs are simple and do not affect one another, where supervisors are trusted, where there are good measures of work quality at the individual level, and where there is no union. An example of such an organization might be a large group of salespersons working alone in separate and distinct geographical areas and selling an uncomplicated product under trustworthy supervisors. Unfortunately, while such organizations are rare, merit pay systems are not.

However, it is not my purpose here to discuss the advantages and disadvantages of merit pay in general, but rather to deal with its specific impact on joint management systems. Since joint management systems, by definition, occur only in unionized organizations, I will briefly comment on Lawler's "where there is no union" criterion. A prime reason for labor's opposition to merit pay (and piecework) systems is that the organizational health of a union rests upon its members' acceptance of common goals and upon their performance of mutually supportive actions. Unions see merit pay as promoting individual goals and the performance of competitive actions. Merit pay sets employees "at each other's throats," while the effective functioning of a union requires its members to be in solidarity.

The key point here is that, while a unionized but traditionally managed organization might be justified in using merit pay as part of a "divide and conquer" strategy, such a strategy in a jointly managed organization is nonsensical. In a jointly managed organization, adversary issues are kept separate from problems that can be solved to the mutual benefit of labor and management. It is just as much in management's interest as it is in labor's that employees be at one with each other and that they embrace common goals and perform mutually supportive actions. In a jointly managed organization, many of these goals are held in common with management and the actions taken to attain these goals are supportive of both managers and co-workers.

Lawler also says that merit pay works well only where there are no interdependent tasks. He says, in effect, that situations where people must cooperate with each other in the performance of their jobs do not favor merit pay for individuals. It would seem to be generally true that most jointly managed organizations are concerned with the performance of interdependent tasks. Further, even in those rare cases where the regular tasks performed by workers might not themselves be interdependent, the tasks performed by both workers and managers in their roles as members of the parallel organization (like problem solving) are highly interdependent.

Before leaving the question of merit pay, we should say a word about the process through which the decision to adopt a merit pay system is made and the process through which such a system, once adopted, is administered. First, it is possible that the members of a primary organization, working through their parallel organization, might decide to adopt a merit pay system. In such a case, we would have to assume that their action is appropriate and that the general propositions discussed above do not apply in their situation. Second, in the event of such a decision, it would be well if the process for administering the merit pay system were designed along democratic lines. For example, all the members of a work group should be involved in deciding which of their number should receive merit raises. When a final decision is made, everyone involved should be informed of the decision and of the logic on which it is based.

A piece rate is defined by Wallace and Fay (1983, p. 272) as a "direct performance payment based on production by a worker who receives a set amount for each piece produced." The same arguments advanced against the use of merit pay in jointly managed organizations apply with equal force to the use of piece rates. However, since decisions regarding merit pay are generally made on more subjective grounds, they are aimed primarily at manipulating employee attitudes and general behavior, while piece rates focus on one thing: production. While they are more honest in this respect, piece rates promote dishonesty on both sides in that they create a constant incentive for management to raise production standards and a constant incentive for labor to conceal its ability to meet higher standards.

Promotion. In traditionally managed workplaces, workers are selected for promotion on the basis of such criteria as seniority, experience, education, training, and individual performance. In a jointly managed workplace, employees also contribute to the organization through their problem-solving activities. In addition, their ability to work cooperatively with others is of the greatest importance. Accordingly, performance evaluation systems should be revised to take account of these new criteria.

It is also important to revise the criteria for evaluating managerial performance. First, they should emphasize the need for facilitative, instead of "take charge," supervision. Second, they should measure managerial performance in action and planning teams. Finally, they should assess every manager on the basis of the promptness and effectiveness with which consensus decisions are implemented. One of the key elements of a joint management system is the linking of the planning and action teams with the primary organization—the link between "the shadow and the rock." This link is the responsibility of the senior manager-members of the organization's action teams. An excellent way to hold them accountable for this "linking pin" function is to make it a major part of their performance evaluations.

It is also necessary to change the process through which managerial performance evaluations are made. A manager's subordinates are in an excellent position to provide input with regard to his or her skill in "facilitative supervision." The other members of his or her action or planning teams should provide written recommendations on his or her performance of the "linking pin" function.

Suggestion Award Systems

It is not uncommon for middle managers, when they are first faced with the need to participate in the design of a joint management system, to propose a suggestion award system as an alternative. They argue, "Let's get the employees' ideas without wasting time on meetings." If they lose this argument, they sometimes propose a suggestion award system in addition to joint management—contending that this will at least cut down on the time that might be wasted in meetings.

I will not deal here with the relative advantages and disadvantages of suggestion award systems versus joint management. Rather, I will simply point out the incompatibility of the two approaches. Suggestion systems offer rewards for ideas. Therefore, it becomes in the individual's self-interest to maximize his or her share in an award by minimizing the number of people involved in presenting the idea. This leads to idea hoarding rather than to open, mutually supportive discussion. Yet open, mutually supportive discussion is required for the success of the autonomous work team and the parallel organization. In cases where individual suggestion award systems have been adopted along with parallel organizations, members of action teams have sometimes withheld their ideas from their teams and submitted them individually. This has created both resentment and opposition to their ideas among their fellow workers. In some cases, members of action teams have even been suspected by their fellow workers of attending meetings only to steal ideas and submit them individually.

In broader terms, the conflict between joint management and suggestion award systems can be said to arise from the tendency of the former to promote cooperation and the tendency of the latter to promote competition.

The Design Issue

The above discussion dealt mainly with the content of compensation and reward systems and pointed out some of the conflicts between traditional systems and joint management. An even larger issue revolves around the process through which compensation (and other administrative) systems are designed. In order for a joint management system to work well, it is not enough to redesign the primary organization's other administrative systems to be compatible with it. A more important condition is that judgments regarding their compatibility be influenced and owned by the members of the organization. This means that the task of reevaluating and redesigning the administrative systems of an organization that has converted to joint management should be assigned to the planning teams of its parallel organization. In this way, the views of the members of the organization regarding the content of its administrative systems can be reconciled. Of course, management has the final say on the content of these systems, subject to appeal by labor through the distributive bargaining mechanism. Where the views of the members of an organization conflict with the views expressed in these pages, it must be assumed that the members' views more nearly fit the special circumstances of that organization. Further, it is the responsibility of action and planning teams to monitor the results of their work and to correct any mistakes they might have made.

Chapter 20

Productivity Gain Sharing

One of the difficulties/opportunities raised by joint management is that it often results in higher rates of productivity. In order to maintain equity, an organization experiencing these gains must alter its compensation system to distribute them to the various parties in a fair manner. If this is not done, rank-and-file employees will have less incentive to continue their participation in the joint management system and, over the long run, it may stop producing gains. This is also an opportunity because gain sharing can increase the enthusiasm with which organization members strive to make joint management work, it can prevent eventual feelings of exploitation on the part of employees and thus help joint management to survive over the long run, and it can help decrease the income gap between managers and employees.

In practice, most productivity gain-sharing plans have been adopted, not to distribute gains already being realized, but as part of an effort to create gains. In the past decade or so, however, many joint management systems have been adopted to increase productivity and improve the quality of working life simply by providing organization members with opportunities to be more autonomous and participative. Few such systems provide for productivity gain sharing. In many cases, after several years of experiencing increases in productivity, organization members have asked, "What about us? Shouldn't we be getting something out of this in the way of dollars and cents?" Unions are generally inclined to rely on collective bargaining to obtain their members' share of the productivity increases. Using this method, a union simply uses whatever information it possesses regarding productivity increases as another argument to support its demands for a wage increase. Leaving aside the question of whether the principle of equity is well served by this approach, it is clear that it does not have the powerful impact on worker motivation that can be achieved by gain sharing. A union's demands for wage increases are generally supported by many arguments. It is almost impossible for even the bargaining committee to get an accurate idea of how important any one argument may have been in producing the end result. In addition, research has shown that positive reinforcement (in this case, the distribution of productivity gains) becomes less and less effective the longer it is delayed (Wofford, 1982). Thus, a collectively bargained increase, even if employees attribute it solely to their increased productivity, would be of little motivational value. Too much time would have elapsed between the desired behavior and the reward.

There are two main criteria for gain-sharing plans that are used in connection with joint management systems. First, they must be equitable. That is, they must provide the members of the organization with a fair share of the gains. Second, they must work well. This means that they must be perceived by the organization members as fair and, in addition, must be tightly linked to the kinds of behavior that make joint management systems work.

Gain sharing is especially important in a time marked by wage rollbacks, layoffs, and concession bargaining. Because gain sharing "opens the books" to labor, it serves as a means of ensuring that a generally troubled economy is not used as a tool in concession bargaining. Because gain sharing involves a joint monthly financial review by labor and management, it can help secure employee acceptance of "concessions" when they are justified.

The remainder of this chapter will (1) distinguish between productivity gain sharing and profit sharing, (2) comment on piece rates and their relationship to gain sharing, (3) describe three of the most common gain-sharing plans, (4) comment briefly on gain sharing in the public sector, and (5) place gain sharing in perspective—commenting on what it can and cannot be expected to accomplish.

Profit Sharing Versus Gain Sharing

Profit sharing and productivity gain sharing are often regarded as one and the same thing. They are, however, quite different. Profits depend on many factors besides productivity. For example, profits are affected by changes in demand, cost of materials, pricing, tax strategy, and marketing effectiveness, among other factors. Thus, it is possible for labor productivity to increase at the same time that profits are decreasing and vice versa. This means that profit-sharing payments, over the short run, bear little relationship to the efforts of an organization's employees. Partly because of this lack of "linkage," profit-sharing plans rarely make payments on a monthly basis. In fact, many profit-sharing plans either pay annually or credit payments to employees' accounts on a yearly basis, making actual payments only when employees retire or leave the firm. Thus, profit sharing violates two of the cardinal principles of motivation theory. Reinforcement theory tells us "the longer the delay between an act and its reinforcement, the less efficient the learning" (Wofford, 1982). Expectancy theory tells us that an employee's motivation depends, in part, on the employee's expectation that his or her performance is tightly linked to a desired outcome (Vroom, 1964). Profit-sharing payments are often delayed and only loosely linked to performance. Productivity gain sharing, on the other hand, lends itself to making prompt payments that accurately reflect the efforts of organization members. While it is an effective motivational device, however, gain sharing has problems of its own. These problems will be discussed later on in this chapter.

Individual Piece Rates

Piece rates are perhaps the most direct form of productivity gain sharing. Since piece rates involve paying an employee a certain amount for each item produced, they form a very close link between productivity and pay. However, they create destructive forms of competition among organization members that can more than offset any advantage that might be gained from their close linkage to performance. High performance by an employee reflects adversely on his or her fellows and tempts management to lower the rate per piece. It is thus in the interest of each individual that co-workers do poor work. Under these circumstances, cooperative and helping behavior is rare. The best case for piece rates can be made in organizations where there is little need for cooperative and helping behaviors. There are few such organizations, however. Jointly managed organizations depend for their success on these behaviors. Their chances for success are seriously hurt by piece rates, merit pay, suggestion systems, or any other individually based incentive plan.

Wofford (1982, p. 68) lists the following five criteria against which incentive plans should be evaluated:

1. Incentives must be tied to performance.
2. They must be valued by the employee.
3. The reward should immediately follow the performance.
4. They should not lead to the loss of other rewards (like social acceptance).
5. They should not lead to counterproductive (like competitive) behaviors.

Wofford argues that individual incentives fail to meet criteria four and five. If this is so, they are clearly inappropriate for jointly managed organizations.

Specific Gain-Sharing Plans

The gain-sharing plans most commonly used in North America are the Scanlon Plan, the Rucker Plan, and Improshare. I will briefly describe these plans below and comment on their applicability to joint management situations.

The Scanlon Plan. In the 1930s an officer of the United Steelworkers of America, Joe Scanlon, in one brilliant stroke created a structure that prefigured the parallel organization and combined this structure with a means of sharing any gains in productivity that it might produce. Scanlon's committee structure is not as comprehensive as that of the parallel organization. Unlike the action and planning teams of the parallel organization, Scanlon committees limit themselves to dealing with production problems and operating as reviewing bodies for suggestions submitted by individual employees. Nevertheless, Scanlon understood—as many of the designers and users of the parallel organization failed to understand—that the provision of participative structures is only half a solution. In addition, rewards should be given for participation, above and beyond the psychological benefits it provides. While the specific formulas vary from case to case, most Scanlon plans provide for these rewards in ways similar to the one outlined below:

1. The value of goods produced is computed for a two- or three-year base period prior to the adoption of the plan.
2. The labor costs for this period (along with any other costs controlled by the work force) are taken as a percentage of the value of the goods produced.
3. This standard percentage is multipled by the value of production (minus rejects and returns) for each month during which the plan is in effect. The result is the "allowed" payroll.
4. The actual payroll for the month is subtracted from the allowed payroll and the difference is the bonus pool.
5. Three-quarters of the bonus pool goes to the employees (up to and including the plant manager) and the remaining quarter goes to the stockholders.

Opportunities for employees to affect the size of the bonus pool are provided by a plant-level "screening committee" and "production committees" in each work area. These committees are made up of representatives from both labor and management. The screening committee figures the monthly bonus and deals with suggestions beyond the authority of the production committees. Worker representatives on the committees are elected. Evaluations of Scanlon plans are virtually unanimous in their finding that these plans promote helping and cooperative behavior. Since this kind of behavior is necessary for the effective operation of parallel organizations and autonomous work teams, jointly managed organizations might do well to consider integrating their systems with the Scanlon Plan.

The Rucker Plan. The Rucker Plan was developed during the 1940s by Allen W. Rucker of the Eddy-Rucker-Nichols Company (U.S. Department of Defense, 1985). The Rucker Plan is similar to the Scanlon Plan in that it establishes an "allowed" payroll based upon past performance and sets up a bonus pool consisting of the difference between the allowed and actual payrolls. However, it is different from the Scanlon Plan in some important respects:

1.   It places less emphasis on building a participative management system (Lawler, 1981). This is the most important difference. While the Rucker Plan gives employees a reason for wishing to increase productivity, it does not give equal attention to providing them with a means of doing so.
2.   The standard percentage (see Step 3 of the illustrative Scanlon Plan method for computing bonuses) is figured, not on the basis of production value, but on the basis of production value *added*. The consequence of this method is that, when the cost of materials and supplies is reduced, the bonus is increased.
3.   Other differences between the Rucker and Scanlon plans include the facts that the Rucker Plan does not require an employee vote of acceptance and that the plan does not necessarily give bonuses to top managers.

While the Rucker Plan does not appear to be as consistent with joint management principles as the Scanlon Plan, its method of figuring a standard percentage may be highly appropriate for firms in which organization members can control material and supply costs.

Improshare. Improshare is a more recent gain-sharing plan. It is apparently being used by an increasing number of firms because of its ease of installation and its lack of emphasis on employee participation (U.S. General Accounting Office, 1981). While the Scanlon and Rucker plans measure productivity at the organizational level, Improshare develops an engineered performance standard for each product. It can be applied at either the plant or group level, but "is based on many of the same principles as are individual incentive plans" (Lawler, 1981). Improshare is designed so that each separate group within the firm can have its own plan, while Scanlon and Rucker do not easily permit this approach.

Further, changes in product mix create distortions in the Scanlon and Rucker plans, but not in Improshare. However, Improshare, as it is presently designed, appears to be in conflict with the principles of joint management (see Introduction). Its main relevance to our discussion here is that it does not depend on the existence of a dollar value for production and, therefore, might—with modifications—meet a need in the public sector.

The Public Sector

Joint management systems are rarer in the public than in the private sector. Chief among the reasons for this are the lack of an economic incentive to increase productivity, the relative weakness of many public-sector unions, the number of parties involved in making policy decisions, and the autonomy of many public-sector middle managers. The lack of an economic incentive arises from the fact that increases in productivity rarely solve the problems of top and middle managers in the public sector. To the contrary, a department head whose unit shows a productivity increase may be "rewarded" with a budget cut. Thus, public-sector managers may be less motivated to adopt joint management systems.

At the worksite level the problem is more specific and perhaps more subject to solution. At this level, employees are probably just as highly motivated as private-sector workers. Unlike private-sector employees, however, their work units can almost never arrive at a value-of-production figure. Therefore, gain-sharing plans of the Scanlon or Rucker type are not generally feasible. However, two alternative approaches have been used to develop incentive plans consistent with joint management principles: the use of engineered production standards aggregated at the group level and the use of arbitrary rewards based on outstanding group behavior.

The first approach is that taken by Improshare. A standard is engineered for each product or service. In the public sector, however, standards are not engineered for all the products and services produced by a major organization. Instead, certain positions that lend themselves to productivity measurement are included and the rest are excluded. For example, seven of the thirteen federal gain-sharing plans listed in an official 1980 report (U.S. General Accounting Office, 1980) were for data transcribers only. Even if standards were developed for all the positions in an agency or department, it is not clear that they could be applied so as to be consistent with joint management principles. Nevertheless, it is important to develop some form of gain sharing in the public sector. Therefore, experimentation should be undertaken to find ways of adapting the group standards approach to make it consistent with joint management principles.

The second approach involves setting criteria for the kinds of behavior that are most appropriate in jointly managed organizations and rewarding the groups and individuals who demonstrate that behavior. The employees of Pima County, Arizona, are currently pioneering this approach. Pima County's management and unions bypass the direct measurement of day-to-day productivity. Their system calls for annual nominations of work teams that have demonstrated cooperative behavior and achieved productivity increases through that behavior. The nominations are evaluated by the county-level planning team and, based on its recommendations, the county-level action team makes cash awards of $1,000 each to the ten most outstanding work teams. Smaller awards are also made to individuals who are nominated because they have made exceptional progress in their own self-development or because they have made outstanding contributions to the organization through their participation in its joint management system. Between the first year of this plan (1983) and its second year, savings achieved by the plan increased from $153,281 to $591,832 (Mazany, 1984).

Gain Sharing in Perspective

Gain-sharing plans, if they are consistent with Wofford's five criteria, would appear to be tailor-made for dealing with two of the three major difficulties/opportunities that joint management raises in connection with compensation systems. A sound gain-sharing plan reinforces the active, responsible, self-developing, participative, cooperative behavior required by joint management. This is not to say that it deals with inconsistencies between traditional job and performance evaluation systems and joint management. Quite apart from the gain-sharing issue, a special effort must be made to redesign these systems so that they allow and reinforce these kinds of behavior. A sound gain-sharing plan also provides a means of equitably distributing the productivity gains that are often produced by joint management systems. Without such a means, after their initial euphoria has worn off the members of the organization are likely to see themselves as being "ripped off." They may then abandon their active, responsible, self-developing, participative, cooperative behavior. At this point, the joint management system is likely to falter and productivity to fall. Whether the distribution is, in fact, equitable depends on the specific provisions of the plan. For example, most gain-sharing plans distribute the bonus pool pro rata to existing wages and salaries. Yet the existing wages of rank-and-file employees rarely if ever include compensation for the management functions they perform as members of the parallel organization. This means that their bonuses, as well as their wages, are inequitable. This kind of inequity, however, is not an integral part of gain sharing. A plan could easily be designed to give an equal bonus to each organization member regardless of base wage or salary. This raises a crucial point: while amounts of compensation must be bargained distributively, methods of distributing compensation can be bargained integratively. The important thing is not to decide in advance whether gain sharing is appropriate and what form it should take, but rather to create a "compensation plans" planning team at the executive level to explore these questions and develop proposals to the action team.

While an "equal bonus" plan would deal with the problem of equitably distributing productivity gains, it would not fully deal with what is perhaps the prime difficulty/opportunity presented by joint management: the fact that joint management spreads management functions more evenly among organization members without commensurately spreading total compensation. In order to deal with this difficulty (or capitalize on this opportunity), other approaches are necessary. In the public sector, a possible approach might be the redesign of job evaluation systems so that they give credit for the management functions performed by rank-and-file workers. In the private sector, this might be accompanied by a more widespread use of producer cooperatives and employee stock ownership plans (see Chapter Twenty-One).

A final characteristic of gain sharing that should be noted is its reliance on the existence of other firms that pay "going wages and fringes" for its existence. This reliance makes gain sharing a marginal approach and rules it out as a societal model. Gain sharing rests upon the idea that the physical and mental effort normally put forth by employees is at a level below that which is feasible. Where a gain-sharing plan is in effect, this level of effort increases. For example, a recent study of twenty-four gain-sharing firms showed average savings of 16.8 percent (U.S. General Accounting Office, 1981). A bonus commensurate with the increase is then appropriate. Should this higher level of effort become the norm, however, the process of determining going wages and fringes would no longer be grounded in reality and there would be a real danger that gain-sharing plans would become simply a means of extracting full effort from workers for what might be no larger a share of society's wealth than they presently receive. This characteristic need not deter individual firms from securing the benefits available from gain sharing at present. It should, however, be a consideration in the formulation of public policy around the concept of gain sharing.

Chapter 21

◠──✦──◡

Employee Ownership

This chapter, along with Chapters Nineteen and Twenty, is concerned with the relationships between joint management and compensation systems. These relationships fall into two closely related groups: those having to do with equity and those having to do with incentives. In our discussions of equity we ask the question "What changes in traditional compensation systems are required to make joint management fair?" In our discussions of incentives, we ask, "What changes are required to make joint management work well?" That is, what kinds of compensation systems will reinforce active, responsible, self-developing, participative, cooperative behavior by organization members? It is important to note that jointly managed workplaces, through their parallel organizations, are in a position to design compensation systems that are tailored to meet their equity and incentive needs. Further, the more closely the parallel organization conforms to the design principles set forth in Chapter Two, the more likely it is to produce effective compensation systems.

At the organizational level, employee ownership affects joint management primarily in terms of incentives rather than equity. That is, an employee's ownership of a share in a firm does not compensate him or her for the performance of management functions. Workers pay for their shares, either with dollars or with wage concessions. Once their ownership of these shares is vested, they are entitled to the proceeds from them, whether or not they participate in the management functions of the company. Equity requires that an employee who participates in a joint management system receive additional compensation, whether or not the firm is employee owned. The issue here is one of equitable compensation compared with other employees of the firm and is not affected by the question of worker ownership. An employee's ownership of a firm does, however, give an incentive to perform management functions. The more effectively these functions are performed, the more the employee's share will be worth.

The implications of worker ownership for joint management systems at the organizational level can best be understood in the context of incentives. At the societal level, however, employee ownership has equity implications of the greatest importance. Widespread employee ownership, if combined with democratic control and joint management, could have a substantial impact on the inequities that lie at the roots of many of our most pressing societal problems.

A share in the ownership of a firm appears to give employees a strong incentive to make the firm successful. A University of Michigan survey found that employee-owned companies were 1.5 times as profitable as comparable companies that were not employee owned (Conte and Tannenbaum, 1980). Another study found that companies with employee stock ownership plans (ESOPs) had twice the annual productivity growth rates of comparable non-ESOP companies (Marsh and McAllister, 1981). Still a third study found that firms in which employees own a majority of the stock create three times as many net new jobs per year as comparable, traditionally owned firms (Rosen and Klein, 1981).

Employee ownership by itself, however, is probably not enough. In addition to wanting the company to be profitable, employees must possess a means of affecting its profitability. From the point of view of the worker ownership advocate, this is where the joint management system comes in. Based on fifty case studies of employee ownership companies, Rosen and Whyte (1983) conclude that employees also need to be involved in the decision-making process. This view is widely held. According to a New York Stock Exchange report (1982), employee ownership companies are four times as likely as other firms to have quality of working life (employee participation) programs.

The joint management system is a tool that organization members can use both to increase productivity and to improve the quality of their working lives. But, like employee ownership, the joint management system is not enough by itself. In addition to the psychological benefits they derive from participation, employees in a jointly managed organization require economic benefits of two kinds. First, they need economic benefits that compensate them for their performance of management functions. Second, they need economic benefits that give them an incentive to contribute fully to the success of the enterprise. The first benefit can be provided by revising the organization's job evaluation system. The second can be provided through changes in the performance evaluation system and through the adoption of gain sharing and employee ownership plans.

This chapter will outline the recent history of employee ownership, describe the two most common means of achieving it, discuss the problems it presents, and argue that it requires a systems approach. Such an approach would integrate employee ownership with joint management and productivity gain sharing.

Recent History

Until recently, employee ownership was a little-used approach to industrial organization. The worker cooperative was its best-known form. In 1974, however, federal law gave substantial tax advantages to companies adopting employee stock ownership plans (ESOPs). Between 1974 and 1981, ESOPs with one hundred or more participating employees increased in number from 435 to 1,918 and the employees involved in these plans increased from 427,546 to 5,154,383 (Bloom, 1984). By 1984, the number of employees covered by ESOPs was approaching ten million (Whyte, 1985). Since there are only about 200 worker cooperatives in the United States, the ESOP is now our dominant form of employee ownership.

The 1974 law, the Employee Retirement and Income Security

Act (ERISA), was followed by a large number of federal laws bearing on ESOPs. The most important of these acts is the Deficit Reduction Act of 1984. This act (among other provisions) allows commercial lending institutions to deduct 50 percent of the interest income they receive from loans to an ESOP. As of early 1985, eleven states had passed laws providing assistance to firms in arranging for employee buyouts (Whyte, 1985).

Employee Ownership Plans

The two most common approaches to employee ownership are the ESOP and the worker cooperative. In terms of numbers of firms and numbers of workers involved, the ESOP dwarfs the employee cooperative.

The Employee Stock Ownership Plan (ESOP). A firm wishing to adopt an ESOP first sets up an employee stock ownership trust. In a "leveraged" ESOP, the trust borrows money from conventional sources and uses it to buy shares of stock newly issued by the company for that purpose. This stock is allocated to individual employees, usually pro rata to compensation. In a nonleveraged ESOP, the company simply contributes new treasury issues of its stock to the trust and these shares are allocated to individual employees. In the leveraged ESOP, the company guarantees the loan made to the trust and pays it off by making annual donations to the trust. Here, a major advantage to the company is that it obtains cheap capital, since federal tax law makes its donations fully deductible whereas only interest payments are deductible in amortizing a conventional loan. In the nonleveraged ESOP, the contributed shares are deductible at market value despite the fact that the company, while it may have diluted the value of its total shares, has spent no cash.

However, employees do not automatically acquire full property rights in the shares allocated to their accounts. For example, they usually cannot dispose of their interests in the shares until they leave the firm or retire. Also, they normally acquire a disposable interest in the shares allocated to their accounts only after two or three years. This "vesting" process is usually completed (that is, they acquire a 100 percent interest in the shares) after ten years. Further, employee owners often do not acquire full voting rights in their stock. While publicly traded firms must allow employees to vote the shares allocated to their accounts, privately held companies need only grant them the right to vote on a limited number of issues. Of the estimated 7,000 ESOPs in existence in 1984, the National Center for Employee Ownership projected from available data that 85 percent did not grant employees significant voting rights (Blasi, 1984).

Even where voting rights are present and a majority of the stock is owned by employees, the amount of control the workers get depends on the following additional factors: how an employee is defined, how voting is structured, how shares are allocated, who selects the trustees, the vesting schedule of the stock, the manner of distribution of the stock, the percentage of ownership, and who chooses the company board of directors (Blasi, 1984). Blasi suggests that control of ESOP firms rests largely with management; he points out that it takes only "one or two undemocratic characteristics to result in a largely undemocratic ESOP." The tax advantages of ESOPs make them attractive tools for raising capital, creating an employee benefit plan, creating a market for firms, saving a company that is "going under," and providing management with a "chip" to trade off during concession bargaining.

The Worker Cooperative. The National Center for Employee Ownership estimated recently that there were about 200 worker cooperatives in the United States. Not only does this estimate of firms heavily favor the ESOP; worker cooperatives also tend to have far fewer employees than ESOP firms. Unlike ESOPs, worker cooperatives are used to bring about employee control as well as employee ownership. Since cooperatives are not as constrained by legislation as ESOPs, they can be more easily designed to accomplish this purpose. Where a state's cooperative incorporation statute is unwieldy, a worker cooperative may choose to incorporate under a general business corporation statute. Ellerman (1984, p. 3) defines a worker cooperative or industrial cooperative as "a company where the 'owners' or members are the people who work in the company. The workers hold the basic 'ownership' or membership rights which consist of (1) the voting rights to elect the board of directors which, in turn, appoints the management, and (2) the rights to the profits or net income of the company. Each member has an equal vote in accordance with the democratic principle of one person/one vote. The net income, which could be positive or negative, is shared among the members according to some agreed-upon formula, such as equally per dollar pay or equally per hour worked." Thus, the control an employee/member can exert in the firm depends not upon the amount of stock he or she owns but upon the simple fact of membership in the cooperative. The rights to the profits of a cooperative also depend upon membership itself rather than on the amount of equity held by the member. Instead of being distributed to investors commensurate with their holdings, profits are distributed to members according to whatever criteria the members decide upon (for example, pro rata to pay or hours worked). These rights to control and profits cannot be held by anyone other than a member. When a member leaves employment with the firm or moves from the community, he or she must sell these rights back to the cooperative.

Like the ESOP, the cooperative is eligible for preferential tax treatment under the Internal Revenue Code. Both approaches can avoid the "double taxation" of net income. Most corporations pay taxes on this income and then distribute it to their shareholders in the form of dividends, at which point the shareholders are also taxed. Worker cooperatives are entitled to deduct from their net income "patronage dividends" to members (Internal Revenue Code, 1954, Sections 1381–1388). Further, only 20 percent of these patronage dividends need to be paid in cash. This gives the cooperative important cash flow advantages in its early years. Of course, in later years, when the remaining 80 percent of the patronage dividends are paid in cash, they cannot be deducted a second time by the cooperative (Gips, 1982).

Unlike the ESOP, the worker cooperative does not receive preferential tax treatment of a nature that makes it attractive to firms wishing to raise capital. Neither does it create an employee benefit plan, create a "chip" for concession bargaining, and so on. It does not provide a tax advantage in raising money, but only in distributing money that has been earned and in sheltering any profits the owner of a privately held firm may realize from selling it to its employees. This, along with the fact that converting to a worker cooperative results in a loss of control by present management, explains why it is not a common form of business organization. However, the Deficit Reduction Act of 1984 took a step toward making it more attractive when it allowed a person selling a firm to his or her employees the same tax advantage under either the ESOP or worker cooperative approach (National Center for Employee Ownership, 1984).

Pitfalls to Avoid in Employee Ownership

Since the ESOP and the worker cooperative represent such different approaches, their pitfalls are best discussed separately. As space does not permit the discussion of these pitfalls in detail, readers desiring further information should contact the National Center for Employee Ownership, 927 South Walter Reed Dr., #6, Arlington, Va. 22204, or the Industrial Cooperative Association, Inc., 58 Day Street, Suite 203, Somerville, Mass. 02144, for additional material.

ESOP Problems. Some of the major problems that often arise with ESOPs are the pass-through of voting rights, their tendency toward being management controlled, the difficulty of maintaining them as employee-owned firms, the potential dilution of stock, the danger of substituting them for pension plans, and the general failure to combine them with systemic structures for employee participation.

Pass-through of voting rights has two aspects. First, ESOPs in privately held companies are required to pass voting rights through to their employee owners only with regard to major issues (dissolution, merger, relocation, and so forth, but not board elections). Only about 15 percent of these companies pass through additional voting rights voluntarily (Rosen, 1985). Second, where a firm guarantees an ESOP loan, any voting rights that are passed through must be passed through pro rata to the amount of stock owned. This interferes with the democratic "one person, one vote" principle.

In many cases it is possible to structure an ESOP to allow for democratic control by the worker owners. However, very few ESOPs are so structured. Since they occur in existing firms in which a group of existing managers hold the power and design the structure, there is little reason to expect them to be structured democratically. Only in unusual circumstances, such as where the union takes the initiative in a buyout, do the employee owners gain any degree of control.

Only those ESOP firms that are 100 percent employee owned can take steps to prevent the purchase of shares by nonemployees. Thus, William Foote Whyte predicts that "unless those designing the ESOP are committed to the long-run maintenance of employee ownership . . . the employee owned firm of today will turn into the firm owned by outside investors the day after tomorrow" (Whyte, 1985, p. 15).

In many cases, new shares of stock are issued by ESOP firms and used either as collateral for loans or to provide an employee benefit. This has led some critics, such as the president of the Profit Sharing Research Foundation, to point out the possibility that the stock of the firm will be diluted in these cases (Metzgar, 1976). The track record of employee-owned firms in the area of increased productivity has lessened the force of this argument.

Where firms do not have pension plans or propose to cancel them upon adopting an ESOP, organized labor is generally opposed. The reason for this is that a safe pension plan is based on diversified holdings, while an ESOP stands or falls with the fate of the one firm.

While ESOP firms are more likely than others to have worker participation programs, many firms either overlook this crucial element entirely or adopt programs that fail to meet workers' expectations. Prior to the adoption of an ESOP, workers typically are not clear on exactly what they expect in the way of participative rights (Hammer and Stern, 1980). In ESOPs that have been created by management initiative, however, Stern, Whyte, Hammer, and Meek (1983, p. 88) have noted a pattern of disillusionment. Workers feel the "apparent contradiction between sharing in ownership and being excluded from any influence in decision making."

Worker Cooperative Problems. The design of worker cooperatives avoids many of the problems that confront ESOPs. The first and most serious problem, however (assuming we accept the desirability of this form of organization), is that there are so few worker cooperatives in existence. The people who normally select the form of employee ownership have little reason to select the worker cooperative.

While it has been estimated that about ten million workers were covered by ESOPs in 1985, there were only about 200 cooperatives, most of them small, in the United States. This suggests that there are good reasons for the people who make the decisions in this matter to choose the ESOP over the cooperative. The first such reason is that, in most cases, the ESOP offers the better tax advantage. The second, and perhaps most important reason, is that the people who normally make these decisions are the managers of existing firms. If they choose the worker cooperative, they will lose control. If they choose the ESOP, they can avoid losing control. Thus, the worker cooperative form of employee ownership is normally selected only where a group of people are starting an enterprise, where a union is active in making the decision to convert an existing firm, or where employees take over a failed company.

My discussion of maintaining worker ownership, as it affects worker cooperatives, draws heavily on the work of Ellerman (1983). Some U.S. worker cooperatives have been sold to outside interests when the group of workers who formed them reached retirement age. In other cases, the cooperatives were so successful that the shares held by the worker-owners became extremely valuable. Then, when worker-owners left the firm or retired, they could not find replacement workers who could afford to buy their shares. The shares, therefore, went on the open market. Thus, the integrity of the cooperative was damaged from two directions. People who were not workers became owners and people who were not owners became workers. A means of avoiding this problem, however, is now available. Most worker cooperatives now use the Spanish "Mondragon" method of setting up an "internal capital account" for each worker-owner. This method assigns workers varying interests in the firm, depending on factors such as their length of service. New employees can join the firm without buying a share equal in size to those held by older employees. The cooperative itself buys the shares of departing or retiring workers. In this way the firm can continue to be 100 percent employee owned.

Even small (twelve- to twenty-member) worker cooperatives need some form of participative governance system. Saglio and Hackman (1982) propose a system with three components: the membership, the board of directors, and the grievance council. In a larger, unionized firm, these components might be built into the labor-management parallel organization, the board of directors, and the union. Many cooperatives, however, assume that democratic governance will occur without being planned and structured. This is generally an incorrect assumption.

A Systems Approach to Employee Ownership

In order to be successful in both human and economic terms, an employee-owned firm would appear to require control, governance, and operations subsystems that meet the following criteria.

Subsystem	*Criteria*
Control subsystem	Employee voting for board of directors, one employee/one vote, employee election of trustees (in an ESOP), and voting rights not restricted to major issues
Governance subsystem	Designed by the employees, representative of all groups, and integrated with union and management administrative subsystems (including job evaluation, performance evaluation, and gain-sharing subsystems)
Operations subsystem	Aimed at training and servicing rank-and-file workers and providing them opportunities for autonomy and participation at the work unit level

Note that gain-sharing plans are not incompatible with worker ownership. Even in a 100 percent worker-owned organization, where the members can expect to eventually enjoy the fruits of their labor, gain sharing provides them prompt feedback about their own productivity and positive reinforcement when their productivity is high. This supplements the more general incentive supplied by worker ownership itself.

Part VII

Applying
Joint Management
Thinking

A well-designed joint management system should be based on the practice of extended integrative bargaining. The adoption of such a system has three critical phases: conversion, administration, and adaptation. The first step in converting to extended bargaining is for the union to propose an extended integrative bargaining structure (the parallel organization) at the distributive bargaining table. The detailed rules, policies, and procedures that govern the parallel organization are then developed in a separate forum (the action team at the bargaining unit level) through the integrative bargaining process. Then the action and planning teams are formed, trained, and put into operation. Once implemented, the parallel organization is administered jointly by labor and management, with each having its own role. Then begins the long process of adapting the administrative structures of labor and management so that they support the philosophy and practices of joint management. Chapter Twenty-Two discusses the conversion process and proposes distinctive roles for labor and management in administering the integrative bargaining system. Chapter Twenty-Three discusses the need to adapt management's administrative subsystems to the joint management system. Chapter Twenty-Four does the same for labor's administrative subsystems.

Chapter 22

Extending the
Bargaining Structure:
Roles for Management
and Unions

This chapter commences with a step-by-step commentary on a proposed process for converting to extended bargaining. This commentary is arranged in chronological order. It begins with an account of
the "mixed" bargaining that must be done in order to build a foundation in the basic labor contract for extended bargaining. It then
describes the integrative bargaining process that develops the structures, policies, and procedures of the extended bargaining system
(the parallel organization). This integrative bargaining occurs at
the executive level, the operating level, the intermediate levels, and
the worksite level of the organization. After commenting on the
conversion process, this chapter deals with the need for training in
integrative bargaining, discusses the roles of the parties in the various steps of the process, and lists a number of conversion activities
that in the past have been carried on by outside consultants. It
should be emphasized that this book is not reporting on an existing
bargaining process and prescribing how it should best be done.
While the parallel organizations now in existence carry on extended
bargaining in a weak form and give us hints of how it might best be
arranged, we must wait for the first experiments in strong forms of
enforceable extended bargaining before we can do more than speculate on what the best arrangements might be. Our best real-life

example at this time is the ECWU/Shell-Sarnia case (see Chapter Five). However, Shell-Sarnia is a "greenfields site" and its learnings have only limited application to the conversion of existing traditional organizations.

The "Mixed" Bargaining Phase

The first step in the conversion process is for the parties to agree that it should be undertaken and to make the necessary commitments. In the past, these "agreements to proceed" have been very general agreements to experiment with employee participation. It has been assumed that labor and management have an equal interest in employee participation and that participation programs must be based on their mutual willingness to cooperate. Frequently, these initial agreements to proceed have been arrived at through the integrative bargaining process before the actual contract talks have begun. They often include provisions allowing the parties to withdraw from the agreements without cause.

However, when the kind of participation being proposed is the participation by large numbers of employees in an extended bargaining process, the nature of the agreement to proceed changes radically. Bargaining is a right that must be established by law or by contract. Labor must take the initiative where it is to be established by contract. It is true that extended bargaining is likely to benefit management by increasing productivity. For this reason, management at the bargaining unit level is likely to look upon it as something of a win/win matter. However, staff officers and middle managers are less likely to take such a positive view. Therefore, while the agreement to proceed must be recorded in the basic labor contract, it is likely to be reached by a combination of distributive and integrative bargaining. It is what Walton and McKersie (1965) call a "mixed issue." Labor is offering to cooperate in an effort to increase productivity, but it is asking for something in return: the right to enforceable extended bargaining.

A number of elements are essential to the agreement to proceed:

1. *Principles.* The parties should agree to a set of principles such as that contained in Chapter Two. This facilitates the design of an effective bargaining system.
2. *Bargaining time.* Management should commit to a minimum amount of release time for each action and planning team. This time would be used for integrative bargaining. It is important that the action team to be formed at the bargaining unit level be named, provided sufficient bargaining time to write a parallel agreement, and given a target date for the ratification of the parallel agreement.
3. *Sustained level of productivity.* Labor should commit itself to maintain the existing level of productivity. This assures management that the time committed to integrative bargaining, training, and administration will not lower this existing level.
4. *Productivity gain sharing.* There should be an assurance that any increases in productivity will be shared between labor and management. The details of the gain-sharing formula can be left to be worked out by the action team at the bargaining unit level.
5. *Administrative resources.* Management should commit itself to providing administrative support (like typing, printing, and so on) to the action and planning teams.
6. *Training.* Management should agree to a minimum amount of release time to be spent in training all members of action and planning teams and in giving orientation training to all employees. Labor should agree to give separate training to its participation stewards and to help give joint training to members of action and planning teams.
7. *Layoffs.* Management should guarantee that gains in labor productivity will not result in layoffs.
8. *Conversion schedule.* The parties should agree to a series of dates by which parallel agreements would be in effect at the bargaining unit level, the operating level, the intermediate levels, and the worksite level.

Many of these elements involve financial commitments that are essential to the success of the integrative bargaining system. It is crucial that these commitments be incorporated into the basic labor contract before integrative bargaining begins. The principal weakness of our experimental efforts at integrative bargaining has been that these commitments have either not been made or have been made but not kept. It is a fact of organizational life that financial pressures will almost always arise to divert money earmarked for low-priority uses. One way to make integrative bargaining a high-priority use is to include it and its specific requirements in the basic labor contract so that they can be enforced. While the following sections describe a proposed rather than an existing process, they are written in the present tense for the sake of clarity.

The Integrative Bargaining Phase

Integrative bargaining begins immediately after the extended bargaining provision of the labor contract is ratified. Initially, this integrative bargaining deals with the design and implementation of the parallel organization. After the parallel organization is in place, it can take up a wide range of problems involving worker well-being and productivity. This chapter, however, deals only with the conversion process. This process would occur at each level of the organization and would consist of three steps: reaching agreement to proceed, designing the system, and implementing the system.

At the Bargaining Unit Level

The first step in the design process has already been taken. The action team at the bargaining unit level has been defined in the labor contract, following the principles of wholeness and representation. Elections now need to be held to secure representation for such groups as middle managers and first-line supervisors. Then the action team can meet and begin its work.

Agreeing to Proceed. This step has already been taken and recorded in the labor contract.

Designing the System. The first task of the action team is to create, through the integrative bargaining process, an agreement at the bargaining unit level that runs parallel to the basic labor contract. The purpose of this parallel agreement is to define the integrative bargaining structure (the parallel organization). It defines the components of this system at the bargaining unit level in detail. It defines the operating- and worksite-level components in general terms. The content areas that the parallel agreement should cover and the process through which it is reached are outlined below.

The parallel agreement at this level summarizes the principles that will guide lower levels in designing their portions of the parallel organization. It also details the policies and procedures that will govern the system as it operates at the bargaining unit level. In large, far-flung organizations with decentralized operations, the formation of planning teams at the top level may be neither necessary nor desirable. The action team may simply write its own charter for this portion of the agreement. In most cases, however, action teams at this level create planning teams to do their developmental work for them. In these cases, the parallel agreement covers such matters as the composition of the planning teams, election procedures for their members, responsibilities of the teams, release time for team members, frequency of meetings, training programs for team members, how problems are identified, how the integrative bargaining process differs from the distributive bargaining process, and how issues and problems are referred from one process to the other.

Instead of one side making a proposal to the other, the action team sits down without either side having formulated a proposal. The members jointly identify the problem they are going to work on together: in this case, the writing of a parallel agreement. Then they define the elements of the problem (for example, how to schedule and assign tasks, how to develop an outline for the agreement, how to ensure that the agreement is understood by the various constituencies, and so forth). They then brainstorm ideas for dealing with each element of the problem. They discuss the ideas, formulate them as alternatives, and select the most reasonable ones. This process leads to a plan and schedule for producing the agreement. Before attempting this process, the action team should complete an intensive training course in integrative bargaining. Without this training, it is unlikely that a group of people accustomed to distributive bargaining techniques could successfully develop a parallel agreement. The final step in the process is a decision on whether the parallel agreement at this level requires ratification and, if so, what the ratification procedures should be.

Implementing the System. Where the top-level structure does not include planning teams, implementation occurs when the action team begins meeting. Where the structure includes planning teams, the initial implementation focus is on holding planning team elections. Since some of the constituencies (like middle managers or first-line supervisors) cut across organizational lines, these elections require a great deal of careful planning. Since the planning team members will be new to the process, the first month or so of their tenure should be devoted to training in integrative bargaining. It is important that this training be completed before the teams hold their first working meetings. In order for them to function effectively, their members must relate to each other in new ways and begin to value new character traits and ways of behaving. They can accomplish this shift better in a protected, nonthreatening environment. Once they have held their first meeting, any attempt to articulate new values and behaviors is almost certain to be resisted.

At the Operating Level

At this level, no agreement to proceed has been reached. In some cases, it might be desirable to poll the employees to get an idea of the level of their enthusiasm before beginning to work on a formal agreement to proceed. However, this poll should be preceded by a general orientation session so that employees would have an accurate idea of what they were being polled on.

Agreeing to Proceed. The labor contract and the parallel agreement at the bargaining unit level do not impose an extended bargaining system on the employees of the organization. Instead, they give the employees in each operating unit the right to carry on integrative bargaining if they so choose. For this reason and because it is usually not feasible to train an entire organization in integrative bargaining at the same time, one of the first tasks of the top-level action team is to find one or two units at the operating level to "pilot" decentralized bargaining. In a large corporation, a pilot unit at the operating level might be an assembly plant with 7,000 employees. In a school system, it might be a school with 50 employees.

While integrative bargaining would be mandatory for the heads of operating units, the pilot unit(s) should not be led by reluctant manager(s) or union leaders. These leaders should, if possible, be enthusiastic about the idea. Once an operations-level manager and union leaders who wish to lead the pilot effort are found, their tentative "agreement to proceed" can take the form of a jointly signed memorandum to all the members of the pilot unit. This memorandum would cover the same elements as the extended bargaining provision of the basic labor contract (see the section entitled "The 'Mixed' Bargaining Phase" earlier in this chapter). The manager should agree to serve personally on the action team and to provide administrative support to the bargaining process. As a general rule of thumb, about one-third of the time of a staff member is required to support bargaining for every 400 or so people. In an organization of fewer than 400 members, it is sometimes feasible for the manager to assign a secretary to provide this support. This is a workable arrangement as long as the secretary's performance evaluation is signed by the cochairs of the action team. The unit's agreement to proceed would not be final until the parallel agreement developed by the unit-level action team was ratified by the employees.

Designing the System. Before the system can be designed, the action team specified by the joint memorandum must be formed. In order to ensure that this action team is "whole" (that is, that all workplace interest groups are represented), some special elections will probably be needed. Before the action team begins to meet, it should complete an intensive course in integrative bargaining.

As soon as this training is complete, the action team begins to develop its parallel agreement. This agreement specifies the purposes and principles underlying the system; gives the composition of the planning and action teams at all levels; sets forth the responsibilities of the teams and of each category of team member; establishes procedures for making decisions and submitting proposals;

lists the steps to be followed and the techniques to be used in solving problems; and establishes administrative guidelines for obtaining release time to attend meeetings, communicating within the bargaining system, holding elections, conducting training, evaluating the system, and filing grievances where provisions of the agreement have been violated. Since operating units need coherent systems and since the levels of the system are highly interrelated, the operations-level action team does not so much write guidelines for the lower levels as actually design the system, down to and including the worksite-level action teams. Of course, where the operations-level unit is large, the lower-level teams are designed in less detail.

The key to producing a workable agreement is the involvement of all unit members in the design process. Organization members should "own" the agreement. In order for this to happen, the members of the action team must stay in close communication with their constituencies. The tentative agreement to proceed should provide for this close communication. For example, in some organizations it might provide for weekly meetings with constituents. Whatever the arrangements are, they should be agreed to in advance or they are almost certain to be resisted later on.

While the action team is working on a draft agreement, all of the members of the operating unit should receive general orientation training in the principles and practices of the parallel organization. As soon as a draft is ready, each member of the action team briefs his or her constituents on the draft and gets their input. Frequently, changes are made in the agreement based on this input. These orientation and briefing sessions require a combined total of perhaps three to five hours.

All unit members are informed of any changes to the agreement and a referendum is held to ratify it. Since the agreement is an attempt to reconcile the views of all the workplace interest groups, it is ratified by all members of the unit. Each middle manager, first-line supervisor, and so on gets one vote, just as does each rank-and-file employee. The action team sets a minimum ratification requirement before submitting the agreement to referendum. The design process at the operating level, beginning at the time the action team is formed and ending when the parallel agreement is ratified, usually takes about six to eight months (my time estimates are only very rough guides; the time required varies greatly, depending on the size and complexity of the organization). Should the agreement fall short of ratification, the action team seeks to reach consensus on whether to modify it and submit it to another ratification vote or to report to the top-level action team that the unit is not yet ready to convert to extended bargaining.

Operating-level action teams should devote a portion of their time during the design phase to solving a few significant problems in the areas of worker well-being and production. This is important because the members of operating units are likely to expect some results from extended bargaining as soon as they learn that it is being contemplated. If no results are forthcoming, they are likely to vote against ratifying the agreement.

Implementing the System. Making the bargaining system fully operational might take another three to five months. Elections must be held to fill the positions on the planning and action teams at the intermediate and worksite levels. The newly elected members must be given training in group dynamics, problem solving, and proposal writing. Often, some of the initial team meetings can benefit from the use of a facilitator who is not a member of the team. The bargaining system can be considered operational when a critical mass of its teams have identified a top-priority problem of their primary organizational unit and have successfully resolved it.

Elections generally occur within a week of the day the parallel agreement is ratified. They are conducted by the operating-level action team, which should have planned them in great detail before the agreement is put up for ratification. Ideally, the agreement will include procedures covering such matters as who counts the ballots, how they are collected, what to do in case of an appeal, and so on. The successful candidates are then announced, along with target dates by which each action team in the unit will have held its first meeting. Team members will already have received three to five hours of orientation in the principles of the parallel organization. They will now receive perhaps six to nine hours of training in the skills necessary to integrative bargaining (like reaching consensus, solving problems, and writing proposals). Action and planning teams should be kept intact during this training so that it can use real rather than "made-up" problems.

It is often useful to have outside facilitators attend the initial meeting or meetings of action and planning teams. A facilitator can remind a team of the lessons it learned during its training and help it get off on the right foot. For example, team members have been trained to follow certain problem-solving steps, but do not know how seriously to take this training. Left to their own devices, they might simply engage in unstructured discussions of the problem.

Certain problems identified by the action and planning teams become "initial testing events" (Herrick and Mazany, 1982). That is, the members of the organization test the integrative bargaining system by observing whether or not it solves these problems. If they are not solved, people take this as a sign that it is not worth their while to invest their time and energy in the bargaining system. Since a great deal of people-energy is required to make the system work, this has some of the earmarks of a "Catch-22" situation. Outside facilitators (who are not members of the action or planning team) are sometimes useful in helping the parties resolve these initial testing events.

At the Worksite Level

The first part of each work unit's participative system has already been designed at the operating level. This part is the worksite-level action team, which will conduct integrative bargaining at the worksite level. The parallel agreement at the operating level outlines the composition, election procedures, responsibilities, and operating procedures of the worksite-level action teams. It also specifies the extent to which individual work units may vary from these guidelines. The second part of the participative system at the worksite level is the autonomous work team. It is the responsibility of the worksite-level action team, once it has been formed and trained, to design more autonomous and teamlike working arrangements for its work unit and submit them to the work unit members for approval. It should be noted here that teamlike working arrangements themselves involve day-to-day and hour-to-hour integrative bargaining among the members of the team.

Agreeing to Proceed. Participation in integrative bargaining is voluntary for rank-and-file employees. Employees can simply decline to stand for election to the worksite-level action team. If the employee slots on an action team cannot be filled, the unit cannot conduct integrative bargaining. The operating-level parallel agreement may also specify polls or referendums to determine a work unit's readiness to conduct integrative bargaining.

One series of steps that might be taken to secure an agreement to proceed is as follows:

1. An election is conducted to fill the participation steward slots on the worksite-level action team.
2. The entire unit is given training in integrative bargaining and on what it would be like to be an autonomous work team.
3. The team develops a parallel agreement covering its own particular operating procedures and submits it to the unit members for ratification.
4. Once the parallel agreement is ratified, the team develops a "team agreement" covering that particular work unit's notion of how it wants to implement the team concept and submits this "team agreement" for ratification. Once both agreements have been ratified, the work unit has agreed to proceed with both parts of its participative system.

This procedure protects employees from abuses of the team concept in two ways. First, a work unit can decide to bargain integratively in its action team, but not to adopt the team concept. Second, the action team, with the input of the work unit members, has control over how the team concept will be carried out. Where a work unit has fewer than ten members, of course, it might decide to include all of them on its action team.

Designing the System. Designing the integrative bargaining system for the worksite-level action team should be a fairly simple matter. Most of the action team's procedures will probably have been specified by the operating-level parallel agreement. The part of the worksite-level agreement dealing with the action team may

simply be a memorandum signed by the unit head and the participation stewards.

Designing new working arrangements (that is, converting to
the autonomous work team) is far more difficult. The members of
the worksite-level action team receive training in how to perform a
sociotechnical analysis and then go through the analytical steps
described in Chapter Fifteen. They stay in close two-way communication with their constituents as they perform these steps. In addition, the action team gives periodic briefings to the rest of the work
unit on its progress. Some changes in working arrangements are
made during the analysis, while others depend on the approval of a
higher authority. Within three to five months, the total unit can
usually reach consensus on a draft description of the unit's new
working arrangements, to include the new duties of the various
members of the unit and the new skills that each member must
acquire before the unit can become a fully functioning autonomous
work team. Normally, this description requires the approval of
someone above the worksite level. As soon as this approval is obtained, it is signed by the members of the action team and, taken
with the joint memorandum describing the integrative bargaining
arrangements of the worksite-level action team, becomes the worksite-level parallel agreement. This agreement becomes a "living
document" and can be changed at any time the team leader and the
team members agree on the need for a change (assuming that the
nature of the change does not affect other work units, in which case
some higher approval would be required).

Implementing the System. Implementing both parts of the
work unit's participative system is the responsibility of the first-line
supervisor. The action team part is implemented first. The supervisor arranges for the necessary training and then authorizes integrative bargaining meetings to be held. In most cases, these initial
integrative bargaining meetings will be mainly concerned with designing new working arrangements. However, it is often wise to
deal with some of the work unit's most pressing problems during
this three- to five-month design period. Otherwise, work unit members may become disillusioned with the integrative bargaining system because it is not producing immediate results. Once the portion

of the agreement dealing with working arrangements is approved, the supervisor acts as facilitator in introducing these arrangements. It is likely that the new working arrangements cannot become fully operative until the supervisor has arranged for some team members to acquire new skills.

It is usually desirable for a group of six to eight work units to convert to autonomous work teams together. In this way, a single training class or series of classes can accommodate the three or four action team members from each of the converting units. In addition, it is often helpful for the action teams to meet together periodically to share their experiences. Autonomous work teams are usually implemented on a pilot basis within each operating-level unit. Perhaps a half-dozen or so worksite-level units may be converted to autonomous work teams on a pilot basis. Then a realistic schedule is adopted for the conversion of the remaining work units. The action teams of work units that are not engaged in converting to autonomous work teams normally bargain other matters until their turn comes. Another approach (the one used by the Cadillac Detroit-Hamtramck plant—see Chapter Five) is to designate all work units as "teams," require each team to elect a leader, and let each team take on as much or as little autonomy as its members wish.

Education and Training

Each step of the conversion process needs to be accompanied by orientation and training in integrative bargaining and in the procedures of the parallel organization. This orientation and training is necessary in order to make the parallel organization minimally effective. A great deal more training is required for optimal effectiveness. In an organization that uses extended integrative bargaining, all employees need to possess management skills. They also need to understand how the parallel organization affects reward structures, planning, controlling, power, conflict, motivation, leadership behavior, and so on. This means that it would be highly desirable for the organization to offer a course on integrative bargaining through the parallel organization or arrange for a local college to develop and offer one. In addition to this joint training, the union should give separate training to its participation stewards and management should give separate training to all managers. This separate training focuses on the specific roles and responsibilities of the parties in extended integrative bargaining.

Roles of the Parties

Agreeing to Proceed. At the top level, the initiative for proposing an extended bargaining system lies with labor. Once the initial agreement to proceed is reached at that level and an action team is formed, it is the joint responsibility of labor and management (acting through the action team) to assist units at the operating level in reaching agreements to proceed. In the same way, labor and management at the operating level are jointly responsible for assisting intermediate- and worksite-level units in reaching their agreements to proceed. However, if management fails to give priority to this activity, it is labor's responsibility to enforce the agreement to proceed and the subsequent parallel agreements.

Designing the System. The design of the system is, at all levels, a joint initiative. Further, the parties to this joint initiative include not just the union and management but all the workplace interest groups: middle management, first-line supervision, staff offices, and so on. More specifically, management's role is to take the administrative actions necessary to convene the action and planning teams (arranging for release time, providing typing and other administrative services, and so on). Everyone's role is to participate in the design of the system, and the union's special role is to ensure that management carries out its role.

Implementing the System. Management takes the necessary administrative actions. Labor and management do some of the training jointly (to combined groups) and some separately to their own constituencies. The union monitors the parallel agreements (that is, sees to it that management takes the necessary administrative actions).

Administering the System. The union does not have the resources to administer an integrative bargaining system, nor would this be an appropriate function for the union if it did have the resources. With regard to administration, the union's role should be reactive. That is, it should watch carefully to see that management is living up to the terms of the parallel agreement (providing release time, providing administrative support, scheduling regular meetings, promptly implementing agreed-upon proposals, and so forth). Where management is not living up to the terms of the agreement, it is the union's job to bring management into compliance—settling the matter informally if possible, but filing a grievance if necessary. The union should ensure that its participation stewards are well-trained and effective integrative bargainers and should make sure that management honors both the parallel agreements and the policies, procedures, rules, and programs that are integratively bargained. However, it is management's job to administer the parallel organization and implement the plans it produces.

Outside Consultants

In many of the experiments with parallel organizations that have taken place during the past seventeen years, outside consultants have played major roles in the conversion process. Labor and management have been regarded as the first two parties and the outside consultants as the "third party." The extended bargaining approach, however, places the responsibility for developing and administering a parallel organization squarely on the shoulders of labor and management. I am providing a list of the functions that have been performed by third parties (Brower, 1983), however, for two reasons. First, a union and management may wish to contract for certain specific functions (for example, functions 8–10). Second, unions and managements should consider how to provide for each of these functions, whether externally or internally:

1. Bringing labor and management together to consider initiating a program
2. Providing an initial organizational diagnosis, with recommendations for structure and training
3. Assisting top management with strategic planning, if needed
4. Chairing the initial meetings of the top-level action team

5. Helping both sides construct a common agenda
6. Demonstrating by example how to conduct a meeting so that it starts on time, follows a planned agenda, and so forth
7. Helping participants identify problems that can best be worked on in smaller groups, and assisting in setting up such groups
8. Training participants in such key skills as agenda building, problem analysis, and problem solving
9. Training internal process facilitators to replace the third party
10. Providing one-on-one consultation with individual managers and union leaders
11. Modeling for all participants a nonjudgmental, open-minded, "fresh slate" attitude, thereby creating the space and opportunity for people on both sides to break free of past behaviors
12. Setting the framework to deal with errors and mistakes as learning opportunities
13. Providing the parties with information about prior experience in other programs that might be useful in avoiding pitfalls or achieving rapid progress
14. Helping the participants plan and conduct self-evaluations of their programs

Chapter 23

How Management Must Change
to Make Joint Management Work

Bargaining and implementing a parallel organization and autonomous work teams are only the first steps in creating an effective, jointly managed organization. It is almost certain that the parallel organization and the autonomous work teams will be at odds with the existing management and labor subsystems. In most cases, the existing management subsystems are based in part on scientific management principles (see Introduction) and the labor subsystems assume the existence of these principles. Thus, an intermediate planning subsystem (the parallel organization) and a worksite-level production subsystem (the autonomous work team) that are based on joint management principles (see Introduction) become locked in conflict with personnel, budget, finance, productivity measurement, and collective bargaining subsystems that are based, at least in part, on scientific management principles.

The outcome of this conflict is easily predicted. Unless a major effort is made to redesign the existing management and labor subsystems, they will gradually erode and destroy or emasculate the parallel organization and the autonomous work teams. Greenfields sites (that is, new organizations) can design all their subsystems concurrently and avoid this problem. In most cases, this is not feasible for existing organizations. The specific changes that need to be made in their other management and labor subsystems are neither clear nor politically possible until the parallel organization and the autonomous work teams are in place. At that point, two conditions emerge to make adaptation more feasible: the inconsistencies come into sharper focus and the parallel organization is available as the redesign vehicle. This chapter discusses the adaptation of management subsystems to joint management principles. Chapter Twenty-Four points out some aspects of labor subsystems (for example, contract negotiation, contract administration, and internal training) that need to be redesigned so as to be compatible with joint management.

The Need for Redesigning Management Subsystems

An effective joint management system changes the ways in which management functions (like planning and controlling) are carried out. It changes the ways in which power and leadership are exercised and spreads these functions out among the members of the organization. In order to work well, it requires certain kinds of behavior (for example, cooperative). Yet the existing management subsystems have probably been designed to support a quite different kind of behavior (for example, competitive). Since people tend to behave in ways that they see as being in their best interests, it is unrealistic to expect them to change from competitive to cooperative behavior unless the management subsystems stop rewarding competitive behavior and begin to reward cooperative behavior. The Introduction shows that joint management requires active, open, informed, helpful, cooperative, responsible, thoughtful behaviors of organization members. The task is to redesign management subsystems so that they support and reward these behaviors.

The Vehicle for Redesigning Management Subsystems

Just as the parallel organization is the logical vehicle for redesigning the worksite-level production subsystem (that is, creating autonomous work teams), so it is the logical vehicle for redesigning the other management subsystems. This is so for three reasons. First, the members of the organization's planning teams represent all its workplace interest groups. Therefore, they can provide a comprehensive understanding of the ways in which the management subsystems affect the behavior of these groups. Second, the parallel organization is specifically designed to reconcile different points of view and produce revised management subsystems that are acceptable to all organization members. Third, where the parallel organization has been folded into the collective bargaining process, the new management subsystems are enforceable. These features of the parallel organization make it possible to redesign existing management subsystems in ways that are technically correct, politically viable, and based on right, not privilege. The impetus for the redesign effort must come from the top. It represents a large investment of staff time and therefore requires an administrative decision by the top-level action team. Most of the redesign will probably be done by the planning team at the level authorized to approve major changes in management subsystems. Subsequently, lower-level planning or action teams can review these revisions and make whatever additional changes are needed at their level.

Adaptation and the Organization's Staff Offices

Many of the activities of the parallel organization are potentially threatening to the staff offices of the primary organization. These offices are responsible for designing rules, policies, and procedures in their functional areas. The parallel organization's planning teams do the same thing. Indeed, one of their first tasks is to conduct comprehensive reviews of the rules, policies, and procedures that govern the management subsystems, with the goal of revising them so that they reinforce the practices of joint management. This situation can lead to competition and conflict. In order to avoid this, the initial review of management subsystems should be conducted in a way that respects the vested interests of the staff offices. The principle of representation requires that all people who have an interest in a problem participate in its solution. An organization's staff offices have an interest in both the process of redesigning the subsystems for which they have staff responsibility and the content of the changes proposed.

Therefore, a number of steps are necessary. First, representatives from the staff offices should meet with the top-level action team to develop a process through which the staff offices can be involved in the overall review of management policies and procedures. Second, this process should provide for representation from staff offices on planning miniteams when they are reviewing subsystems for which the staff offices are responsible. Third, in addition to being represented on such planning teams, the staff offices should be charged with serving the planning teams by providing them with staff assistance. It should be clear that the person providing the staff assistance is not a member of the planning team and has no voice in its decisions. Finally, the top manager should inform all staff officers that a major criterion in their performance evaluations will be the effectiveness with which they provide this staff assistance to the parallel organization. The top manager should evaluate them on this criterion only after consultation with the action and planning teams. Ehn (1988) has written an excellent book on the relationship between the design expert (in this case, the staff specialist) and the user (in this case, the planning team).

A Checklist for the Adaptation of Management Subsystems

Each organization must, of course, review its own management subsystems to discover the specific ways in which they fail to support joint management. However, it should be helpful at this point to make some general comments on the ways in which this failure often manifests itself. We have treated compensation subsystems in Part Six of this book and so will only briefly touch upon them here. This section focuses on the personnel, budget, financial, and productivity measurement subsystems.

Personnel

Education. Most education subsystems in traditionally managed organizations are mainly concerned with tuition reimbursement. Further, they often reimburse employees only for courses that are directly connected with the employees' jobs. In jointly managed organizations, formal education takes a more prominent role. In an auto mirror plant in Bolivar, Tennessee, for example, courses requested by workers (for example, industrial engineering, first aid, typing, and music) were held before or after the beginning of each shift. These courses were held during time gained by groups of workers who were able to reach production standards in less than eight hours (Macy, 1982).

Maccoby (1981, p. 231) suggests that "what is most lacking for the education of leaders in our culture is education in the humanities, first of all in clear writing and speaking, but also in religion, ethical philosophy, depth psychology and history." Jointly managed organizations rely on the assumption of leadership roles by almost all of their members at one time or another. It follows that their tuition reimbursement criteria should include courses not directly related to the performance of the employee's assigned tasks.

Career Ladders. It is necessary in jointly managed organizations that managers plan and solve problems with their subordinates on an equal basis. This means that, during action and planning team meetings, they must treat their subordinates' views with the utmost respect. The existence of bottom-to-top career ladders facilitates this respectful treatment. The less comprehensive the career ladder subsystem, the less likely it is for managers to observe the "equality in meetings" principle. This is especially true where upward mobility is barred by credentialism. For example, doctors sometimes find it difficult to take nurses' opinions seriously and nurses find it hard to plan and solve problems on an equal basis with nurse assistants. Where a manager's subordinates are also his or her potential successors, however, the "mental leap" involved in accepting them as equals becomes less strenuous.

It is important that organizations converting to joint management assign a top-level planning team the task of reviewing its job structure with several specific goals in mind. First, the planning team should identify all credentials requirements (and other qualifications) that are not essential and recommend their elimination. Second, where there are essential qualifications requirements that prevent classes of employees from being promoted to given jobs, the team should recommend opening the door to lateral transfers so that the employees can become qualified for the promotions through experience. Third, where certain credentials are found to be essential and where these credentials prevent even lateral transfers, the team should develop and recommend educational programs that would give all employees the opportunity to obtain these credentials.

Hiring and Promotion. Traditionally managed organizations typically leave hiring and promotion decisions to people occupying managerial positions. The people who must work with the newly hired employee or for the newly promoted manager are rarely consulted. While this approach may work well in traditional firms, it conflicts with the fourth principle of joint management (that is, let workers and managers think together). Decisions regarding hiring and promotion powerfully affect all the members of an organization. If workers and managers are to think together at all, they should certainly think together about these decisions. The specific ways in which this is accomplished may vary from organization to organization. The rank-and-file employees of the Pima County, Arizona, Health Department elect representatives to sit on the panels that interview and rate candidates for managerial positions. Autonomous work teams often interview job applicants and recommend candidates for selection.

The successful adaptation of hiring and promotion systems does not depend so much on changing the criteria as on changing the process. Certainly, it is desirable that the criteria for hiring and promotion include participative attitudes and participative skills. But it is more important that the hiring and promotion processes themselves be participative. If elected representatives of the various workplace interest groups sit on interview panels and participate in the making of hiring and promotion decisions, it is likely that hiring and promotion criteria will be modified to include participative attitudes and skills. In any event, the main object is not to screen out candidates who do not possess these attitudes and skills. Almost everyone has the potential to learn them. Rather, the main object is to inform candidates that, given the culture of the organization, they must learn these attitudes and skills if they wish to be successful.

Job Evaluation. This subject has been treated at length in Chapter Nineteen. The crucial point is that the criteria used in job evaluation must reflect the principles of joint management. This means that these principles, as they are understood and agreed to by the members of the organization, should be readily available in written form. Usually, they are printed in the prefaces of the parallel agreements developed at the top and operating levels of the organization. The planning team that is assigned the task of reviewing the organization's job evaluation subsystem should ask itself, with regard to each set of job evaluation criteria, "Do these criteria place a high wage or salary value on the tasks that are crucial to joint management?" For example, do they reward the exercise of discretion by the individual worker? Do they reward the learning of a number of skills? Do they reward the joint exercise of coordination and control by autonomous work team members? Do they reward an emphasis on teaching by autonomous work team leaders and avoid rewarding these leaders for coordinating and controlling their team members? Do they reward managers and workers for thinking together? Where the answer to any of these (or similar) questions is "No," the planning team should revise the critiera so that the answer becomes "Yes."

Merit Pay. As suggested in Chapter Nineteen, compensation systems that reward competitive behavior are difficult to adapt to the needs of joint management. Where the pay of the individual worker is based on the quantity and quality of the product or service he or she produces, management systems that depend for their success on helping, cooperative behavior will not work well. Thus, the only effective way to "adapt" such a system is to change it so that it rewards group, rather than individual, achievements. For example, a merit pay system might be adapted by prohibiting the award of a merit raise to any person in a work unit unless every other person in that work unit also receives one. This would promote cooperation, rather than competition, within the unit. It would also, however, promote competition among units. Therefore, it should be considered only where the units involved do not depend on each other for help and are not vulnerable to each other's hostile actions. In most cases, the best way to deal with merit pay systems is probably to discontinue them and "start from scratch."

Performance Evaluation. The planning team charged with reviewing an organization's job evaluation system must ask itself whether the system rewards *tasks* that are consistent with the principles of joint management. The team that reviews the performance evaluation system must ask itself whether the system rewards *behaviors* that are consistent with joint management. Performance evaluation criteria can reward these behaviors in three ways. First, they can emphasize results. Where workers and managers are evaluated according to the results they achieve rather than according to the steps they take to achieve these results, they are free to use their discretion and exercise their ingenuity. Second, performance evaluation criteria can give leaders credit for the results achieved by their followers. This makes it in the interests of the leaders to train and educate their followers and make sure they have the tools and raw materials to get the job done. In a traditionally managed organization, where leaders are often rewarded according to their force and charisma, it is not uncommon for leaders to be threatened by the achievements of subordinates and to hide these achievements from top management. In a jointly managed organization, where leaders are rewarded for results, a leader who convinces top management that he or she has created a team of high achievers is placed in line for promotion. Finally, the criteria can include the responsibilities assigned to each position by the organization's parallel agreements. For example, a given managerial position might be responsible for making time available for training and group meetings, for participating in the planning process, and for promptly implementing programs developed during this process. A worker in an autonomous work group might be responsible for participating in a scheduling session with fellow workers each morning. Performance evaluation criteria should cover these responsibilities. However, elected representatives are accountable to their constituents—not to management—for the quality of their performance. Therefore, their performance should not be evaluated by management.

It is clear from this discussion that the process of performance evaluation, as well as its content, needs to be adapted. The people who are most knowledgeable about the performance of managers, with regard to some of the above critiera, are their subordinates. Therefore, they should be part of the managerial evaluation process. However, the use of peer evaluations is not recommended. These evaluations tend to promote divisiveness rather than solidarity and to discourage cooperative and helping behaviors. The responsibilities assigned to participation stewards and other union officers by the organization's parallel agreements are a special case, since their constituents evaluate their performance. To illustrate, a participation steward is normally responsible for, among other things, maintaining two-way communication with constituents. The quality of this two-way communication is assessed by his or constituents at election time.

Promotion from Within. One of the most destructive ideas that can be applied to joint management is the traditional "new blood" theory. This theory relies on hiring people from outside the organization to bring new ideas to bear on its problems. There are two major reasons that this theory is dysfunctional in jointly managed situations. First, joint management radically increases the number of organization members whose ideas can be brought to bear on problems. Jointly managed organizations rarely experience shortages of new ideas. Therefore, the argument that new ideas are needed from outside the organization loses its force. Second, joint management develops a large pool of "home grown" talent that can be used to fill vacancies. One of the main results of its principles (for example, giving workers more discretion, training workers in more than one skill) and of the practices that put these principles into operation (that is, the autonomous work team and the parallel organization) is to prepare people to assume higher-level responsibilities. Finally, going outside to fill positions above the entry level is seen by organization members as a betrayal of the expectations raised by joint management. People who have developed new skills under joint management have higher opinions of themselves and see themselves as deserving of promotion. When the organization goes outside itself to fill a higher-level position, it is making a powerful statement that it disagrees with these higher opinions and that it wishes to subvert the joint management process.

In addition to the modifications in hiring and promotion systems that have been discussed above, the tendency of some organizations to cling to the "new blood" idea can be overcome by including provisions against new blood in the top-level parallel agreement. For example, this agreement could require the approval of the top-level action team before an outsider is hired when a qualified organization member is available.

Suggestion Awards. Individual suggestion award systems make it difficult for organization members to solve problems informally in autonomous work teams or to participate in the work of planning or action teams. Much as they might enjoy the psychological benefits of team problem solving and well as they might understand the advantages of having the team own the solution, people are sometimes tempted to forgo these benefits and advantages by the possibility of an individual reward. Like merit pay, however, suggestion award systems do not die easily. Some organizations ease them out by degrees, first combining them with team achievement awards and then decreasing, over time, the portion of the total award budget devoted to individual awards. Others make their team awards so much larger than their individual awards that it makes economic sense for people to share their ideas (Mazany, 1986). If it is feasible, however, individual suggestion award systems should simply be discarded.

Training. The two dominant components of traditional training systems are skills training and management training. Skills-training programs instruct employees in the technical aspects of their jobs (how to operate equipment, how to process papers, and so forth). Management training emphasizes the manipulation of people and other resources in order to get the work out. Jointly managed organizations may need to modify their policies with regard to skills training in order to ensure that it is available for purposes of promotion and lateral transfer. The main change usually needed with regard to skills training, however, is simply to provide more of it. The more skilled people are at the technical aspects of their work, the more independently they can function. The more independently its members can function, the more effective is the jointly managed organization. Management training generally needs major shifts in both content and concept. What constitutes good management in a traditional organization does not necessarily constitute good management in a jointly managed one. In the former case, for example, opening one's books to employees might be disastrous. In the latter, it might be a very wise move.

In addition, the concept of management training must change. Instead of being geared to give people who are in authority over other people the ability to exercise that authority, it needs to give all members of the organization the ability to jointly plan and solve problems with other members. In a jointly managed organization, all employees have some management functions and must be trained to carry out these functions. The specific forms of this training are discussed in Chapter Twenty-Two.

Budget Administration

The budget is an intermediate-range planning tool. It estimates the resources that will be required (generally over periods ranging from six months to five years) for the various functions of the organization. It then serves as the basis for the allocation of resources to these functions. The budget process generally starts when top management issues guidelines. These guidelines are often revised by each successively lower level of management and reissued in more specific form. The lower levels of the organization then develop estimates and submit them up through the hierarchy. The estimates are consolidated and revised at each successively higher level until they reach the top level where budget decisions are normally made.

This process is appropriate for jointly managed organizations with one important change. This change involves the inclusion of the parallel organization in the budget process. The parallel organization is essentially a vehicle for intermediate-range planning. Therefore, it is well suited to be used by line managers for budget formulation purposes. This means that the action team at each level should discuss the guidelines issued by higher levels and make appropriate recommendations to the senior manager-member before more specific guidelines are issued for lower levels. At the autonomous work team level, where the basic building block of the budget is produced, the guidelines should be discussed by the action team in an open meeting attended by any other interested employees. The action team should attempt to reach consensus on the written budget estimate before it is submitted to the next higher organization level. As the budget estimates rise through the hierarchy for revision and consolidation, they should be reviewed by the appropriate action and planning teams. These teams advise the accountable manager on any revisions that are necessary and attempt to reach consensus on the revised and consolidated versions submitted to higher levels.

Financial Administration

The financial administration carries out the financial aspects of the plans made during the budget process. It involves both day-to-day decisions and short-range planning. The day-to-day decisions are affected by the parallel organization only in that they may be made in accordance with rules, policies, and procedures it has developed. The short-range plans (for example, a decision to spend money on a piece of equipment) are often appropriate for discussion by action and planning teams.

The principal change that may need to be made in a financial management system before it will be in harmony with joint management, however, has to do with the extent to which it is decentralized. A decentralized financial management system tends to encourage innovation and the exercise of discretion at lower levels of the organization. For example, a lower-level manager who has control of his or her budget can begin to think about achieving results as well as about completing any prescribed steps that may be required by higher levels. Where financial administration is centralized, a lower-level manager who overruns the budget can count on being bailed out by adjustments made at higher levels. By the same token, a lower-level manager who has managed to save money through increased efficiency (and would like to use the saved money to try an innovative project) can count on the saved money being gathered up to bail out someone else. Neither efficiency nor innovation are encouraged by a centralized financial administration system.

Yet joint management systems depend on organization members to be both efficient and innovative. They are trained in problem solving and given as much discretion as they can handle. This includes managers as well as workers. By discouraging innovation and efficiency, centralized financial management systems put themselves in opposition to the principles and practices of joint management. Planning teams reviewing centralized financial administration systems should consider such alternatives as profit centers and other means of decentralizing financial decisions to the lowest feasible level. In this context, procurement decisions and personnel decisions that cost money should be regarded as financial decisions.

Productivity Measurement

The way an organization measures its productivity has a powerful effect on the way its members behave. In some offices, productivity is defined as the number of papers of a certain kind that get processed each day. In these offices, people adopt behaviors that allow them to process large numbers of papers. In plants that use Scanlon plans, productivity is defined as the ratio between the labor bill and the value of production. In these plants, people adopt behaviors that tend to reduce this ratio. The more productivity is measured in terms of end results, the more people adopt behaviors consistent with joint management. The Scanlon Plan ratio is an excellent example of this kind of measurement. Not only does it reflect an end result, it reflects an end result within the control of the organization members. They can control the value of production by controlling both the amount and the quantity of what they produce. Three kinds of behavior that can be influenced by productivity measurement are especially desirable in jointly managed organizations: cooperation, discretion, and innovation.

Cooperation. If productivity is measured at the individual level, people tend to compete, rather than cooperate, with each other. If it is measured at the team level, cooperation within the teams is enhanced, but the teams themselves are likely to compete with each other. If it is measured at a very high level (like the corporate level), neither individuals nor groups feel that they can influence it. Accordingly, they do not let it influence them. The planning team that is reviewing productivity measurement systems should look for that level in the organization somewhere between the individual and the corporate level where the following conditions exist: (1) individuals and small groups feel that they can influence the measurement, and (2) there is no significant need for cooperation with other units of the organization at the same level. Measuring productivity at this optimum level does not preclude measuring it at higher levels as well. In fact, an initial step in the formation of an autonomous work team by a worksite-level action team is to define the work unit's primary task. This step, in effect, defines what constitutes productivity within the work team.

Deciding the level at which productivity should be measured often places labor and management on the horns of a dilemma. From the point of view of maximizing incentives and creating cooperative behaviors, measuring productivity at the plant level often produces the best results. However, from the point of view of union solidarity, measuring productivity at the plant level can produce harmful results. It leads, in some cases, to "whipsawing" and to turning local union against local union.

Discretion and Innovation. The first principle of joint management is that members of the organization should be allowed maximum discretion in the performance of their duties. Where much discretion is allowed, it is possible for people to try new and innovative ways to achieve the organization's goals. To the extent productivity is defined in terms of the steps people take to achieve these goals, they are limited to taking these steps and prevented from trying different approaches. In addition, it is virtually impossible to measure all the steps a person might take in the course of a day's work that would help the organization reach its goals. Yet, where productivity is measured in terms of taking certain steps, we all tend to focus our energy on taking these steps and tend to leave other things undone. To the extent productivity is measured in terms of goals rather than steps, people tend to constantly ask themselves what steps are available to them to help reach these goals. This question leads to exercising discretion and to trying new approaches. Of course, policies and procedures are necessary in order to ensure some degree of uniformity and predictability. However, the procedures should be kept to a minimum and should not serve as the basis for measuring productivity.

Problems

Perhaps the two biggest problems that organizations face in modifying their management subsystems are (1) the substantial effort and resources required by such a project and (2) the probable resistance of the existing staff offices. One approach to dealing with the first problem is to ensure that the top manager personally attends the initial orientation seminars given before the organization commits itself to joint management. These seminars should discuss the adaptation stage of converting to joint management and explain how crucial it is to a successful conversion. The second problem can be resolved if the top manager clearly defines the role of the planning team vis-à-vis existing staff offices, holds the staff offices accountable for providing technical assistance to the planning team as it conducts its review of management subsystems, and—as a first adaptive step—changes the reward system for the staff office heads and for the staff specialists so that it is in their best interests to support the planning team in its review and modification of management subsystems.

Chapter 24

How Labor Must Change
to Make Joint Management Work

Section 8(d) of the National Labor Relations Act requires employers and employee representatives to meet at reasonable times and confer in good faith with respect to wages, hours, and other terms and conditions of employment. The phrase "other conditions of employment" has been interpreted fairly broadly by the courts. However, some management consultants advise nonunion employers using quality circles to restrict these circles to production problems (carefully sidestepping conditions of employment) in order to avoid the "company union" proscription of the act (Bohlander, Jorgensen, and Werther, 1983). This proscription, Section 8(a)(2), has been interpreted to prohibit employers from taking an active part in organizing committees to represent employees.

In unionized organizations, employers avoid this prohibition by inducing labor to jointly sponsor employee participation systems. This tactic has been successful in preventing suits under Section 8(a)(2). After all, it is normally the union that brings these suits and, in these cases, the union is a cosponsor of the system. However, the intent of the section (to prevent management from undermining the union by controlling the collective bargaining process) is being effectively violated. Employees are often convinced that the union is only "going along" with the participative system and that they have management, not their union, to thank for any benefits they experience from it.

In the past, when integrative and distributive bargaining were carried on together at the bargaining unit level, integrative bargaining was controlled by the union and was no threat to union solidarity. What must be recognized now is that integrative bargaining has expanded and, as a practical matter, is being carried on separately from distributive bargaining in many jointly managed workplaces. We must also recognize that integrative bargaining is, in most cases, now being dominated by management. Since integrative bargaining "feels good" to the people involved, since it is extremely effective when carried on separately from distributive bargaining, and since it is regarded by employees as management driven, it tends to alienate employees from their union. Often employees will ally themselves with management in inducing the union to "go along" with particular changes (like the weakening of seniority provisions) that are regarded as necessary to the participative system. In these ways, the union becomes the "bad guy" and management becomes the "good guy" in the eyes of some employees.

For these reasons, when I speak of the adaptation of contract negotiation and contract administration to employee participation systems, I am speaking of labor reasserting itself in the area of integrative bargaining. Integrative bargaining has expanded its influence tremendously in the past decade. At the same time, it has slipped out of the regular collective bargaining process and has been taken over by management. It is up to labor to recognize that employee participation activities are, in effect, collective bargaining and to reclaim its lead role in these activities. It is impossible to say exactly what tactics will work best in reclaiming this lead role until more local unions have made the attempt. This book proposes the use of the parallel organization as the integrative bargaining mechanism because its visibility, concreteness, and permanent nature should facilitate folding it into the collective bargaining process. This chapter suggests some of the steps that unions might take to reclaim their role in integrative bargaining in the context of the parallel organization.

The adaptation of collective bargaining and contract administration to joint management has already begun in real life. Chapter Five describes the successful effort of ECWU Local 800 to make the Shell-Sarnia *Good Work Practices Handbook* grievable. Shell-Sarnia is a greenfields site where a participative system was installed when the plant began operation. Local 800 was reacting to its members' disenchantment with this system when it went to the brink of strike in 1988 over the enforceability issue.

This book is geared to a more typical situation: that of the existing traditionally managed workplace. It proposes that the parallel organization be used as a mechanism for decentralized, integrative bargaining at all levels of the organization and gears its discussion to the changes needed in contract negotiation and administration for this to happen.

I note in Chapter Twenty-Three that the parallel organization is well suited to serve as the vehicle for adapting the management subsystems of the organization so that they are consistent with joint management principles. This means that the work of adapting these subsystems is done jointly by management and labor after the parallel organization is developed and installed. The work of adapting the labor subsystems (contract negotiation and contract administration), on the other hand, is done independently by the union. It need not wait until the parallel organization is available. Indeed, if a union were to begin adapting its own subsystems before initiating a move toward joint management, it would place itself in a very strong position to ensure a well-designed participative system.

However, local unions are pretty much on their own when it comes to adapting to joint management. It is, therefore, difficult for them to anticipate the changes they should make until they are actually involved in the joint management process. This chapter aims at being helpful to unions by first summarizing the arguments for adapting their collective bargaining sytems and then discussing some changes that might be made in their bylaws and in the way they approach contract negotiation, contract administration, and training. These changes are aimed at strengthening both the joint management system and the union itself.

The Argument for Change

The first argument for change arises from the fact that joint management is not realizing its full potential. In some instances, there have been marked gains in productivity and human well-being. In others, these gains have been less impressive. While many flaws have contributed to the "less impressive" cases, the most common complaint is the "lack of top management support." The complaint is that top management does not compel lower levels of management to live by the rules of the participative system and to implement the solutions it develops. What we have failed to realize is that top management normally gives its energy and support only to crises. It will compel middle and lower levels of management to cooperate in making joint management work only if joint management assumes the dimensions of a crisis. An excellent way to convert joint management to crisis status and thus gain the attention and support of top management is to bargain and enforce it. This is the approach taken by ECWU Local 800 in 1988.

The second argument for change involves the survival of organized labor and is introduced in the opening paragraphs of this chapter. It is clear that parallel organizations are vehicles for collective bargaining. As most parallel organizations are presently structured, they are imperfect and ineffective vehicles and are potentially dangerous to organized labor, but they are vehicles nonetheless. Section 8(a)(2) of the National Labor Relations Act states, in part: "It shall be an unfair labor practice for an employer to dominate or interfere with the formation or administration of any labor organization." An example of behavior that has been found illegal under this section is an employer's "taking an active part in organizing a . . . committee to represent employees" (U.S. Department of Labor, 1971). Bohlander, Jorgensen, and Werther (1983) advise employers to avoid being found in violation of the act by restricting the role of the participation team to that of improving production methods. A collective bargaining mechanism that is not controlled by labor is clearly a danger to labor. As one worker responded when asked what role his union was playing in his work unit, "You call that a union? Now take QWL [a participative system that had been adopted by his

unit], that's a real union!" If labor does not adapt its contract negotiation and administration systems to embrace joint management,
joint management will further weaken organized labor's hold on
the minds and hearts of workers.

A third argument might be stated: "If labor does take the
initiative in integrative bargaining, it might become stronger in
unionized plants and become better able to organize nonunion
workplaces." Some employees who are extremely active in employee
participation systems have histories as inactive and cynical union
members. As one worker at the Cadillac Detroit-Hamtramck plant
said, "No, I've never been much of a one for the union. I've never
been active in it. But I like being active on problem-solving teams. It
makes me want to get up in the morning and come to work." This
suggests the existence of a pool of union members who have not
involved themselves in the traditional union activities, but who
might become active as participation stewards if labor were to take
the lead role in integrative bargaining. It also suggests the use of
extended integrative bargaining as an organizing tool. In nonunion
plants, employees often respond positively to employers who offer
them the opportunity to become involved in problem solving that is
limited to production problems. They might be even more receptive
to a union that offered them the opportunity to become directly
involved in bargaining both conditions of employment and solutions to production problems.

Changes Needed

Unions need to make four crucial changes:

1. Bargain for the establishment of parallel organizations consis-
    tent with the four design principles
2. Bargain for the enforceability of these parallel organizations
    and the agreements reached by their action teams
3. Require that all workers who serve on action or planning teams
    or who act as program "coordinators" be union officers (that is,
    that these positions be official, elective union positions)
4. Devote major resources to setting up and maintaining training
    programs for participation stewards

These changes would place labor on a strategic course involving decentralization, multilateral bargaining, and the maintenance of management accountability. A "whole" parallel organization used as a mechanism for integrative bargaining would necessarily decentralize the integrative part of collective bargaining. By involving large numbers of members in this mainstream activity, unions would increase their levels of internal democracy. A whole parallel organization also means multilateral bargaining. Action and planning teams include representatives from all workplace interest groups, and the rules, procedures, policies, programs, and work methods developed must be agreed to by all the interest groups. Another key feature of the parallel organization is that it does not change the authority structure. Management continues to make the final decisions and management continues to be accountable for results. To tamper with this arrangement would create conflict-of-interest situations, impair management's ability to perform, and weaken labor's ability to protect its members. This is not to say, however, that hour-to-hour and day-to-day decisions about how to work should not be delegated to workers and to their team leaders to the maximum feasible extent.

I recognize that, in many workplaces (for example, the Pima County government), most workers are not union members. This makes it difficult to implement the part of Change 3 that deals with workers sitting on action and planning teams. Where the penetration of the union is substantial, Change 3 creates an added incentive for nonaffiliated workers to join the union. Where only a small portion of the work force belongs to the union, other strategies must be developed. For example, nonaffiliated workers serving on action or planning teams can be made "honorary" union officers for the duration of their service. The remaining sections of this chapter discuss the detailed changes that might be made in local bylaws, the ways that contract negotiation and administration might be affected by the three crucial changes, and the kind of training needed by participation stewards.

Local Bylaws

The four crucial changes should be reflected in the local bylaws. This would help make it clear to members that they owe their opportunities to participate in decision making to their union. The articles on objectives, duties of local officers, duties of stewards, and collective bargaining are among those affected.

Objectives. This article might be clarified by an additional paragraph dealing with the improvement of working conditions. This additional objective would define the aims of the union in proposing, jointly developing, jointly operating, and monitoring a parallel organization and autonomous work teams. For example, such an objective might read: "To increase the influence of the worker over strategic planning and over work methods and conditions of employment at all levels of the organization."

Duties of Local Officers. This article would be revised to reflect the responsibilities of union officers in connection with serving on action and planning teams. For example, the article might assign the president of the local union the duty of serving as the senior union member on the action team at the bargaining unit level. This article could also be revised to authorize additional officers to serve as coordinators for the participation system. It might establish several "system coordinator" positions, which would be paid by management. The United Auto Workers Region 5 "New Directions" platform calls for the election of these "clipboard people" (Slaughter, 1989). This is an excellent platform plank, but it is not enough. When a worker is elected to one of these positions, he or she should become a recognized union officer as a result of election. These positions should appear in the bylaws along with the president, secretary, treasurer, and so on.

Duties of Stewards. This article would be divided into two parts: one part dealing with existing stewards and the other with participation stewards. The latter would probably require their election in accordance with the provisions of the applicable parallel agreement. It might describe their duties as "representing their constituents in working jointly with management to develop plans and solutions to problems through the integrative bargaining process." The existence of these provisions should help make it clear to the rank and file that employees sitting on action or planning teams are acting as union officers and are representing union members.

Collective Bargaining. This article would describe two collective bargaining processes: distributive bargaining and integrative bargaining. In addition to describing the composition and procedures of the bargaining committee, it would summarize in a general way the composition and procedures of the parallel organization. It would establish guidelines and procedures for such matters as deciding whether an item should be handled by the bargaining committee or by the top-level action team. It would also specify the levels at which parallel agreements are authorized and would specify the consensus agreements that would be grievable (for example, all parallel agreements down to and including the parallel agreement for each autonomous work team; all consensus agreements regarding conditions of employment, work methods, and strategic planning that are signed by both labor and management).

Contract Negotiation

Under joint management, four additional kinds of agreements can be negotiated in addition to the basic labor contract: parallel agreements, conditions of employment agreements, work-methods agreements, and strategic planning agreements. Parallel agreements establish the rules, policies, and procedures of the participative system itself. "Conditions of employment" agreements deal with matters that might otherwise have been bargained at the bargaining unit level. Work-methods agreements address production problems, and strategic planning agreements affect long-term marketing, financial, and other plans. All of these additional agreements would be reached through the process of integrative bargaining.

However, it is probable that certain aspects of the joint management system should be bargained in the distributive bargaining relationship and included in the basic labor contract rather than in the parallel agreement at the bargaining unit level. Two aspects that might be so bargained are the general agreement to proceed with the development and installation of a joint management system and specific provisions dealing with the enforceability of each of the four kinds of agreements reached through the parallel organization.

Bargaining Parallel Agreements. The remainder of the joint management system might be best developed through the integrative bargaining process. This process would probably begin with the establishment of an action team at the bargaining unit level. This action team might form a whole and representative design team. The design team could develop the bargaining unit level (executive level) parallel agreement. This agreement could:

> Establish the general management principles upon which the system would be based
> State the design principles that would guide operating and worksite levels of the organization in developing their own parallel agreements
> Give the purposes of the joint management system and describe its structure in specific terms at the bargaining unit level and in general terms at lower levels
> Set forth the election procedures governing top-level action and planning teams
> Establish the organization and the operating procedures of these top-level teams along with the responsibilities and roles of their members
> Establish mechanisms for enforcing both the provisions of parallel agreements at all levels of the organization and the rules, policies, and procedures developed by the action and planning teams

After the parallel agreement at the bargaining unit level is approved by the action team and ratified by the membership, parallel agreements could be bargained at the operating, intermediate, and worksite levels. The process through which these agreements would be bargained is, of course, quite different than that which is used in distributive bargaining. The guiding principle of the integrative bargaining process is consensus. Its key constraint is that the senior management members of the action teams at the executive, operating, intermediate, and worksite levels are authorized to make the final design decisions. Should the union wish to appeal a design decision, its recourse would be to take it up in the distributive bargaining process. The principles to be observed and the specific steps to be taken in bargaining joint management systems are discussed in Chapter Twenty-Two. To bargain these systems is, in effect, to jointly design them. Accordingly, bargaining them must follow the design principles described in Chapter Two: joint management systems should be whole, self-designed, and representative. Further, the administrative structures of labor and management should be adapted to be consistent with the principles and philosophy of joint management (see Introduction).

Using the Parallel Organization as a Bargaining Mechanism. Each action and planning team of the parallel organization would be a forum for bargaining work methods and conditions of employment. These teams would produce rules, policies, procedures, and programs (work rules, fiscal procedures, procurement policies, personnel policies, personnel procedures, training programs, and so on) that would be designated as enforceable by the basic labor contract.

The process that action and planning teams would use to produce enforceable rules, policies, and procedures is quite different from distributive bargaining. The integrative bargaining process uses problem-solving techniques (see Chapter Seventeen) and relies on reaching consensus rather than compromising and trading off. Further, integrative bargaining does not rely on strikes and lockouts as immediate sanctions. Management makes the final decisions. If labor disagrees with a management decision, it can refer the matter to its bargaining committee to be handled through distributive bargaining. Only then can sanctions be applied. When an action team reaches consensus, it means that management has joined in a decision regarding conditions of employment, work methods, or the governance of the parallel organization. Once these decisions are made, they are enforceable. It is also important to realize that integrative bargaining is not bipartite. This kind of bargaining recognizes that neither labor nor management is monolithic. The views of the people making up different occupational groups, different levels of management, and different organizational units not only differ but sometimes conflict with each other. The reconciliation of these different views requires a new process: multilateral bargaining. Multilateral bargaining possesses a new and unique feature when applied to the workplace: the weaker parties have their rights enforced for them by the stronger parties. That is, in order to gain the benefits of social integration (Herrick, 1985), labor and management agree to enforce the agreements arrived at through the consensus of all the workplace interest groups. In this way, groups that lack the power to enforce their own rights (like first-line supervisors, middle managers, and nonunion office workers) can rely on the two parties with the power to see that the rules of the participative system are followed and that the policies, procedures, and programs bargained through the system are implemented. In effect, multilateral bargaining is a step toward the kind of "associational unionism" advocated by Heckscher (1988).

The rules, policies, and procedures that are produced by action and planning teams differ from those produced through adversary bargaining in both substance and form. Their substance is different because their principal purpose is not to protect one party from the other but to record a mutually agreed-upon solution to a common problem. They appear in the form of instructions (manual sections, memoranda, and so on) signed by both labor and management rather than as provisions of the labor contract. They deal with conditions of employment, work methods, and, in some cases, strategic plans.

Contract Administration

Under extended bargaining, the union must administer three additional kinds of contracts: decentralized agreements dealing with conditions of employment, parallel agreements, and decentralized agreements dealing with work methods. In addition, where the parallel organization participates in strategic planning, the union must consider the extent to which consensus plans constitute agreements. I will not comment on this question, since there is so little experience available at this time on which to base any comments.

Enforcing Conditions of Employment. It would seem that conditions of employment bargained in the parallel organization should be enforced using the existing grievance procedure and working through the regular stewards. However, I can only speculate on this, since (to my knowledge) no formal grievance has ever been filed on a rule, policy, or procedure bargained in a parallel organization. It might be helpful, however, to listen to an AFSCME field representative talk about a grievance that was nearly filed in 1981 on behalf of an employee in Pima County, Arizona: "I heard that Chuck [the department head] had assigned Joe to a different maintenance unit without following the procedures agreed to under QWL. I went down there and asked him what was going on. He said, 'But that was just QWL. I thought it was voluntary.' I said, 'Think again,' and he put Joe back in his old unit." This story suggests that, where a basic labor contract makes conditions of employment bargained in the parallel organization enforceable, managers will be even less likely to violate them. This point is supported by the recent Shell-Sarnia experience.

Enforcing the Parallel Agreements. It is possible that some unions might wish to develop separate systems for enforcing their parallel agreements. A case can be made for a grievance procedure jointly designed by labor and management and contained in the top-level parallel agreement. This arrangement might be desirable, since, while management might not regard the enforceability of parallel agreements as desirable, once the union has carried this point it is in the interests of both parties to design as effective an enforcement system as possible. Further, it will be necessary to deal with violations by labor as well as by management representatives. While the specifics of any enforcement system will depend on the needs of the organization and on the views of its members, the following criteria might be useful:

1. The system should facilitate the resolution of complaints informally and at the lowest level possible.
2. Its decisions should consider the points of view of all parties and should be acceptable to all parties.
3. It should serve as a strong incentive to everyone to abide by the parallel agreements.

One approach to meeting these criteria would be to use the action teams to consider complaints. Any member of the organization could complain that a provision of a parallel agreement was being violated. The first step in the complaint procedure might be for the steward representing the complainer to arrange an informal meeting between the complainer and the person who is thought to be violating the provisions of a parallel agreement. If the complaint cannot be resolved to the complainer's satisfaction, the steward could raise the complaint orally in the lowest-level action team on which the complainer is represented. If the complaint cannot be resolved in this forum, it might be referred to the next higher action team, which would discuss it with both the complainer's steward and the person being complained against. This procedure could be repeated at higher and higher levels of the organization until the complaint is resolved.

An action team's finding that a manager has failed to abide by the provisions of a parallel agreement should be entered in his or her personnel file and become a factor in considering that member for promotion. This kind of enforcement system should improve the effectiveness of the joint management system substantially. This improvement might well occur without any complaint ever getting past the informal discussion stage. The simple existence of the grievance procedure would send a powerful message to all organization members that they should take the joint management system seriously. Why should a manager risk a negative finding in his or her personnel folder by such behavior as failing to schedule action team meetings or failing to implement agreed-upon decisions?

Enforcing Work Methods. Some work methods have a major impact on conditions of employment and others do not. One way to handle the enforcement of work-methods agreements would be for the action or planning team to discuss this question when it is reaching consensus on the work method itself. At this time, the team could also reach consensus on whether the work method has a major impact on conditions of employment. If the team agrees that it does, it could be put in writing and signed by both labor and management. This would make it enforceable under the regular grievance procedures. If the team agrees that it does not have this impact, it would not be signed by both labor and management and so would not be enforceable under the grievance procedures. Rules, policies, and procedures arrived at in action and planning teams, however, should rarely need to be enforced. They have the advantage of having been agreed to by all the affected parties before being put into effect. One of the major reasons that unions and managements develop joint management systems is that they lead to internally controlled organization members. That is, all the parties tend to abide by the rules, polices, and procedures of the organization without any control being exercised over them by others. They "own" the rules, policies, and procedures and so they voluntarily abide by them.

Nevertheless, enforcement procedures are necessary. They help the parties to the problem-solving process take the process seriously. They protect the organization from the tendency of the new manager to change procedures that have been working well, simply to make a mark on the organization. They protect the gains realized by the union and its members.

Training Implications and Their Costs

We can only speculate on whether an extended bargaining system of this nature would require more or fewer union resources. There are two factors to be taken into account in considering this question: the cost of administering such a system and the impact of the system on present costs.

One of labor's major costs of administering an extended bargaining system would be the cost of training. It is important that the union conduct its own separate training program to instruct participation stewards and combined-function union officers in their responsibilities to their constituents and to the union as an institution. This does not mean that the union should conduct separate training in communications, problem solving, proposal writing, and so on. Training in these skills, along with the specifics of the joint management system and information on the organization's other management subsystems (budget, personnel, and so on), can appropriately be organized by management, so long as a union co-instructor is used. The responsibilities of union representatives to their constituents and the responsibilities of management representatives to theirs, however, should be taught by labor and management separately. Since there would be perhaps five times as many participation stewards as regular stewards in a local union, the cost of their training will be substantial.

Another cost would be the provision of staff assistance to the participation stewards and combined-function union officers in carrying out these responsibilities. This staff assistance would range from giving advice on the telephone to attending a particular problem-solving meeting. In addition, there would be some cost involved in enforcing the "conditions of employment" agreements reached at all levels of the parallel organization. Where the enforcement of the parallel agreements themselves is handled by the parallel organization, it would probably not place much of an additional burden on the union. Experience suggests that the costs of administering the basic labor contract would decrease under an extended bargaining situation. Typically, joint management systems have resulted in marked declines in the numbers of grievances filed.

Problem Areas

The problems with extended bargaining revolve around the additional resources it would require in its initial stages and the fact that its consequences are unknown. While it might well lower the administrative costs of the union in the long run, it would require an initial investment (or the transfer of resources from existing activities) in the short term. It is always difficult to invest money now in the expectation of future benefits. The possible consequences of enforcing the administrative issuances of all levels of management, when these issuances deal with conditions of employment and are agreed upon in action teams, are upsetting. Might the union get mired down in an impossible task? If there were a large number of grievances against these locally bargained working conditions, how could the staff cope with them? Further, how could the conflicts that might arise between the locally bargained conditions and the provisions of the basic contract be resolved? These concerns are serious and valid. The stakes, however, are high. Labor must change in some radical way that more nearly meets the needs of workers if it is to survive. Further, the answers to many of these questions about integrative bargaining may not be known, but they are knowable. Unions could experiment with extended bargaining in the 1990s in much the same way that they experimented with early parallel organizations and autonomous work teams in the 1970s and 1980s.

Part VIII

⟋⟍⟋⟍

The Social Impact of Jointly Managed, Participative Organizations

This part discusses the societal implications of joint management at three levels: the individual, the organization, and society. Chapter Twenty-Five makes the case that, if properly designed and maintained, joint management systems *can* improve human well-being and increase productivity. Whether a given system accomplishes these things depends, in large part, on whether it is self-designed, whole, and representative, and whether the existing management and labor subsystems are adapted to its principles and practices. Chapter Twenty-Six comments on the ways that working arrangements, and specifically joint management, affect other aspects of our lives, such as economics, political freedom, and social values. It also suggests roles that labor, education, church, and government might play to ensure that the total impact of joint management on society is positive. It suggests a lead role for labor and advocates a coalition of organized labor and organized religion. The preceding seven parts of the book discuss joint management and how to go about putting it in place. This part talks about why well-designed joint management systems are a good idea.

The Social Impact of Jointly Managed Participative Organizations

Chapter 25

People and Productivity

The most asked but least answered set of questions about joint management (and about participative management generally) is: "Will it improve worker well-being and will it increase productivity?" I do not attempt to answer these questions here. Instead, I address a different set of questions: "*Can* joint management improve worker well-being and *can* it increase productivity?"

The first set of questions assumes that joint management is a constant: that the same design decisions are made in each case and that these decisions are made through the same process. Researchers examining these questions typically look at a given number of instances of joint management and report that, in X percent of these cases, people or productivity were affected positively. Yet the natures of the systems concerned are likely to be radically different. To lump them together for purposes of analysis is like lumping a dozen different kinds of food together and reporting that X percent of all food is helpful in preventing cancer. It might be a true report, but it would hardly be useful to people interested in reducing their chances of getting cancer. Of course, some sort of "lumping together" is necessary if one is to draw conclusions based on more than one case. One way to accomplish this might be to first grade each joint management system being researched on the extent to which it is whole, self-designed, and representative and the extent to which labor and management administrative systems have been adapted to joint management philosophy and practices. These grades could then be related to the people and productivity consequences of the systems. We might then use the results to develop hypotheses on the criteria, or combinations of criteria, that are important to a system's success. Based on this research, an evaluation system might be developed capable of predicting the success of any given joint management system. It would then be possible to answer the question "What kinds of joint management systems are most likely to improve human well-being and increase productivity?" The answers to this question would certainly be useful to unionists and to managers.

There would be difficulties, both theoretical and practical, in developing such an evaluation system. The theoretical difficulty arises from systems theory, which suggests that the criteria are interdependent. A low ranking on any one criterion might prevent the total system from producing significant results. The practical difficulty is that many other factors clearly influence the success of a joint management system (industry, size of organization, the economy, existing labor-management relations, financial health of the firm, the personalities involved, and so on). These factors would also have to be taken into account in the design of an effective evaluation system.

While it is impossible to answer the first question posed at the beginning of this chapter (Does joint management improve worker well-being and increase productivity?), it is useful to discuss the second question (Can joint management have these results?). While even this simpler question cannot be answered absolutely (due to the factors other than joint management that influence worker well-being and productivity), we can draw tentative conclusions on the basis of reports such as those described below.

The Well-Being of Organization Members

Job security, high wages, safe working conditions, and fair administrative systems contribute to the well-being of the workers and managers who make up an organization. Other measures of well-being include such items as job satisfaction, general happiness, trust of management, trust of co-workers, and so on. This section abstracts these kinds of information from a number of published accounts reporting on jointly managed organizations.

Lawler (1986) reports that an attitude survey taken in a number of locations of the Ford Motor Company having QWL (that is, joint management) showed employees to be more satisfied as a result of being involved in the thinking side of their jobs. He also reports a drop in grievances at the General Motors Tarrytown, New York, facility from 2,000 in 1972 to 32 in 1978 (a QWL program was initiated at this facility in 1973). In a recent survey at Ford, says Lawler, over 90 percent of the employees were in favor of QWL. He concludes from these and other cases that QWL projects lead to improved employee well-being.

In a jointly authored book chapter, Raymond Williams of AT&T and Glen Watts, formerly president of the Communications Workers of America, also present evidence supporting the position that joint management leads to improved human well-being (1986). They describe a study in AT&T that showed that QWL team members were more satisfied with their jobs than was the work force in general. The same study revealed that these team members felt they had grown personally in skills and confidence. Benjamin Boylston of the Bethlehem Steel Corporation (1986) reports similar findings. He cites a survey done in that corporation's Lebanon, Pennsylvania, plant a year after labor-management participative committees were formed. The data in this case showed improvements in employee attitudes and communications.

Macy (1982) reports similar results in connection with the first joint management experiment in the United States. After evaluating the first fifty-five months of the United Auto Workers/Harman International Industries project in a Bolivar, Tennessee, auto mirror plant, Macy wrote that "the Bolivar program resulted in positive changes in the area of employment security. More jobs were created, as the employment level rose 55 percent" (p. 205). Macy also reported that Bolivar employees were generally positive about the project. These findings are especially impressive in the light of the pioneering nature of the Bolivar project. Another early experiment in joint management, the United Mine Workers/Rushton Coal Mine project, was terminated by the union for a variety of reasons.

However, Goodman (1982) reports higher safety ratings for the experimental sections of the mine, an increase in favorable job attitudes, and increases in job skills. In addition, some workers in the experimental sections received wages above the regular contract wage. Gardell (1982) reports on a "workplace democratization" project entered into by the AB Almex Company and its three unions. Interviews conducted with workers showed that this project, which featured the use of autonomous work teams, increased the workers' sense of their worth and dignity. Further, while 50 percent of the workers in Almex's nonautonomous departments felt that the main benefit they received from their work was money, only 20 percent of the employees in the autonomous departments held this view. The project also appeared to affect stress and energy levels in a positive manner. In the nonautonomous departments, 18 percent of the workers reported experiencing stress very often or quite often, compared with 7 percent in the autonomous departments. As regards energy, 22 percent of the nonautonomous workers said that they were often (or quite often) so tired from the day's work that they had trouble doing something else like getting together with friends or spending time on a hobby. The comparable figure for the autonomous departments was only 2 percent. An employee involvement program combined with a modified Scanlon Plan at Eggers Industries resulted in improved employee morale (Dulworth, 1985). Union vice-president Hearley commented that he himself was "a lot happier at work."

While joint management is less common in the public sector, a number of efforts have reported improvements in human well-being. For example, John Venios, president of Service Employees International Union Local 246, is quoted as saying that a joint management effort begun in 1979 in the New York City Department of Sanitation had reduced grievances by more than three-quarters and substantially improved job satisfaction (Contino, 1986).

Another public-sector system, based on an agreement between AFSCME and the board of supervisors of Pima County, Arizona, reported increases in security, equity, and job satisfaction. The same effort, however, reports decreases in perceived autonomy. Interviews with workers and supervisors in Pima County suggest strong benefits in the area of human well-being (Herrick, 1983–84).

Jerry Robles, heavy equipment operator, notes that there is less distance now between the blue-collar and white-collar (predominantly Anglo) employees of his department. "Before, they were always grouchy. You'd ask them a question and they'd snap back at you. Now they're real nice about it. Before, you'd pass by and wave at them and they wouldn't wave back. I don't know if it's because of QWL, but they've gotten friendlier" (p. 61). Ray Borquez, assistant crew supervisor, also comments on ethnic relations. "In QWL, Anglos and Mexicans accept each other's ideas and share in the situation. . . . Before, we didn't have this. We were Mexicans and that's all there was to it. I'm a grown man, fifty some odd years old, but I have feelings about these things" (p. 62). Ron Ayers, assistant to the director, gives another example. "Hey, it's been a positive force on my life. . . . My wife and my boys and I, we deal with . . . things jointly. I'll tell you, there's even less fighting between my boys, Jimmy and Brian" (p. 62).

Few of the above accounts give us any hints regarding the extent to which the joint management systems involved meet the criteria of wholeness, self-design, representation, and integration. Neither do they tell us about such factors as the state of the economy at the time the system was initiated. Nevertheless, we can conclude from these accounts that it is possible, under favorable circumstances, for joint management systems to impact positively on human well-being. It is reasonable to suppose that, at this stage in the evolution of joint management, most of the systems reported on meet only very imperfectly the four criteria suggested above. Thus, we can modify our conclusion to read: "Under somewhat favorable circumstances, joint management systems can impact positively on human well-being." If the four criteria were more fully met, the impact might be even more positive.

Productivity

Changes in productivity are, perhaps, even more sensitive to factors outside the joint management system than are changes in human well-being. We cannot conclude, simply because productivity increases follow the installation of a joint management system, that the system has produced these changes. Neither can we conclude, from the fact that published accounts of joint management efforts almost always report productivity increases, that these increases will always occur. Certainly, successful systems are more likely to be "written up" than are failures. Nevertheless, the following abstracts strongly suggest that joint management *can* lead to increased productivity. This section abstracts information regarding productivity changes from a number of published accounts of joint management systems.

Katz, Kochan, and Gobeille (1983) report limited support for the hypothesis that quality of working life efforts improve both industrial relations and economic performance. They evaluated eighteen General Motors plants with QWL programs and assigned them high or low QWL program ratings, using twenty criteria ranging from whether the plant had held off-site training or problem-solving discussions with hourly workers to whether or not it had promotional programs, such as plant T-shirts, jackets, and pens. Over the two-year period following the installation of the joint management systems, the plants with high ratings outperformed the others on a number of economic measures. For example, they had an average 1.5 percent improvement in their quality index, while the plants with low ratings had a 0.2 percent decrease. The plants with the most QWL activity had a 1.8 percent increase in absenteeism while the others had a 20.6 percent increase.

While most evaluations of Scanlon plans (see Chapter Twenty for a description of the plan) combine data from union and nonunion plants, we will use these data in our discussion of joint management on the grounds that the Scanlon committee structure by itself constitutes a union of sorts, albeit a questionable one under Section 8(a)(2) of the NLRA. Lawler and Ledford (1981–82) concluded on the basis of two reviews of published Scanlon Plan cases that it has about an 80 percent chance of success. While they concede that many failures go unreported, Lawler and Ledford say that they have experienced well above a 50 percent success rate in their own work. A survey of the literature by Moore and Ross (1978) found thirty successes and fourteen failures. Most of the reasons given for the failures suggest that they could have been avoided (poor formula, negative management attitudes, and so forth). Moore and Ross also cite another group of firms that reported an average bonus of 10 percent above going wages over a ten-year period. In describing the 1981 installation of a Scanlon plan at Eggers, Dulworth (1985) tells us that bonuses have been paid every month since the trial period, ranging from 2.2 to 33.6 percent of employees' gross pay. He also writes that, in 1983, profits rose from the previous year by about 14 percent.

According to Lawler (1986), the evidence, while incomplete, indicates that productivity improvements can be obtained through QWL programs. He mentions a report of the Ford Sharonville plant stating that the plant's customer complaints dropped by 70 percent. Sharonville also showed annual cost improvements of almost 7.2 percent for 1982 to 1984, while 2.5 percent was common during this time for other Ford plants.

QWL activities were sponsored by Honeywell and Teamsters Local 1145 in Minneapolis beginning in 1981. Scrap and rework as a percentage of sales decreased from 6.5 percent in 1981 to 4.0 percent in 1984 (Boyle, 1986). Camens (1986) cites a number of examples of savings accomplished by labor-management participation teams in the steel industry. Just to mention one of these examples, he describes one team that developed a tool availability program for a blast furnace at a cost of $16,000, which saved $330,000 per year. After studying the UAW/Harman effort over a seven-year period, from 1972 to 1979, Macy (1982) concluded "there is little question as to the positive behavioral and financial outcomes for the company" (p. 215). Output per hourly employee per day rose 23 percent. Net product reject rates declined by 47 percent and scrap decreased by 16 percent. "Not all results were positive, as the rate of manufacturing supplies rose 22 percent and the rate of machine down time increased slightly" (p. 206). Goodman (1982) reports on the UMW/ Rushton project, saying "our best estimate is that there was a slightly positive effect on productivity on the order of 3 to 4 percent" (p. 241).

We also find some evidence of increased productivity through joint management in the public sector. This evidence is rarer, in part because productivity is difficult to measure in many public-sector operations. The New York City Sanitation Department's Bureau of Motor Equipment increased its productivity by 24 percent during the first year of its joint management program (Contino, 1986). The eight "profit centers" of this bureau increased profits from $1.15 million per year to $2.4 million, a gain of 109.3 percent. One of the few hard measures available to evaluate the joint management system in Pima County, Arizona, is road grading efficiency. This measure rose from 14 percent of standard in 1980 (when the system was installed in the Department of Transportation) to 119 percent during the first three months of 1983. Estimated savings over the two-and-one-quarter-year period was $12.2 million (Herrick, 1983–84).

The Real Issue

The issue is not whether joint management "works." In many cases, unions and managements join together in sponsoring participative systems and these systems produce gains in human well-being and productivity. In some cases, unions and managements join together toward the same end and the resultant systems fail. Whether joint management works or not depends on the nature of the design process, the design features of the system, and environmental factors. In general, I believe that, if a system were participatively designed and based on the principles of wholeness, representation, and adaptation, it would very probably "work." This book proposes specific approaches to achieving participative design, wholeness, and representation. It also proposes approaches to adapting labor and management administrative systems to the principles and practices of joint management.

The issue is to discover the specific design features and the specific design processes that will serve labor and management best as "points of departure" as they begin the task of converting their organizations to joint management. Discovering these features and processes is a job that is best accomplished through a combination of ethnographic research and evaluation. The hypotheses we need to investigate do not involve the general relationships among job characteristics or the relationships of job characteristics to productivity. What we need to do is to investigate such hypotheses as "Where union bylaws define all worker representatives on action and planning teams as union officers, the effectiveness of both the parallel organization and the union will increase." A list of thirty-four such hypotheses is included in a *Human Relations* article (Herrick, 1985).

Chapter 26

Joint Management
and Social Policy

Joint management is a powerful idea. It can provide benefits to the rich and to the poor, to the middle and working classes, and to Republicans and Democrats. Its compensation policies can lessen the income gaps between these groups. It can give managers and workers alike the freedom to develop their positive traits. It can reinforce cooperative and gentle behavior and offer managers and employees mutual respect based on right behavior. It can open up public policy options with the potential for enabling us to better compete abroad and to improve our material and our psychological standards of living here at home.

Joint management is also a dangerous idea. It can obscure the legitimate conflicts of interest between labor and management. It can weaken the protections that workers have created for themselves over the years through their unions. It can place managers in positions of great paternalistic power and so make it difficult for them to develop their positive character traits. It can seduce workers into surrendering their dignity and their power to benevolent dictatorships. It can help destroy the labor movement.

Whether for good or for evil, we have opened Pandora's box and released both its sorrows and its redeeming virtue: hope. Now strong action must be taken to avoid the sorrows and bring the hope to fruition. The main responsibility for taking this action falls squarely on the shoulders of the labor movement. Only labor can act to adapt its contract negotiation and administration systems to joint management. Only labor can broaden its enforcement mechanisms to cover parallel agreements and the rules, policies, procedures, and programs produced by parallel organizations. Only labor can initiate the decentralization of integrative bargaining.

To date, unions have typically either enthusiastically entered into joint arrangements with management, without sufficiently integrating these arrangements into the collective bargaining process (like the United Auto Workers, Communications Workers of America, and the United Steel Workers of America), or reluctantly allowed their locals to enter into joint arrangements under certain specified conditions (like the International Association of Machinists and Aerospace Workers). Both policies are likely to lead to the further weakening of labor and strengthening of management. Therefore, this chapter on joint management and social policy must be written conditionally. That is, the implications of joint management for the world we live in can be either very positive or very negative, depending on the actions taken or not taken by organized labor. This chapter assumes that labor will act to integrate joint management and collective bargaining, but makes an occasional comment on the consequences of not doing so.

Societal Implications

Most of the chapters of this book have been based on a combination of personal experience and the reported experiences of others. This chapter is more speculative. It draws inferences from experiences in the workplace and applies these inferences to some major aspects of life: economics, political freedom, and religion. Industrial organization is not a dry, specialized subject, interesting only to academicians. It is a key element of a larger system (society) and powerfully affects this larger system in myriad ways.

Economics. Let us assume that the principles and practices of joint management, if properly applied in all unionized workplaces, would have results comparable to those described in Chapter

Twenty for the seven Scanlon Plan companies over a ten-year period (see Moore and Ross, 1978). This seems reasonable, since, while all joint management efforts may not be able to apply gain sharing, they can all use the knowledge we have gained about parallel organizations and autonomous work teams—and the seven Scanlon plants did not enjoy the benefits of this knowledge. Nevertheless, although the form of parallel organization they used was incomplete, they produced monthly bonuses averaging 10 percent of pay. Since most Scanlon plans return $1 to the company for every $3 paid in bonuses, these companies probably enjoyed a return of about 3.3 percent of payroll over the ten-year period.

Returns such as these applied to the approximately 17 percent of the work force that is now unionized would improve the economy in several ways. In the public sector, assuming that the bonuses could not be obtained through either gain sharing or collective bargaining, the lion's share of the benefits would accrue to the taxpayer, in the form of either increased services or reduced taxes. In the private sector, the standards of living of the unionized work force would increase, as would the taxes paid by this work force, the profits realized by its companies, and the ability of these companies to compete on the foreign market. The point here is that the order of productivity increases that might be realized through joint management, when applied to a significant segment of the work force, would have a substantial impact on the country's total economy. However, it should be noted that this conclusion is based on the performance of the Scanlon Plan and that this plan uses a form of the parallel organization. Experience suggests that joint management approaches that are dominated by management (and are not monitored by labor-management teams at all levels of the organization) rarely produce long-term productivity increases.

Political Freedom. Even if we assume that the economy might benefit from a widespread application of joint management principles and practices—whether or not unions move to integrate these principles and practices into collective bargaining—the same cannot be said for our political freedom. I will, therefore, speculate on the consequences of two possible courses of events.

First, let us suppose that unions continue their present strategy: neither adequately protecting themselves from joint management nor integrating it into their collective bargaining mechanisms: the "occasional dabbling" strategy (Parker, 1985). It seems likely that this strategy, if continued, will substantially contribute to nationwide decline in union membership. In effect, management will control a major portion of the collective bargaining process and workers will respond by asking themselves, "What do we need a union for now that we have QWL?" (Showalter and Yetman, 1983).

It is clear that workers place a high value on having more control over the special problems facing their departments, divisions, sections, and work units. Over the past fifteen years, a variety of joint management systems (variously called QWL, employee involvement, labor-management participation circles, and so forth) have evolved that, in varying degrees, have allowed workers more control over these problems. However, participative systems in nonunion workplaces have also been effective in satisfying employee needs. An AFL-CIO report (1984) reports that it is extremely difficult to organize plans with participative systems. "Unions won only 8 percent of the campaigns in manufacturing industries with QWL plans (as opposed to 36 percent in these industries overall)."

It seems clear that many workers want participative systems. It also seems clear that management has taken the lead role in providing these systems, both in nonunion and in union workplaces. This has been made possible, in large part, by our failure to recognize that most participative systems carry on a form of collective bargaining and should, therefore, be union driven. The courts have failed to recognize this in their recent decisions (for example, *NLRB* v. *Streamway Division,* 1982). Unions have also failed to recognize the fact that participation systems are their "bread and butter." While they have often "gone along" with management in sponsoring these systems in unionized workplaces, they have been willing to allow management to do the lion's share of the work and get the lion's share of the credit. While they have brought suit against management for creating participative systems in nonunion workplaces, they have not devoted major resources to creating competitive systems in unionized plants. It is certainly of major importance that decisions such as *NLRB* v. *Streamway* be overturned. But it is also crucial that labor take the lead in shaping the course of participation in unionized workplaces.

The decision that organized labor is now pondering (that is, how to relate to employee participation) may be a factor in determining whether the trade union movement continues to be a force in North American society. Should labor cease to be such a force, a chain of events may be set in motion that might seriously weaken our civil liberties. First, the power vacuum created by a weakened labor movement is likely to be occupied by government. The dominant mechanism for protecting workers' rights in this country is still collective bargaining. As this mechanism becomes weaker, it tends to be replaced by state and federal labor legislation. In this way, government becomes stronger. At the same time, the ability of a democracy to maintain itself depends, in part, on the existence of power centers independent of government (for example, a free press, the church, labor unions). These rallying points give people the means to join together and resist arbitrary governmental actions. Should labor cease to be the prime mechanism for worker protection, government would not only gain power by assuming this role—it would also have one less "rallying point" to deal with should it be tempted to use its power in an arbitrary way.

On the other hand, let us suppose that unions do modify their bargaining structures to include decentralized integrative bargaining. This action, by meeting the needs of employees to exercise decentralized control over their working conditions (and by meeting these needs within the framework of the union movement), should help labor reverse the decline in its membership. Unions would have an important additional benefit to offer prospective members. In addition, to decentralize integrative bargaining would also be to decentralize power and influence within unions. This should tap an important source of new energy for the labor movement: the energy of the rank-and-file worker. It should also reduce friction and increase loyalty between workers and their unions. Such a reversal would tend both to prevent government from usurping the protective role now performed by unions and to maintain labor as a "rallying point." It would also give far more union members practical day-to-day experience in the operation of a democratic system.

The number of members directly involved in the collective

bargaining process would increase by factors ranging from the hundreds to the thousands. Further, they would be involved in a kind of bargaining (integrative bargaining) that develops skills and attitudes appropriate for use in their off-the-job lives. This experience should better equip them to participate in the larger political system.

Societal Values. The values of a society are shaped, in part, by its economics and its form of industrial organization. Fromm (1955) tells us that people adapt themselves; they want to act as they have to act. In a democratic nation with a free trade union movement, however, people can have some control over their form of industrial organization, thus choosing the way they "have to act." One example of the way people's values are shaped by the form of industrial organization under which they work is contained in the Scanlon Plan. In plants with successful Scanlon plans, workers are more likely to engage in coordination, teamwork, and the sharing of information. Conversations with people who work in Scanlon organizations convince me that these behavioral changes are accompanied by value shifts. These people often state with conviction that the financial rewards from the plan are of secondary value. What really matters is the way feelings of concern and helpfulness among the organization's members are increased. It is possible that, if feelings of concern and helpfulness were increased among the members of a critical mass of North American work organizations, these feelings would spill over into people's off-the-job lives and thus impact on societal values.

Institutional Roles in Joint Management

This book makes the case that joint management, if properly initiated and designed, has the potential for freeing people to be more caring, more cooperative, and more productive. If widely adopted, it also has the potential for improving our standard of living and for revitalizing labor unions. The institutions of organized labor, education, and government, therefore, have clear stakes in the way joint management is initiated and designed. The stake of organized religion, while less obvious, is equally real. If we accept the notion that joint management systems can result in increased feelings of cooperation and caring among organization members, we must also accept the notion that there might be a role for religious institutions in promoting joint management. Caring and cooperation are, after all, secular terms for describing spiritual values.

The Role of Labor. A new and potentially highly effective form of collective bargaining is evolving in North America. It uses different processes and techniques and has different ground rules, but it does contain many of the elements of collective bargaining. Organized labor, for the most part, has failed to recognize the fact that QWL, employee involvement, labor-management participation committees, the team concept, and so on are, in effect, watered-down and potentially dangerous forms of collective bargaining. It does have a vague notion that these activities have their down sides. Accordingly, it either resists them or "occasionally dabbles" in them (Parker, 1985). The first step that unions need to take is to wake up to the fact that QWL, employee involvement, and so forth are not soft, pop sociological creations dreamed up by academics. They are a real and shiny 1990 model of collective bargaining. Further, this shiny late model has management in the driver's seat. Organized labor should neither ease itself into the comfortable passenger seat nor run the shiny new model off the road. A more constructive strategy would be for labor to get into the driver's seat itself.

The question, then, becomes how to get into the driver's seat. At first glance, this would not appear to be difficult. Section 8(a)(2) of the National Labor Relations Act (NLRA) prohibits management from being in the driver's seat. Boal (1985) suggests that "QWL programs will undoubtedly soon be subjected to legal challenge." Boal is talking here about management-instituted QWL programs in unionized settings. However, there are two problems with taking such programs to court. First, it is a classic case of "throwing out the baby with the bathwater." Of course, nonunion QWL programs should be taken to court. Where there is no union presence, there is no means of protecting employees from abuses. Where there is a union presence, however, instead of bringing suit the union might more profitably follow the approach laid out in

Chapter Twenty-Four for integrating the program into its collective bargaining system. The second problem lies in the vulnerability of Section 8(a)(2) of the NLRA. Should this section of the law be amended or further weakened by interpretations such as that of the Sixth Circuit Court of Appeals (*NLRB* v. *Streamway,* 1982), the field would be open to the managements of both union and nonunion workplaces to co-opt a major portion of the collective bargaining process and, by so doing, deal another blow to organized labor.

However, while the present situation with regard to joint management presents labor (and society in general) with a serious problem, it also offers a great opportunity. In my view, labor should take the lead role in initiating joint management systems. I have gone into some detail in Chapter Twenty-Two regarding the delineation of roles between labor and management in the initiation of these systems. In order to position itself so that it can be effective in its role, I would suggest that labor take the following actions: first, begin an immediate program to fold joint management into collective bargaining in existing sites; second, take the initiative in bargaining parallel organizations in workplaces where there is no joint management effort; third, protect Section 8(a)(2) from amendment; fourth, enforce Section 8(a)(2) in nonunion workplaces; fifth, democratize its own internal management; and, finally, propose a tripartite commission to comprehensively review the NLRA in the light of the present situation.

Each international union might select a group of strong locals that are engaged in joint management. It could then offer its resources and technical assistance to these locals to undertake the adaptation process described in Chapters Twenty-Two and Twenty-Four. In effect, this would be an experimental program. There is no way of anticipating all the problems and solutions that might be involved in this adaptation process. The only way to discover these problems and their solutions is to go ahead and do it. Just as labor and management began to develop a joint management technology in the 1972 UAW/Harman experiment, so must labor now begin to develop a technology for folding joint management into collective bargaining.

As soon as labor has gained some experience in the adaptation process, it could begin to bargain for extended integrative bargaining in all unionized workplaces. It could also use its new capability in organizing drives. Whether the task were to organize a nonunion workplace or to increase the penetration of a weak local, labor's position would be strengthened if it were able to offer prospective members the opportunity to participate personally in decentralized integrative bargaining.

Should the "company union" section of the NLRA be stricken (or even softened), it is unlikely that labor would be left with the ability to fold joint management into collective bargaining. To eliminate this section would allow managements to control collective bargaining. To rewrite it so that it would not apply to joint management would limit labor's role to the negotiation of wages and fringes. This issue should be given a high priority by the lobbying arms of organized labor.

In addition to ensuring the continued existence of Section 8(a)(2), labor should ensure that it is not violated by nonunion employees. While any worker or any "real" union can file a charge with the National Labor Relations Board at no cost (Boal, 1985), the law is "permissive" (that is, it is not enforced unless charges are filed). Thus, many programs resembling joint management exist in nonunion firms. Unions could publicize the fact that it is open to workers to file such charges. They could also monitor the newspapers and other sources of information and file charges themselves when appropriate. Labor's organizing ability could be strengthened by the legal monopoly it has on joint management. However, it could be seriously weakened if labor does not choose to enforce its monopoly. It should be noted here that this monopoly may no longer be limited to the private sector. A U.S. Supreme Court decision in 1983 may have opened the door to future application of the NLRA in the public sector (Wermiel, 1983).

Parallel organizations are highly democratic mechanisms for collective bargaining. They are decentralized, open to all, and their positions of power are filled by eléction, not by appointment. A union that integrated the parallel organization into its collective bargaining structure would be taking a giant step toward making its own internal administration more democratic. The internal democratic systems of North American unions above the workplace level are imperfect. Only one union does not fit the oligarchical pattern (Lipset, Trow, and Coleman, 1956). The one-party oligarchy ("one group which controls the administration, usually retains power indefinitely, rarely faces organized opposition, and when faced with such opposition often resorts to undemocratic procedures to eliminate it" [p. 3]) is the usual pattern. These top-level oligarchical structures would not be in harmony with the kind of workplace-level democracy that would be created by decentralized integrative bargaining. Unions might well consider reviewing their constitutions and bylaws, with a view toward making themselves more democratic (Herrick, 1983, Chapter Sixteen). This, of course, is already being done by groups such as Teamsters for a Democratic Union (TDU). On March 13, 1969 (largely due to the efforts of TDU), Teamster members gained the right to vote directly for their eighteen top officers ("Teamsters," April 1989).

The "de facto" separation of distributive and integrative bargaining that has been evolving over the past seventeen years has major implications for the total labor-management relationship as it is defined by labor law. In addition, the way may now be legally open for the inclusion of the public sector in federal labor law (Wermeil, 1983). The process used in developing such a law might be modeled after the process used in Massachusetts to develop the chapter of the Massachusetts General Laws authorizing the Joint Labor Management Committee for Police and Firefighters. This chapter was developed by representatives of the labor and management organizations that later carried it out. It was then enacted into law virtually without change by the state legislature. The success of the law is attributed, at least in part, to this "multilateral bargaining" process (Brock, 1982). Labor might consider proposing a national presidential commission made up of representatives from labor, management, and religion to develop a body of federal labor law supportive to our economy, political freedom, and social values (Herrick, 1983, Chapter Sixteen). The experience gained through folding joint management into collective bargaining in unionized workplaces that now use joint management systems would be invaluable in framing a new body of labor law.

The Role of Education. One of the functions of education is to provide workers (and managers) with the knowledge, attitudes, and skills needed in the workplace. It follows that, as the workplace becomes more participative, schools should provide students with knowledge about participation and with participative attitudes and skills. Providing information about participation is relatively easy. This kind of information can be worked into courses such as social studies, business, and government. Providing participative attitudes and skills is far more difficult. This would require the restructuring of school districts, schools, departments, and classrooms so that they are managed along more participative lines.

Many school districts (for example, Dade County, Fla.; Detroit, Mich.; Rochester, N.Y.; Petaluma, Calif.; Pittsburg, Pa.; Hammond, Ind.) are installing systems that allow some degree of participation at the school level. In some of these districts, students and parents are included on the school-level committees.

In addition to these school-level efforts, some work is being done to make the actual learning process at the classroom level more participative. The Institute for Democratic Learning at Ohio University is the catalyst for a number of projects of this nature.

However, there are problems with both of these approaches. While the school-level approach tends to improve the management of the school, it involves only small numbers of students and has not resulted in participative classrooms. On the other hand, while the classroom-level experiments get to the heart of the matter, they are dependent on the efforts of exceptional teachers. They are also extremely difficult to maintain over extended periods of time in schools that are not participatively managed.

I would suggest that state legislators reallocate major portions of the money now being spent on alternative schools, dropout programs, and other programs focusing on specific school-related problems. This money would have a greater and more lasting effect if it were spent to fund experiments linking the school-level and classroom-level participative approaches through the use of the parallel organization. Just as the aim of the parallel organization in industry is to support and nurture the autonomous work team, the aim of the school-level "reform" effort should be to support and nurture the participative classroom. Specific school-related problems are symptoms of systemic problems. The development of participative classrooms embedded in participatively managed schools would be a systemic approach to these systemic problems. It would address root causes, rather than symptoms.

   The Role of Government. In one sense, it is inappropriate to talk about a separate role for government. The role of government is to carry out the wishes of the people, not to have wishes of its own. I have already discussed one possible governmental action that might be consistent with the wishes of labor unions (that is, the formation of a presidential commission to review existing labor law). However, we may give some examples of things that governments have done to carry out the wishes of the people with regard to joint management without ascribing to government a greater independence of action than it should have.

   The actions of local governments have mainly concerned their own employees. For example, New York City, Boston, Redwood City (Calif.), San Mateo (Calif.), Columbus (Ohio), and Pima County (Ariz.) are a few of the local governments that have entered into joint management arrangements with the unions representing their employees. The public schools of Detroit are now developing a joint management system.

   Massachusetts and New York are examples of states that are developing joint management systems with the unions representing state employees. California, Florida, and South Carolina have passed "school-based management" laws requiring, among other things, the establishment of committees at the school level that include parents and teachers. Many states, including Massachusetts, Michigan, and Pennsylvania, have passed laws facilitating the "buyout" of troubled firms by their employees.

   The federal government has established a Bureau of Labor-Management Relations and Cooperative Programs in the U.S. Department of Labor. A 1974 law, the Employee Retirement and Income Security Act (ERISA), gave substantial tax advantages to employee stock ownership plans and has been followed by thirteen pieces of federal legislation tending in the same direction (see Chapter Twenty-One). It should be noted that organized labor is far from unanimous in its support of the steps taken to date by the federal government. A UAW member at the Rouge complex outside Detroit asks, in a book published by the Labor Education and Research

Project (Parker, 1985, p. 120), "Is it ironic that the same administration which destroyed PATCO, undermined the NLRB, and rendered OSHA useless should be promoting labor-management cooperation through QWL? Or is it logical?" This underscores the need to ensure that both labor and management are involved in the initial development of any future labor legislation. The opportunities provided by the legislative process to make suggestions and criticisms after legislation is drafted are not adequate in this case.

The Role of Organized Religion. In seeking to promote spiritual growth among its members, the church relies on techniques such as prayer, meditation, Bible study, and sermons. Churches also provide a link between spiritual growth and political action. Along with labor unions and other "rallying points" that are independent of government, they provide people a way to locate other people of like mind and find some protection as they join together to dissent from a government position or policy (for example, administration policy in Central America).

Organized religion has other, less used approaches available to it for promoting spiritual growth. One of these approaches is to influence secular arrangements in the workplace, since these arrangements can either hinder or help people develop spiritually. For example, a piecework system (paying each worker according to the number of items he or she produces) can lead to envious, jealous, and destructive behavior and to angry, uncaring feelings toward one's fellow workers. It does this by making it in each individual's best interest to withhold information and help from others in order to prevent them from driving production standards up. Parallel organizations, autonomous work teams, and gain-sharing plans, on the other hand, foster cooperation and consideration of others. They do this by making it in the best interest of each individual to share information and to give help and support to others. Further, parallel organizations are designed to reconcile the various views of the different workplace interest groups and enable them to spend their work days in greater harmony one with the other. The habitual practice of more caring and helpful behavior must certainly contribute to the spiritual growth of the people concerned.

It follows that organized religion has a major interest and

role in promoting the forms of industrial organization that are conducive to spiritual growth. Two recent encyclicals of the Catholic Church have called for workers to participate in both decision making and in the fruits of their labor (John XXIII, 1965; John Paul II, 1985). Whether for the purpose of promoting spiritual growth or out of a desire to assist the growing American underclass, some U.S. churches have involved themselves in this cause. A number of individual churches have launched programs to assist in the formation of worker cooperatives, among them the Church of the Messiah in Detroit and the Presbyterian Church of Gladwyne, Pennsylvania. In July 1988, the national Episcopal Church Convention committed itself to raising $24,000,000 over the next six years for use as grant and investment money in assisting the underclass to form worker cooperatives (Hooper, 1989).

I would suggest that churches take action to:

1. Increase the support and technical assistance a few churches are already giving to the formation of worker cooperatives, especially for the disadvantaged
2. Develop the capability of providing technical assistance to unions and managements as they convert to and engage in extended integrative bargaining
3. Join with organized labor in lobbying for national legislation strengthening labor's position and defining a labor-management relationship leading to spiritual growth by all organization members

People acting under the egis of a religious organization would be highly credible to both parties and would bring a spiritual dimension to the task of providing technical assistance to unions and managements engaged in joint management. Groups of "workplace missionaries" could be formed by different denominations at regional levels. If it is true that secular arrangements in the workplace can either promote or deter spiritual growth—and if one of the goals of the church is to promote such growth—groups of workplace missionaries could advance this goal. These missionaries could be trained in the principles, practices, and processes of joint management. Since the principles are consistent with those of most major religions, the missionaries could integrate their religious and management training and base their consulting work on this integrated view of the workplace.

A coalition of unions and churches formed for the purpose of bringing about revisions in federal law as it affects labor-management relations would further the goals of both institutions. We need strong unions, in both the private and public sectors. We also need governance structures in the workplace and within unions that are consistent with the democratic governance structures outside the workplace. Finally, we need working arrangements that are favorable to both spiritual and economic values. Fortunately, these needs are consistent with each other. They are not, however, consistent with existing labor law. For example, existing law does not provide labor effective guarantees against unfair labor practices. Neither does it provide society effective guarantees against undemocratic and corrupt unionism, nor does it provide labor and management incentives to carry out constructive roles in initiating and administering joint management systems. Organized religion could bring pressure to bear for the enactment of new labor legislation and could participate in its development by being represented on the presidential commission that might be formed for this purpose (Herrick, 1983, Chapter Sixteen).

Glossary

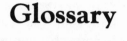

Action team. A small team of organization members, each representing a workplace interest group, that is responsible for supporting and operating the joint management system within its corresponding unit of the primary organization. Each action team includes the head of its corresponding unit, who sits as senior manager-member (see Chapter Thirteen). Action teams at intermediate and higher levels rarely engage in formal problem-solving exercises, but rather review and approve the solutions that have been integratively bargained by their planning teams.

Autonomous work team. A team of people seeking to accomplish the same primary task under conditions characterized by "joint optimization," "facilitative supervision," "a redundancy of functions," and "minimum critical specification" (see Chapter Fifteen).

Combined-function union officer. A union officer who is concerned with both the distributive and the integrative aspects of the labor-management relationship. All officers who have responsibility for bargaining or administering the basic labor contract are combined-function union officers.

Distributive bargaining. Bargaining carried on in an adversary manner for the purpose of distributing finite resources. It usually occurs at contract time and at the bargaining unit level.

Executive level. This level of management occurs only in larger organizations. It plans, controls, budgets, and sets policies—but does not engage in operations (for example, the corporate level, the school system level, the county manager's level).

Extended bargaining. Integrative bargaining carried out by action and planning teams at the bargaining unit level and below. Extended bargaining is enforceable. Unionists who engage in it do so in the capacity of union officers.

Facilitative supervision. Supervisory behavior that serves employees instead of exercising power over them; facilitative supervision provides people the necessary supplies, materials, tools, skills, and reward systems and leaves them to get the job done (see Chapter Eleven).

Integrative bargaining. Bargaining carried on in a cooperative manner for the purpose of solving mutual problems. Until recently, integrative bargaining was mixed with distributive bargaining and carried on at the bargaining unit level.

Intermediate levels. These are the levels between the operating level and the worksite levels of management (for example, the levels between the plant manager and the work units or autonomous work teams).

Joint management. A situation in which organized labor cosponsors the participation of employees in the management process. Labor's cosponsorship can be active or passive. This book proposes an active form of cosponsorship: decentralized integrative bargaining through the parallel organization.

Jointness. A situation in which labor and management jointly pursue mutual goals (for example, safety). Jointness does not necessarily involve the participation of rank-and-file workers.

Joint optimization. Designing the social and technical systems of an organization so that they are mutually supportive.

Minimum critical specification. A management principle that allows for maximum adaptability by giving employees as much discretion as possible in deciding what work methods to apply in each work situation.

Multilateral bargaining. Bargaining by more than two parties. Decentralized integrative bargaining is multilateral because it recognizes that there are subgroups with different interests within both labor and management. Multilateral bargaining aims at finding resolutions acceptable to all parties when there are more than two parties concerned.

Operating level. The lowest level of management that has substantial policy and procedure-making authority (for example, the manager of an auto assembly plant, the head of a county department of transportation, the principal of a school).

Parallel agreement. A written agreement that defines the responsibilities of the parties in administering a parallel organization. Parallel agreements are negotiated at every level of the organization by every organizational unit. At the worksite level, they can be used to describe the methods of operation of autonomous work teams.

Parallel organization. A system of interlinked labor-management teams that develop and act upon (that is, approve, revise, or disapprove) work methods or administrative rules, policies, and procedures. Parallel organizations have the potential to be mechanisms for decentralized integrative bargaining and strategic planning.

Participation steward. A union officer who specializes in integrative bargaining. Participation stewards represent discrete constituencies of workers on action or planning teams. Ideally, all worker members of action and planning teams should be recognized as participation stewards.

Planning miniteam. Since planning teams must represent all workplace interest groups, they are usually too large to do effective problem solving. Therefore, they generally organize themselves into a number of "miniteams," each consisting of four to six members. These miniteams develop solutions to problems and present them to the total planning team for approval before they are submitted to the appropriate action team.

Planning team. A team of organization members, each representing a workplace interest group, that provides staff assistance to an executive- or operating-level action team. Planning teams develop administrative rules, policies, procedures, and programs and submit them to their action teams for approval.

Primary organization. A system of organizational units headed by managers that implements work methods and administrative rules, policies, and procedures and makes day-to-day and hour-to-hour operating decisions.

Primary work unit. The group of people who actually produce the product or service. Where major authorities have been delegated to the work unit and the unit leader is a trainer and boundary maintainer, this group of people is called an autonomous work team.

Redundancy of functions. A management principle that maximizes adaptability by providing employees skills in addition to those required in their everyday work; this allows their work units to deal effectively with "variances" in supply, demand, and other environmental conditions.

Redundancy of parts. A management principle that minimizes training costs by breaking tasks down into simple operations and requiring each employee to learn only one of these operations.

Senior manager-member. The member of an action team who heads that team's corresponding unit in the primary organization. Senior manager-members serve as the main links between the parallel and the primary organizations.

Variance. A variation from the norm in supply, demand, or other condition (for example, a large order for only one of a number of services provided by a work unit, the absence of an employee who normally performs a given task in a work unit, and so forth).

Workplace interest group. A group of organization members who share similar points of view and self-interests due to their common occupation, level in the hierarchy, organizational unit, and so on (for example, middle managers, first-line supervisors, employees of a given subunit, nurses).

Worksite level. The level of organization that actually produces the good or provides the service. This level may be organized as a work unit or as an autonomous work team (for example, a seven-to ten-person work team in an auto assembly plant, a ten-to twelve-person road maintenance team).

References

Adams, J. S. "Inequity in Social Exchange." In L. Berkowitz (ed.), *Advances in Experimental Social Psychology.* Vol. 2. Orlando, Fla.: Academic Press, 1965.

AFL-CIO. *Statistical and Tactical Information Report Number 18.* Washington, D.C.: AFL-CIO, 1984.

AFL-CIO. *The Changing Situation of Workers and Their Unions: A Report by the AFL-CIO Committee on the Evolution of Work.* Washington, D.C.: AFL-CIO, 1985.

Ahlin, J. E. "Arbetsmiljosanering—fornyelse genom demokratisering av planeringsprocessen [Changing the work environment—Renewal through democratization of the planning process]." Stockholm: Royal Institute of Technology, 1974.

Anderson, H. J. *Primer of Labor Relations: A Guide to Employer-Employee Conduct.* Washington, D.C.: Bureau of National Affairs, 1975.

Argyris, C. "Interpersonal Barriers to Decision Making." *Harvard Business Review,* 1966, *44,* 84–97.

Bacharach, S. B., and Lawler, E. J. *Power and Politics in Organizations.* San Francisco: Jossey-Bass, 1981.

Bahr, M. "The Union Makes Us Strong; Participation Makes Us Stronger." *Workplace Democracy,* 1988, *62,* 12–15.

Bales, R. F., and Strodtbeck, F. L. "Phases in Group Problem-Solving." *Journal of Abnormal and Social Psychology*, 1951, *46*, 485–495.

Bansler, J. *Systemudvikling: teori og historie i skandinavisk perspecktiv* [System development: theory and history in Scandinavian perspective]. Lund, Sweden: Studentlitteratur, 1987.

Baron, R. A. *Behavior in Organizations: Understanding and Managing the Human Side of Work*. Newton, Mass.: Allyn & Bacon, 1983.

Bennis, W. G., and Shepard, H. A. "A Theory of Group Development." *Human Relations*, 1965, *9*, 415–457.

Bernstein, P. *Workplace Democratization: Its Internal Dynamics*. New Brunswick, N.J.: Transaction Books, 1976.

Blair, J. D., Cohen, S. J., and Hurvitz, J. V. "Quality Circles: Practical Considerations for Public Managers." *Public Productivity Review*, 1982, *6* (1–2), 9–18.

Blasi, J. R. "The Sociology of Worker Ownership and Participation." In B. D. Dennis (ed.), *Proceedings of the Thirty-seventh Annual Meeting*. Madison, Wis.: Industrial Relations Research Association, 1984.

Bloom, S. M. "The Economics of Employee Ownership." In B. D. Dennis (ed.), *Proceedings of the Thirty-seventh Annual Meeting*. Madison, Wis.: Industrial Relations Research Association, 1984.

Boal, E. "Legal Challenges to QWL." In M. Parker, *Inside the Circle: A Union Guide to QWL*. Boston: South End Press, 1985.

Bohlander, G. W., Jorgensen, G. J., and Werther, W. B., Jr. "The Legal Side of Productivity Through Employee Involvement." *National Productivity Review*, 1983, *2*, 394–401.

Boyle, F. A. "An Evolving Process of Participation: Honeywell and Teamsters Local 1145." In J. M. Rosow (ed.), *Teamwork: Joint Labor-Management Programs in America*. Elmsford, N.Y.: Pergamon Press, 1986.

Boylston, B. C. "Employee Involvement and Cultural Change at Bethlehem Steel." In J. M. Rosow (ed.), *Teamwork: Joint Labor-Management Programs in America*. Elmsford, N.Y.: Pergamon Press, 1986.

Braverman, H. *Labor and Monopoly Capital: The Degradation of*

Work in the Twentieth Century. New York: Monthly Review Press, 1976.

Brock, J. *Bargaining Beyond Impasse: Joint Resolution of Public Sector Labor Disputes.* Boston: Auburn House, 1982.

Brower, M. J. "Massachusetts: Lessons from Efforts That Failed." In N. Q. Herrick (ed.), *Improving Government: Experiments With QWL Systems.* New York: Praeger, 1983.

Camens, S. "Labor-Management Participation Teams in the Basic Steel Industry." In J. M. Rosow (ed.), *Teamwork: Joint Labor-Management Programs in America.* Elsmford, N.Y.: Pergamon Press, 1986.

Cattell, R. B., and Stice, G. F. *The Dimensions of Groups and Their Relations to the Behavior of Members.* Champaign, Ill.: Institute for Personality and Ability Testing, 1960.

Christie, R., and Geis, F. (eds.). *Studies in Machiavellianism.* Orlando, Fla.: Academic Press, 1970.

Cohen-Rosenthal, E., and Burton, C. E. *Mutual Gains: A Guide to Labor-Management Cooperation.* New York: Praeger, 1987.

Conte, M., and Tannenbaum, A. *Employee Ownership.* Ann Arbor: University of Michigan Survey Research Center, 1980.

Contino, R. "Productivity Gains Through Labor-Management Cooperation in the NYC Department of Sanitation, Bureau of Motor Equipment." In J. M. Rosow (ed.), *Teamwork: Joint Labor-Management Programs in America.* Elmsford, N.Y.: Pergamon Press, 1986.

Doyle, M., and Straus, D. *How to Make Meetings Work.* New York: Jove Publications, 1976.

Dulworth, M. "Employee Involvement and Gainsharing Produce Dramatic Results at Eggars Industries." *Labor-Management Cooperation Brief.* Washington, D.C.: U.S. Department of Labor, 1985.

Eckstein, H. *Division and Cohesion in Democracy.* Princeton, N.J.: Princeton University Press, 1966.

Ehn, P. *Work-Oriented Design of Computer Artifacts.* Stockholm: Arbetslivscentrum, 1988.

Ellerman, D. P. "Theory of Legal Structure: Worker Cooperatives." Unpublished paper of the Industrial Cooperative Association, Somerville, Mass., November 1983.

Ellerman, D. P. *What Is a Worker Cooperative?* Somerville, Mass.: Industrial Cooperative Association, 1984.

Emery, F. E. *Characteristics of Sociotechnical Systems.* London: Tavistock Institute of Human Relations, Doc. 527, 1959.

Emery, F. E. "The Next Thirty Years: Concepts, Methods and Anticipations." *Human Relations,* 1967, *20,* 199–237.

Emery, F. E. "Introduction." In F. E. Emery (ed.), *Systems Thinking.* New York: Penguin Books, 1969.

Emery, F. E., and Trist, E. L. "Sociotechnical Systems." In F. E. Emery (ed.), *Systems Thinking.* New York: Penguin Books, 1969.

Emery, F. E., and Trist, E. L. *Towards a Social Ecology: Contextual Appreciation of the Future in the Present.* New York: Plenum Press, 1973.

Feldman, R., and Betzold, M. *End of the Line.* New York: Weidenfeld & Nicolson, 1988.

Fiedler, F. *A Theory of Leadership Effectiveness.* New York: McGraw-Hill, 1967.

Fisher, A. B. "Behind the Hype at GM's Saturn." *Fortune,* Nov. 11, 1985.

"Forum." *QWL Focus,* 1984, *4* (1).

French, J. R., Jr., and Raven, B. H. "The Bases of Social Power." In D. Cartwright (ed.), *Studies in Social Power.* Ann Arbor: University of Michigan Press, 1959.

Fromm, E. *The Sane Society.* Greenwich, Conn.: Fawcett, 1955.

Gardell, B. "Worker Participation and Autonomy: A Multilevel Approach to Democracy in the Workplace." *International Journal of Health Services,* 1982, *12* (4), 527–558.

Goodman, P. "The Rushton Quality of Work Experiment." In R. Zager and M. P. Rosow (eds.), *The Innovative Organization: Productivity Programs in Action.* Elmsford: N.Y.: Pergamon Press, 1982.

Granath, J. Å. "Produktionsteknik och rumslig gestaltning [Production technology and spatial form]." *IACTH,* 1986, *6.*

Halperin, K., Snyer, C. R., Shenkkel, R. F., and Houston, B. K. "Effects of Source Status and Message Favorability on Acceptance of Personality Feedback." *Journal of Applied Psychology,* 1976, *61,* 85–88.

Halpern, N. "Sociotechnical Systems Design: The Shell-Sarnia Experience." In J. Cunningham and T. White (eds.), *Quality of Working Life, Canadian Cases.* Ottawa: Labour Canada, 1984.

Halpern, N. "Novel Organization Working at Shell Canada Facility." *Oil and Gas Journal,* Mar. 25, 1985, pp. 88–93.

Hammer, T. H., and Stern, R. N. "Employee Ownership: Implications for the Organizational Distribution of Power." *Academy of Management Journal,* 1980, *23* (1), 78–100.

Hayes, F. O'R. *Productivity in Local Government.* Toronto: Lexington Books, 1977.

Heckscher, C. C. *The New Unionism: Employee Involvement in the Changing Corporation.* New York: Basic Books, 1988.

Henriksson, J. "Industrial Working Environment: The Employees' Participation in Planning." Unpublished paper, Stockholm, Aug. 1983.

Herbst, P. G. *Sociotechnical Design.* London: Tavistock, 1974.

Herbst, P. G. *Alternatives to Hierarchies.* Leiden: Martinus Nijhoff, 1976.

Herrick, N. Q. (ed.). *Improving Government: Experiments with QWL Systems.* New York: Praeger, 1983.

Herrick, N. Q. "QWL: An Alternative to Traditional Public-Sector Management Systems." *National Productivity Review,* 1983–84, *3* (1), 54–67.

Herrick, N. Q. "Parallel Organizations in Unionized Settings: Implications for Organizational Research." *Human Relations,* 1985, *38* (10), 961–981.

Herrick, N. Q. "Learning from Mistakes." *Society,* 1986, *23* (3), 30–35.

Herrick, N. Q., and Mazany, T. "The Initial Testing Event: A Predictable Crisis in the Early Life of a QWL System." *Work Life Review,* 1982, *1* (2), 26–30.

Hooper, J. "Spotlight on Co-ops: $24,000,000 Pledged to Co-ops." *The WARM Times,* May 1989.

Ivancevich, J. M. "An Analysis of Control, Bases of Control, and Satisfaction in an Organizational Setting." *Academy of Management Journal,* 1970, *13,* 427–436.

John XXIII. *Mater et Magistras.* Rome: The Vatican, 1965.

John Paul II. *Slavorum Opostali.* Rome: The Vatican, 1985.

Johnson, D. W., and others. "Effects of Cooperative, Competitive, and Individualistic Goal Structures on Achievement: A Meta-Analysis." *Psychological Bulletin,* 1981, *89,* 47-62.

Jones, C. M. "Major Obstacles to QWL's Development in the Canadian Federal Public Service." In N. Q. Herrick (ed.), *Improving Government: Experiments With QWL Systems.* New York: Praeger, 1983.

Kanter, R. M. *The Change Masters: Innovation for Productivity in the American Corporation.* New York: Simon & Schuster, 1983.

Katz, H. C., Kochan, T. A., and Gobeille, K. R. "Economic Performance and QWL Programs: An Interplant Analysis." *Industrial and Labor Relations Review,* 1983, *37* (1), 3-17.

Kaufman, A. "Human Nature and Participatory Democracy." In W. E. Connolly (ed.), *The Bias of Pluralism.* New York: Atherton, 1969.

Kerr, S., and Jermier, J. "Substitutes for Leadership: Their Meaning and Measurement." *Organizational Behavior and Human Performance,* 1978, *22,* 375-403.

Latham, G. P., and Baldes, J. J. "The Practical Significance of Locke's Theory of Goal Setting." *Journal of Applied Psychology,* 1975, *60,* 122-124.

Lawler, E. E. *Pay and Organizational Development.* Reading, Mass.: Addison-Wesley, 1981.

Lawler, E. E. *High-Involvement Management.* San Francisco: Jossey-Bass, 1986.

Lawler, E. E., and Ledford, G. E., Jr. "Productivity and the Quality of Work Life." *National Productivity Review,* Winter 1981-82, *1* (1), 23-26.

Levin, D. P. "U.A.W.'s Challenge from Within." *New York Times,* June 18, 1989, p. F5.

Lipset, S. M., Trow, M. A., and Coleman, J. S. *Union Democracy.* Garden City, N.Y.: Anchor Books, 1956.

Locke, E. A. "Toward a Theory of Task Motivation and Incentive." *Organizational Behavior and Human Performance,* 1968, *3,* 157-189.

Maccoby, M. *The Leader: A New Face for American Management.* New York: Ballantine Books, 1981.

McMahon, J. T., and Perritt, G. W. "Toward a Contingency Theory of Organizational Control." *Academy of Management Journal*, 1973, *16*, 624.

Macpherson, C. B. *Democratic Theory: Essays in Retrieval*. Oxford: Oxford University Press, 1973.

Macpherson, C. B. *The Life and Times of Liberal Democracy*. Oxford: Oxford University Press, 1977.

Macy, B. "The Bolivar Quality of Work Life Program: Success or Failure?" In R. Zager and M. P. Rosow (eds.), *The Innovative Organization: Productivity Programs in Action*. Elmsford, N.Y.: Pergamon Press, 1982.

Manners, G. E., Jr. "Another Look at Group Size, Group Problem-Solving and Member Consensus." *Academy of Management Journal*, 1975, *18*, 715-724.

Marsh, T., and McAllister, D. "ESOP's Tables." *Journal of Corporation Law*, 1981, *6*, 551-623.

Maslow, A. H. *Toward a Psychology of Being*. (2nd ed.) New York: D. Van Nostrand, 1968.

Mazany, T. *Third Party Annual Report on the Pima County Quality of Working Life Management System*. Tucson, Ariz.: Pima County, 1984.

Mazany, T. "Making Participation Make Sense: A Task for Collective Bargaining." *Work Life Review*, 1986, *5* (2), 13-23.

Mehrabian, A. *Tactics of Social Influence*. Englewood Cliffs, N.J.: Prentice-Hall, 1970.

Memorandum of Agreement Between the Saturn Corporation and the UAW, 1985.

Metzgar, B. "Elements of a Sharing-Participative System." *Profit Sharing*. Evanston, Ill.: The Profit Sharing Research Foundation, 1976.

Miles, R. H. *Macro Organizational Behavior*. Santa Monica, Calif.: Goodyear, 1980.

Mill, J. S. "That the Ideally Best Form of Government is Representative Government." In M. Cohen (ed.), *The Philosophy of John Stuart Mill: Ethical, Political and Religious*. New York: Modern Library, 1961.

Mintzberg, J. *The Nature of Managerial Work*. New York: Harper & Row, 1973.

Moore, B. E., and Ross, T. L. *The Scanlon Way to Improved Productivity: A Practical Guide.* New York: Wiley, 1978.

Nadler, E. G. "Yielding, Authoritarianism, and Authoritarian Ideology Regarding Groups." *Journal of Abnormal and Social Psychology,* 1959, *58,* 408–410.

Nagle, J. H. *Participation.* Englewood Cliffs, N.J.: Prentice-Hall, 1987.

National Center for Employee Ownership. *Employee Ownership: A Legislative Guide.* Arlington, Va.: National Center for Employee Ownership, 1984.

National Labor Relations Board v. *Streamway Division,* 691 F2d 288 (6th Cir., 1982).

" 'New Directions for Labor' Conference Draws Over 1,000 to Detroit." *Labor Notes,* 1989, *124,* 8.

New York Stock Exchange. *People and Productivity.* New York: New York Stock Exchange, 1982.

Nicholas, J. M. "The Comparative Impact of Organizational Development Interventions on Hard Criteria Measures." *Academy of Management Review,* 1982, 7 (4), 331–542.

Parker, M. *Inside the Circle: A Union Guide to QWL.* Boston: South End Press, 1985.

Parker, M., and Slaughter, J. *Choosing Sides: Unions and the Team Concept.* Boston: South End Press, 1988.

Pasmore, W., Francis, C., Haldeman, J., and Shani, A. "Sociotechnical Systems: A North American Reflection on Empirical Studies of the Seventies." *Human Relations,* 1982, *35* (12), 1179–1202.

Pateman, C. *Participation and Democratic Theory.* London: Cambridge University Press, 1970.

Pfeffer, J. *Power in Organizations.* Marshfield, Mass.: Pitman, 1981.

Pima County. *QWL Monthly Training Program.* Tucson, Ariz.: Pima County, 1984.

Porter, L., and Lawler, E. E. *Managerial Attitudes and Behavior.* Homewood, Ill.: Irwin, 1968.

Rankin, T., and Mansell, J. "Integrating Collective Bargaining and New Forms of Work Organization." *National Productivity Review,* Autumn 1986, pp. 338–347.

Raven, B. H. "A Comparative Analysis of Power and Power Preference." In J. T. Tedeschi (ed.), *Perspectives on Social Power.* Hawthorne, N.Y.: Aldine, 1974.

Ronchi, D., and Morgan, W. R. "Springfield, Ohio: Persisting and Prevailing." In N. Q. Herrick (ed.), *Improving Government: Experiments with QWL Systems.* New York: Praeger, 1983.

Rosen, C. "Growth vs. Equity: The Employee Ownership Solution." *ILR Report,* 1985, *22* (2), 19-23.

Rosen, C., and Klein, K. "Job Creation Performance of Employee Owned Companies." *Monthly Labor Review,* Aug. 1981, pp. 15-19.

Rosen, C., and Whyte, W. F. *Encouraging Employee Ownership: The Government's Role.* New York: Democracy Project Report, Nov. 1983.

Rosenbaum, M. E., and others. "Group Productivity and Process: Pure and Mixed Reward Structures and Task Interdependence." *Journal of Personality and Social Psychology,* 1980, *39,* 626-642.

Sachs, S. "Employee Participation: The Next Stage." *Workplace Democracy,* 1988, *61,* 4.

Saglio, J. H., and Hackman, J. R. "The Design of Governance Systems for Small Worker Cooperatives." Working paper of the Industrial Cooperative Association, Somerville, Mass., Oct. 1982.

Schumpeter, J. A. *Capitalism, Socialism and Democracy.* (3rd ed.) New York: Harper & Row, 1950.

Seashore, S. E. *Group Cohesiveness in the Industrial Work Group.* Ann Arbor: Institute for Social Research, 1954.

Shaw, M. E. *Group Dynamics: The Psychology of Small Group Behavior.* (2nd ed.) New York: McGraw-Hill, 1976.

Sherif, M., and others. *Intergroup Conflict and Cooperation: The Robbers' Cave Experiment.* Norman: University of Oklahoma Press, 1961.

Showalter, J., and Yetman, D. "Pima County: The Dilemma of Weak Unions and QWL." In N. Q. Herrick (ed.), *Improving Government: Experiments With QWL Systems.* New York: Praeger, 1983.

Slaughter, J. "UAW Leadership to Face More Challenges From 'New Directions' Candidates." *Labor Notes,* 1989, *120,* 1.

Sorcher, M., and Danzig, S. "Chartering and Changing the Organizational Climate." *Personnel,* 1969, *46,* 16-28.

Steers, R. M., Ungson, G. R., and Mowday, R. T. *Managing Effective Organizations*. Boston: Kent, 1985.

Steiner, I. D. *Group Process and Productivity*. Orlando, Fla.: Academic Press, 1972.

Stern, R. N., Whyte, W. F., Hammer, T., and Meek, C. B. "The Union and the Transition to Employee Ownership." In W. F. Whyte (ed.), *Worker Participation and Ownership*. Ithaca, N.Y.: ILR Press, 1983.

Stogdill, R. "Personal Factors Associated With Leadership: A Survey of the Literature." *Journal of Psychology*, 1948, *25*, 35–71.

Susman, G. I. *Autonomy at Work: A Sociotechnical Analysis of Participative Management*. New York: Praeger, 1979.

Tannenbaum, A. S. "Control in Organizations: Individual Adjustment and Organizational Performance." *Administrative Science Quarterly*, 1962, *7*, 236–257.

Taylor, F. W. *The Principles of Scientific Management*. New York: Harper, 1911.

"Teamsters Win Right to Vote." *Labor Notes*, 1989, *121*, 1.

Thomas, K. "Conflict and Conflict Management." In M. Dunnette (ed.), *Handbook of Industrial and Organizational Psychology*. Skokie, Ill.: Rand McNally, 1976.

Tichy, N. "An Analysis of Clique Formation and Structure in Organizations." *Administrative Science Quarterly*, 1973, *18* (2), 194–208.

Trist, E. L. "The Sociotechnical Perspective." In A. H. Van de Ven and W. F. Joyce (eds.), *Perspectives on Organizational Design and Behavior*. New York: Wiley, 1981.

Trist, E. L., and Bamforth, K. "Some Social and Psychological Consequences of the Long-Wall Method of Goal Setting." *Human Relations*, 1951, *1*, 3–58.

Trist, E. L., Higgin, C., Murray, H., and Pollock, A. *Organizational Choice:* London: Tavistock, 1963.

Trist, E. L., Susman, G., and Brown, G. "An Experiment in Autonomous Working in an American Underground Coal Mine." *Human Relations*, 1977, *30*, 201–236.

Tuckman, B. W. "Development Sequence in Small Groups." *Psychological Bulletin*, 1965, *63*, 384–399.

U.S. Congress, Senate Committee on Labor and Public Welfare. *Worker Alienation Hearings.* 1972, 92nd. Cong., 2d sess.

U.S. Department of Defense. *Guide for the Design and Implementation of Productivity Gain Sharing Programs.* (DOD 5010.31-G) Washington, D.C.: U.S. Department of Defense, 1985.

U.S. Department of Health, Education, and Welfare. *Work in America.* Cambridge, Mass.: MIT Press, 1973.

U.S. Department of Labor. *Federal Labor Laws and Programs.* Washington, D.C.: U.S. Government Printing Office, 1971.

U.S. General Accounting Office. *Ways to Improve Federal Management and Use of Productivity Based Reward Systems.* (FPCD-81-24) Washington, D.C.: U.S. General Accounting Office, 1980.

U.S. General Accounting Office. *Productivity Sharing Programs: Can They Contribute to Productivity Improvement?* (AFMD-81-22) Washington, D.C.: U.S. General Accounting Office, 1981.

Vogl, G. C. "Quality of Work Concept: General Motors Corporation–United Auto Workers Approach." *Work Life Review,* 1984, *3* (2), 26.

Vroom, V. H. *Work and Motivation.* New York: Wiley, 1964.

Vroom, V. H., and Yetton, P. W. *Leadership and Decision Making.* Pittsburgh: University of Pittsburgh Press, 1973.

Wahba, M. A., and Birdwell, L. G. "Maslow Reconsidered: A Review of Research on the Need Hierarchy Theory." *Organizational Behavior and Human Performance,* 1976, *15,* 212–240.

Wallace, M. J., Jr., and Fay, C. H. *Compensation Theory and Practice.* Boston: Kent, 1983.

Walton, R. E., and McKersie, R. B. *A Behavioral Theory of Labor Negotiations.* New York: McGraw-Hill, 1965.

Webber, R. A., Morgan, M. A., and Browne, P. C. *Management: Basic Elements of Managing Corporations.* (3rd ed.) Homewood, Ill.: Irwin, 1985.

Wermiel, S. "Justices Rule 5-4 that U.S. Age-Bias Law Supersedes State and Local Regulations." *Wall Street Journal,* March 3, 1983, p. 4.

Whyte, W. F. "Employee Ownership Yesterday, Today, and Tomorrow." *ILR Report,* 1985, *22* (2), 7–14.

Williams, L. "Industrial Democracy Has Been With Us from the Start." *Workplace Democracy,* 1988, *62,* 8–11.

Williams, R., and Watts, G. "The Process of Working Together: CWA's/AT&T's Approach to QWL." In J. M. Rosow (ed.), *Teamwork: Joint Labor-Management Programs in America.* Elmsford, N.Y.: Pergamon Press, 1986.

Wofford, J. C. *Organizational Behavior: Foundation for Organizational Effectiveness.* Boston: Kent, 1982.

Zand, D. E. "Trust and Managerial Problem Solving." *Administrative Science Quarterly,* 1972, 7, 229–238.

Index

A

AB Almex Company, well-being at, 378

Accountability: ambiguity of, 144; and consensus, 52

Action teams: at all levels, 39–40; aspects of, 199–217; background on, 199–200; chairs of, 216–217; and combined-function union officers, 215–216; and communication lines, 66; communication problems of, 257–260; composition of, 201–203; concept of, 13, 399; decision-making authority of, 58; and enforcement, 368; at executive level, 202, 203–204, 206–207, 208, 209; formation of, 210–211; functions of, 203–210; initiating function of, 206–207; in integrative bargaining, 329, 331–333, 335–336; at intermediate level, 202, 207, 208, 209; lowest-level, 16–17; membership in, 60; monitoring function of, 209; at operations level, 202–203, 206–207, 208, 209; in parallel organization, 37, 209; in parallel organization, 37,

58; and participation stewards, 210–211, 214–215; problem solving function of, 209–210, 217; and process principles, 50–54; purpose of, 201; reviewing function of, 207–208; roles of members on, 211–217; sanctioning function of, 203–206; and senior manager-member, 212–213; and subordinate managers, 213–214; and workplace interest groups, 42; at worksite level, 63–64, 201–202, 207, 208, 209–210, 217

Adams, J. S., 164

Adaptation: for budget administration, 351–352; design for, 47–49; examples of, 85–86, 93–94, 100–101, 106; for financial administration, 352–353; by labor, 356–371; by management, 341–355; for personnel, 344–351; problems of, 355, 370–371; for productivity measurement, 353–355; and staff offices, 343–344

Administration: actions of, 205; adaptation for, 351–353; of contracts, 366–369; policies of, 205–206; roles in, 338–339

415